The Fundamental Concepts of Metaphysics

Studies in Continental Thought

Martin Heidegger

The Fundamental Concepts of Metaphysics
World, Finitude, Solitude

Translated by
William McNeill
and
Nicholas Walker

Indiana University Press
Bloomington and Indianapolis

Published in German as *Die Grundbegriffe der Metaphysik. Welt—Endlichkeit—Einsamkeit* ©1983, 1992 by Vittorio Klostermann, Frankfurt am Main. Publication of this work was supported by funding from Inter Nationes, Bonn.

The paper used in this publication meets the minimum requirements of American National Standard for Information Sciences—Permanence of Paper for Printed Library Materials, ANSI Z39.48-1984.

Manufactured in the United States of America

Library of Congress Cataloging-in-Publication Data

Heidegger, Martin, 1889–1976.
    [Grundbegriffe der Metaphysik. English]
    The fundamental concepts of metaphysics : world, finitude, solitude / Martin Heidegger ; translated by William McNeill and Nicholas Walker.
        p. cm.—(Studies in Continental thought)
    Translation of: Die Grundbegriffe der Metaphysik
    Includes bibliographical references.
    ISBN 0-253-32749-0 (cloth : alk. paper)
    1. Metaphysics. I. Title. II. Series
B3279.H48G76513   1995
110—dc20   94-43451
                1 2 3 4 5 00 99 98 97 96 95

In Memory of Eugen Fink

He listened to this lecture course with
thoughtful reticence, and in so doing
experienced something unthought of
his own that determined his path.

Presumably this is where we must look
for the reason why, over the past decades,
he repeatedly expressed the wish that
this lecture should be published before
all others.

Martin Heidegger
26 July 1975

Contents

PART ONE

Awakening a Fundamental Attunement in Our Philosophizing

Chapter One

*The Task of Awakening a Fundamental Attunement
and the Indication of a Concealed Fundamental
Attunement in Our Contemporary Dasein*

Chapter Two

The First Form of Boredom: Becoming Bored by Something

Chapter Three

The Second Form of Boredom: Being Bored with
Something and the Passing of Time Belonging to It

Chapter Four

The Third Form of Boredom:
Profound Boredom as 'It Is Boring for One'

Contents

Chapter Three

*The Beginning of the Comparative Examination,
Taking the Intermediate Thesis That the Animal
Is Poor in World as Our Point of Departure*

Chapter Four

*Clarification of the Essence of the Animal's Poverty in World by
Way of the Question Concerning the Essence of Animality, the
Essence of Life in General, and the Essence of the Organism*

Contents

Translators' Foreword

The text of Martin Heidegger's 1929–30 lecture course presented here is of special interest on at least three counts. First, we have a preliminary appraisal of about 90 pages documenting Heidegger's conception of philosophy and metaphysics during this period. Developing an adequate concept of what is meant by the term 'metaphysics' was undoubtedly central to the revision Heidegger's thought was undergoing around this time—as witnessed by his inaugural Freiburg lecture "What Is Metaphysics?"[1]—and the analyses given in this 1929–30 course provide us with a detailed insight in this respect. In particular, they address the relation between λόγος and φύσις, and the conception of πρώτη φιλοσοφία, first philosophy, as it develops in and after Aristotle.

Second, a major part of the interest aroused in this lecture course stems from its penetrating analyses (covering some 130 pages of German text) of the mood or "fundamental attunement" [*Grundstimmung*] of boredom. Prior to the publication of this course, the only fundamental attunement to receive detailed treatment from Heidegger was that of anxiety [*Angst*]. The analysis of anxiety assumed a pivotal role in his magnum opus *Being and Time*,[2] and anxiety remained the central focus in "What Is Metaphysics?," manifesting *Dasein* (Heidegger's term for human existence with respect to its openness to being) not so much in terms of the "being held in limbo" [*Hingehaltenheit*] that will be shown to characterize the various forms of boredom, but as a "being held out into the Nothing" [*Hineingehaltenheit in das Nichts*]. The prominence of the mood of anxiety in fact led many readers to assume that there was but *one* fundamental attunement that could be attributed to *Dasein*. In the 1929–30 course, however, Heidegger emphatically denies that this is the case. Indeed, he already appeals to the attunement of "profound boredom" in the 1929 inaugural lecture.[3] Furthermore, the recent publication of the early lecture entitled "The Concept of Time" indicates that Heidegger was well aware of the possibility of understanding boredom in terms of a lengthening of time as early as 1924, and perhaps earlier.[4] With respect to the general

---

1. *"Was ist Metaphysik?,"* delivered 24 July 1929, is published in *Wegmarken*, Gesamtausgabe, Vol. 9 (Frankfurt: Klostermann, 1976), pp. 103–22. [Trans. D. F. Krell in *Martin Heidegger: Basic Writings* (New York: Harper Collins, 1993), pp. 93–110.]
2. See *Sein und Zeit* (Tübingen: Niemeyer, 1979), especially §40. [Trans. J. Macquarrie and E. Robinson, *Being and Time* (Oxford: Blackwell, 1987).]
3. *"Was ist Metaphysik?,"* op. cit., p. 110. [Trans. p. 99.]
4. See *Der Begriff der Zeit* (Tübingen: Niemeyer, 1989), pp. 19–22. [Trans. W. McNeill, *The Concept of Time* (bilingual edition) (Oxford: Blackwell, 1992), pp. 14–17.]

significance of the attunement of boredom for Heidegger's thought, it is worth remarking that in the mid-1930s boredom comes to be identified by Heidegger as being "the concealed destination" of modernity in the scientific era.[5] We should also note that the concept of the "while" [*Weile*] which is central to the investigations on boredom (see below) continued to play a crucial role in Heidegger's later thinking.

Third, the 1929–30 course shows Heidegger venturing into the realms of positive science—specifically biology—and doing so at great length. The move is astonishing, because Heidegger will nowhere else take the experimental results of science so seriously in support of possible metaphysical claims. The engagement with experimental biology occurs in the course of examining the possibility of an ontology of 'life', the term referring primarily to the 'natural' life of plants and animals, but also encroaching, uncannily, no doubt, on what Heidegger, in the 1946 "Letter on Humanism," would call our "scarcely fathomable, abyssal bodily kinship with the animal."[6] The task of elaborating such an ontology of life is already intimated in *Being and Time,* where Heidegger insists that it would have to occur "by way of a privative interpretation,"[7] yet the appeal to experimental science is nevertheless unexpected. The difficulty in understanding animal life, with which Heidegger concerns himself here—in particular the problems involved in differentiating the animal's being from that of humans—is an issue that will continue to appear in Heidegger's later works, though only by way of much briefer (and eminently problematic) comments.

Finally, one ought to draw special attention to the concluding analyses of the apophantic λόγος, which is treated much more extensively than in *Being and Time,* and to Heidegger's reflections on the ontological difference (i.e., the difference between being and beings)—reflections which, as he himself indicates, herald the imminent collapse of ontology as such.

Even by the standard of the majority of Heidegger's works, *The Fundamental Concepts of Metaphysics* poses immense problems of translatability. One major difficulty is that the English word *boredom,* which translates the German *Langeweile,* is unable to convey the temporal sense which Heidegger makes central to his phenomenological analyses. The German *Langeweile* literally means 'long while', and Heidegger, taking this up, will argue that the various forms of boredom are ultimately nothing other than various ways in which

5. See *Beiträge zur Philosophie (Vom Ereignis),* Gesamtausgabe, Vol. 65 (Frankfurt: Klostermann, 1989), §76, p. 157.
6. '. . . die kaum auszudenkende abgründige leibliche Verwandtschaft mit dem Tier.' In *Wegmarken,* op. cit., p. 326. [Trans. *Basic Writings,* op. cit., p. 230 (translation modified).]
7. *Being and Time,* op. cit. §10, p. 50. [Trans. p. 75.]

time temporalizes.[8] A further problem was posed by Heidegger's use of complicated etymological chains which cannot be adequately rendered in English. For example, the chain *Benehmen, Benommenheit, Genommenheit, Hingenommenheit, Eingenommenheit, Vernehmen*—terms used to describe the activity of the animal (although some of them are also pertinent to human *Dasein*)—is a series of variations on the German *nehmen,* to take, and its past participle *genommen.* We have chosen to render this chain as *behaviour, captivation, withholding, being taken, absorption,* and *apprehending* in order to adequately convey the meaning. Here, as elsewhere, we have aimed to produce a readable translation that will allow an accurate sense of what is being discussed to emerge from the text as a whole. Where the etymological connection in the German is particularly important (as in the above cases), we have indicated the relevant German terms in parentheses. In general, we have opted for minimal intervention in the form of translators' commentary, preferring to confine translators' notes (indicated by Tr) to one or two essential pointers.

The translators would like to thank Indiana University Press for their patience during the preparation of this volume, which took longer than expected. Will McNeill thanks the British Academy in London for their provision of a Postdoctoral Research Fellowship in the Humanities which provided financial assistance during the course of this work; the German Literature Archive in Marbach for their hospitality and for allowing access to the manuscripts of the lecture course, and the DAAD which funded my visit there. Warm thanks also to Kathleen Jones for her careful correction and revision of the proofs. Nicholas Walker and Will McNeill would also like to thank David Wood of Vanderbilt University, Nashville, and, and David Farrell Krell of DePaul University, Chicago, for their helpful comments on some of the more difficult passages.

The publication of this work has been funded by a subvention from Inter Nationes, Bonn, and we are most grateful to them for their support.

William McNeill
Nicholas Walker

---

8. See especially §33 of the course, on "The essential meaning of the word 'boredom' or '*Langeweile*'. . . ."

The Fundamental Concepts of Metaphysics

PRELIMINARY APPRAISAL

The Task of the Course and Its Fundamental
Orientation, Starting with a General
Elucidation of the Title of the Course

Chapter One

The Detours toward Determining the Essence of
Philosophy (Metaphysics), and the Unavoidability of
Looking Metaphysics in the Face

§1. The incomparability of philosophy.

a) Philosophy neither science, nor the proclamation of a worldview.

The course is announced under the title "The Fundamental Concepts of
Metaphysics." Presumably there is little we can think of that falls under this
title, and yet it is completely clear as regards its form. It sounds, for instance,
like the course titles: The Fundamental Features of Zoology; The Fundamental Elements of Linguistics; Outline of the History of the Reformation, and
suchlike. This indicates that we are faced with a fixed discipline, called
'metaphysics'. It is then a matter of depicting its most important aspects—
while avoiding lengthy details—within the scope of a semester. Since metaphysics is the central discipline in the whole of philosophy, the treatment of
its fundamental features becomes a condensed report on the main contents of
philosophy. Because philosophy is the universal science, as opposed to the
so-called individual sciences, it will give our studies the right breadth and round
them off. In this way everything is completely in order—and the business of
the university can begin.

Indeed it has long since begun, and is underway to such an extent that some
are already beginning to sense something of the barrenness and waywardness
of this activity. Has something perhaps already shattered at the very heart of
the machinery? Is it now held together only by the obtrusiveness and banality
of organisation and of convention? Is there a falseness and a hidden despair
somewhere in all this activity? What if it were a *prejudice* that metaphysics is
a fixed and secure discipline of philosophy, and an *illusion* that philosophy is
a science that can be taught and learned?

Yet why do we need explicitly to ascertain such things? After all, it has long been known that in philosophy, and especially in metaphysics, everything is uncertain, that innumerable different views, standpoints, and schools conflict with one another and begin to fray at the edges—a questionable back and forth of opinions, as against the clear truths and advances, the so-called secure results of the sciences. Here lies the source of the whole disaster. Philosophy, especially as metaphysics, has indeed not yet reached the maturity of science. Philosophy moves on an inferior level. It has not yet succeeded in achieving what it has been attempting since Descartes (the beginning of modernity), namely to raise itself to the rank of a science, of absolute science. Thus all we have to do is to put our every effort into seeing that it one day succeeds in this. Then it will stand unshakable and assume the secure path of a science—for the benefit of mankind. Then we will know what philosophy is.

Or is all this talk of philosophy as the absolute science a delusion? Not simply because the individual or a particular school may never achieve this goal, but because positing this goal is itself fundamentally an error and a misunderstanding of the innermost essence of philosophy. Philosophy as absolute science—a high, unsurpassable ideal. So it seems. And yet perhaps even to judge philosophy according to the idea of science is the most fateful debasement of its innermost essence.

Yet if philosophy in general and fundamentally is *not* science, then what is it doing, what right does it then have in the sphere of the sciences at the university? Does not philosophy then merely become the proclamation of a *worldview?* And the latter? What else is it than the personal conviction of an individual thinker, brought into a system that drums up a few supporters for a while, who then turn around and construct their own systems? Is philosophy not then like some great marketplace?

In the end, the interpretation of philosophy as proclamation of a worldview is just as mistaken as characterizing it as science. Philosophy (metaphysics)—neither science nor the proclamation of a worldview. What then remains for it? At the outset we have made only the negative assertion that it cannot be fitted into such frameworks. Perhaps it cannot be determined as something else, but *can be determined only from out of itself and as itself—comparable with nothing else* in terms of which it could be positively determined. In that case philosophy is something that *stands on its own,* something *ultimate.*

b) The essence of philosophy not to be determined via the detour of comparing it with art and religion.

Can philosophy in general not be compared to anything else? Perhaps it may be compared, albeit only negatively, with *art* and with *religion,* by which we do not mean an ecclesiastical system. Yet why then can we not equally well compare philosophy with science? In what was said above, however, we were not simply comparing philosophy with science; we wished instead to determine it *as* science. Yet it would not even occur to us to determine philosophy *as* art or *as* religion. The comparison of philosophy with science is an unjustified debasement of its essence. Comparing it with art and religion, on the other hand, is a justified and necessary determination of their essence as equal. Yet equality here does not mean identity.

Will we therefore be able to grasp philosophy in its essence by taking a detour through art and religion? Quite irrespective of all the difficulties that such a route presents, we shall never grasp the essence of philosophy through these comparisons either—however much art and religion are treated on a level equal to philosophy—unless we have already managed to look philosophy in the face to begin with. For only then can we differentiate art and religion from it. Thus this route too is closed, even though we shall encounter both, art and religion, along our path.

We find ourselves repeatedly rebuffed by all these attempts to grasp philosophy by way of comparison. It has become manifest that all these routes are in themselves impossible detours. In constantly being rebuffed we are being driven into a corner with our question of what philosophy, what metaphysics, itself is. How are we to experience what philosophy itself is, if we have to forego all such detours?

c) The escape route of determining the essence of philosophy via a historical orientation as an illusion.

There remains one final way out: we shall inquire in the realm of history. After all, philosophy—if it does exist—has not existed only since yesterday. Indeed, we may now wonder why we did not immediately take this route via history, instead of struggling with fruitless questions. By way of historical orientation we shall straightaway obtain information about metaphysics. There are three things we can ask about: [1.] Where does the word 'metaphysics' come from, and what is its initial meaning? Here we encounter the strange history of a strange word. [2.] Through the simple meaning of the word we can arrive at whatever it is that is defined as metaphysics. We become acquainted with a discipline of philosophy. [3.] Finally, by means of this definition we can push our way through to the *matter* itself that is *named* therein.

This is a clear and didactic task. Yet in all this we shall fail to experience what metaphysics itself is unless we already know this beforehand. Without this knowledge, however, all reports on the history of philosophy remain mute. We become acquainted with opinions *about* metaphysics, but not with metaphysics itself. Thus, this last remaining way also leads to a dead end. Indeed, this route contains the greatest illusion, because it always pretends that on the basis of historical knowledge we might know, understand, or have what we are looking for.

§2. Determining philosophy from out of itself,
taking our lead from a word of Novalis.

a) The withdrawal of metaphysics (philosophizing) as a human activity into the obscurity of the essence of man.

We have ultimately failed, then, in all these attempts to characterize metaphysics by way of detours. Yet have we not gained anything in so doing? Yes and no. We have not gained a definition or anything like that. No doubt we have gained an important and perhaps essential insight into what is peculiar about metaphysics: that we ourselves avoid confrontation with it, steal away from metaphysics itself and take to detours; yet also that no other choice remains than to ready ourselves and to *look metaphysics in the face,* so as not to lose sight of it again.

Yet how is it possible to lose sight of something that we have not yet caught sight of at all? How can metaphysics withdraw from us when we are not at all in a position to follow it to wherever it draws us? Are we really unable to see where it slips away to, or do we merely draw back in terror when faced with the peculiar effort entailed in grasping metaphysics directly?

The negative result is this: philosophy does not permit itself to be grasped or determined by way of detours or as something other than itself. It demands that we do not look *away* from it, but apprehend it from out of itself. Philosophy itself—what do we know of it, what and how is it? It itself *is* only whenever we are philosophizing. *Philosophy is philosophizing.* That does not seem very informative. Yet however much we seem merely to be repeating the same thing, this says something essential. It points the *direction* in which we have to search, indeed the direction in which metaphysics withdraws from us. Metaphysics as philosophizing, as our own human activity—how and to where can metaphysics as philosophizing, as our own human activity, withdraw from us, if we ourselves are, after all, human beings? Yet do we in fact know what we ourselves are? What is man? The crown of creation or some wayward path, some great misunderstanding and an abyss? If we know so little about man, how can our essence not be alien to us? How can philosophizing as a human activity fail to conceal itself from us in the obscurity of this essence? Philosophy—as we are presumably superficially aware—is not some arbitrary enterprise with which we pass our time as the fancy takes us, not some mere gathering of knowledge that we can easily obtain for ourselves at any time from books, but (we know this only obscurely) something to do with the whole, something extreme, where an ultimate pronouncement and interlocution occurs on the part of human beings. For why else would we have come along here? Or have we arrived here only because others also come along, or because we happen to have a free period just between five and six when it is not worth going home? Why are we here? Do we know what we are letting ourselves in for?

b) Homesickness as the fundamental attunement of philosophizing, and the questions concerning world, finitude, individuation.

Philosophy—an ultimate pronouncement and interlocution on the part of man that constantly permeates him in his entirety. Yet what is man, that he philosophizes in the ground of his essence, and what is this philosophizing? What are we in this? Where do we want to go? Did we once just stumble into the universe by chance? Novalis on one occasion says in a fragment: "Philosophy is really homesickness, an urge to be at home everywhere."[1] A strange definition, romantic of course. Homesickness—does such a thing still exist today at all? Has it not become an incomprehensible word, even in everyday life? Has not contemporary city man, the ape of civilization, long since eradicated homesickness? And homesickness as the very determination of philosophy! But above all, what sort of witness are we presenting here with regard to philosophy? Novalis—merely a poet, after all, and hardly a scientific philosopher. Does not Aristotle say in his *Metaphysics:* πολλὰ ψεύδονται ἀοιδοί:[2] Poets tell many a lie?

Yet without provoking an argument over the authority and significance of this witness, let us merely recall that art—which includes poetry too—is the sister of philosophy and that all science is perhaps only a servant with respect to philosophy.

Let us remain with the issue and ask: What is all this talk about philosophy as homesickness? Novalis himself elucidates: "an urge to be everywhere at home." Philosophy can only be such an urge if we who philosophize are *not* at home everywhere. What is demanded by this urge? To be at home everywhere—what does that mean? Not merely here or there, nor even simply in every place, in all places taken together one after the other. Rather, to be at home everywhere means to be at once and at all times within the whole. We name this *'within the whole'* and its character of wholeness the *world.* We are, and to the extent that we are, we are always waiting for something. We are always called upon by something as a whole. This 'as a whole' is the world.

We are asking: *What is that—world?*

This is where we are driven in our homesickness: to being as a whole. Our very being is this restlessness. We have somehow always already departed

---

1. Novalis, *Schriften.* Ed. J. Minor (Jena, 1923). Vol. 2, p. 179, Frgm. 21. [Tr: The term "urge" translates the German *Trieb,* more literally "drive" or "instinctual drive." *Trieb* and its cognates (e.g., *treiben, vertreiben, wegtreiben, zutreiben*) are prominent both in the analyses of boredom and in the discussions of animal life which constitute the two major themes of the course.]

2. *Aristotelis Metaphysica.* Ed. W. Christ (Leipzig, 1886). A 2, 983a 3f.

toward this whole, or better, we are always already on the way to it. But we are driven on, i.e., we are somehow simultaneously torn back by something, resting in a gravity that draws us downward. We are underway to this 'as a whole'. We ourselves are this underway, this transition, this 'neither the one nor the other'. What is this oscillating to and fro between this neither/nor? Not the one and likewise not the other, this 'indeed, and yet not, and yet indeed'. What is the unrest of this 'not'? We name it *finitude*.

We are asking: *What is that—finitude?*

Finitude is not some property that is merely attached to us, but is *our fundamental way of being*. If we wish to become what we are, we cannot abandon this finitude or deceive ourselves about it, but must safeguard it. Such preservation is the innermost process of our being finite, i.e., it is our innermost becoming finite. Finitude only *is* in truly becoming finite. In becoming finite, however, there ultimately occurs an *individuation* of man with respect to his Dasein. Individuation—this does not mean that man clings to his frail little ego that puffs itself up against something or other which it takes to be the world. This individuation is rather that *solitariness* in which each human being first of all enters into a nearness to what is essential in all things, a nearness to world. What is this *solitude,* where each human being will be as though unique?

What is that—individuation?

What is all this, taken together: world, finitude, individuation? What is happening to us here? What is man, that such things happen to him in his very ground? Is what we know of man: the animal, dupe of civilization, guardian of culture, and even personality—is all this only the shadow in him of something quite other, of that which we name *Dasein?* Philosophy, metaphysics, is a homesickness, an urge to be at home everywhere, a demand, not blind and without direction, but one which awakens us to such questions as those we have just asked and to their unity: what is world, finitude, individuation? Each of these questions inquires into the whole. It is not sufficient for us to know such questions. What is decisive is whether we really ask such questions, whether we have the strength to sustain them right through our whole existence. It is not sufficient for us to simply abandon ourselves to such questions in an indeterminate and vacillating manner. Rather this urge to be at home everywhere is in itself at the same time a seeking of those ways which open up the right path for such questions. For this, in turn, we require the hammer of conceptual comprehension [*Begreifen*], we require those concepts [*Begriffe*] which can open such a path. We are dealing with a conceptual comprehension and with concepts of a *primordial* kind. *Metaphysical concepts* remain eternally closed off from any inherently indifferent and noncommittal scientific acumen. Metaphysical concepts are not something that we could simply learn in this way, nor something which a teacher or anyone calling themselves a philosopher might require to be simply recited and applied.

Above all, however, we shall never have comprehended these concepts [*Begriffe*] and their conceptual rigor unless we have first been *gripped* [ergriffen][3] by whatever they are supposed to comprehend. The fundamental concern of philosophizing pertains to such being gripped, to awakening and planting it. All such being gripped, however, comes from and remains in an *attunement* [Stimmung]. To the extent that conceptual comprehending and philosophizing is not some arbitrary enterprise alongside others, but happens in the *ground* [Grunde] of human Dasein, the attunements out of which our being gripped philosophically and our philosophical comprehension arise are always necessarily *fundamental attunements* [Grundstimmungen] of Dasein. They are of the kind that constantly, essentially, and thoroughly attune human beings, without human beings necessarily always recognizing them as such. *Philosophy in each case happens in a fundamental attunement.* Conceptual philosophical comprehension is grounded in our being gripped, and this is grounded in a fundamental attunement. Does not Novalis ultimately mean something like this when he calls philosophy a homesickness? Then this poet's word would not be at all deceptive, if only we extract what is essential from it.

And yet, what we have gained from all this is certainly not some definition of metaphysics, but something else. We saw that in our initial attempts to characterize metaphysics we were brought back time and again from all our detours and forced to grasp metaphysics in terms of itself. Even as we did so, metaphysics withdrew from us. Yet to where did it draw us? Metaphysics drew itself back and draws itself back into the obscurity of the essence of man. Our question: What is metaphysics? has transformed itself into the question: What is man?

Certainly we have found no answer to this either. On the contrary, man himself has become more enigmatic for us. We ask anew: What is man? A transition, a direction, a storm sweeping over our planet, a recurrence or a vexation for the gods? We do not know. Yet we have seen that in the essence of this mysterious being, philosophy happens.

---

3. [Tr: A play on cognates of *Griff* and *greifen* features throughout the course, and is difficult to render adequately in English. The noun *Begriff* is standard German for "concept," and is related to the verbs *greifen,* to "grasp" or "seize" (both literally and figuratively), and *begreifen,* to "grasp" or "comprehend" (in the mind). In this section, Heidegger stresses the importance of our conceptual thought being "gripped" or "seized" (*ergriffen*) by being drawn into a fundamental attunement; in §3, he will refer to philosophical concepts (*Begriffe*) as *Inbegriffe,* "comprehensive" or "inclusive" concepts (the *Inbegriff* normally means the quintessence or epitome of something, so that Heidegger's usage also has the sense of "quintessential concept"); in §7, the philosophical concept or *Begriff* is described as an "attack" (*Angriff*) upon man. In all these usages, the notion of being gripped, seized, or taken hold of is central.]

§3. Metaphysical thinking as comprehensive thinking:
dealing with the whole and gripping existence
through and through.

We are at the stage of a *preliminary appraisal.* This appraisal is meant to bring the *task* of the course closer to us, and at the same time to clarify our *overall orientation.* With regard to the title "Fundamental Concepts of Metaphysics," which initially seemed clear, we immediately saw that we are basically at a loss concerning our intentions as soon as we ask more closely what metaphysics is. Yet this is something that we must have some vague knowledge of, after all, if we are somehow able to take up a position with respect to what is at issue. If we pursue this question of what metaphysics is via *those* ways which directly present themselves to us and which have been trodden since time immemorial—if we determine philosophy as a science or as the proclamation of a worldview; or if we attempt to compare philosophy with art and religion; or if, finally, we resort to determining philosophy via a historical orientation, then the result is that in all these moves we are making detours. They are detours not only in the sense that they would be longer, but in the sense that we merely circumvent the matter. These detours [*Umwege*] are really false trails [*Holzwege*], paths which suddenly stop, which lead up a blind alley.

Yet these considerations and attempts that we have now roughly sketched show us something essential: that we may by no means shirk the task of grasping philosophy and metaphysics itself immediately, directly; that this is precisely what is difficult: to really stay with what is being asked about here, and not to steal away on detours. This staying is what is particularly difficult, especially because as soon as we seriously inquire about philosophy, philosophy withdraws from us into a peculiar obscurity of its own where it properly resides: as human activity in the ground of the essence of human Dasein.

We therefore had direct and apparently arbitrary recourse to a word of Novalis, according to which philosophy is a homesickness, an urge to be at home everywhere. We attempted to interpret this word. We tried to *extract* something from it. In so doing, it turned out that this demand to be at home *everywhere,* which means to exist among beings *as a whole,* is nothing other than a peculiar questioning about the meaning of this 'as a whole' which we call *world.* What happens here in this questioning and searching, in this back and forth, is the *finitude* of man. What occurs in such becoming finite is an ultimate *solitariness* of man, in which everyone stands for him- or herself as someone unique in the face of the whole. Thus it turned out that this questioning by way of conceptual comprehension is ultimately grounded in a *being gripped* which must determine and attune us, and on the basis of which we are first able to conceptually comprehend, and are first able to grasp, the matter of our inquiry. All being gripped is rooted in an attunement. What Novalis names *homesickness* is ultimately the *fundamental attunement of philosophizing.*

If we return to the initial point of departure of our preliminary appraisal and ask anew: What is meant by the title "The Fundamental Concepts of Metaphysics"?, then we will now no longer simply conceive of it as corresponding to "Fundamental Features of Zoology," or "Fundamental Elements of Linguistics." Metaphysics is not some discipline of knowledge in which we interrogate a restricted field of objects in a particular respect with the aid of some technique of thinking. We shall forego classifying metaphysics as one scientific discipline alongside others. Initially we must leave open what metaphysics is in general. We can see only this much: metaphysics is a fundamental occurrence within human Dasein. Its fundamental concepts are indeed concepts, yet these—according to logic—place something before us [*sind Vorstellungen*] whereby we represent to ourselves something universal or something in general, something with respect to the universal that many things have in common with one another. On the basis of such representation of the universal, we are in a position to determine individual items that stand before us, e.g., to determine this thing as a lectern, that thing as a house. The concept is thus something like a determinative representation. The fundamental concepts of metaphysics and the concepts of philosophy, however, will evidently not be like this at all, if we recall that they themselves are anchored in our being gripped, in which we do not represent before us that which we conceptually comprehend, but maintain ourselves in a quite different comportment, one which is originarily and fundamentally different from any scientific kind.

Metaphysics is a questioning in which we inquire into beings as a whole, and inquire in such a way that in so doing we ourselves, the questioners, are thereby also included in the question, placed into question.

Accordingly, fundamental concepts are not universals, not some formulae for the universal properties of a field of objects (such as animals or language). Rather they are concepts of a properly peculiar kind. In each case they comprehend the whole within themselves, they are *comprehensive concepts* [Inbegriffe]. Yet they are also comprehensive in a second sense which is equally essential and which ties in with the first: they also in each case always comprehend within themselves the comprehending human being and his or her Dasein—not as an addition, but in such a way that these concepts are not comprehensive without there being a comprehending in this second sense, and vice-versa. No concept of the whole without the comprehending of philosophizing existence. Metaphysical thinking is comprehensive thinking in this double sense. It deals with the whole and it grips existence through and through.

Chapter Two

Ambiguity in the Essence of Philosophy (Metaphysics)

Our understanding of the title of the course and the specification of our task have thus been transformed, but also the fundamental comportment in which we are to maintain ourselves in all discussions. To put it more clearly: whereas we previously knew nothing at all of a fundamental comportment of philosophizing and merely entertained the indifferent expectation of acquiring some knowledge, we now for the very first time have some idea that something like a fundamental comportment is demanded. At first we might think that fundamental concepts of metaphysics or fundamental features of linguistics all presuppose interest, yet that they ultimately presuppose merely an indifferent expectation of something that can be more or less penetratingly acquired as knowledge. We, however, are saying that it is not like this at all. It is essentially and necessarily a matter of a certain readiness. Confused and groping though this fundamental comportment may be and must at first remain—it has in this uncertainty precisely its specific vitality and strength, which are needed here if we are to understand anything at all. If we fail to summon up enthusiasm for the adventure of human existence, an appetite for the entirely enigmatic nature and fullness of Dasein and of things, an independence from schools of thought and learned opinions, and yet in all this a deep desire to learn and to listen, then our years at university—however much knowledge we amass—are an inner loss. Not only that, but the years and times to come will then assume a tortuous and tedious course that will in the end become a smug contentment. This alone we understand: there is a different kind of attentiveness demanded here than when taking note of research results or of a scientific proof and memorizing them, or rather, merely accumulating them in the great box of our memory. And yet the extrinsic arrangement of everything is the same: lecture theatre, lectern, lecturer, listeners, except that there it is about mathematics, there about Greek tragedy, and here about philosophy. If, however, philosophy is something totally different from science, and yet the exterior form of science still remains, then philosophy hides itself so to speak, it does not appear directly. What is more, it presents itself as something which it is not at all. This is neither simply a whim of philosophy, nor a fault, but belongs to the positive essence of metaphysics. What does? *Ambiguity.* Our preliminary appraisal of philosophy is incomplete until we have provided some indication of this ambiguity which is a positive characteristic of the essence of metaphysics and of philosophy.

   With regard to the essential ambiguity of metaphysics we shall discuss three things: [1.] The ambiguity in philosophizing in general; [2.] The ambiguity in our philosophizing here and now in the comportment of listeners and in the comportment of the lecturer; [3.] The ambiguity of philosophical truth as such.

We are not discussing this ambiguity of philosophy in order to develop a psychology of philosophizing, but in order to clarify the fundamental orientation demanded of us, so that we may let ourselves be guided by greater perspicacity in the coming discussions and leave false expectations aside, be they too high or too low.

§4. *The ambiguity in philosophizing in general:*
the uncertainty as to whether or not philosophy is
science or the proclamation of a worldview.

We already have a rudimentary awareness that philosophy presents itself as and looks like a science, and yet is not. Philosophy presents itself as the proclamation of a worldview and likewise is not this. These two kinds of semblance, of looking like . . ., are allied, and it is through this that the ambiguousness first becomes obtrusive. If philosophy appears in the semblance of science, then we are also referred to a worldview. Philosophy looks like the scientific grounding and presentation of a worldview, and yet is something else.

This dual semblance of being a science and worldview brings about a constant *insecurity* in philosophy. On the one hand, it seems as though one could not furnish philosophy with enough scientific knowledge and experience—and yet this 'never enough' of scientific knowledge is always too much at the decisive moment. On the other hand, philosophy—so it seems at first—demands that its knowledge be practically applied, as it were, and transformed into factical life. Yet it is always evident too that this moral concern remains superficial to philosophizing. It looks as though creative thinking and moral concern with a worldview could be welded together to produce philosophy. Because philosophy is for the most part familiar only in this *ambiguous double face as science and as proclamation of a worldview,* one tries to reproduce this double face in order to be completely true to it. This then produces those hybrids which, without marrow, bones, or blood, eke out a literary existence [*Dasein*]. In this way a scientific treatise arises with moralising directives added on or strewn throughout it. Or else what arises is more or less a good sermon using scientific expressions and forms of thought. Both can look like philosophy, although neither is. Or the converse may happen: something may present itself as a strictly scientific treatise, dry, heavy, without any moralising resonance or any hint of worldview, mere science—and yet it is laden with philosophy through and through. Or a private conversation may take place without any scientific terminology or pretensions, a commonplace discussion—and yet be of the most rigorous philosophical comprehension through and through.

Thus philosophy parades in the marketplace in manifold illusory forms or even disguises. One moment it looks like philosophy and is not philosophy at all, the next it looks nothing like philosophy and yet is precisely philosophy. Philosophy can be recognized only by whoever becomes intimately acquainted with it, i.e., takes trouble over it. This is so in a quite special sense in the case of our own undertaking in this course.

§5. The ambiguity in our philosophizing here and now in the comportment of the listener and of the teacher.

The ambiguity of philosophy always becomes more acute, however,—rather than vanishing—wherever we are explicitly concerned with it, as is the case in our situation here and now: philosophy as a subject to be taught, an examination subject, a discipline in which people do their doctorates as in other disciplines. For those who study and lecture, philosophy has the appearance of a general subject on which lectures are held. Accordingly, our comportment toward such a lecture is that we take it in or pass it by. In this way nothing else happens at all, it is simply that something fails to happen. After all, what do we have academic freedom for? We can profit even further and save ourselves the ten Marks enrollment fee. True, that is not enough for a pair of skis, but it will provide a pair of decent ski poles, and perhaps these are indeed far more essential than a philosophy lecture. The lecture could indeed be a mere deception—who can know?

Perhaps, however, we have also passed by an essential opportunity. The uncanny thing is that we do not notice this at all and perhaps indeed never notice it; that it makes no difference to us at all if we pass it by, and that here in the halls of the university we can nevertheless hold just as important speeches as others who listen to philosophy and perhaps even quote Heidegger. And if instead of passing it by we attend the lecture, is the ambiguity then removed? Has something obvious changed? Is not everyone sitting there just as attentively or just as bored? Are we better than our neighbour because we comprehend more quickly, or are we merely more skillful and eloquent, perhaps because we have the philosophical terminology more at our fingertips than others on account of a few philosophy seminars? Yet maybe, despite all this, we lack something essential that someone else—it might even be some female student—perhaps precisely possesses.

We—you as listeners—are incessantly surrounded and watched over by something ambiguous: philosophy. And even the teacher—what can he not prove, what a forest of concepts and terminology he can move around in, playing with some sort of scientific construction until the poor listener takes fright! He can present himself as though with him philosophy came into the world as absolute science for the first time. What can he not report about the world situation, the spirit and future of Europe, the approaching world era and the new Middle Ages, using the most modern catchphrases! He can talk with such unparalleled seriousness about the situation of the university and its running, ask what man is, whether a transition or a vexation for the gods. Is he perhaps some sort of play actor—who can know? If not, what kind of contradictory beginning is this, if philosophizing is an ultimate pronouncement, something extreme in which man is individuated with respect to his Dasein, whereas the teacher addresses the masses? Why, if he is philosophizing, does he abandon his solitude and run around in the marketplace as a professor in public? Above all, however, what a dangerous beginning this ambiguous stance is!

Do we merely address the masses or—if we look more closely—do we not persuade them, persuade them on the grounds of an authority that we do not at all have, but which for various reasons usually disseminates somehow in various forms, even when we do not intend this at all? For what is this authority based upon by which we silently persuade? Not on the fact that we are appointed by a higher power, nor on the fact that we are wiser and cleverer than others, but only on the fact that we are not understood. Only so long as we are not understood does this dubious authority work for us. Yet if we are understood, then it will become apparent whether we are philosophizing or not. If we are not philosophizing, then this authority will collapse of its own accord. Yet if we are philosophizing, then this authority was never there in the first place. It will then become clear for the first time that philosophizing fundamentally belongs to each human being as something proper to them, that certain human beings merely can or must have the strange fate of being a spur for others, so that philosophizing awakens in them. Thus the teacher is not exempt from ambiguity, but through the very fact that he presents himself as a teacher he brings a certain semblance with him. Thus every philosophical lecture—whether it is a philosophizing or not—is an ambiguous beginning in a way unknown to the sciences.

Regarding everything that has been said concerning the ambiguity of philosophizing in general and of ours in particular, one might reply: Factically there may always be a certain semblance, a lack of genuineness, an unjustified authoritative influence at work in things, but in the first and final instance all this can be decided on the purely factual grounds of proof. The individual carries weight only insofar as he or she supplies the grounds of proof, and through what has been proven compels the others to agree. After all, what has not already been proven in philosophy and presented as proven—and yet! How do things stand regarding proofs? What can really be proven? Perhaps what is provable is always only that which is essentially irrelevant. Perhaps that which can be proven and consequently must be proven is fundamentally of little value. Yet if philosophizing deals with something essential, then can and must what is essential therefore be unprovable? Can philosophy move in arbitrary assertions? Or—is it not permissible to establish philosophizing on the basis of the either/or of 'provable' or 'unprovable' at all? How do things stand then in general concerning the truth of philosophy? Is the character of truth pertaining to philosophy anything like the evidence of a scientific proposition, or is it something fundamentally different? With this we touch upon the question of the innermost ambiguity of philosophy.

§6. The truth of philosophy and its ambiguity.

In our preliminary appraisal thus far we have, in a provisional way, gained a characterization of metaphysics as a comprehensive thinking, a questioning which in every question, and not just in its results, questions the whole. Every question concerning the whole also comprehends within itself the questioner, puts the questioner into question from the perspective of the whole. We have sought to characterize the whole from one perspective, which looks like something psychological, the perspective of what we called the ambiguity of philosophizing. Thus far we have considered this ambiguity of philosophy in two directions: first, the ambiguity of philosophizing *in general* and, second, the ambiguity of *our* philosophizing *here and now*. The ambiguity of philosophy in general means that it presents itself as science and as worldview and is neither. It makes us unsure as to whether philosophy is a science and worldview or not.

This general ambiguity becomes more acute, however, precisely whenever we venture to present something explicitly as philosophy. In this way the semblance is not overcome, but intensified. There is a semblance in a dual sense which affects you, the listeners, and me; a semblance that can never be overcome at all for reasons we shall see. This semblance is much more persistent and dangerous for the teacher, because a certain undesired authority always speaks for him, which has the peculiar and obscure effect of persuading others. Such persuasion is an effect whose danger only rarely becomes transparent. This persuasion, however, which lies in every philosophy lecture, would not vanish even if one were to make the demand that everything had to be brought back to grounds of evidence alone and could be decided only within the realm of what has been proven. To presuppose that ambiguity could ultimately be overcome in principle by limiting matters to what can be proven goes back to an underlying presupposition: that even in philosophy what is essential is in general whatever can be proven. Yet perhaps that is a mistake. Perhaps what can be proven is only whatever is essentially irrelevant, and perhaps everything which first needs to be proven carries no intrinsic weight in itself.

Thus this last attempt to overcome ambiguity by limiting things to whatever is provable leads us to the question of what the character of philosophical truth and knowledge is in general, the question of whether there can be any talk of provability here at all.

We shall initially leave aside the peculiar fact that the question of philosophical truth has seldom been posed, and that when it has, this has been done in a distinctly provisional way. That this is so is not due to chance, but has its grounds precisely in the ambiguity of philosophy. To what extent? The ambiguity of philosophy misleads man into making sound common sense the ally and guide of philosophy, an ally which prescribes with equal ambiguity what is to be thought of philosophy and of its truth.

We said that philosophizing is an extreme and ultimate pronouncement and interlocution. Even everyday awareness knows that philosophy is such a thing, although it misinterprets this knowledge as having the sense of a worldview or absolute science. To begin with, philosophy presents itself first as something that concerns and is understood by everyone, and second as something ultimate and supreme.

a) Philosophy presents itself as something that concerns everyone and is understood by everyone.

Philosophy is something that concerns everyone. It is not the prerogative of one human being. Perhaps this is not in doubt. From this, however, our general awareness tacitly concludes that what *concerns* [an*geht*] everyone must be *understood* [ein*gehen*] by everyone. It must be accessible for everyone *straightaway*. This 'straightaway' means: it must be immediately clear. Immediately— that is to say: clear to everyone just as they are, without further effort on the part of clear and sound common sense. What everyone understands straightaway in this manner, however—as everyone knows—are such statements as 2 times 2 is 4, whatever can be calculated, whatever does not lie outside everyone's calculations or outside whatever everyone can reckon with straightaway. Reckoning itself is something we can understand like 2 times 2 is 4. In order to grasp such a thing, the most negligible amount or even no expenditure of human substance is required. We understand these truths for everyone without ever bringing our human essence into play from its very ground. I understand that, human beings understand that, whether they are a scholar or a peasant, whether a person of honour or a villain, whether human beings are near to themselves and agitated or lost and caught up in something arbitrary. Philosophy concerns everyone. Therefore it is for everyone, as everyone thinks straightaway. Philosophical truth, precisely if it concerns everyone, must be understood by everyone according to this everyday criterion. This directly implies that *what* concerns everyone contains in itself the *manner* and *way in which* it is understood by everyone. Whatever everyone can understand prescribes in general what can be true, what a truth in general and what a philosophical truth must look like.

b) Philosophy presents itself as something ultimate and supreme.

α) Philosophical truth in its semblance of
absolutely certain truth.

Philosophy is something ultimate, extreme. This is precisely something everyone must have and be able to have *in their secure possession*. As what is supreme, it must, after all, also be what is most sure—this is clear to everyone. It must be what is most certain. What everyone understands without any strenuous human effort must have *supreme certainty*. And behold—what is accessible to everyone straightaway like 2 times 2 is 4 is something we know in its extreme and developed form as mathematical knowledge. It is, after all, as everyone likewise knows, the highest, most rigorous, and most certain knowledge. We would thus possess the idea and measure of philosophical truth, arising out of what philosophizing is and should be. To crown it all, we are aware that Plato, whom we would be reluctant to deny philosophical charisma, had inscribed above the entrance to his Academy: οὐδεὶς ἀγεωμέτρητος εἰσίτω: No one shall have entry who is not well-versed in geometry, in mathematical knowledge. Did not Descartes, who determined the fundamental orientation of modern philosophy, want nothing other than to furnish philosophical truth with the character of mathematical truth and wrest mankind from doubt and unclarity? From Leibniz the saying has been handed down: *"Sans les mathématiques on ne pénètre point au fond de la Métaphysique":* Without mathematics one cannot penetrate into the ground of metaphysics. This is surely the most profound and sweeping confirmation of what is proposed straightaway and for everyone as absolute truth in philosophy.

Yet if it is as clear as day that philosophical truth is absolutely certain truth, why does precisely this endeavor on the part of philosophy never succeed? Regarding this endeavor concerning absolute truth and certainty, do we not instead throughout the history of philosophy constantly see one catastrophe after another? Thinkers such as Aristotle, Descartes, Leibniz, and Hegel have to put up with being refuted by a doctoral candidate. These catastrophes are so catastrophic that those concerned do not even notice them.

Must we not conclude, from our experience hitherto concerning the destiny of philosophy as absolute science, that this goal must finally be relinquished as a task? One might object to this conclusion, first, that even though two and a half thousand years' history of Western philosophy represent a considerable time, they are still not sufficient to allow us to draw this conclusion as regards the entire future. Second, we cannot therefore in principle conclude and decide in this way about what is yet to come on the basis of the past—the possibility that philosophy may after all one day succeed must remain open in principle.

To these two objections it must be said: We are not denying philosophy the character of absolute science because it has not yet attained this status hitherto, but because this idea of the essence of philosophy is ascribed to philosophy on the grounds of its ambiguity, and because this idea undermines the essence of philosophy at its core. This is why we gave a rough indication of the provenance of this idea. What does it mean to uphold mathematical knowledge as the measure of knowledge and as the ideal of truth for philosophy? It means nothing less than making that knowledge which is absolutely non-binding and emptiest in content into the measure for that knowledge which is the most binding and richest in itself, i.e., that knowledge which deals with the whole. Thus we do not at all need to leave open the possibility that philosophy will ultimately succeed in its putative concern of becoming absolute science, because this possibility is not a possibility of philosophy at all.

If we reject this connection between mathematical knowledge and philo-sophical knowledge on principle right from the start, the motive for this rejection is as follows: although it objectively comprises a great wealth, math-ematical knowledge is in itself, in terms of its content, the emptiest knowledge imaginable, and as such is at the same time the least binding for man. For this reason we are faced with the strange fact that mathematicians can make great discoveries when only seventeen years old. Mathematical knowledge does not necessarily need to be borne by the inner substance of man. Such a situation is impossible in principle for philosophy. This emptiest and at the same time least binding knowledge as regards human substance—mathematical knowl-edge—cannot become the measure for the richest and most binding knowledge imaginable: philosophical knowledge. This is the real reason—at first indicated only in a rough way—why mathematical knowledge cannot be proposed as the ideal of philosophical knowledge.

β) The emptiness and non-binding character of the argument of
formal contradiction. The truth of philosophy as rooted in the
fate of Dasein.

If we meet these objections in this way and uphold the proposition that philosophical knowledge, in short, is not mathematical in the broad sense, that it does not have this character of absolute certainty, are we not then threatened by another, much *more acute objection* which undermines all our discussions hitherto? Cannot someone without difficulty come up to us and say: Stop—you keep saying in an uncompromising tone that philosophy is not a science, is not absolutely certain knowledge. Yet this, precisely this—that it is not absolutely certain knowledge—is, after all, supposed to be absolutely certain, and you are proclaiming this absolutely certain proposition in a philosophical lecture. Surely we have here the whole sophistry of this unscientific conduct. To assert with a claim to absolute certainty that there is no absolute certainty: this is surely the most cunning method that can be thought up, but one that is distinctly short-lived. For how is it to resist the objection just brought forward?

Because this argument which we are now being confronted with does not just stem from the present day, but emerges time and again, we must constantly keep it in view and grasp it in its formal transparency. Is this argument not convincing? The argument is: it is contradictory to assert with absolute certainty that there is no absolute certainty, for this refutes itself. For then there is at least *this* certainty: that there is no certainty. Yet that means after all: there is *a* certainty. This argument, however, is as convincing as it is worn out; it is so worn out that it has always remained ineffective. It cannot be by chance that this apparently unshakable argument nevertheless carries no weight. We shall not appeal once more, however, to the ineffectiveness of this argument in past history, but shall ponder two things.

First: precisely because this argument is so easy to bring up at any time, it has essentially nothing to say. It is completely empty and non-binding. It is an argument that does not relate to philosophy at all with respect to its inner content, but is a formal argumentation which forces every speaker back into self-contradiction. If the argument were able to have the force and range expected of it in such circumstances, then surely—at least for those who want to see everything based upon such certainty and certain proofs—it would have to be proven in advance that this empty trick employing formal self-contradiction were intrinsically appropriate for sustaining and determining philosophy in its essence, philosophy in the extreme and as a whole. This proof has so far not only not been delivered, its necessity is not even recognized or understood at all by those who argue by means of this argument.

Second: this argument which hopes to demolish our proposition that philosophy is not a science and does not possess any absolute certainty is not relevant at all. We are not in fact claiming, and will never claim, that it is absolutely certain that philosophy is not a science. Why do we leave this uncertain? Perhaps because we still keep open the possibility that it may after all be a science? By no means, but rather because we are not at all absolutely certain and cannot be certain whether we are philosophizing at all in all these discussions. If we are not certain of what we are doing in this sense, how could we wish to impose absolute certainty on what we do?

We are uncertain about philosophizing. Could not philosophy have its intrinsic and absolute certainty precisely in this? No, for the fact that we are uncertain

about philosophizing is not some accidental property of philosophy in relation
to us, but belongs to philosophy itself, if it is indeed a human activity. Philosophy has a meaning only as human activity. *Its truth is essentially that of human
Dasein.* The truth of philosophizing is in part rooted in the fate of Dasein.
This Dasein, however, occurs in freedom. Possibility, change, and predicament
are obscure. Dasein stands before possibilities it does not foresee. It is subject
to a change it does not know. It constantly moves in a predicament it does not
have power over. Everything that belongs to the existence of Dasein belongs
just as essentially to the truth of philosophy. If we put things this way, then
we do not know this with absolute certainty, nor do we know it as something
probable. Probability is merely the conceptual counterpart of a presupposed
absolute certainty. We know all this in a unique kind of knowing which is
distinctive as a hovering between certainty and uncertainty—in a knowing that
we first grow into through philosophizing. For if we simply state these things
in this way, we only give rise once more to the illusion of apodictic propositions
in which there is no participation on our part. This illusion disappears whenever we transform the content.

Yet if we ourselves do not know whether we are philosophizing or not, does
not everything then really begin to vacillate? Indeed. Everything should start
to vacillate. From our point of view, we simply cannot demand anything else.
Only if we were assured that we, that each of us, were a god or God himself
might this not happen. Then philosophy too would have become utterly superfluous, and especially our discussion about it. For God does not philosophize, if indeed (as the name already says) philosophy, this love of . . . as
homesickness for . . ., must maintain itself in nothingness, in finitude. Philosophy is the opposite of all comfort and assurance. It is turbulence, the turbulence into which man is spun, so as in this way alone to comprehend Dasein
without delusion. Precisely because the truth of this comprehension is something ultimate and extreme, it constantly remains in the perilous
neighbourhood of supreme uncertainty. No knower necessarily stands so close
to the verge of error at every moment as the one who philosophizes. Whoever
has not yet grasped this has never yet had any intimation of what philosophizing means. What is ultimate and extreme is what is most perilous and insecure,
and this becomes more grave through the fact that it is proper and self-evident
that what is ultimate and extreme must be what is most certain for everyone.
Philosophy too appears on stage in the light of this illusion. In revelling in the
idea of philosophy as absolute knowledge, one tends to forget this perilous
neighbourhood of philosophizing. Perhaps one remembers it later in a hang-
over, without this remembering becoming decisive for action. For this reason
too the proper fundamental stance rarely awakens, a stance that would be equal
to this innermost ambiguity of philosophical truth. This elementary readiness
for the perilousness of philosophy is something with which we are not yet

acquainted. Because it is unfamiliar and above all not something actual, a dialogue that is a philosophizing is rarely or never at all attained among those who busy themselves with philosophy, yet do not philosophize. So long as this elementary readiness for the intrinsic perilousness of philosophy is lacking, a confrontation that is a philosophizing will never occur, no matter how many articles are launched against one another in journals. They all want to prove their own truths in the face of one another, and in so doing forget the single, actual, and most difficult task of driving one's own Dasein and that of others into a fruitful questionableness.

γ) The ambiguity of the critical stance in Descartes
and in modern philosophy.

It is no accident that with the advent of the increased and explicit tendency to raise philosophy to the rank of an absolute science in Descartes, a peculiar ambiguity of philosophy simultaneously works itself out in a special way. Descartes' fundamental tendency was to make philosophy into absolute knowledge. Precisely with him we see something remarkable. Here philosophizing begins with *doubt,* and it seems as though everything is put into question. Yet it only seems so. Dasein, the I (the ego), is not put into question at all. This illusion and this ambiguity of a critical stance runs right through the whole of modern philosophy up to the most recent present. It is, at most, a scientifically critical but not a philosophically critical stance. All that is ever put into question—or less still, remains open and is not followed up—is knowledge, consciousness of things, of objects or of subjects as well, and this only so as to reinforce the assuredness that has already been anticipated—*yet Dasein itself is never put into question.* A fundamental Cartesian stance in philosophy cannot in principle put the Dasein of man into question at all; for it would thereby destroy itself at the outset in its most proper intention. It, and with it all philosophizing of the modern era since Descartes, puts nothing at all at stake. On the contrary, the fundamental Cartesian stance already knows in advance, or thinks it knows, that everything can be absolutely strictly and purely proven and grounded. In order to prove this, it is critical in a non-binding and unperilous way—critical in such a way that it is inherently assured in advance that nothing, supposedly, can happen to it. Why this is so, we shall come to understand later. So long as we take such a stance toward ourselves and toward things we stand outside philosophy.

§7. The struggle of philosophizing against the insurmountable ambiguity of its essence. Philosophizing stands on its own as the fundamental occurrence in Dasein.

Insight into the multiple ambiguity of philosophizing acts as a deterrent [*abschreckend*] and ultimately betrays the entire fruitlessness of such activity. It would be a misunderstanding if we wished in the slightest to weaken this impression of the hopelessness of philosophizing, or to mediate it belatedly by indicating that in the end things are not so bad after all, that philosophy has achieved many things in the history of mankind, and so on. This is merely idle talk that talks in a direction leading away from philosophy. We must rather uphold and hold out in this terror [*Schrecken*]. For in it there becomes manifest something essential about all philosophical comprehension, namely that in the philosophical concept [*Begriff*], man, and indeed man as a whole, is in the *grip of an attack* [Angriff]—driven out of everydayness and driven back into the ground of things. Yet the attacker is not man, the dubious subject of the everyday and of the bliss of knowledge. Rather, *in philosophizing the Da-sein in man launches the attack upon man.* Thus man in the ground of his essence is someone in the grip of an attack, attacked by the fact 'that he is what he is', and already caught up in all comprehending questioning. Yet being comprehensively included in this way is not some blissful awe, but the struggle against the insurmountable ambiguity of all questioning and being.

Yet it would be just as perverse to see in philosophy a despairing activity that perhaps wears itself out, something gloomy, morose, 'pessimistic', turned toward everything dark and negative. It would be wrong to take philosophizing in this way—not because it also has its sunny sides in addition to this supposed shadow, but because this assessment of philosophizing is not drawn from philosophizing itself at all. In this assessment of philosophizing—and precisely of our own attempts too—authors of the most varied worldviews and directions and their supporters find themselves in agreement today.

Yet this assessment of philosophizing, which is by no means new, stems from the social atmosphere—once again, distinctly transparent in itself—of the normal human being and his or her guiding convictions that what is normal is what is essential, that whatever is average and therefore universally valid is what is true (the eternal average). This normal human being takes his or her petty pleasures as the measure of what joy should be. This normal human being takes his or her shallow fears as the measure of what terror and anxiety should be. This normal human being takes his or her smug comforts as the measure of what security and insecurity can be. It ought at least to have become questionable by now whether philosophizing as the ultimate and extreme pronouncement and interlocution may be dragged before such a judge, and whether we wish to let our attitude toward philosophy be dictated to us by this judge; or whether we are resolved to try something else, i.e., whether we wish to put ourselves, our being human, on the line. Is it really so sure that the interpretation of human existence [*Dasein*] in which we move today—according to which, for example, philosophy is one so-called cultural asset among others, and perhaps a science, something that needs to be cultivated—is it so sure that this interpretation of existence [*Dasein*] is the highest? Who can guarantee to us that man in this present-day self-conception has not raised some mediocre aspect of himself to the status of a god?

Thus far, we have attempted to grasp philosophizing itself—albeit only in a provisional way—in contrast to our initial detours. We have done so in two ways. First, we clarified philosophical questioning by way of our interpretation of a word of Novalis: philosophizing is homesickness, the urge to be at home everywhere. Second, we characterized the unique ambiguity proper to philosophizing. From all this we may conclude that philosophy is something autonomous that stands on its own. We may neither take it as a science among others, nor as something that we find only whenever we question the sciences with respect to their foundations. Philosophy does not exist because there are sciences, but vice-versa: there *can* be sciences only because and only if there is philosophy. Yet the grounding of the sciences, i.e., the task of furnishing their ground, is neither the sole nor the principal task of philosophy. Rather philosophy permeates the whole of human life (Dasein) even when there are no sciences, and not only in such a way as to merely gape belatedly at life (Dasein) as something at hand, ordering and determining it according to universal concepts. Philosophizing itself is rather a fundamental way of Da-sein. It is philosophy which, in a concealed way for the most part, lets Da-sein first become what it can be. Yet the Dasein concerned never knows what the Da-sein of man *can* be in individual epochs. Rather its possibilities are first formed precisely and only in Da-sein. Such possibilities, however, are those of factical Dasein, i.e., of the confrontation it must have with beings as a whole.

Philosophizing is not some belated reflecting on nature and culture as something at hand, nor is it a thinking up of possibilities and laws that can subsequently be applied to whatever is at hand.

All these are views which make an occupation and a business out of philosophy, albeit in a very exalted form. In contrast to this, philosophizing is something that lies prior to every occupation and constitutes the fundamental occurrence of Dasein, something autonomous that stands on its own and is quite different in nature to the kinds of comportment within which we commonly move.

The philosophers of antiquity already knew this and had to know it in their first decisive commencements. A word handed down to us from Heraclitus reads: ὁκόσων λόγους ἤκουσα, οὐδεὶς ἀφικνεῖται ἐς τοῦτο, ὥστε γινώσκειν ὅτι σοφόν ἐστι πάντων κεχωρισμένον.[1] "However many men I heard the statements of, none has managed to recognize that being wise, the σοφόν [philosophy], is something separated off from everything else." In Latin, what is separated off is called *absolutum*, something that is at its own proper place, or more precisely, something that first forms its own proper place for itself. Plato says in one of his major dialogues[2] that the difference between the philosophizing human being and the one who is not philosophizing is the difference between being awake (ὕπαρ) and sleeping (ὄναρ). The non-philosophizing human being, including the scientific human being, does indeed exist, but he or she is asleep. Only philosophizing is wakeful Dasein, is something totally other, something that stands incomparably on its own with respect to everything else. Hegel (to name a philosopher of the modern era) designates philosophy as the inverted world. He means that compared to what is normal for the normal human being, philosophy looks like something upside down, yet is fundamentally that orientation which is proper to Dasein itself. This may suffice not as an authoritative proof, but merely as an indication that I am not inventing a concept of philosophy here, nor arbitrarily presenting you with some private opinion.

Philosophy is something primordial that stands on its own, yet for this very reason it is not something isolated. Rather, as something extreme and primary, it is already comprehensive of everything, so that any application of it comes too late and is a misunderstanding.

At issue is nothing less than regaining this originary dimension of occurrence in our philosophizing Dasein, in order once again to 'see' all things more simply, more vividly, and in a more sustained manner.

---

1. H. Diels, *Die Fragmente der Vorsokratiker*. Ed. W. Kranz (Berlin, 1934ff.). Fifth edition. Vol. 1, Frgm. 108.
2. Plato, *Res Publica. Platonis Opera*. Ed. I. Burnet (Oxford, 1902ff.). Vol. 4, 476 c f., 520c, 533c.

Chapter Three

Justifying the Characterization of Comprehensive Questioning
Concerning World, Finitude, Individuation as Metaphysics.
Origin and History of the Word 'Metaphysics'

Philosophical concepts, fundamental concepts of metaphysics, have proved to be comprehensive concepts—comprehensive concepts in which the whole is always questioned, and comprehensive concepts which, in their questioning, always include and comprehend whoever is comprehending as well. We therefore determine metaphysical questioning as comprehensive questioning. It may have been conspicuous that in so doing, we have constantly equated philosophy and metaphysics, philosophical and metaphysical thinking. Yet in philosophy there is, after all, besides metaphysics also 'logic' and 'ethics', 'aesthetics', 'philosophy of nature', and 'philosophy of history'. With what right do we grasp philosophizing as such as metaphysical thinking? Why do we give the discipline of metaphysics such precedence over all others?

The disciplines of philosophy which are familiar under these headings—disciplines whose factical existence is by no means as harmless as it might seem for the fate of philosophizing—these disciplines have grown out of a scholastic concern with philosophy. Yet we are not at all in danger of arbitrarily giving one discipline of philosophy—metaphysics—precedence over the others, because we are not now dealing with disciplines at all. The intention of our preliminary appraisal is precisely to destroy this idea of metaphysics as a fixed discipline.

Metaphysics is comprehensive questioning. The questions: What is world, finitude, individuation? constitute such comprehensive questioning.

Yet with what right do we then still claim the title 'metaphysics' for comprehensive questioning thus characterized? This question, which is indeed legitimate, can be answered only by a brief discussion of the history of the word and its meaning. We have now already gained a certain pre-understanding of philosophizing, on the basis of which we can make the traditional meaning of the word 'metaphysics' speak to us. Yet in so doing we are *not taking* the essence of philosophy *from* this word 'metaphysics'. On the contrary, *we are first giving this word its meaning on the basis of an understanding of philosophy.*

Why do we still use the word 'metaphysics' and 'metaphysical' to designate philosophizing as comprehensive questioning? Where does this word come from, and what does it mean originally?

In the introduction to a lecture 'about' metaphysics it would seem reasonable, and would be tempting, to examine in more detail the history of the word and what it designates, the changes in its meanings and in our ways of viewing metaphysics. We shall forego this for reasons that have already been sufficiently discussed. Nevertheless, a brief indication of the history of the word is not only possible here, it is also indispensable. We shall conclude our preliminary appraisal with a discussion of the concept and word 'metaphysics'. We shall then have gained a general elucidation of the title of our lecture and our intent.

§8. The word 'metaphysics'. The meaning of φυσικά.

The word 'metaphysics', to put it negatively at first, is not a primal word [*Urwort*]. By a primal word we understand one that has been formed out of an essential and originary human experience as the *enunciation* of that experience. Here it is not necessary for this primal word also to have arisen in some primal time [*Urzeit*]; it can be relatively late. The relatively late character of a primal word does not speak against its being a primal word. The expression 'metaphysics', however, although we wish to designate something proper and authentic by it, is not a primal word. It goes back to the Greek wording which reads, when broken down: μετὰ τὰ φυσικά, or to put it in full: τὰ μετὰ τὰ φυσικά. We shall initially leave untranslated this wording, which later became amalgamated into the expression 'metaphysics'. We shall note merely that it serves to designate philosophy.

a) Elucidation of the word φυσικά. φύσις as the self-forming prevailing of beings as a whole.

We shall begin our elucidation of the context of the word with the last-mentioned term: φυσικά. In it lies φύσις, which we customarily translate as *nature*. This word itself comes from the Latin *natura*—*nasci*: to be born, to arise, to grow. This is also the fundamental meaning of the Greek φύσις, φύειν. Φύσις means that which is growing, growth, that which has itself grown in such growth. We here take growth and growing, however, in the quite elementary and broad sense in which it irrupts in the primal experience of man: growth not only of plants and animals, their arising and passing away taken merely as an isolated process, but growth as this occurring in the midst of, and permeated by, the changing of the seasons, in the midst of the alternation of day and night, in the midst of the wandering of the stars, of storms and weather and the raging of the elements. Growing is all this taken together as one.

We shall now translate φύσις more clearly and closer to the originally intended sense not so much by growth, but by the 'self-forming prevailing of beings as a whole'. Nature is not, for instance, to be taken in the narrow, present-day sense as the object of natural science, yet neither is it to be taken in a broad, pre-scientific sense, nor in Goethe's sense. Rather this φύσις, this prevailing of beings as a whole, is experienced by man just as immediately and entwined with things in himself and in those who are like him, those who are with him in this way. The events which man experiences in himself: procreation, birth, childhood, maturing, aging, death, are not events in the narrow, present-day sense of a specifically biological process of nature. Rather, they belong to the general prevailing of beings, which comprehends within itself human fate and its history. We must bring this quite broad concept of φύσις closer to us in order to understand this word in *that* meaning in which the philosophers of antiquity used it, who are wrongly called 'philosophers of nature'. Φύσις means this whole prevailing that prevails through man himself, a prevailing that he does not have power over, but which precisely prevails through and around him—him, man, who has always already spoken out about this. Whatever he understands—however enigmatic and obscure it may be to him in its details—he understands it; it nears him, sustains and overwhelms him as that which *is:* φύσις, that which prevails, beings, beings as a whole. I emphasize once more that φύσις as beings as a whole is not meant in the modern, late sense of nature, as the conceptual counterpart to history for instance. Rather it is intended more originally than both of these concepts, in an originary meaning which, prior to nature and history, encompasses both, and even in a certain way includes divine beings.

b) λόγος as taking the prevailing of beings as a whole out of concealment.

Man, insofar as he exists as man, has always already spoken out about φύσις, about the prevailing whole to which he himself belongs. Man has done so not only through the fact and for the purpose of talking specifically *about* things; for to exist as man already means: to make whatever prevails come to be spoken out. The prevailing of prevailing beings, i.e., their ordering and constitution, the law of beings themselves, comes to be spoken out. What is spoken out is that which has become manifest in speaking. In Greek, speaking is called λέγειν; the prevailing that has been spoken out is the λόγος. Therefore—it is important here to note this from the outset, as we shall see more precisely from the evidence—it belongs to the essence of prevailing beings, insofar as man exists among them, that they are spoken out in some way. If we conceive of this state of affairs in an elementary and originary way, we see that what is spoken out is already necessarily within φύσις, otherwise it could not be spoken from out of it. To φύσις, to the prevailing of beings as a whole, there belongs this λόγος.

The question for us is: What does this λέγειν, this speaking out accomplish? What occurs in the λόγος? Is it only a matter of the fact that what beings as a whole are is brought to a word, formulated, comes to word? To come to word—what does that mean? What the Greeks early on (and not just in their later philosophy, but as soon as they philosophized, i.e., from out of the ground of their understanding of existence [*Dasein*]) assigned to λέγειν, to the 'bringing to word' as its fundamental function, we can take with irrefutable clarity from the opposite concept, which the most ancient philosophers already opposed to λέγειν. What is the opposite of λέγειν? A 'not letting come to word'? How is this understood by the Greeks, by the very ones who use the word φύσις which we have elucidated? We can learn something of this from a word of Heraclitus, whom we have already mentioned: ὁ ἄναξ, οὗ τὸ μαντεῖόν ἐστι τὸ ἐν Δελφοῖς, οὔτε λέγει οὔτε κρύπτει ἀλλὰ σημαίνει.[1] "The master, whose Oracle is at Delphi, neither speaks out, nor does he conceal, but gives a sign [signifies]." Here it becomes clear that the opposite concept to λέγειν, to 'bringing to word', is κρύπτειν, keeping concealed and in concealment. From this it necessarily follows that the fundamental function of λέγειν is to take whatever prevails from concealment. The opposite concept to λέγειν is concealing [*Verbergen*]; the fundamental concept and the fundamental meaning of λέγειν is 'taking out of concealment', *revealing* [Entbergen]. Revealing, 'taking from concealment', is that happening which occurs in the λόγος. In the λόγος the prevailing of beings becomes revealed, becomes manifest.

For these stages of thinking, which are originary in an elementary way, it is the λόγος itself which becomes manifest; the λόγος lies in prevailing itself. Yet if prevailing is torn from concealment in the λόγος, then it must, as it were, try to conceal itself. The very same Heraclitus tells us in addition (without explicitly drawing attention to this connection), as emerges from another fragment, why φύσις came to be revealed and torn from concealment explicitly in λέγειν. In the collection of fragments one sentence stands alone which to this day has never been understood or comprehended in its profundity: φύσις . . . κρύπτεσθαι φιλεῖ.[2] "The prevailing of things has in itself a striving to conceal itself." You can here see the innermost connection between concealment and φύσις, and at the same time the connection between φύσις and λόγος as revealing.

c) λόγος as the saying of what is unconcealed (ἀληθέα). ἀλήθεια (truth) as something stolen, something that must be torn from concealment.

What it properly means to say that the λόγος is revealing is something we may take from another word of Heraclitus: σωφρονεῖν ἀρετὴ μεγίστη, καὶ σοφίη

1. H. Diels, op. cit., Frgm. 93.
2. Ibid., Frgm. 123.

ἀληυθέα λέγειν καὶ ποιεῖν κατὰ φύσιν ἐπαΐοντας.[3] "The highest that man has in his power is to meditate [upon the whole], and wisdom [lucidity] is to say and to do what is unconcealed as unconcealed, in accordance with the prevailing of things, listening out for them." You can thus see clearly the intrinsic relation between the opposite concept κρύπτειν and that which the λόγος says, ἀληθέα, that which is unconcealed. We usually translate this word by our colourless expression 'that which is true'. The highest that man has in his power is to say what is unconcealed, and together with this to act κατὰ φύσιν, i.e., fitting in with and adapting to the entire prevailing and fate of the world in general. Acting κατὰ φύσιν takes place in such a manner that he who thus speaks out listens to things. Only now have we gained the innermost context in which the primal word φύσις stands in the philosophy of antiquity: φύσις, the prevailing of what prevails; λόγος, the word, that which takes this prevailing from concealment. Everything that occurs in this word is a matter of σοφία, i.e., for the philosophers. In other words, philosophy is meditation upon the prevailing of beings, upon φύσις, in order to speak out φύσις in the λόγος.

We must keep in mind this connection which I have now clarified, especially that between φύσις and λόγος, in order to understand why in a later era Aristotle, when reporting on the most ancient of the Greek philosophers and speaking of them as his forebears, calls them the φυσιολόγοι. Yet the φυσιολόγοι are neither 'physiologists' in the contemporary sense of physiology as a special science of general biology, one which, as opposed to morphology, deals with the life-process; nor are they philosophers of nature. The φυσιολόγοι is rather the genuine primordial title for a questioning about beings as a whole, the title for those who speak out about φύσις, about the prevailing of beings as a whole, those who see that it is spoken out, who bring it to revealedness (truth).

We are thus able to see what φύσις initially means with respect to the strange and still problematic title τὰ μετὰ τὰ φυσικά, though we are not yet adequately prepared to delimit precisely what lies in the said title τὰ μετὰ τὰ φυσικά. The meaning of φύσις, however, has now been clarified. At the same time, we have gained an insight which is no less decisive for all that follows, an insight into the context in which φύσις stands for the Greeks themselves.

Initially, of course, one could say that it is self-evident that speaking out about beings should be true, and that our meditation should maintain itself in truth. Yet what is at issue is by no means the claim that this speaking out should be true, that statements about φύσις should be true and not false. It is rather a matter of comprehending what truth means here, and how the truth

---

3. Ibid., Frgm. 112.

of φύσις is understood by the Greeks in this commencement. We shall understand this only if we come to understand the Greek word ἀλήθεια, which we are not at all able to do by way of our corresponding German expression. Our German word *Wahrheit* [truth] has the same character as the words *Schönheit* [beauty], *Vollkommenheit* [completeness], and suchlike. However, the Greek word ἀ-λήθεια, un-concealment, corresponds to the German word *Un-schuld* [in-nocence], *Un-endlichkeit* [in-finity]: that which is not guilty, not finite. Correspondingly, ἀληθέα means that which is not concealed. The Greeks thus implicitly understand something negative in the innermost essence of truth, something that corresponds to the German *un-*. The α- is termed α-*privativum* in linguistics. It expresses the fact that something is lacking in the word it prefixes. In truth beings are torn from concealment. Truth is understood by the Greeks as something stolen, something that must be torn from concealment in a confrontation in which precisely φύσις strives to conceal itself. Truth is innermost confrontation of the essence of man with the whole of beings themselves. This has nothing to do with the business of proving propositions at the writing desk.

Φύσις is assigned to the λόγος and to ἀλήθεια, to truth in the sense of revealedness, for σοφία. This primal meaning of the Greek expression for truth is not as harmless as people believe and have hitherto taken it to be. Truth itself is something stolen. It is not simply there; rather, as a revealing, it ultimately demands the engagement of man as a whole. Truth is in part rooted in the fate of human Dasein. It itself is something concealed, and as such is something higher. This is why Heraclitus says: ἁρμονίη ἀφανὴς φανερῆς κρείττων.[4] "Higher and more powerful than the harmony lying open to the day is the harmony which does not show itself (is concealed)." This tells us that what φύσις conceals is precisely what is proper to it, that which does not lie open to the day. The fact that in the later period up to Aristotle the function of the λόγος emerges more and more clearly as that of ἀποφαίνεσθαι is merely in keeping with this. This means that the λόγος has the task of compelling the ἀφανής, that which conceals itself and does not show itself (that which is not self-showing), to show itself, the task of making it manifest.

The Greek concept of truth presented here manifests to us an intimate connection between the prevailing of beings, their concealment, and man. Man as such, insofar as he exists, in the λόγος tears φύσις, which strives to conceal itself, from concealment and thus brings beings to their truth.

When in *Being and Time* I emphatically pointed to this primal meaning of the Greek concept of truth, this was not done merely in order to provide a better and more literal translation of the Greek word. Nor is it a matter of

---

4. Ibid., Frgm. 54.

artificially playing around with etymologies and constructing something on the basis of such etymologies. What is at stake, rather, is nothing less than first making visible the fundamental position of man in antiquity with respect to the prevailing of beings (φύσις) and their truth (and thereby gaining an insight into the essence of philosophical truth), by way of an elementary interpretation of the concept of truth in antiquity.

This word for truth in antiquity is a primal word precisely on account of its 'negativity'. It testifies that truth is a fate of the finitude of man and, so far as the philosophy of antiquity is concerned, has nothing to do with the harmlessness and indifference of proven propositions. Yet this word for truth in antiquity is as old as philosophy itself. It does not need to be and cannot be more ancient, nor indeed more recent, because the understanding of truth that is spoken out in this primal philosophical word first emerges with philosophizing. The seemingly late emergence of the word is no objection to its fundamental meaning, but the reverse: its innermost belonging together with the fundamental experience of φύσις as such.

d) The two meanings of φύσις.

Let us keep in mind this primal meaning of truth (the revealedness of prevailing beings, φύσις), and let us now attempt to grasp more precisely the meaning of φύσις. We shall pursue the history of the fundamental meaning of this word, in order to arrive at an understanding of what φυσικά initially means in the title μετὰ τὰ φυσικά.

α) The ambivalence of the fundamental meaning of φύσις: that which prevails in its prevailing. The first meaning of φύσις: the φύσει ὄντα (as opposed to the τέχνη ὄντα) as regional concept.

The fundamental meaning of φύσις is already ambivalent in itself, although this ambivalence does not clearly emerge at first. Yet it soon makes itself visible. Φύσις, that which prevails, means not only *that which itself prevails,* but that which prevails in its prevailing or the *prevailing* of whatever prevails. And yet—as a consequence of the incisive confrontation with whatever prevails, that which prevails manifests itself in its undecidedness. Precisely what prevails as all-powerful for immediate experience claims the name φύσις for itself. Yet such is the vault of the heavens, the stars, the ocean, the earth, that which constantly threatens man, yet at the same time protects him too, that which supports, sustains, and nourishes him; that which, in thus threatening and sustaining him, prevails of its own accord without the assistance of man. Φύσις, nature, is here already understood in a narrower sense, yet one that is still broader and more originary than the concept of nature in modern natural science, for instance. Φύσις now means that which of itself is always already at hand, continually forming and passing away of its own accord, as distinct from that which is of human making, that which springs from τέχνη, from skill, invention, and production. Φύσις, that which prevails, in this distinct and yet narrower meaning now designates a distinctive region of beings, certain beings among others. The φύσει ὄντα are opposed to that which is τέχνη, that which arises on the basis of a preparation and production, of a meditation proper to man. Φύσις now becomes a regional concept. Yet nature in this narrower sense, which is nevertheless fairly broad, is that which for the Greeks neither arises nor passes away. Again, Heraclitus tells us: κόσμον τόνδε, τὸν αὐτὸν ἁπάντων, οὔτε τις θεῶν οὔτε ἀνθρώπων ἐποίησεν, ἀλλ' ἦν ἀεὶ καὶ ἔστιν καὶ ἔσται πῦρ ἀείζωον, ἁπτόμενον μέτρα καὶ ἀποσβεννύμενον μέτρα.[5] "This kosmos [I deliberately leave the word untranslated] is always the same throughout everything, and neither a god nor any human being created it, rather this φύσις always was, always is, and always will be an ever-flaming fire, flaring up according to measure and extinguishing according to measure."

β) The second meaning of φύσις: prevailing as such
as the essence and inner law of the matter.

In the expression φύσις, however, prevailing as such, which lets everything that prevails be as that which it is, is equiprimordially and just as essentially understood. Φύσις now no longer means one region among others, indeed it does not mean a region of beings at all, but the *nature of beings.* Nature now has the meaning of *innermost essence,* as when we say: the nature of things, and in so doing mean not only the nature of natural things, but the nature of each and every being. We speak of the nature of spirit, of soul, of the nature of the work of art, of the nature of the matter. Here φύσις does not mean that which prevails itself, but its *prevailing* as such, the essence, the inner law of a matter.

What is now decisive is that one of these two concepts of φύσις does not, for instance, suppress the other, but that they both continue alongside one another. Indeed, they are not only alongside one another, for the insight gradually awakens that *both meanings* which come to the fore in φύσις right from the commencement, albeit unaccentuated, express something equally essential and therefore persist in *that* questioning which in principle questions concerning the prevailing of beings as a whole: philosophy.

We cannot here pursue more closely the historical process which in the philosophy of antiquity leads to an increasingly distinct prominence of these

5. Ibid., Frgm. 30.

two fundamental meanings, and in this way establishes two directions of questioning which intrinsically belong together and continually challenge one another. I shall merely indicate that it took centuries for these two concepts of φύσις to develop, and this in the case of a people entrusted in their hearts with the passion of philosophizing. We barbarians, on the other hand, think that such things happened overnight.

§9. *The two meanings of* φύσις *in Aristotle. Questioning concerning beings as a whole and questioning concerning the essentiality (the being) of beings as the dual orientation of questioning in* πρώτη φιλοσοφία.

We shall cast only a brief glance at that stage of ancient philosophizing where it reaches its pinnacle: the state of the problem in Aristotle. The transformations and fates of Greek man are the commencements of philosophy up to Aristotle. Leaving all that in the background, we shall look merely at the bare facts of the problem.

I have already indicated that the prevailing of whatever prevails, and that which prevails itself, manifests itself, as soon as it is taken from concealment, as that which is: beings. Beings impose themselves as a whole in their manifold character and fullness and attract investigation, which becomes involved with particular areas and domains of beings. This means that together with questioning about φύσις as a whole, particular orientations of questioning awaken; particular paths of knowledge are embarked upon; from out of philosophizing there grow individual philosophies, which we later call sciences. Sciences are ways and kinds of philosophizing, not the reverse: philosophy is not a science. The Greek word for science is ἐπιστήμη. ἐπίστασθαι means: to stand before a matter, to know one's way around in it. ἐπιστήμη therefore means approaching a matter, knowing one's way around in it, being in control of it, penetrating the contents of the matter. Only in Aristotle does this word take on the decided meaning of 'science' in a broad sense, i.e., the specific meaning of theoretical investigation in the sciences. Sciences arise which relate to different domains, to the vault of the heavens, to plants and animals and suchlike. That ἐπιστήμη which relates to φύσις in whatever sense is the ἐπιστήμη φυσική—physics, not yet in the narrow meaning of contemporary modern physics, but physics that also comprises all the disciplines of biology. The ἐπιστήμη φυσική is not merely an amassing of facts in the different domains, but is originally just as much a reflecting upon the inner lawfulness of this entire domain itself. Questions are asked concerning what life itself is, what the soul is, what arising and passing away (γένεσις and φθορά) are, what happening is as such, what movement, position, and time are, what the emptiness is in which that which is moved moves, what that which moves itself is as a whole and what the Prime Mover is. All this falls into ἐπιστήμη φυσική, i.e., there is as yet no clear structuring of any individual sciences or of an accompanying philosophy of nature. This ἐπιστήμη φυσική has as its object everything that in this sense belongs to φύσις and that the Greeks designate as τὰ φυσικά. The questioning proper to these sciences dealing with φύσις is the supreme question of the Prime Mover, of what this whole of φύσις is in itself as this whole. Aristotle designates this ultimate determinant within the φύσει ὄντα as the θεῖον, as the divine, without yet associating this with any particular religious view. Questions are thus asked concerning beings as a whole, and ultimately concerning the divine. The ἐπιστήμη φυσική is assigned to such questioning. We have a lecture course on this physics handed down from Aristotle himself, Φυσικὴ ἀκρόασις or, as we would say today, though inaccurately, the philosophy of nature.

How do things now stand concerning the second meaning of φύσις in the sense of essence? The prevailing of what prevails here can be grasped as that which determines whatever prevails as a being, that which makes beings beings. In Greek, beings are called the ὄν, and that which makes beings beings is the essence of beings, their being. The Greeks designate the latter as οὐσία. Thus for Aristotle οὐσία, the essence of beings, is still called φύσις. We thereby have two meanings of φύσις that are found together in Aristotelian philosophy: firstly φύσις as beings as a whole, and secondly φύσις in the sense of οὐσία, the essentiality of beings as such. What is decisive is that these two orientations of questioning, contained in the unitary meaning of φύσις, are explicitly amalgamated by Aristotle. There are not two different disciplines; rather he designates questioning concerning beings as a whole and questioning concerning what the being of beings, their essence, their nature is, as πρώτη φιλοσοφία, as First Philosophy. Such questioning is philosophizing of the first order, philosophizing proper. Philosophizing proper is a questioning concerning φύσις in this dual sense: questioning concerning beings as a whole, and together with this, questioning concerning being. This is how things stand for Aristotle. At the same time Aristotle says nothing, or we have nothing handed down, about how he thinks these two orientations of questioning in their unity, to what extent precisely this questioning in its dual orientation constitutes philosophizing proper in a unitary way. This question is open and is open to this day, or rather is not even posed any more today.

Looking back we may sum up. We are now asking with what right we may claim the title 'metaphysics' as a proper designation for philosophizing, when, after all, we simultaneously reject metaphysics in the traditional sense as a discipline of philosophy. Initially we are attempting to justify the legitimacy and kind of use we are making of the title 'metaphysics' for our considerations by way of a brief orientation concerning the history of the expression. This orientation leads us back into the philosophy of antiquity and at the same time provides us with information about the commencements of Western philosophy itself in the tradition in which we stand. In the context of clarifying the main expression in the title τὰ μετὰ τὰ φυσικά, we considered φύσις in connection with the λόγος. The prevailing of beings as a whole intrinsically strives to conceal itself. Commensurate with this, a peculiar confrontation is associated with this prevailing, a confrontation in which φύσις is revealed. We shall now provisionally leave aside this connection between φύσις and truth, i.e., unconcealment as spoken out in the λόγος. We shall have to take it up again later. For now, we are interested only in the development of the two fundamental meanings of φύσις, of that which prevails in its prevailing. Therein lies on the one hand that which prevails itself, namely beings, and on the other hand beings taken in their prevailing, i.e., in their being. With respect to these two fundamental orientations, the expression φύσις develops into these two fundamental meanings: φύσις as φύσει ὄντα, beings as they are accessible in physics, in the investigation of nature in the narrower sense, and φύσις in its second meaning as nature, just as we use this expression today whenever we speak of the nature of the matter, of the essence of the matter. Φύσις in the sense of that which constitutes the being and essence of a being is οὐσία. The separation of these two meanings of φύσις: beings themselves and the being of beings, and the history of these meanings and their development culminate in Aristotle, who precisely grasps questioning concerning the φύσει ὄντα as a whole (φύσις in the first sense) and the question concerning οὐσία, the being of beings (φύσις in the second sense), in one, and designates this questioning as πρώτη φιλοσοφία, prima philosophia, First Philosophy, philosophy in the proper sense. Philosophizing proper asks after φύσις in this dual sense: after beings themselves and after being. To the extent that philosophy asks about beings themselves, it does not take just any arbitrary thing as its object, but directs its questioning toward these beings as a whole. Insofar as the fundamental character of these beings and their being is movement, the original question concerning them goes back to the first mover, that which is ultimate and extreme, which is simultaneously designated the θεῖον, the divine, without any connotations of a particular religious meaning. This is how the matter stands in Aristotelian philosophy. Philosophizing proper is for Aristotle this dual questioning: concerning the ὂν καθόλου and concerning the τιμιώτατον γένος, concerning beings in general, concerning being, and concerning that being which properly is. Yet the way in which these are intrinsically connected was not further elaborated by Aristotle, and we find nothing in what has been handed down from him that would provide us with information as to how this *unitary* problematic looks which takes as its object φύσις in this dual sense, nor are we given any information as to how that problematic is explicitly grounded from out of the essence of philosophy itself.

*§10. The formation of the scholastic disciplines of logic, physics,
and ethics as the decline of philosophizing proper.*

What Aristotle achieved with respect to philosophy proper has been handed down to us in individual lecture courses and treatises. In these we find ever new approaches and attempts at philosophizing proper, but nothing of an Aristotelian system such as was first invented later, just as there is no system of Platonic philosophy in the Dialogues of Plato.

Aristotle died around 322–21 B.C. Since then, however, philosophy has long become the victim of ambiguity. The philosophy of antiquity reached its acme with Aristotle, and its descent and proper decline begins with him. In Plato and Aristotle the formation of schools becomes unavoidable. What effect does this have? Living questioning dies out. The proper grip that held philosophical questioning is absent. And this is all the more so since what once meant being gripped in this way has come to be something known and has been spoken out. What has been spoken out is taken on its own and made into a useful result, something that can be applied, something for everyone to learn and repeat. That means that everything belonging to Platonic and Aristotelian philosophy, the wealth of treatises and dialogues that has been handed down, is uprooted and is no longer comprehended as something rooted. Nevertheless a rich stockpile of philosophy is now available with which their descendants and epigones must somehow come to terms. Platonic and Aristotelian philosophy succumbs to the fate which no philosophy escapes: it becomes philosophy of the schools. However, because the enrootedness of this philosophizing has been lost, the school and those who come after are left with the task of somehow stitching together the divergent elements which are now splitting apart, with the result that philosophy comes to be accessible for everyone and can be repeated by everyone. Everything that had once grown out of the most diverse questions—extrinsically unconnected, but all the more intrinsically rooted—now becomes rootless, heaped together in subjects according to viewpoints that can be taught and learned. The context and its rootedness are replaced by an ordering within subjects and scholastic disciplines. The question is which viewpoints now regulate the ordering of this rich material, which is no longer taken hold of at its core or in its vitality.

The viewpoint of this scholastic ordering was a direct result of the main themes that have already become familiar to us. We saw that, on the one hand, philosophy is concerned with φύσις. In clarifying the expression φύσις in the sense of that which subsists independently for itself and grows and prevails from out of itself, we distinguished it from those beings that are on the basis of their being produced by man. From here we gain the opposite concept to φύσις, one which comprises everything referring to human deed and action, including man in his activity, in his conduct, in his stance, in that which the

Greeks designate ἦθος, from which our expression 'ethics' comes. ἦθος means man's stance, the stance taken by man, in his self-conduct as a being who is distinct from nature in the narrower sense, from φύσις. Thus we have two fundamental areas which come to light as major themes for our appraisal. Now insofar as φύσις and ἦθος are dealt with in philosophy, they are explicitly spoken out and discussed in the λόγος. Insofar as the λόγος, speaking about things, comes first in everything to do with teaching, an appraisal of the λόγος itself comes first.

When the attempt is made to slot the entire stock of ancient philosophizing into scholastic disciplines, then this simultaneously means that the manner of knowing is no longer a living philosophizing from out of the problems themselves, but takes place in the manner in which domains of knowledge are elsewhere dealt with in the sciences. The manner in which these domains of philosophy are dealt with now becomes a science, ἐπιστήμη in the Aristotelian sense. There arises the ἐπιστήμη λογική, followed by the ἐπιστήμη φυσική; and the ἐπιστήμη ἠθική completes things. In this way there ensue three disciplines of philosophy scholastically conceived: logic, physics, ethics. This process of the scholastic development and thereby of the decline of philosophizing proper begins already in the era of Plato, in his own school academy. In the classical tradition it is reported from the Hellenistic period that this separation of disciplines was made possible through Plato himself, and was for the first time founded by one of his pupils and director of the Academy, Xenocrates. This division not only maintained itself through the centuries in the Platonic Academy, but also passed over into the school of Aristotle, into Peripatetic philosophy, and was then taken over from them by the Stoics. We find the evidence for this in Sextus Empiricus: πλὴν οὗτοι μὲν ἐλλιπῶς ἀνεστράφθαι δοκοῦσιν, ἐντελέστερον δὲ παρὰ τούτους οἱ εἰπόντες τῆς φιλοσοφίας τὸ μέν τι εἶναι φυσικὸν τὸ δὲ ἠθικὸν τὸ δὲ λογικόν· ὧν δυνάμει μὲν Πλάτων ἐστὶν ἀρχηγός, περὶ πολλῶν μὲν φυσικῶν [περὶ] πολλῶν δὲ ἠθικῶν οὐκ ὀλίγων δὲ λογικῶν διαλεχθείς· ῥητότατα δὲ οἱ περὶ τὸν Ξενοκράτην καὶ οἱ ἀπὸ τοῦ περιπάτου ἔτι δὲ οἱ ἀπὸ τῆς στοᾶς ἔχονται τῆσδε τῆς διαιρέσεως:[1] In a more complete way the philosophers divided up those who say it is the task of philosophy to deal with that which concerns physics, ethics, and logic; a distinction prefigured in Plato, who as leader was the first to be concerned a great deal with φυσικά as with ἠθικά and no less with λογικά; this distinction was first explicitly introduced by those around Xenocrates and the pupils of Aristotle in Peripatos, as well as the Stoics.

Yet for us it is not sufficient simply to take note of this fact. Rather what is decisive is that from the commencement this scholastic structuring prefigures

---

1. Sextus Empiricus, *Adversus Mathematicos.* Ed. I. Bekker (Berlin, 1842). Book VII, Section 16. [Tr: The following passage is Heidegger's rendition of the Greek.]

the conception of philosophy and of philosophical questioning for the following period, so that philosophy in the post-Aristotelian era—with a few exceptions—becomes an affair of schooling and learning. Those philosophical questions that emerge or are known from earlier times are inevitably accommodated within one of these disciplines and dealt with according to its methodological schema of question and proof.

§11. The changeover from the technical meaning
of μετά *in the word 'metaphysics' to a meaning*
conceived in terms of content.

a) The technical meaning of μετά: after (*post*).
Metaphysics as the technical title for an
embarrassment in the face of πρώτη φιλοσοφία.

During these centuries of the decline of ancient philosophy, in the period from 300 B.C. until into the first century B.C., the writings of Aristotle were almost forgotten. He himself had published very little at all. What remained was kept merely in manuscripts, lecture drafts, and transcripts of lectures, just as it had arisen. When people became concerned with all this material of Aristotelian philosophy in the first century B.C. and wished to make it accessible to the schools, they saw themselves faced with the task of gathering and ordering the entire corpus of Aristotelian treatises. It was thus quite natural for them to regard all the material from the perspective available to them, i.e., taking the three disciplines of logic, physics, and ethics as their guiding thread. For those who were gathering together the Aristotelian writings, there arose the task of dividing the entire corpus of handed-down material into these three disciplines, which for their part were not put in question.

If we put ourselves in the position of those who first gathered together all this material, then we have before us the material of Aristotelian philosophy and the three disciplines. However, among the treatises of Aristotle there were also to be found those in which he himself sometimes says that they present πρώτη φιλοσοφία, philosophizing proper, those which ask concerning beings in general and concerning the being that properly is. Those who were arranging the Aristotelian writings were unable to accommodate these treatises in any of the three disciplines into which scholastic philosophy was divided. On account of this fixed framework of the three disciplines of philosophy, they were not in a position to take on board what Aristotle designates as philosophy proper. In the face of Aristotle's philosophy proper, there arose the *embarrassment* of its not belonging in any of the disciplines. On the other hand, one could least of all leave aside precisely what Aristotle designates as philosophizing proper. Thus the question arose of where to put philosophy proper within the schema of these three disciplines which the school was not in a position to expand or alter. We must be quite clear about this situation: what is essential in philosophy could not be accommodated. The philosophy of the schools fell into an embarrassment in the face of philosophizing.

There remains only one way out of this embarrassment. One tries to see whether philosophy proper does not have some connection to what is familiar in the schools. And indeed it does. In these treatises we find in part questions similar to those found in *that* lecture course which lays the foundations of 'physics'. It is evident that there is a certain relatedness between the questions that Aristotle treats in First Philosophy and those questions which philosophy of the schools discusses under physics, although what Aristotle treats in First Philosophy is much broader and very much more fundamental. There is therefore no possibility of simply classifying First Philosophy within physics, but only the possibility of placing it *alongside, behind* physics, of classifying it *after* physics. Behind, following after, is μετά in Greek, so that philosophy proper was placed behind physics: μετὰ τὰ φυσικά. Philosophy proper henceforth comes under the title τὰ μετὰ τὰ φυσικά. What is essential here is that we are faced with the awkward situation that through this designation, philosophy proper is not characterized according to content, according to its particular problematic, but by a title that is supposed to indicate its position in the extrinsic order of the writings: τὰ μετὰ τὰ φυσικά. What we call 'metaphysics' is an expression which arose from being at a loss as to what to do, the title for an embarrassment, a purely technical title which says nothing at all as regards content. τὰ μετὰ τὰ φυσικά are πρώτη φιλοσοφία.

This classification of Aristotelian writings has been maintained throughout the entire tradition and has passed over into the major edition of Aristotelian writings, the Berlin Academy edition, in which the writings on logic are followed by those on physics, then those on metaphysics, and finally the ethical and political writings.

b) The meaning of μετά with respect to content: over beyond
(*trans*). Metaphysics as a designation and interpretation of πρώτη
φιλοσοφία with respect to content: science of the suprasensuous.
Metaphysics as a scholastic discipline.

For a long time τὰ μετὰ τὰ φυσικά remained such a technical title, until—we do not know when or how or through whom—this technical title was assigned a meaning with respect to content and the phrase was compressed into one word, the Latin expression *metaphysica*. In Greek μετά means after, behind, as in the words μετιέναι (to go after), μετακλαίειν (to cry after), μέθοδος, method, i.e., the way in which I go after a matter.

μετά has a further meaning in Greek, however, which is connected with the first. If I go behind a matter and go after it, in so doing I move away from one matter and over to another, i.e., I turn myself 'around' in a certain respect. We have this meaning of μετά in the sense of 'away from something toward something else' in the Greek word μεταβολή (changeover [*Umschlag*]). In condensing the Greek title τὰ μετὰ τὰ φυσικά into the Latin expression *metaphysica,* the μετά has altered its meaning. The meaning of changeover, of 'turning away from one matter toward another', of 'going from one over to another', came out of a purely positional meaning. τὰ μετὰ τὰ φυσικά now no longer means that which comes after the doctrines on physics, but that which deals with whatever *turns away* from the φυσικά and *turns toward* other beings, toward beings in general and toward that being which properly is. This *turnaround* happens in philosophy proper. The πρώτη φιλοσοφία is metaphysics in this sense. This turning away of philosophy proper from nature as one particular domain, from any such domain at all, is a *going over beyond* individual beings, *over to* this other.

Metaphysics becomes the title for knowledge of that which lies out beyond the sensuous, for the *science* and *knowledge of the suprasensuous.* This may be clarified from the Latin meaning. The first meaning of μετά, after, means *post* in Latin, the second means *trans.* The technical title 'metaphysics' now becomes a designation for πρώτη φιλοσοφία with regard to its content. Metaphysics in this meaning with respect to content now assumes a particular interpretation and conception of πρώτη φιλοσοφία. The business of classifying in scholastic philosophy—and above all its embarrassment—is the cause of a quite specific interpretation to which philosophizing proper as metaphysics is henceforth subject. Hitherto—apart from the unsatisfactory elucidation of the developmental history of the word—insufficient attention has been paid to the fact that this changeover is by no means as inconsequential and harmless as it may appear. This changeover in the title is by no means something trivial. Something essential is decided by it—*the fate of philosophy proper in the West.* The questioning of philosophy proper is conceived in advance as metaphysics in its second meaning with respect to content, it is forced in a particular direction and into particular approaches. Thus the title 'metaphysics' has given rise to analogous word-formations which are correspondingly thought of with respect to content: meta-logic, meta-geometry, which ranges beyond Euclidian geometry; Baron von Stein called people who construct practical politics based upon philosophical systems metapoliticians. There is even talk of a meta-aspirin whose effects go beyond those of conventional aspirin.[1] Roux speaks of the metastructure of protein. Metaphysics itself however comes to be installed as

---

1. Cf. J. Wackernagel, *Vorlesungen über Syntax mit besonderer Berücksichtigung von Griechisch, Lateinisch und Deutsch.* Second edition (Basel, 1928). Zweite Reihe, p. 248.

the title for one discipline alongside others. The initial technical meaning was meant to indicate the position of πρώτη φιλοσοφία, which was not understood, and then changed over into a characterization of philosophizing proper in terms of its content. In this meaning it is the title for one philosophical discipline which is classified alongside the rest.

The origin of the word 'metaphysics' and its history is initially important for us only in this quite essential respect, namely that we recall the changeover from the technical meaning to one in terms of content, and remember the associated thesis of how metaphysics thus conceived comes to be classified in the order of scholastic disciplines. We cannot present the history of this discipline itself in any detail. There are many kinds of things we could say about it. And yet—such things remain fundamentally unproductive, unless we understand them from out of a living problematic of metaphysics.

§12. The inherent incongruities of the traditional concept of metaphysics.

We are concerned with a different question, namely with what right we retain the title 'metaphysics', and that means at the same time what meaning we accord it, given that we nevertheless reject it as a scholastic discipline. We sought to find the answer to this question via the history of the word. What did this history tell us? It acquainted us with two meanings: the initial technical one and the subsequent one referring to content. The first evidently cannot detain us any longer. We are taking 'metaphysics' in its second meaning, with respect to its content, when we say that philosophy is metaphysical questioning. We are thus taking metaphysics as the title for πρώτη φιλοσοφία, not just as a mere title, but in such a way that this word expresses what philosophizing proper is. Everything would thus be fine: we are sticking to the tradition. And yet—in such keeping to the tradition there lies the real difficulty. For is the meaning of metaphysics in respect of its content drawn from a real understanding of πρώτη φιλοσοφία and arrived at as an interpretation of the latter? Or is not *the reverse* the case, namely that πρώτη φιλοσοφία has been conceived in accordance with a relatively arbitrary interpretation of metaphysics? This is indeed so. The development of the second meaning of metaphysics showed us that the expression 'metaphysics' was taken in respect of its content to refer to knowledge of the suprasensuous. The title 'metaphysics' has kept this sense throughout the tradition, though this is precisely the meaning that we may *not* assume for it. Rather for us the reverse task arises, namely *of first providing the title now at hand with its meaning from out of an originary understanding of* πρώτη φιλοσοφία. In short, we are not to interpret πρώτη φιλοσοφία in terms of metaphysics, but must on the contrary *justify the expression 'metaphysics' via an originary interpretation of what is at issue in the* πρώτη φιλοσοφία *of Aristotle.*

If we make this demand, then it is based on the conviction that the traditional title 'metaphysics', conceived in terms of its content as knowledge of the suprasensuous, is not drawn from an originary understanding of πρώτη φιλοσοφία. To give this conviction foundation, we would now have to show two things: *first,* how an originary understanding of πρώτη φιλοσοφία is to be gained in Aristotle, and *second,* that the traditional concept of metaphysics is deficient with respect to this.

We can show the first, however, only if we ourselves have already developed a more radical problematic of philosophy proper. Only then do we have the torch with which to illuminate the concealed and unexcavated foundations of πρώτη φιλοσοφία and thus of ancient philosophy, so that we may decide what is fundamentally happening there. Yet, we are supposed to first enter such philosophizing proper via these lectures. Accordingly we must renounce the first task. Yet then we cannot bring to light the unsuitability of the traditional meaning of metaphysics with respect to πρώτη φιλοσοφία either—and our refutation of this traditional title remains quite arbitrary.

In order to show roughly, however, that this is not the case, we shall give some indication of the inherent incongruities of this traditional concept. These, however, stem purely from the fact that the concept was not gained from a πρώτη φιλοσοφία understood in an originary way. Rather the arbitrariness of the word-formation pointed the way to an interpretation of πρώτη φιλοσοφία.

We make three assertions concerning the traditional concept of metaphysics: [1.] it is *trivialized;* [2.] it is intrinsically *confused;* [3.] it is *unconcerned* about the real problem of that which it is supposed to designate. Instead, this title 'metaphysics', in the meaning referring to its content, is dragged through the history of philosophy, from time to time even modified somewhat, yet never understood in such a way that 'metaphysics' itself might become problematic with regard to that which it attempts to designate.

a) The trivialization of the traditional concept of metaphysics: the metaphysical (God, immortal soul) as a being that is at hand, albeit a higher one.

The traditional concept of metaphysics is *trivialized.* In order to see this, we shall start with the popular concept of metaphysics, pursue its origin, and show to what extent it leads us out of philosophy, and is thus trivial. (Certainly we must note that metaphysics as a title is reserved initially for the whole of 'ontology', which, however, is at the same time theology.)

Whenever the word 'metaphysics' or 'metaphysical' is used today in ordinary writings, this usage is also intended to convey the impression of something about it which is profound, mysterious, and not directly accessible, the impression of something which lies behind everyday things, in the realm pertaining to ultimate reality. That which lies out beyond the ordinary experience of the senses, beyond the sensuous, is the suprasensuous. Intentions like those designated by names such as theosophy and occultism are readily associated with it. All these tendencies—which are especially on the rise today and like to represent themselves as metaphysics, which is why literary types keep talking about a resurrection of metaphysics—all these are only substitutes, taken more or less seriously, for the fundamental orientation toward, and establishment of, the suprasensuous as it initially asserts itself in the West through Christendom, through the Christian dogma. The Christian dogma itself acquired a particular form by taking over ancient philosophy, especially that of Aristotle, in a specific direction in order to systematize the content of Christian faith. This systematization is not an extrinsic ordering, but entails an *interpretation of content*. Christian theology and dogma took control of ancient philosophy and reinterpreted it in a quite specific (Christian) manner. Through Christian dogma, ancient philosophy was forced into a quite specific conception which maintained itself throughout the Renaissance, Humanism and German Idealism, and whose untruth we are only slowly beginning to comprehend today. The first to do so was perhaps Nietzsche. In Christian dogma as the laying down of propositions of a specific religious form, God and man must be what is at issue in an exceptional sense. These two, God and man, thus become the primary objects not only of faith, but also of theological systematology: God as the absolutely suprasensuous; man not only, nor indeed solely and predominantly as a creature of this earth, but with respect to his eternal fate, his immortality. God and immortality are the two terms for the world beyond, with which this faith is essentially concerned. This world beyond becomes the properly metaphysical, and it claims a specific philosophy for itself. Even at the beginning of modern philosophy, we see how its founder, Descartes, in his major work *Meditationes de prima philosophia* (meditations on philosophy proper) explicitly says that First Philosophy has as its objective the proof of the existence of God and of the immortality of the soul. At the beginning of modern philosophy, which is readily passed off as a break with philosophy hitherto, we find that what is emphasized and held onto is precisely what has been the *proper concern of medieval metaphysics*.

Taking over Aristotelian First Philosophy into the structure and further construction of the theological dogmatics of the Middle Ages was in a certain sense made easier in a purely extrinsic way by the fact that Aristotle himself in the Sixth Book of the *Metaphysics,* at the point where he speaks of First Philosophy, divides the latter—as we have already heard—into two fundamental orientations of questioning, without making their unity itself into a problem. According to this division, the issue is on the one hand *beings as such,* i.e., that which pertains to every being as a being, to every ὄν insofar as it is an ὄν. The question is asked: what belongs to a being, insofar as it is a being, quite irrespective of whether it is this one or that one? What belongs to it insofar as it is something like a being at all? First Philosophy poses this question of the *essence* and the *nature* of beings. *At the same time* however it *also* poses the question concerning *beings as a whole,* in inquiring back to the *supreme* and *ultimate,* which Aristotle also designates τιμιώτατον γένος, the most original being, which he also calls the θεῖον. With respect to this divine being he also names First Philosophy θεολογική, theological knowledge: the λόγος that is concerned with θεός, not in the sense of a creator God or a personal God, but simply with the θεῖον. We thus find prefigured in Aristotle this *peculiar connection* between *prima philosophia* and *theology.* On the basis of this connection, mediated via a particular interpretation of Arabic philosophy, the assimilation of the content of Christian faith to the philosophical content of Aristotle's writings was made easier when the Middle Ages became acquainted with Aristotle, and above all with his metaphysical writings. Thus it comes about that the suprasensuous, the metaphysical according to the *usual* concept, is at the same time that which is known in *theological* knowledge, a theological knowledge which is not a theology of *faith,* but theology of *reason,* rational theology.

What is essential is that the object of *First Philosophy* (metaphysics) is now a *specific,* albeit *suprasensuous being.* In our question concerning the medieval understanding of metaphysics we are not now dealing with the question concerning the legitimacy of any knowledge of this suprasensuous being, nor with the question concerning the possibility of any knowledge of the existence of God or the immortality of the soul. All these are questions that come later. It is instead a matter of the *principle fact* that the suprasensuous, the metaphysical, is *one* domain of *beings* among others. Metaphysics thereby enters the *same level* as other knowledge of *beings* in sciences or in practico-technical knowledge, with the sole difference that this being is a higher one. It lies *over* . . ., beyond, *trans* . . ., which is the Latin translation of μετά. The μετά *no longer* indicates a particular *orientation* of thinking and knowing, a peculiar *turnaround* in the face of everyday thinking and inquiry, but is merely a sign for the *place* and the *order of those beings* which lie *behind* and *above* other beings. Everything, however—both this suprasensuous being and the sensuous—is in a certain way *at hand in the same manner.* Knowledge of both—regardless of relative distinctions—moves within *the same everyday orientation* of knowledge and proof of things. The very fact of the proofs of God—quite apart from their force of persuasion—already documents this orientation of such metaphysics. Here the fact that philosophizing is a *fundamental orientation that stands on its own* completely disappears. Metaphysics is levelled down and trivialized into everyday knowledge, except that it deals with the suprasensuous which, moreover, is proven by revelation and church doctrine. The μετά, as indicating a place of the suprasensuous, reveals nothing at all of that peculiar turnaround which philosophizing ultimately entails. This now means that the metaphysical is itself one being among others, it means that what I go out to, in moving away from the physical, is in principle not distinguished from the physical, except through the distinction persisting between the sensuous and suprasensuous. Yet this is a complete misinterpretation of the θεῖον which, in Aristotle, is at least left to stand as a problem. When what is metaphysical is taken as some being, albeit a higher being, that is at hand among others, then we encounter the *trivialization* and *superficiality* of the concept of metaphysics.

b) The confused state of the traditional concept of metaphysics: the combining of the two separate kinds of lying out beyond (μετά) as pertaining to *supra*sensuous beings and to the *non*sensuous characteristics of the being of beings.

The traditional concept of metaphysics is intrinsically *confused.* We saw that in Aristotle, alongside theology—which is supposedly to be knowledge of the suprasensuous—there was yet another direction of questioning. Το πρώτη φιλοσοφία, there belonged equally originally the question concerning the ὄν η ὄν, the knowledge of beings as such. Thomas Aquinas also straightforwardly took over this second direction of questioning from Aristotle. When that happened, he naturally had to try to bring his questioning into some kind of correlation with that of Aristotle. In the direction of questioning concerning the ὄν η ὄν, the question is raised of what pertains to every being as such, what a being is and what properties it would proffer, so to speak, whenever I consider it in general: *ens communiter consideratum* or the *ens in communi. Beings in general* likewise become the object of *prima philosophia.* Here it becomes apparent that whenever I ask about what pertains to every being as such, I necessarily pass *over beyond* each individual being. I pass beyond to the most general determinations of beings: the fact that every being is a something, is one thing and not another, that it is distinct, opposed, and so on. All these determinations: something, unity, otherness, difference, opposition, are ones that lie out beyond every individual thing, yet in *their* lying beyond are entirely different from God's lying beyond with respect to any particular thing. These *two fundamentally different kinds of lying beyond* come to be combined into *one* concept. The question is not raised at all of what the μετά means *here;* rather this is left undetermined. We can say more generally that in the first case, in theological knowledge, it is a matter of knowledge of the nonsensuous in the sense of that which lies beyond the senses as a being in its own right. In the second case, whenever I emphasize such things as unity, multiplicity, otherness, things that I cannot taste or weigh, it is a matter of something nonsensuous, not of something *supra*sensuous, but of something *un*sensuous which is not accessible through the senses. There is no mention at all of any distinction or of any problem persisting between suprasensuous and unsensuous in their mutual and contrasting relation to the sensuous. Viewed in this way, insofar as the state of the problem in Aristotle and in Aristotelian philosophy is simply taken over, the intrinsic concept of metaphysics is *in itself confused.*

c) The unproblematic nature of the traditional concept of metaphysics.

Because the traditional concept of metaphysics is thus trivialized and confused in itself, it simply cannot come about that metaphysics in itself or the μετά in its proper sense is made a problem. To put it the other way around: because philosophizing proper as a completely free questioning on the part of man is not possible during the Middle Ages, since completely different orientations are essential during that period; because fundamentally there is no philosophy in the Middle Ages: for this reason the taking over of Aristotelian metaphysics according to the two directions already characterized is structured from the outset in such a way that not only a dogmatics of faith, but also a dogmatics of First Philosophy itself arises. The peculiar process of ancient philosophy being taken over into the content of the Christian faith and thereby, as we have seen with Descartes, into modern philosophy, was brought to a halt for the first time by Kant, who established a proper questioning. Kant really got a grip on the matter for the first time, and attempted in one particular direction to make *metaphysics itself a problem.* We cannot go into this tendency proper to Kantian philosophizing in detail. In order to understand all this, we must free ourselves entirely from the interpretation of Kant that emerged in the 19th century, partly via German Idealism, and has become standard. Whoever wishes to consider these things in more detail can take a look at my book, *Kant and the Problem of Metaphysics.*[1]

---

1. [Tr: *Kant und das Problem der Metaphysik* (Frankfurt: Klostermann, 1973). [Trans. Richard Taft, *Kant and the Problem of Metaphysics* (Bloomington: Indiana University Press, 1990).]]

§13. The concept of metaphysics in Thomas Aquinas as historical
evidence for the three features of the traditional concept of
metaphysics.

I would now like to provide some brief evidence for what I have presented in quite a general fashion, namely the three features of the traditional concept of metaphysics: its trivialization, its confusion, and its unproblematic nature, so that you do not think that this is only one view of the history of metaphysics from some particular standpoint. The evidence may be provided via a brief indication of the concept of metaphysics in Thomas Aquinas. Aquinas spoke several times about the concept of metaphysics, not systematically, but on various occasions, in particular in his commentary on Aristotelian metaphysics. The concept of metaphysics is dealt with in various books of this commentary, most clearly and characteristically however in the general introduction, the *Prooemium.*[1] Here we find a strange state of affairs from the outset, namely that Thomas Aquinas straightaway equates *prima philosophia, metaphysica,* and *theologia* or *scientia divina,* as he also often puts it: knowledge of the divine. The *scientia divina* in the sense of this theology is to be separated from the *scientia sacra,* that knowledge which springs from revelation and is connected with man's faith in an exceptional sense. To what extent is this equating of *prima philosophia, metaphysica,* and *theologia* surprising? After all, it will be said that this is in fact the opinion of Aristotle, and this proves that Thomas Aquinas was the purest Aristotelian there was, if we disregard the fact that Aristotle did not yet know the expression 'metaphysics'.

So it seems—and yet everything is quite different. This will become apparent when we ask how Aquinas grounds this equating of First Philosophy, metaphysics and theology. From his perspective, this grounding is indeed brilliant and a prime example of the manner and way in which he and the medieval thinkers came to terms, in a transparent and apparently entirely undebatable form, with material which had been handed down. For Thomas Aquinas it is a matter of grounding why one and the same science must be called First Philosophy, metaphysics, and theology.

He proceeds from the premise that the highest knowledge (which we shall now always call metaphysical for short)—highest knowledge in the sense of the natural knowledge which man is to attain of his own accord—is the *scientia regulatrix,* which governs all other knowledge.[2] This is why Descartes, because he was intent on grounding the sciences in their entirety, later with the same orientation had to go back to the *scientia regulatrix,* to the *prima philosophia*

---

1. Thomas Aquinas, *In: XII. Libros Metaphysicorum (Aristoteles Commentarium). Prooemium S. Thomae. Opera Omnia* (Parma, 1652ff.). Vol. XX, pp. 245f.
2. Ibid., p. 245.

which governs everything. A *scientia regulatrix,* a science regulating every-thing—we may recall the same thing in Fichte's *Science of Knowledge*—is one *quae maxime intellectualis est,*[3] one that is evidently the most intellectual. *Haec autem est, quae circa maxime intelligibilia versatur:*[4] Most intellectual is that kind of knowledge which deals with what is most knowable. That which is knowable in the highest sense is nothing other than the *mundus intelligibilis,* of which the early Kant speaks in his work *De mundi sensibilis atque in-telligibilis forma et principiis* (1770). Thomas Aquinas says: *Maxime autem intelligibilia tripliciter accipere possumus:*[5] What is most knowable we can divide threefold. With respect to this threefold divisibility of the *maxime intelligibilia,* he distinguishes a threefold character of this science. Something is most know-able and supremely knowable, which at the same time means most suprasensu-ous, [1.] *ex ordine intelligendi,* in terms of the order and levels of knowing, [2.] *ex comparatione intellectus ad sensum,* in terms of a comparison of the under-standing, of intellectual knowledge, with the sensuous, and [3.] *ex ipsa cognitione intellectus,* in terms of the kind of knowing of the intellect itself.[6] What does this mean?

1. Something is knowable in the highest sense *ex ordine intelligendi,* in terms of the order and levels of knowing. For the Middle Ages knowing is quite generally the grasping of things in terms of their causes. Something is known in the highest sense whenever I go back to its *ultimate cause,* to the *causa prima.* According to faith, however, the *causa prima* is God as creator of the world. Thus something is *maxime intelligibile* if it presents in itself the *prima causa,* the highest cause. These highest causes are the object of knowing proper, the theme of *prima philosophia: Dicitur autem prima philosophia, inquantum primas rerum causas considerat.*[7] Thus *prima philosophia* is knowledge of the highest cause, of God as the creator—a train of thought which was completely alien to Aristotle in this form.

2. Something is *maxime intelligibile ex comparatione intellectus ad sensum,* in terms of a comparison of knowledge of the understanding with sensuous knowledge. Aquinas says: *sensus sit cognitio particularium,*[8] through the senses we know what is individuated, dispersed, and in this sense not completely determined. *Intellectus . . . universalia comprehendit,*[9] the intellect on the other hand grasps that which is not this or that, does not have this or that particular property, is not here and now, but which pertains to everything in common.

3. Ibid.
4. Ibid.
5. Ibid.
6. Ibid.
7. Ibid., p. 246.
8. Ibid., p. 245.
9. Ibid.

The *scientia maxime intellectualis* is therefore that *quae circa principia maxime universalia versatur,*[10] which relates to what pertains universally and pervasively to all beings. This, however, is what Aristotle wants to see brought to light in knowledge of the ὄν ᾗ ὄν, and what Aquinas consequently characterises as *ens qua ens,* as that which belongs to beings as such: the determinations that are always already and necessarily co-present in them, such as, for example, *unum, multa, potentia, actus* and suchlike. (*Quae quidem sunt ens, et ea quae consequuntur ens, ut unum et multa, potentia et actus*[11]). In short, what is *maxime intelligibile* in this second sense is that which we designate as *categories,* categorial knowledge, knowledge of the most general determinations of concepts, which has passed over into modern metaphysics as the purely rational knowledge of the categorial. The strange thing now is that Aquinas calls these determinations that pertain to beings as such the *transphysica. Haec enim transphysica inveniuntur in via resolutionis, sicut magis communia post minus communia.*[12] These are those determinations that lie over beyond the physical, over beyond the sensuous. These most general determinations of beings as such are found by way of a regressive resolution of what is less general into what is general. Aquinas assigns this kind of knowledge to the concept *metaphysica: Metaphysica, in quantum considerat ens et ea quae consequuntur ipsum.*[13] We here see the strange state of affairs—I emphasize the context—that metaphysics is ultimately synonymous with First Philosophy and theology, yet the specific meaning of metaphysics is interpreted by Aquinas in *that* sense according to which metaphysics is synonymous with the expression *ontology,* which was first formed *later*—ontology which considers the ὄν ᾗ ὄν and is later named *metaphysica generalis.* For Aquinas, metaphysics is in this sense identical with ontology.

   3. Something is most knowable *ex ipsa cognitione intellectus,* in terms of the kind of knowing of the intellect itself. Aquinas says: *maxime intelligibilia, quae sunt maxime a materia separata:*[14] most knowable is that which is free of matter, i.e., that which, in accordance with its own content and its own manner of being, is least determined by what constitutes the individuation or the particularity of a being. *Ea vero sunt maxime a materia separata, quae non tantum a signata materia abstrahunt, "sicut formae naturales in universali acceptae, de quibus tractat scientia naturalis," sed omnino a materia sensibili. Et non solum secundum rationem, sicut mathematica, sed etiam secundum esse, sicut Deus et intelligentiae.*[15] Pure space and pure number are also free of matter. But this

---

10. Ibid.
11. Ibid.
12. Ibid., p. 246.
13. Ibid.
14. Ibid., p. 245.
15. Ibid.

freedom rests on a *ratio* that reasons by abstraction. This freedom is nothing subsisting by itself, unsensuous, spiritual, as is the case with God and the angels. These spiritual creatures are the highest in the manner of their being and accordingly are also what is most highly knowable. They are those things or beings—if we may here use the title 'thing' in the broadest sense—which exist independently by themselves. The knowledge of that which is beyond and spiritual in the supreme sense is knowledge of God himself, the *scientia divina,* and as such theology: *Dicitur enim scientia divina sive theologia, inquantum praedictas substantias considerat.*[16]

Thus we see how Aquinas, in his unified orientation toward the concept of the *maxime intelligibile* and in the skillful interpretation of a threefold meaning, attempts to bring together the traditional concepts that hold for metaphysics, so that *First Philosophy* deals with the *first causes* (*de primis causis*), *metaphysics* with *beings in general* (*de ente*) and *theology* with *God* (*de Deo*). All three together are a unified science, the *scientia regulatrix.* I no longer need return to the point that the intrinsic problematic of this *scientia regulatrix* was in fact in no way taken up here or even dimly seen, but that these three directions of questioning are instead systematically held together in a quite different way, one essentially determined by faith. In other words, the concept of philosophizing or of metaphysics in this manifold ambiguity is not oriented toward the intrinsic problematic itself, but instead *disparate determinations of passing over and beyond* are here joined together.

Before I proceed further with this theme, I shall once more summarize what has been said. I have attempted to clarify why we are using the expression 'metaphysics', even though we cannot accept it in its traditional meaning. The reason we may not do so is to be found in the inherent incongruity contained in the traditional concept of metaphysics. An ambiguity is already implied in the concept of First Philosophy that evolves in antiquity in Plato and Aristotle. We saw that Aristotle orients philosophizing proper in two directions: as the question of being, namely that each thing that is, insofar as it is, is something, that it is one thing and not another, and suchlike. Unity, multiplicity, opposition, manifoldness, and so on are determinations that pertain to every being as such. The elaboration of these determinations is a task to be elaborated by philosophizing proper. Yet with this there simultaneously arises the question concerning that being which properly is, which Aristotle designates the θεῖον. He characterizes it more clearly in the context of the ἐπιστήμη θεολογική. So far as we know, Aristotle did not become aware of the disharmony and the problem that lies in this dual orientation of philosophizing. It lies in the fact that questioning concerning what equality, difference, and opposition are, how

16. Ibid., p. 246.

they relate to one another and how they belong to the essence of beings, is something totally different from the question concerning the ultimate ground of beings.

The incongruity and the problem can be seen more distinctly in the theology of the Middle Ages which was oriented toward Christian revelation. Questioning concerning the formal categories is something other than the question of God. A certain uniformity and belonging together of these two directions of questioning is attained only because it is said in both cases that what is at issue is knowledge of such things as are free of matter, free of the sensuous in some way or other. The formal concept of equality is abstract: in it we disregard the sensuous; God is indeed not abstract, but precisely the opposite, the most concrete thing that there is, yet he too is free of matter, he is pure spirit. This inherent disharmony in the two directions of questioning belonging to philosophizing proper becomes intensified in the Middle Ages through the fact that the Aristotelian concept of theology came to be grasped in the sense of a quite specific conception of God as absolute person, oriented around Christian revelation. What was to be found as an unspoken problem in Aristotle was presented as firm truth in the Middle Ages, so that the unproblematic nature of the situation, which in a certain sense is found in Aristotle, now becomes raised to a principle. Thus it comes about that from here on the entire content of metaphysics is from the outset determined by an orientation toward theology in the Christian sense. Here theology is no longer classified alongside or in connection with the first-mentioned questions concerning the determinations of being in general, as in Aristotle; rather the whole of metaphysics is explicitly assigned to the knowledge of God. From here theology acquires its proper import, which is later reflected in the fact that metaphysics proper in Kant is conceived as theology. In the Middle Ages and later on no real problem is seen in this Aristotelian concept of philosophizing proper, but only the problem of simultaneously orienting these different titles around one science. Aquinas attempts this in the *Prooemium* to his commentary on Aristotle's *Metaphysics*. I shall not go any further into how he grounds it in detail.

I emphasize only the incongruity and difficulty lying in the fact that Aquinas says that this science, which is the highest and which we name metaphysics in equating these three titles, deals on the one hand with the ultimate cause, with God who created the world and all that is, yet at the same time also deals with those determinations that pertain to every being, the *universalia,* the abstract categories, and simultaneously with that being which is supreme according to its specific manner of being, namely pure absolute spirit. We see in the interpretation of those three titles—as knowledge of the *ultimate* (in the sense of causation), of the *most general* (in the sense of abstraction), and of the *supreme or highest being* (in the sense of its specific manner of being)—that these limit-concepts come to be fused together in the vague concept of the universal or general. Hence Aquinas, in a certain way correctly, yet completely covering over the problem, is able to say that metaphysics can deal: [1.] *de ente, ut communiter consideratum,* i.e., with beings insofar as they are considered in general, i.e., with respect to that which is common to every being; [2.] *de ente, ut principaliter intentum,* with beings as intended, contemplated, understood in the most original sense, namely with respect to God. These are determinations that both have the character of what is highest, what is ultimate, yet are completely different in their inner structure, so that no attempt whatsoever is made to comprehend them in their possible unity.

§14. The concept of metaphysics in Franz Suarez and the fundamental character of modern metaphysics.

This connection of the medieval concept of metaphysics with antiquity and the complete covering over of the real problem, which is only latently there in Aristotle, must be kept in mind if we want to comprehend anything at all about modern metaphysics, about its development, about Kant's position, or about the development of German Idealism. It must also be noted, however, that Aquinas and medieval philosophy, in the sense of High Scholasticism, are important only to a lesser extent for the development of modern metaphysics, which also determines the state of the problem for us. Direct influence on the development of modern metaphysics was exercised by one theologian and philosopher who, in the 16th century, with quite specific theological intentions, set himself the task of interpreting Aristotelian metaphysics anew: the Spanish Jesuit Franz Suarez. Suarez' significance as a theologian and philosopher is far from being acknowledged to the extent merited by this thinker, who must be placed even above Aquinas in terms of his acumen and independence of questioning. His significance for the development and formation of modern metaphysics is not merely formal in the sense that under his influence the discipline of metaphysics took shape in a specific form. Just as important is his moulding of the problems concerning content, problems which then reawakened in modern philosophy. He lived from 1548 to 1617 and worked at a renewal of the scholasticism that flourished in the 16th century in Spain, partly under the influence of humanism. The Jesuit school in Salamanca played a decisive role in these endeavours. In the year 1597 Suarez published a major work: *Disputationes metaphysicae* (2 volumes, Salamanca). The subtitle of this work is characteristic: *in quibus et universa naturalis theologia ordinate traditur, et quaestiones ad omnes duodecim Aristotelis libros pertinentes, accurate disputantur.* The work thus has a dual aim: *on the one hand* to treat the entirety of natural theology (i.e., that which precedes revelation) in its inner structure, and *simultaneously* to discuss in an appropriate manner all the questions belonging to the twelve books of Aristotle's *Metaphysics*. In contrast to earlier scholasticism, Suarez indeed saw that the twelve books of Aristotle form a whole that is inherently disordered, although he did not realize that this book is not one written by Aristotle, but a compilation of treatises put together by his students. He sought to overcome this disorder by giving the main problems a systematic order. Independent discussion of the whole area of the problem with respect to natural theology goes back to Suarez, whereas in Aquinas there was only an application of metaphysical thoughts, as well as the commentary on Aristotelian metaphysics. By contrast, Suarez first undertook an independent development of the metaphysical problem which was of particular influence especially for the beginning of modern philosophy, for Descartes. Descartes, who studied in the Jesuit school of La Flèche and attended lectures on metaphysics, logic, and ethics there, became thoroughly acquainted with Suarez, whom he consulted time and again even during his later period.

We wish to clarify for ourselves one of the aims of this significant work which has not yet been exhausted by far. In the preface, the *Prooemium* to his *Disputationes metaphysicae,* Suarez says: *Ita enim haec principia et veritates metaphysicae cum theologicis conclusionibus ac discursibus cohaerent, ut si illorum scientia ac perfecta cognitio auferatur, horum etiam scientiam nimium labefactari necesse sit.*[1] By this he means that metaphysical truths are so necessary for proper theological knowledge that if they are disregarded, theology proper, in the sense of the theology of revelation, threatens to become all too insecure. Suarez explicitly emphasizes that he is here excluding all questions pertaining merely to logical problems: *quae vero ad puram philosophiam aut dialecticam pertinent (in quibus alii metaphysici scriptores prolixe immorantur), ut aliena a praesenti doctrina, quoad fieri possit, resecabimus.*[2]

The first *Disputatio* treats: *De natura primae philosophiae seu metaphysicae,* of the essence of First Philosophy or metaphysics. Suarez begins in the introduction[3] by discussing the various designations of metaphysics (*varia metaphysicae nomina*), and does so with independent recourse to Aristotle. Here he finds that metaphysics is designated as *sapientia* (σοφία), as *prudentia* (φρόνησις), then as *prima philosophia* (πρώτη φιλοσοφία), then as *naturalis theologia* (θεολογική)—which Suarez here interprets in a sense quite unlike that of antiquity (*quoniam de Deo ac divinis rebus sermonem habet, quantum ex naturali lumine haberi potest*[4])—and finally as *metaphysica.*

---

1. Suarez, *Disputationes Metaphysicae. Prooemium. Opera Omnia.* Ed. C. Berton (Paris, 1856ff.). Vol. XXV, p. 1.
2. Ibid.
3. Suarez, *Disputationes Metaphysicae.* Disp. I. Ibid., pp. 1ff.
4. Ibid., p. 2.

Suarez says that this natural theology or First Philosophy is called meta-physics because it deals with God (*ex quo etiam metaphysica nominata est*[5]). He thereby gives the expression a different meaning from that of Aquinas. Aquinas uses the expression *metaphysica* insofar as it treats *de ente in communi*. Suarez, on the other hand, says it is called metaphysics because it is theology. He remarks that this title 'metaphysics' does not stem from Aristotle himself, but from his interpreters (*quod nomen non tam ab Aristotele, quam ab ejus interpretibus habuit*[6]). However, he is of the opinion that Aristotle did put together this collection.

He explains the expression 'metaphysics' in a sense that deviates from the explanation given by Aquinas, and brings in another point of view which is significant in the history of metaphysics: *de his rebus, quae scientias seu res naturales consequuntur.*[7] Metaphysics deals with that which follows after natural things, *et ideo metaphysica dicta est, quasi post physicam, seu ultra physicam constituta; post (inquam) non dignitate, aut naturae ordine, sed acquisitionis, generationis, seu inventionis; vel, si ex parte objecti illud intelligamus, res, de quibus haec scientia tractat, dicuntur esse post physica seu naturalia entia, quia eorum ordinem superant, et in altiori rerum gradu constitutae sunt.*[8] The Meta-*physics* is not concerned, then, with such books as come after those about physics, rather 'coming after' is now taken in the sense of *content:* knowledge of the suprasensuous is later than that of the sensuous. In the order of appropriation, in the order in which knowledge of the suprasensuous arises, in the sequence of investigation, metaphysical knowledge is placed after knowledge of physics. Suarez stresses the μετά in the sense of *post* and understands this *post* in the sense of the stages of knowledge proceeding from the sensuous to the suprasensuous. At the same time however he brings into play the interpretation in terms of content: μετά, afterwards, that which comes afterwards, which exceeds the sensuous.

I cannot here go into the more detailed construction of the *Disputationes metaphysicae*. It must be emphasized, however, that metaphysics underwent essential development under the influence of Suarez, both in its posing of the problems and in its specific character as a scholastic discipline. Here it must be noted that Suarez sides very positively with Thomas Aquinas and assigns a particular authority to him in all these questions.

From what I have said about the history of the word 'metaphysics' we have seen that medieval philosophy, strengthened by the significance of Suarez, came to have a decisive influence upon the development of modern philosophy.

5. Ibid.
6. Ibid.
7. Ibid.
8. Ibid.

It does not follow from this, however, that the problematic of modern philosophy is completely identical to what was previously dealt with in metaphysics. It is often pointed out that modern philosophy begins with critique, with the critical grounding of philosophy, and that it was precisely Kant who placed the possibility of metaphysics in doubt. Certainly—and yet modern philosophy is intimately bound up with scholasticism and the motives behind its problems. The hint about the aforementioned character of modern metaphysics is not of much help so long as the problem is not comprehended in terms of metaphysics itself. These correct claims about the inception of modern metaphysics with critique have their own story. They do not in themselves provide any understanding of what has taken place from Descartes to Hegel.

In order to avoid misinterpretations and at the same time to prepare for later discussion, I shall briefly discuss the *fundamental character of modern metaphysics*. Whenever we attempt to characterize modern philosophy as we have done for antiquity and the Middle Ages, we are faced with the fact that the concept of metaphysics has become fixed, but that nevertheless something new is occurring. If whatever is new is something that belongs to metaphysics and not to so-called epistemology, then we must ask: What metaphysical character does whatever is new, and which begins with modern philosophy, have with respect to metaphysics in general? You can see from this question that we ought already to have the living problematic of metaphysics in our possession, whereas for the time being we can state merely the following in the form of an assertion: Metaphysical thinking is comprehensive questioning in a dual sense, because it asks concerning beings as a whole, and because the questioner himself is always conceptually included among these beings. That beings as a whole are asked about in antiquity as in medieval philosophy may have become more or less clear. Much less certain, indeed virtually unintelligible by contrast, is the second point, namely how in ancient philosophy the one who is questioning metaphysically is himself put into question by this questioning. Yet it is precisely this point, the fact that comprehensive questioning conceptually includes the questioner, that gives us the possibility of understanding what is new in modern metaphysics in terms of its metaphysical content.

What is the fundamental trait of modern metaphysics? Modern metaphysics is determined by the fact that the entirety of the traditional problematic comes under the aspect of a new science, which is represented by *mathematical natural science*. The less explicit train of thought is this: if metaphysics asks concerning the first causes, concerning the most general and highest meaning of beings, in short concerning what is highest, ultimate, and supreme, then this kind of knowing must be commensurate with what is asked about. Yet that means: it must itself be *absolutely certain*. Thus, via the guiding thread of the mathematical idea of knowledge, the entire problematic of traditional metaphysics assumes the task of carrying out this demand in the strict sense and thus also of raising metaphysics, understood in terms of its content, to the *formal level of an absolute science.* The problem of absolute certainty is above all the fundamental problem of modern philosophy, not in the sense of an epistemology, but sustained and guided by the problem of the content of metaphysics itself. We see this most clearly at the place where modern philosophy explicitly begins, in Descartes, but especially in Fichte. Fichte's main work bears the title *Science of Knowledge* [*Wissenschaftslehre*]. It is that science which has knowledge in the absolute sense as its object and thereby grounds metaphysics. The development of modern metaphysics is sustained by this priority of the problem of certainty with a view to metaphysical knowledge. From there the modification of the body of problems and disciplines occurs.

Yet whenever we take things in this way we do not yet have a proper understanding of what is happening in this concern for absolute certainty in metaphysics. What is ultimate must also be capable of being known in the ultimate sense. Yet what is the status of the concerns of metaphysics for an ultimate certainty? It always tends to be pointed out as a particular characteristic that modernity since Descartes no longer starts from the existence of God or from proofs of God, but from consciousness, from the I. We can see that the I, consciousness, reason, person, spirit indeed stand at the centre of the problematic. If we heed this fact and ask whether this central position of the I, of self-consciousness, does not in the end express the fact that in modern philosophy the questioning I is also put into question, then we must say: This is indeed the case, yet in a peculiar way. For the I, consciousness, the person is taken into metaphysics in such a way that *this I is precisely not put in question.* This does not mean a simple failure to put into question. Rather the I or consciousness is precisely placed at the basis as the *most secure and unquestioned foundation* of this metaphysics, so that in modern metaphysics a *quite specific* comprehensive questioning manifests itself, an inclusive comprehending of the questioner in the *negative* sense, in such a way that the I itself becomes the foundation for all further questioning. Here we find the innermost connection between the priority of the problem of the subject and of the question of certainty, and the question concerning the content of traditional metaphysics. This may suffice on the one hand to show the different nature of modern metaphysics, and on the other hand in order to make it clear that this concern for ultimate certainty and the orientation toward the I and consciousness is meaningful only if the *old problematic is entirely maintained.* So much as regards our historical orientation.

§15. Metaphysics as a title for the fundamental problem of
metaphysics itself. The result of our preliminary appraisal and the
demand to take action in metaphysics on the basis of being
gripped by a metaphysical questioning.

Whenever we survey our whole discussion of the concept of metaphysics, we see that this title expresses a knowledge that is directed toward *beings as a whole*. At the same time, we can see that this expression '*as a whole*' is a term which contains the *real problem*—the problem that *must first be posed in general* and cannot be made to vanish out of existence by taking over various opinions from the tradition. It is thus clear that we cannot simply take the title 'metaphysics' in its traditional meaning. We are taking over the expression 'metaphysics' as the title of a problem, better, as a *title* for the *fundamental problem of metaphysics itself,* which lies in the question of what it, metaphysics, itself is. This question: *What is metaphysics, what is philosophizing?,* remains inseparable from philosophy and is its constant companion. The more properly philosophy happens, the more incisively this question is posed. We shall see repeatedly that this question of what philosophy itself is does not accompany philosophy as something added on later, but inherently belongs to philosophy itself, whereas the question of what mathematics, physics, or philology is can fundamentally be neither posed nor solved by these sciences.

If, in considering what we want from our *preliminary appraisal,* we simultaneously survey this discussion of the concept of metaphysics and of our position with respect to it, then it must be said that all these discussions have in no way achieved any clarity concerning what metaphysics itself is. In our discussion of the word 'metaphysics' we too end up with a question: What is it that we call 'philosophizing'? In this respect the result of our preliminary appraisal is thoroughly negative, even though we had resolved to renounce the usual way of characterizing philosophy and to ask about philosophy in the sense it demands of us, as something that is ultimate and that stands on its own. We are now no longer interpreting metaphysics or philosophy in terms of the sciences, nor comparing it with art and religion, but instead have taken account of the fact that it is something that stands on its own, something that must be comprehended on its own terms. Accordingly, the demand was not to shirk in the face of philosophy, but to inquire concerning philosophy itself. And so we set out in pursuit of philosophy itself. Or have we indeed shirked in the face of it after all? We must concede: Although we dealt directly with philosophy itself—indeed precisely because of this—we have shirked in the face of philosophy. This has merely happened in an inconspicuous and ambiguous way. We have indeed not spoken of other things, of science, art, or religion, but of philosophy—yet not directly and concretely *from out of it,* but *about* it. We are speaking *from out of it* only when we move in advance within a *metaphysical questioning.* Yet precisely this has not happened. We merely said *about* this questioning that it is comprehensive, i.e., a questioning that in each case comprehends beings as a whole within every question and takes the questioner himself into the question as well, puts him into question. Yet we have not understood that metaphysical questioning is comprehensive questioning so long as we have not let ourselves really be put into question through really inquiring into the whole. No matter how extensively we are concerned *about it,* everything remains a misunderstanding unless we are *gripped* by such questioning. In the attempt to deal with philosophy itself we have become victims of an ambiguity. Although we have spoken *of* philosophy, we have not yet spoken *from out of it.* We have indeed dealt *with* philosophy, but not taken action *within* philosophy itself. What is decisive, however, is that we emerge from this dealing with . . . and *take action within metaphysics itself.* This means nothing other than the fact that we must now really and properly question.

We have already indicated the questions we are posing: What is world? What is finitude? What is individuation? Yet these questions were set up almost coincidentally; they appear arbitrary. That is indisputable. At first it appears arbitrary and incomprehensible why precisely these questions are being posed. Yet whatever the case: if we wish to acknowledge these questions as metaphysical, are they not quite empty and general, so indeterminate that they leave *us* indifferent and do not touch *us* fundamentally, let alone grip us? Or must we first develop these questions so that they then grip us, so that in this way we come to be gripped as demanded? Ought we therefore to pose these questions and bring about a suitable attunement for them? If we were to proceed in this way, we would only fall back again onto the level which we wished to abandon and must abandon. We would have theoretical discussions (science) which we would then subsequently bring to fruition in terms of a worldview. The entire superficiality of philosophizing would thereby be restored. It is not a matter of developing these questions as theoretical and then bringing about an attunement *in addition* or *alongside.* On the contrary, we must first of all let these questions arise in their necessity and possibility *from out of a fundamental attunement,* and seek to preserve them in their independence and unambiguousness. Accordingly, we properly undertake such questioning whenever we set about awakening a fundamental attunement of our philosophizing. This is the first and proper fundamental task of this lecture course and the beginning of an actual living philosophizing.

Awakening a Fundamental Attunement in Our Philosophizing

Chapter One

The Task of Awakening a Fundamental Attunement and
the Indication of a Concealed Fundamental Attunement in
Our Contemporary Dasein

*§16. Coming to a preliminary understanding about the
significance of awakening a fundamental attunement.*

a) Awakening: not ascertaining something at hand, but letting what is asleep become wakeful.

Our fundamental task now consists in awakening a fundamental attunement in our philosophizing. I deliberately say: in *our* philosophizing, not in some arbitrary philosophizing nor even in philosophy in itself, for there is no such thing. It is a matter of awakening *a* fundamental attunement which is to sustain our philosophizing, and not *the* fundamental attunement. Accordingly, there is not merely one single attunement, but several. Which one concerns us? From where are we to derive such an attunement? We are faced with a choice concerning which fundamental attunement to awaken here. Yet we are faced not only with this choice, but also with the much more difficult question of the path upon which we are to awaken this or that fundamental attunement in our philosophizing.

Attunements—are they not something we can least of all invent, something that comes over us, something that we cannot simply call up? Do they not form of their own accord, as something we cannot forcibly bring about, but into which we slip unawares? If so, then we cannot and may not forcibly bring about such an attunement artificially or arbitrarily, if we are going to allow it to be an attunement. It must already be there. All we can do is *to ascertain it.* Yet how are we to ascertain a fundamental attunement of philosophizing? Can an attunement be ascertained as generally at hand, can it be demonstrated as a universally admitted fact? Is attunement in general something we take note of as something at hand, just as we notice, for example, that some people are fair and others dark? Is attunement something that one simply has or does not have? Of course, people will say, attunement is perhaps something other than the colour of the hair and skin of human beings, yet something which nevertheless can be ascertained with regard to human beings. How else should we know about such attunements? Thus we will have to undertake a survey to give us the fundamental attunement we are seeking. Granted that this could be carried out, even merely within the circle of those present here and now—are we really so sure that those we ask are in each case in a position to inform us about how this fundamental attunement of their Dasein is there 'in them'? Perhaps such a thing as the fundamental attunement we are seeking is precisely something that cannot be ascertained in this way by an inquiry. It could be that it pertains to ascertaining an attunement not merely that one has the attunement, but that one is attuned in accord with it.

We can see already that any so-called objective ascertaining of a fundamental attunement is a dubious, indeed impossible undertaking. Accordingly, it is also meaningless to ask in general about the pervasiveness and universality of attunement or to brood over the universal validity of something ascertained in this way. In other words, it is not necessarily an objection to our claim of a fundamental attunement being there in our Dasein if one of you, or even many, or all of you assure us that you are unable to ascertain such an attunement in yourselves when you observe yourselves. For in the end there is nothing at all to be found by observation—no matter how astute, even if it were to call upon psychoanalysis for help.

Thus we shall not speak at all of 'ascertaining' a fundamental attunement in our philosophizing, but of *awakening* it. Awakening means making something wakeful, *letting* whatever is sleeping *become wakeful.*

b) The being-there and not-being-there of attunement cannot be grasped via the distinction between consciousness and unconsciousness.

'Whatever is sleeping' is in a peculiar way absent and yet there. When we awaken an attunement, this means that it is already there. At the same time, it expresses the fact that in a certain way it is *not* there. This is strange: attunement is something that is simultaneously there and not there. If, in the customary manner, we now wished to continue philosophizing in a formal way, we could say straightaway: Something that is simultaneously there and not there has that kind of being which intrinsically contradicts itself. For being-there [*Da-sein*] and not-being-there [*Nicht-Da-sein*][1] is a straightforward con-

---

1. [Tr: In order to render the German meaningfully in this context, it has been necessary to translate *Da-sein* as "being-there" and the associated *Weg-sein* as "being-away." Readers should note that there is little consistency in the hyphenation of *Da-sein* and *Nicht-Da-sein* ("not-being-there") in the German text; accordingly, we have translated the inconsistencies and indicated the German where helpful.]

tradiction. Yet whatever is contradictory cannot be. It is—and this is an ancient proposition of traditional metaphysics—intrinsically impossible, just as a round square cannot be. We shall see that we must not only put in question this venerable principle of metaphysics, which is based on a quite specific conception of being, but also cause it to shatter in its very foundations.

After all, what we generally know about things, we know in terms of an unambiguous either/or. Things are either at hand or not at hand. Is this not valid for man also? Certainly—either someone is there or not there. Yet at the same time one must recall that the state of affairs here is quite different from the case of a stone. For we know from experience of ourselves as human beings that something can be at hand in us and yet not be, that there are processes that belong to us yet do not enter our consciousness. Human beings have a consciousness, and something can be at hand in them of which they know nothing. In that case it is presumably at hand in them, but not at hand in their consciousness. A stone either has a property or does not have it. We, on the contrary, can have something and at the same time not have it, that is, not know of it. We speak, after all, of the unconscious. In one respect it is at hand, and yet in another respect it is not at hand, namely insofar as it is not conscious. This strange 'at hand and yet at the same time not at hand' arises from the possibility of being conscious of something unconscious. This distinction between not being there [*Nicht-Dasein*] in the sense of the unconscious and being there [*Dasein*] in the sense of what is conscious also seems to be equivalent to what we have in mind by awakening, specifically by the awakening of whatever is sleeping. Yet can we straightforwardly equate sleep with the absence of consciousness? After all, there is also absence of consciousness in being unconscious (which cannot be identified with sleep), and *a fortiori* in death. This concept of the nonconscious, there-fore, is much too broad, irrespective of the question as to whether it is at all suitable. Furthermore, sleep is not simply an absence of consciousness. On the contrary, we know that a peculiar and in many cases extremely animated consciousness pertains precisely to sleep, namely that of dreams, so that here the possibility of characterizing something using the distinction 'con-scious/unconscious' indeed breaks down. Waking and sleeping are not equiv-alent to consciousness and unconsciousness.

We can thus see already that we will not get by with the distinction between 'unconscious' and 'conscious'. To awaken an attunement cannot mean simply to make conscious an attunement which was previously unconscious. To awaken an attunement means, after all, to let it *become awake* and as such precisely to let it *be*. If, however, we make an attunement conscious, come to know of it and explicitly make the attunement itself into an object of knowl-edge, we achieve the contrary of an awakening. The attunement is thereby precisely destroyed, or at least not intensified, but weakened and altered.

And yet the fact remains: whenever we awaken an attunement, this entails that it was already there, and yet not there. On the negative side, we have seen that the distinction between being there [*Dasein*] and not being there [*Nichtdasein*] is not equivalent to that between consciousness and unconsciousness. From this, however, we may conclude something further: If attunement is something that belongs to man, is 'in him', as we say, or if man has an attunement, and if this cannot be clarified with the aid of consciousness and unconsciousness, then we will not come close to this matter at all so long as we take man as something distinguished from material things by the fact that he has consciousness, that he is an animal endowed with reason, a rational animal, or an ego with pure life-experiences that has been tacked on to a body. This conception of man as a living being, a living being that in addition has reason, has led to a complete failure to recognize the essence of attunement. The awakening of attunement, and the attempt to broach this strange task, in the end coincide with the demand for a complete transformation of our conception of man.

In order not to make the problem all too complicated here at the outset, I shall not enter into the question of what sleep properly is. For in a methodological respect one could say that we will acquire information about the essence of awakening only if we clarify what sleeping and waking mean. I shall mention merely that the task of clarifying such phenomena as sleeping and waking cannot be addressed extrinsically as one particular question. Rather, such clarification can occur only on the presupposition that we possess a fundamental conception of how a being must be structurally determined such that it can sleep or be awake. We do not say that the stone is asleep or awake. Yet what about the plant? Here already we are uncertain. It is highly questionable whether the plant sleeps, precisely because it is questionable whether it is awake. We know that the animal sleeps. Yet the question remains as to whether its sleep is the same as that of man, and indeed the question as to what sleep in general is. This problem is intimately bound up with the question concerning the structure of being pertaining to these various kinds of beings: stone, plant, animal, man.

In contrast to the many misinterpretations of sleep in modernity, we see already in the philosophers of antiquity that the fundamental character of sleep shows itself to have been grasped in a much more elementary and immediate manner. Aristotle, who has written a treatise specifically on waking and sleeping (Περὶ ὕπνου καὶ ἐγρηγόρσεως), a treatise which has a peculiar character of its own, has noticed something remarkable in saying that sleep is an ἀκινησία. He does not connect sleep with consciousness or unconsciousness. Rather, he says that sleep is a δεσμός, a being bound, a peculiar way in which αἴσθησις is bound. It is not only a way in which perception is bound, but also our essence, in that it cannot take in other beings which it itself is not. This characterization of sleep is more than an image, and opens up a broad perspective which has by no means been grasped in its metaphysical intent. For fundamental metaphysical reasons we must forego entering into the problem of sleep, and must attempt to clarify on *another path* what it means to awaken an attunement.

c) The being-there and not-being-there of attunement on the grounds of man's being as being-there and being-away (being absent).

That it is by no means a matter of the distinction between consciousness and unconsciousness in the case of man when we speak of this simultaneous being-there [*Da-sein*] and not-being-there [*Nicht-Da-sein*] becomes clear from an occurrence that happens when we are quite awake, if for the moment we posit awakeness as conscious life in contrast to unconscious life (sleep). How often it happens, in a conversation among a group of people, that we are 'not there', how often we find that we were *absent,* albeit without having fallen asleep. This not-being-there, this being-away [*Weg-sein*], has nothing at all to do with consciousness or unconsciousness in the usual sense. On the contrary, this not-being-there can be highly conscious. In such being absent we are precisely concerned with ourselves, or with something else. Yet this not-being-there is nonetheless a *being-away.* Think of the extreme case of madness, where the highest degree of consciousness can prevail and yet we say: The person is de-ranged, displaced, away and yet there. Nor are being-there and being-away identical with waking and sleeping. Why we nevertheless rightly conceive of them in these terms will become apparent later.

We see that this *potential* to be away ultimately belongs to the way in which man is in general. Yet man has the *potential* to be away in this manner only if his being has the character of being-*there* [Da-*sein*]. *We name the being of man being-there, Da-sein,* in a sense yet to be determined and in distinction to the being at hand of the stone. In the end, this being-away pertains to the essence of being there [*Dasein*]. It is not something which happens arbitrarily from time to time, but is an essential characteristic of man's very being that indicates *how* he is, so that a human being—insofar as he or she exists—is, in his or her being there, also always already and necessarily away in some manner. All this transpires in such a way that the distinction between 'conscious' and 'unconscious' turns out not to be a primary one, but can be ascertained both in being there and in being away.

An attunement is to be awakened. Yet this means that it is there and not there. If attunement is something that has the character of 'there and not there', then attunement itself has to do with the innermost essence of man's being, with his Dasein. *Attunement belongs to the being of man.* The possibility and manner of this 'there and not there' has now already been brought closer to us, although we do not yet see it correctly by any means. For as long as we speak in this way—that attunement is there and not there—we take it as something that both appears and does not appear in man. Yet the being-there and being-away of man is something totally different from being at hand or not being at hand. We speak of being at hand or not being at hand, for example, with respect to a stone (e.g., roughness is not at hand in this erratic), or in a particular conception relating to a physical process or indeed even to a so-called emotional experience. Being at hand and not being at hand decide concerning being and non-being. Yet what we have designated as being there [*Dasein*] and being away [*Wegsein*] are something in the being of man. They are possible only if and so long as man *is*. *Being away is itself a way of man's being.* Being away does not mean: not being at all. It is rather a *way* of Da-sein's being-there. The stone, in its being away, is precisely *not* there. Man however must be *there* in order to be able to be away, and only so long as he is there does he in general have the possibility of an 'away'.

Accordingly, if attunement indeed belongs to the being of man we may not speak of it or take it as though it were at hand or not at hand. Yet people will reply: Who will deny us that? Attunements—joy, contentment, bliss, sadness, melancholy, anger—are, after all, something psychological, or better, psychic; they are emotional states. We can ascertain such states in ourselves and in others. We can even record how long they last, how they rise and fall, the causes which evoke and impede them. Attunements or, as one also says, 'feelings', are events occurring in a subject. Psychology, after all, has always distinguished between thinking, willing, and feeling. It is not by chance that it will always name feeling in the third, subordinate position. Feelings are the third class of lived experience. For naturally man is in the first place the rational living being. Initially, and in the first instance, this rational living being thinks and wills. Feelings are certainly also at hand. Yet are they not merely, as it were, the adornment of our thinking and willing, or something that obfuscates and inhibits these? After all, feelings and attunements constantly change. They have no fixed subsistence, they are that which is most inconstant. They are merely a radiance and shimmer, or else something gloomy, something hovering over emotional events. Attunements—are they not like the utterly fleeting and ungraspable shadows of clouds flitting across the landscape?

One can certainly take attunements this way, as shades and side-effects of other emotional events. Indeed hitherto they have basically always been taken this way. This characterization is indisputably correct. Yet one would not wish to claim, either, that this ordinary conception is the sole possible one or even the decisive one simply because it lies closest and can most easily be accommodated within the ancient conception of man. For attunements are not a mere emotional event or a state, in the way that a metal is liquid or solid, given that attunements indeed belong to the being of man. Therefore, we must now ask: How are we to grasp attunement *positively* as belonging to the essence of man, and how are we to relate toward man himself if we wish to awaken an attunement?

Before pursuing this question, let us review what has been said thus far regarding the task of our lecture course. We are confronting the task of awakening a fundamental attunement in our philosophizing. Attunements are something that cannot be straightforwardly ascertained in a universally valid way, like a fact that we could lead everyone to see. Not only can an attunement not be ascertained, it ought not to be ascertained, even if it were possible to do so. For all ascertaining means bringing to consciousness. With respect to attunement, all making conscious means destroying, altering in each case, whereas in awakening an attunement we are concerned to let this attunement be as it is, as this attunement. Awakening means letting an attunement be, one which, prior to this, has evidently been sleeping, if we may employ this image to begin with in accordance with linguistic usage. Attunement is in a certain way there and not there. We have seen that this distinction between being-there and not-being-there has a peculiar character, and is by no means equivalent to the distinction between a stone's being at hand or not being at hand. The not being at hand of the stone is not a particular manner of its being at hand, but the complete opposite of the latter. By comparison, being away, absence in its various forms, is not something like the exclusive opposite of being there. Rather all being away presupposes the being there pertaining to Dasein. We must be-there [*da-sein*] in order to be able to be away. Only as long as we are-there [*da-sind*] can we be away at all, and vice-versa. Hence being away, or this 'there and not there', is something peculiar, and attunement is connected in some as yet obscure way with this peculiar manner of being.

We also touched upon the fact that it is fundamentally misleading to say that an attunement is there, for in such a case we take attunement as something like one existing property that appears amongst others. In contrast to this conception, which denies that attunements are existing things, we brought ordinary opinion to bear, as found in psychology and in the traditional view of things. Attunements are feelings. Alongside thinking and willing, feeling is the third class of experience. This classification of experiences is carried out on the basis of the conception of man as a rational living being. This characterization of feelings is not something to be disputed in the first instance. But we concluded with the question as to whether this characterization of attunements, which is correct within certain limits, is decisive, and whether it is the essential one. By contrast, we saw that first, attunements are not beings, not things that somehow simply appear in the soul; second, attunements are not that which is most inconstant and fleeting either, contrary to what people think. It is a matter of showing what is *positive,* by way of contrast with our negative thesis. We must bring attunements and their essence a few steps closer to us in order to counterpose our positive thesis to these two negative ones.

§17. Provisional characterization of the phenomenon of attunement: attunement as a fundamental way of Dasein, as that which gives Dasein its subsistence and possibility. The awakening of attunement as a grasping of Da-sein as Da-sein.

A human being we are with is overcome by grief. Is it simply that this person has some state of lived experience that we do not have, while everything else remains as before? If not, what is happening here? The person overcome by grief closes himself off, becomes inaccessible, yet without showing any animosity toward us; it is simply that he becomes inaccessible. And yet we may be with him as before, or perhaps even more frequently, and may be more accommodating toward him. He does not alter anything about his comportment toward things or toward us either. Everything remains as before, and yet everything is different, not only in this or that respect but—irrespective of the sameness of *what* we do and *what* we engage *in*—the *way* in which we are together is different. Yet this is not some subsequent effect of the attunement of grief being at hand in him, but belongs rather to his grief as part of it.

What does it mean to say that in such an attunement this human being is inaccessible? The manner and way in which we can be with him, and in which he is with us, has changed. It is the grief that constitutes this way (the way in which we are together). He draws us into the manner in which he is, although we do not necessarily feel any grief ourselves. Our being with one another, the being-there of our Da-sein, is different, its attunement has shifted. Upon closer consideration of this context, which we shall not pursue any further now, we can already see that attunement is not at all inside, in some sort of soul of the Other, and that it is not at all somewhere alongside in our soul. Instead we have to say, and do say, that the attunement imposes itself on everything. It is *not* at all '*inside*' in some interiority, only to appear in the flash of an eye; but for this reason it is *not at all outside either.* Where and in what way is it, then? Is this attunement, grief, something concerning which we may ask where it is and in what way it is? Attunement is not some being that appears in the soul as an experience, but the way of our being there with one another.

Or let us consider other possibilities. A human being who—as we say—is in good humour brings a lively atmosphere with them. Do they, in so doing, bring about an emotional experience which is then transmitted to others, in the manner in which infectious germs wander back and forth from one organism to another? We do indeed say that attunement or mood is infectious. Or another human being is with us, someone who through their manner of being makes everything depressing and puts a damper on everything; nobody steps out of their shell. What does this tell us? Attunements are *not side-effects,* but are something which in advance determine our being with one another. It seems as though an attunement is in each case already there, so to speak, like an atmosphere in which we first immerse ourselves in each case and which then attunes us through and through. It does not merely seem so, it is so; and, faced with this fact, we must dismiss the psychology of feelings, experiences, and consciousness. It is a matter of *seeing* and *saying* what is happening here. It is clear that attunements are not something merely at hand. They themselves are precisely a fundamental manner and fundamental way of being, indeed of being-there [*Da-sein*], and this always directly includes being with one another. Attunements are ways of the being-there of Da-sein, and thus ways of being-away. An attunement is a way, not merely a form or a mode, but a way [*Weise*]—in the sense of a melody that does not merely hover over the so-called proper being at hand of man, but that sets the tone for such being, i.e., attunes and determines the manner and way [*Art und Wie*] of his being.[1]

Thus we have the positive correlate of our first negative thesis, namely that attunement is not a particular being. In positive terms, attunement is a fundamental manner, the *fundamental way in which Dasein is as Dasein.* We now also have the counterthesis to our second negative thesis that attunement is not something inconstant, fleeting, merely subjective. Rather because attunement is the originary way in which every Dasein is as it is, it is not what is most inconstant, but that which gives Dasein *subsistence and possibility* in its very foundations.

We must learn to understand from all this what it means to take so-called 'attunements' in the correct way. It is not a matter of taking up an opposite stance to psychology and delimiting more correctly a kind of emotional experience, thus improving psychology, but rather a matter of first opening up a general perspective upon the *Dasein* of man. Attunements are the fundamental ways in which we *find* ourselves *disposed* in such and such a way. Attunements are the '*how*' [*Wie*] according to which one is in such and such a way. Certainly we often take this 'one is in such and such a way'—for reasons we shall not go into now—as something indifferent, in contrast to *what* we intend to do, *what* we are occupied with, or *what* will happen to us. And yet this 'one is in such and such a way' is not—is never—simply a consequence or side-effect of our thinking, doing, and acting. It is—to put it crudely—the presupposition

1. [Tr: In addition to its common meaning of 'way' or 'manner' of doing something, the German word *Weise* has the more literary meaning of a 'tune' or 'melody'.]

for such things, the 'medium' within which they first happen. And precisely *those* attunements to which we pay no heed at all, the attunements we least observe, those attunements which attune us in such a way that we feel as though there is no attunement there at all, as though we were not attuned in any way at all—these attunements are the most powerful.

At first and for the most part we are affected only by particular attunements that tend toward 'extremes', like joy or grief. A faint apprehensiveness or a buoyant contentment are less noticeable. Apparently not there at all, and yet there, is precisely that *lack of attunement* in which we are neither out of sorts nor in a 'good' mood. Yet even in this 'neither/nor' we are never without an attunement. The reason we take lack of attunement as not being attuned at all, however, has grounds of a quite essential nature. When we say that a human being who is good-humoured brings a lively atmosphere with them, this means only that an elated or lively attunement is brought about. It does not mean, however, that there was no attunement there before. A lack of attunement prevailed there which is seemingly hard to grasp, which seems to be something apathetic and indifferent, yet is not like this at all. We can see once more that attunements never emerge in the empty space of the soul and then disappear again; rather, Dasein as Dasein is always already attuned in its very grounds. There is only ever a change of attunement.

We stated in a provisional and rough and ready manner that attunements are the 'presupposition' for, and 'medium' of thinking and acting. That means as much as to say that they reach more primordially back into our essence, that in them we first meet ourselves—as being-there, as a Da-sein. Precisely because the essence of attunement consists in its being no mere side-effect, precisely because it leads us back into the grounds of our Dasein, the essence of attunement remains concealed or hidden from us; for this reason we initially grasp the essence of attunement in terms of what confronts us at first, namely the extreme tendencies of attunement, those which irrupt then disappear. Because we take attunements in terms of their extreme manifestations, they seem to be one set of events among others, and we overlook this peculiar being attuned, the primordial, pervasive attunement of our whole Dasein as such.

From this it becomes clear that awakening attunements is a manner and means of grasping Da-sein with respect to the specific 'way' ['*Weise*'] in which it is, of grasping Da-sein as Da-sein, or better: of letting Da-sein be as it is, or can be, as Da-sein. Such awakening may perhaps be a strange undertaking, difficult and scarcely transparent. If we have understood our task, then we must now see to it that we do not suddenly start to deliberate *about* attunements again or even *about* awakening, but inasmuch as this awakening is an acting, we must *act* in accordance with it.

*§18. Making sure of our contemporary situation and of the
fundamental attunement that pervades it as the presupposition for
awakening this fundamental attunement.*

Yet even if we keep to this, we shall still meet difficulties, which are necessary and merely make clear to us as we run through them that this awakening of a fundamental attunement is not something that one can simply undertake like picking a flower, for instance.

a) Four interpretations of our contemporary situation: the opposition of life (soul) and spirit in Oswald Spengler, Ludwig Klages, Max Scheler, and Leopold Ziegler.

We must awaken a fundamental attunement, then! The question immediately arises as to *which* attunement we are to awaken or let become wakeful in us. An attunement that pervades *us* fundamentally? Who, then, are *we*? What do we mean here in referring to '*us*'? We, this number of individual human beings assembled here in this room? Or 'us' insofar as we are faced with specific tasks of study in the sciences here at university? Or 'us' insofar as we, in belonging to the university, are simultaneously involved in the process of our spiritual education? And this history of spirit—is it merely a German occurrence, or is it Western and indeed European? Or should we draw the circle in which we stand even wider? We mean 'us', but in what situation, and how are we to demarcate and delimit this situation?

The broader the perspective we have on this situation, the fainter our horizon becomes, and the more indeterminate our task. And yet—we sense that the broader the perspective we take, the more passionately and decisively it will take hold of us—of each one of us.

At this point, however, a clear task also imposes itself which we can evidently no longer evade. If we are to awaken a fundamental attunement in ourselves and wish to do so, then to this end we must *make sure of our situation.* Yet which attunement are we to awaken for *ourselves today?* We can answer this question only if we know *our* situation well enough to gather from it which fundamental attunement pervades us. Since something essential and ultimate is evidently at issue in awakening the fundamental attunement and in our intention to do so, this situation of ours must be seen in its greatest possible breadth. How are we to satisfy this demand? If we examine things more closely, then not only does the demand to characterize our situation prove not to be a new one, but this task has already been fulfilled in a manifold sense. For us it will merely be a case of highlighting the *unitary character* of the way our situation has been presented, and of retaining its *pervasive fundamental trait.*

If we look around for the explicit characterizations (interpretations, depictions) of our contemporary situation that come into question, then we may concentrate upon and very briefly acquaint ourselves with *four* of them. In such cases the choice is never free from arbitrariness. Such arbitrariness, however, is rendered innocuous by what we gain.

The best-known interpretation of our situation, one that was provocative for a short period, is the one that has come to be expressed in the slogan "decline of the West."[1] What is essential for us is what underlies this 'prophecy' as its fundamental thesis. Reduced to a formula, it is this: the decline of life in and through spirit. What spirit, in particular as reason (*ratio*), has formed and created for itself in technology, economy, in world trade, and in the entire reorganization of existence symbolised by the city, is now turning against the soul, against life, overwhelming it and forcing culture into decline and decay.

The *second* interpretation moves in the same dimension, except that the relation of soul (life) to spirit is seen differently. Commensurate with this different vision, it does not settle for a prediction of the decline of culture through spirit, but comes to repudiate spirit. Spirit is seen as the adversary of the soul.[2] Spirit is a sickness which has to be exorcised in order to liberate the soul. Freedom from spirit here means: let's return to life! Life, however, is now taken in the sense of the obscure simmering of drives, which is simultaneously grasped as the breeding ground of the mythical. This is the opinion proffered by the popular philosophy of Ludwig Klages. It is essentially determined by Bachofen and above all by Nietzsche.

A *third* interpretation likewise keeps to the dimension of the first two, but sees neither a process of the decline of spirit in life, nor does it seek to uphold a struggle of life against spirit. Instead it attempts to find a balance between life and spirit, and regards this as its task. This is the view represented by Max Scheler during the final period of his philosophizing. It is expressed most clearly in his lecture at Lessing College, "Man in the epoch of balance."[3] Scheler sees man in the epoch of a balance between life and spirit.

A *fourth* interpretation basically moves within the orbit of the third, and simultaneously includes the first and second within it. Relatively speaking, it is the most unoriginal and philosophically most fragile. We mention it only because it introduces a historical category for characterizing our contemporary situation and looks toward a new Middle Ages. The term 'Middle Ages' is here

---

1. O. Spengler, *Der Untergang des Abendlandes.* Vol. 1 (Vienna and Leipzig, 1918). Vol. 2 (Munich, 1922). [Trans. H. Werner, *The Decline of the West* (New York: Oxford University Press, 1991). Abridged version.]

2. L. Klages, *Der Geist als Widersacher der Seele.* Vols. 1 and 2 (Leipzig, 1929).

3. M. Scheler, *Der Mensch im Weltalter des Ausgleichs.* In: M. Scheler, *Philosophische Weltanschauung* (Bonn, 1929), pp. 47ff. [Trans. O. A. Haac, *Philosophical Perspectives* (Boston: Beacon Press, 1958).]

not supposed to mean a renaissance of the particular historical epoch that we know and indeed conceive of in very different ways. Rather the title moves in the same direction as the third interpretation. What is meant is a middle or mediating epoch that is to bring about a new sublation of the opposition between 'life and spirit'. This fourth interpretation is represented by Leopold Ziegler in his book *The European Spirit*.[4]

This is merely a kind of summary in terms of stereotypes pointing out what is known today, what is spoken of, and what in part has already been forgotten again, interpretations that are partly borrowed second- and third-hand and moulded into an overall picture, views that subsequently penetrate into the higher journalism of our age and create the spiritual space—if one may say such a thing—in which we move. If one were to take this pointer concerning the four interpretations of our situation as more than what it is, namely a mere pointer, then it would necessarily be unfair, because it is too general. And yet, the essential thing that matters to us is the fundamental trait of these interpretations, or better, the perspective in which they all see our contemporary situation. In terms of a stereotype once more, this perspective is that of the relation between life and spirit. It is no accident that we find this fundamental trait of these interpretations of our situation in the distinction and opposition provided by this formula.

In view of this distinction and of these two catchwords it will initially be said that this simply invokes something which is already well known; how can this help us grasp what is peculiar about the contemporary and future situation of man? Yet it would be a misunderstanding if one were to take these two terms merely as though they designated two components of man, as it were: soul (life) and spirit, two components that have always been ascribed to man and whose relation has always been one of conflict. Rather these terms are concerned with specific fundamental orientations of man. If we take the expressions in this way, then we can easily see that what is at issue here is not some theoretical elucidation of the relation between spirit and soul, but what Nietzsche means by the terms *Dionysian* and *Apollonian*. Thus all four interpretations also point back to this common source, to Nietzsche and to a particular conception of Nietzsche. All four interpretations are only possible given a particular reception of Nietzsche's philosophy. This hint is not meant to put the originality of the interpretations into question, but is merely intended to indicate the place and source where the confrontation proper must occur.

---

4. L. Ziegler, *Der europäische Geist* (Darmstadt, 1929).

b) Nietzsche's fundamental opposition between the Dionysian and Apollonian as the source of the four interpretations of our contemporary situation.

We cannot here enter into the concrete details of how Nietzsche conceives of this fundamental opposition. We shall characterize it only to the extent necessary for us to see what is at stake. The extent to which we can forego this task of interpreting the four depictions of our situation and their source will be seen more clearly later.

This Dionysos/Apollo opposition sustains and guides Nietzsche's philosophizing from early on. He himself knew this. This opposition, taken from antiquity, inevitably revealed itself to the young classical philologist who wanted to break with his discipline. Yet he also knew that however much this opposition is maintained in his philosophizing, it became transformed for him in and through this philosophizing. Nietzsche himself knew: "Only whoever transforms himself is related to me." I would like deliberately to draw on the final interpretation, which he gave in his major and decisive work, in that work which he was never to complete in the form in which he harboured it within him: *The Will to Power*. The heading of the second section of the fourth book reads: "Dionysos."[5] Here we find peculiar aphorisms, and the whole work is in general a cluster of essential thoughts, demands, and valuations. To begin with, I shall provide evidence of how clearly Nietzsche, around this period shortly before his collapse, saw that this opposition had been determinative for him from early on. Even before his doctorate, Nietzsche was called to Basel in 1869 as Professor Extraordinarius.

> *Around 1876* I had the horror of seeing everything I had hitherto wanted *compromised* as I understood where Wagner was now heading: and I had very strong ties with him, through all the bonds of a deep unity of need, through gratitude, through the lack of any substitute and through the absolute deprivation that I saw before me.
>
> Around the same time, I appeared to myself as though inescapably *incarcerated* in my philology and teaching activity—in a contingent and stopgap period of my life—: I no longer knew how to escape, and was tired, exhausted, worn out.
>
> Around the same time, I understood that my instinct was heading in the opposite direction to that of Schopenhauer: toward a *justification of life*, even in its most frightful, most ambiguous, and most deceptive aspects:—for this I held the formula 'Dionysian' in my hands.[6]

5. F. Nietzsche, *Der Wille zur Macht*. Gesammelte Werke (Musarionausgabe) (Munich, 1920ff.). Vol. XIX, pp. 336ff. [Trans. W. Kaufmann and R. J. Hollingdale, *The Will to Power* (New York: Random House, 1968), pp. 520ff.]

6. Ibid., p. 337, no. 1005.

Later we then read:

> Apollo's illusion: the *eternity* of beautiful form; the aristocratic legislation *'thus it shall be always!'*
>
> Dionysos: sensuousness and cruelty. Transitoriness could be interpreted as enjoyment of productive and destructive energy, as *constant creation.*[7]

There follows a section in which Nietzsche then interprets this opposition in what is probably its most beautiful and decisive form and connects it with its source:

> The word *Dionysian* expresses an urge for unity, a reaching beyond the person, the everyday, society, reality, beyond the abyss of passing away: a passionate and painful swelling over into more obscure, more full, more lingering states; an enraptured yes-saying to the overall character of life as that which is the same, of the same power, of the same bliss in the midst of all change; the grand pantheistic shared joyfulness and compassion that approves and sanctifies even the most frightful and questionable aspects of life; the eternal will to creation, to fruitfulness, to return; the feeling of unity in the necessity of creating and de-stroying.
>
> The word *Apollonian* expresses the urge for complete being-for-oneself, for the typical 'individual', for everything that simplifies, sets in relief, makes things strong, clear, unambiguous and typical: freedom under the law.
>
> The further development of art is just as necessarily linked to the antagonism of these two forces of nature and art as is the further development of mankind to the antagonism of the sexes. The fullness of power and moderation, the highest form of self-affirmation in one cool, noble, aloof beauty: the Apollonianism of the Hellenic will.[8]

There then follows his characterization of the origin of this interpretation, and thereby his most profound analysis of the Greek world:

> This opposition of the Dionysian and the Apollonian within the Greek soul is one of the greatest enigmas that I felt attracted by in view of the essential nature of the Greeks. I was fundamentally concerned with nothing other than surmising why precisely the Greek Apollonianism had to grow out of a Dionysian under-ground: the Dionysian Greek needed to become Apollonian: that is, to shatter his will for the immense, for the multiple, the uncertain, the horrifying, upon a will for measure, for simplicity, for classification in rules and concepts. The immeasurable, the desolate, the Asiatic lies at his foundation: the courage of the Greek consists in the struggle with his Asiatic nature: beauty is not bestowed upon him, just as little as logic, or as the naturalness of morals,—it is captured, willed, fought for—it is his *conquest.*[9]

7. Ibid., pp. 359f., no. 1049.
8. Ibid., pp. 360f., no. 1050.
9. Ibid.

One final point, in order to indicate how this opposition became decisively transformed into *"The two types: Dionysos and the Crucified"*:

> [. . .] Here I locate the *Dionysos* of the Greeks: the religious affirmation of life, of life as a whole, not denied or divided; (typical—that the sexual act awakens profundity, mystery, reverence).
>
> Dionysos versus the 'Crucified': there you have the opposition. [. . .] The God on the cross is a curse on life, a sign to redeem oneself thereof;—Dionysos dismembered is a *promise* of life: it will be eternally born again and come home out of destruction.[10]

It does not require many words to see that here in Nietzsche an opposition was alive that in no way came to light in the four interpretations provided of our situation, but merely had a residual effect as material passed on, as a literary form.

Which of the four interpretations is the more correct in Nietzsche's sense is not to be decided now. Nor indeed can we show here that none is correct, because none can be correct, insofar as they all mistake the essence of Nietzsche's philosophy, which for its part rests on strange foundations. These foundations indeed show themselves to be based on a quite ordinary and metaphysically highly questionable 'psychology'. Yet Nietzsche can afford that. Nevertheless, this is no *carte blanche*.

We know only that Nietzsche is the source of the interpretations we have mentioned. We are not saying this in order to accuse these interpretations of being derivative or to detract from their originality in any way, but in order to designate the direction from out of which an understanding is to be gained, and to show where the place of the confrontation proper lies (cf. the George-circle, psychoanalysis).

c) Profound boredom as the concealed fundamental attunement of the interpretations of our situation provided by the philosophy of culture.

All these questions are secondary for us. We are not even asking whether all these interpretations of our situation are correct or not. In such cases most things always tend to be correct. And yet it is essential to mention them. For what is going on in these interpretations? We are claiming that what is going on is a *diagnosis* of culture in which, with the aid of the aforementioned categories of life and spirit, we pass through and beyond world history at a single stroke. In this way, what is contemporary is indeed meant to be located

---

10. Ibid., pp. 364f., no. 1052.

in its *setting* [Stelle], its *situation* is supposed to be determined. Yet we ourselves are not at all concerned, let alone affected by this world-historical determination of where we are, by the settling of accounts with our culture. On the contrary, the whole affair is something sensational, and this always means an unconceded, yet once again illusory appeasement, albeit of a merely literary and characteristically short-lived kind. This whole approach of cultural diagnosis, which is non-binding and is interesting for just this reason, then becomes even more exciting by being developed and reconstituted, whether explicitly or not, into *prognosis.* Is there anyone who does not wish to know what is coming, so that they can prepare themselves for it, so as to be less burdened, less preoccupied and affected by the present! These world-historical diagnoses and prognoses of culture do not involve us, they *do not attack us.* On the contrary, they release us from ourselves and present us to ourselves in a world-historical situation and role. These diagnoses and prognoses of culture are the typical marks of what is called 'philosophy of culture' and is now making an impact in many weaker or even more fantastic variations. This philosophy of culture does not grasp us in our contemporary situation, but at best sees only what is contemporary, yet a contemporaneity which is entirely without us, which is nothing other than what belongs to the eternal yesterday. We have deliberately characterized these interpretations of our situation using foreign words: diagnosis, prognosis [*Diagnose, Prognose*], because their essence does not grow out of anything original. They lead a literary existence—albeit one that is by no means accidental.

If, however, philosophy of culture in its interpretation of our contemporary situation precisely fails to *take hold of us* or even *grip us,* then we would be mistaken if, in the considerations we made, we thought that in order to grasp our fundamental attunement we first had to be certain of our situation in this way.

It could, however, be said that perhaps it is only this particular kind of interpretation of our situation that is inadequate—a claim for which, moreover, we would first require evidence, something that we have so far not provided as such. In any case we will need some kind of pointers to let us see *where* we now stand. *Culture,* surely, is precisely the expression of our soul—indeed, it is a widespread opinion today that both culture and man in culture can only be properly and philosophically comprehended through the idea of expression or symbol. We have today a philosophy of culture concerned with expression, with symbol, with symbolic forms. Man as soul and spirit, coming to expression in forms that bear an intrinsic meaning and which, on the basis of this meaning, give a sense to existence [*Dasein*] as it expresses itself: this, roughly speaking, is the schema of contemporary philosophy of culture. Here too almost everything is correct, right down to the essential. Yet we must ask anew: Is this view of man an essential one? What is happening in these interpretations, quite apart from the classification of man in culture as provided by the philosophy of culture? Man, perhaps even contemporary man, is in this way set out in terms of the expression of his achievements. And yet the question remains as to whether setting man out in this way *concerns and grips his Da-sein,* or indeed brings it to being, whether this setting-out that is oriented toward expression not only factically misses the essence of man, but *must* necessarily miss it, quite irrespective of all aesthetics. In other words, such philosophy attains merely the *setting-out* [Dar-stellung] of man, but never his *Da-sein.* Not only does it factically fail to attain it, but it is of necessity unable to attain it, because in itself it blocks the path to doing so.

Perhaps—precisely if and because we are striving to awaken a fundamental attunement—we must indeed proceed from an 'expression' in which we are merely set out. Perhaps this awakening of a fundamental attunement indeed looks like an ascertaining [*Fest-stellung*], yet is something other than setting-out or ascertaining. Accordingly, if we cannot escape the fact that everything we are saying looks like a setting out of our situation, and seems as though it is ascertaining an attunement that underlies this situation and ex-presses itself [*sich aus-drückt*] in the situation; if we cannot deny this semblance and even less cast it aside, then this is saying merely that *ambiguity* is precisely now setting in for the first time. Is this surprising? If our introductory characterization of the essential ambiguity of philosophizing, of *our* philosophizing, was not some hollow cliché that was intended merely to say something peculiar about philosophy, then *ambiguity* must impose its power now at the *beginning.* We will not wish to believe that such ambiguity is to be remedied in the slightest by our declaring or asserting in advance that there exists a theoretical difference between setting out our spiritual situation and awakening a fundamental attunement. That does not relieve us of anything at all. The more proper our beginning is, the more we shall leave this ambiguity in play, and the harder the task will be for each individual to decide for him- or herself whether he or she really understands or not.

If the kind of interpretation of our situation provided by philosophy of culture leads us onto an erroneous path, then we are not to ask: *Where do we stand?,* but must ask: *How do things stand with us?* Yet if things stand in some way or other—in this way or that—with us, then this does not take place in a void: we are still standing somewhere. We would do well to infer from *where* we are standing *how* things stand with us. Thus we must after all first set out our own situation; perhaps we merely have to characterize it differently than the aforementioned interpretations. Yet this is not necessary at all. We already know enough about our situation without going into those interpretations in more detail or adding another one. Nor do we have to reject them as incorrect. We already know enough about our situation merely by ascertaining *that there are these interpretations*—the prevalence of philosophy of culture—and that they determine our existence [*Dasein*] in many ways, even if we cannot say precisely how.

We now ask anew: What does the fact that these diagnoses of culture find an audience among us—albeit in quite different ways—tell us about what is happening here? What is happening in the fact that this higher form of journalism fills or even altogether delimits our 'spiritual' space? Is all this merely a fashion? Is anything overcome if we seek to characterize it as 'fashionable philosophy' and thus to belittle it? We may not and do not wish to resort to such cheap means.

We said that this philosophy of culture at most sets out what is contemporary about our situation, but does not take hold of *us*. What is more, not only does it not succeed in grasping us, but it unties us from ourselves in imparting us a role in world history. It unties us from ourselves, and yet does so precisely as anthropology. Our flight and disorientation [*Verkehrung*], the illusion and our lostness become more acute. The *decisive question* now is: What lies behind the fact that we give ourselves this role and indeed *must* do so? Have we become too *insignificant* to ourselves, that we require a role? Why do we find no meaning for ourselves any more, i.e., no essential possibility of being? Is it because an *indifference* yawns at us out of all things, an indifference whose grounds we do not know? Yet who can speak in such a way when world trade, technology, and the economy seize hold of man and keep him moving? And nevertheless *we* seek a *role for ourselves*. What is happening here?, we ask anew. Must we first make ourselves interesting to ourselves again? Why *must* we do this? Perhaps because we ourselves have become *bored* with ourselves? Is man himself now supposed to have become bored with himself? Why so? *Do things ultimately stand in such a way with us that a profound boredom draws back and forth like a silent fog in the abysses of Dasein?*

We do not ultimately need any diagnoses or prognoses of culture in order to make sure of our situation, because they merely provide us with a role and untie us from ourselves, instead of helping us to want to find ourselves. Yet how are we to find ourselves—in some vain self-reflection, in that repugnant sniffing out of everything psychological which today has exceeded all measure? Or are we to find ourselves in such a way that we are thereby *given back* to ourselves, that is, given back to *ourselves*, so that we are *given over* to ourselves, given over to the task of becoming what we are?

We may not, therefore, flee from ourselves in some convoluted idle talk about culture, nor pursue ourselves in a psychology motivated by curiosity. Rather we must find ourselves by binding ourselves to our being-there [*Dasein*] and by letting such *being*-there [*Da*-sein] become what is *singularly* binding for us.

Will we find ourselves via this indication of that *profound boredom,* which perhaps none of us know at first? Is this questionable profound boredom actually supposed to be the *sought-after fundamental attunement* that must be *awakened?*

Chapter Two

The First Form of Boredom: Becoming Bored by Something

§19. The questionableness of boredom. Awakening
this fundamental attunement as letting it be awake,
as guarding against it falling asleep.

By drawing attention to this profound boredom, it now seems as though we have done what we were attempting to avoid from the outset, namely ascertaining a fundamental attunement. Yet have we ascertained a fundamental attunement? By no means. We cannot ascertain one at all; indeed we are quite unable to do so, since it is entirely possible for everyone to deny that such an attunement is there. We have not ascertained one at all—indeed everyone will say we have arbitrarily asserted that such an attunement is at hand. Yet what is at issue is not whether we deny it or assert it. Let us simply recall what we asked: Do things ultimately stand in such a way with us that a profound boredom draws back and forth like a silent fog in the abysses of Dasein?

Nevertheless, so long as this boredom remains questionable, we cannot awaken it. Or can we perhaps do so after all? What does it mean to say that this boredom is questionable for us? Initially this amounts to saying in formal terms that we do not know whether this attunement pervades us or not. Who, 'we'? *We* do not know this. This not knowing and not being acquainted with this boredom—does it not precisely also belong to the way in which we are, to *our* situation? Why do we not know about it? Because it is perhaps not there at all? Or—because we *do not want* to know about it? Or do we know about it after all? Are we 'merely' lacking courage concerning what we know? In the end we do not want to know of it, but constantly seek *to escape* it. If we constantly seek to escape from it in this way, we ultimately have a bad conscience in so doing, we cling to the excuses associated with such bad conscience, and are consoled by persuading ourselves and proving to ourselves that we do not know of it—therefore it is not there.

How do we escape this boredom [*Langeweile*], in which we find, as we ourselves say, that *time* becomes drawn out, becomes long [*lang*]?[1] Simply by at all times making an effort, whether consciously or unconsciously, to pass the time, by welcoming highly important and essential preoccupations for the

---

1. [Tr: Heidegger is here alluding to the literal meaning of the German word for boredom, *Langeweile*: literally 'long while'. The temporal sense of *Weile* and its stretching will be important for the following analyses of the attunement of boredom.]

sole reason that they take up our time. Who will deny this? Yet do we then still need to first ascertain the fact that this boredom is there?

Yet what does it mean to say that we *drive away* [vertreiben] and *shake off* boredom? We constantly cause it to *fall asleep.* For evidently we cannot annihilate it by passing the time, however intensively. We 'know'—in a strange kind of knowing—that boredom can return at any time. Thus it is already there. We shake it off. We succeed in making it fall asleep. We wish to know nothing of it. This does not at all mean that we do not wish to be conscious of it, but rather that we do not wish to let it be awake—it, this boredom which, in the end, is already awake. With open eyes it looks into our Da-sein (albeit entirely from a distance), and with this gaze already penetrates us and attunes us through and through.

Yet if it is already awake, then surely it does not need to be awakened. Indeed not. Awakening this fundamental attunement does not mean making it awake in the first place, but *letting it be awake, guarding against it falling asleep.* We can easily see from this that our task has not become any easier. Perhaps this task is essentially more difficult, similar to the way in which we can experience at any time that it is easier to wake someone up by startling them than to guard against them falling asleep. Yet whether our task is difficult or easy is not what is essential here.

We here face a far more essential difficulty. Not to let boredom fall asleep is a strange or almost insane demand [*Zumutung*]. Is it not entirely opposed to what all natural and sound human comportment is concerned with every day and every hour, namely to pass the time and precisely not to let boredom arise, that is, to shake it off and make it fall asleep whenever it approaches? And *we* are supposed to let it be awake! Boredom—who is not acquainted with it in the most varied forms and disguises in which it arises, in the way it often befalls us only for a moment, the way it torments and depresses us for longer periods too. Who does not know that we have already set about suppressing it and are concerned to drive it away as soon as it approaches; that this does not always succeed, that indeed precisely when we set upon it with all the means at our disposal it becomes stubborn, obstinate; that it then really does persist and returns more frequently, slowly propelling us to the threshold of melancholy [*Schwermut*]? Even when we succeed in shaking it off—do we not then know at the same time that it may well return? Do we not have the strange knowledge that what we have fortunately seen driven away and made to vanish could at any time be there once again? And does this belong to it if it shows itself to us in this way?

Yet to where does it vanish, and from where does this insidious creature that maintains its monstrous essence in our Dasein return? Who is not acquainted with it—and yet, who can say freely what this universally familiar phenomenon properly is? What is this boredom, such that faced with it we set ourselves the demand to let *it,* this very attunement, be awake? Or is this boredom that is familiar to us here in this way, and of which we now speak so indeterminately, a mere shadow of our actual boredom? We indeed asked and are repeatedly asking: Have things ultimately gone so far with us that a *profound* boredom draws back and forth like a silent fog in the abysses of Dasein?

*§20. The fundamental attunement of boredom, its
relation to time, and the three metaphysical questions
concerning world, finitude, individuation.*

This *profound boredom* is the *fundamental attunement.* We pass the *time,* in order to master it, because time becomes long in boredom. Time becomes long for us. Is it supposed to be short, then? Does not each of us wish for a truly long time for ourselves? And whenever it does become long for us, we pass the time and ward off its becoming long! We do not want to have a long time, but we have it nevertheless. Boredom, long time: especially in Alemannic usage, it is no accident that 'to have long time' means the same as 'to be homesick'. In this German usage, if someone has long-time for . . . this means he is homesick for. . . . Is this accidental? Or is it only with difficulty that we are able to grasp and draw upon the wisdom of language? Profound boredom—a homesickness. Homesickness—philosophizing, we heard somewhere, is supposed to be a homesickness. Boredom—a fundamental attunement of philosophizing. *Boredom—what is it?*

Boredom, *Langeweile*—whatever its ultimate essence may be—shows, particularly in our German word, an almost obvious *relation to time,* a way in which we stand with respect to time, a feeling of time. Boredom and the question of boredom thus lead us to the problem of time. We must first let ourselves enter the problem of time, in order to determine boredom as a particular relation to it. Or is it the other way around, does boredom first lead us to time, to an understanding of *how time resonates in the ground of Da-sein* and how it is only because of this that we can 'act' and 'manoeuvre' in our customary superficial way? Or are we failing to ask correctly concerning either the first relation—that of boredom to time—or the second—that of time to boredom?

Yet after all we are not in fact posing the problem of time, the question of what time is, but are posing the three quite different questions of what *world, finitude,* and *individuation* are. Our philosophizing is meant to be moving and maintaining itself in the direction of, and along the path of these three questions. What is more, these three questions are supposed to spring *from a fundamental attunement* for us. This attunement, profound boredom—if only we knew what it is, or were even pervaded by this attunement! Yet even assuming that we were pervaded by this fundamental attunement, what in the world does boredom have to do with the question concerning world, finitude, and individuation? We can perceive that this fundamental attunement of boredom is tied up with time and the problem of time. *Or are our three questions ultimately tied up with the question of time?* Is there not an ancient conviction that the world and time both originated together, that both are equally old, equally original and related to one another? Is there not a less venerable, self-evident opinion according to which whatever is finite is temporal? Then finitude would be bound up with time just as much as world. Are we not acquainted with the ancient doctrine of metaphysics according to which something individual becomes this individual thing by virtue of its specific position in time, so that like the first two questions of world and finitude, the problem of individuation would also be a problem of time? Time for its part stands in a relation of boredom to *us*. Boredom is accordingly the fundamental attunement of our philosophizing, in which we develop the three questions of world, finitude, and individuation. Time is thereby itself something that determines us in the working out of these three guiding questions. If time is tied up with boredom, and on the other hand is somehow the basis for our three questions, then the fundamental attunement of boredom constitutes an exceptional relation to time in human Dasein, and thereby offers an exceptional possibility of answering the three questions. Perhaps all this is indeed the case. Yet if so, then what has been said after all remains only a pre-cursory opening up of a broad and as yet obscure perspective. All this is meant merely to serve toward making more comprehensible the state of helplessness we shall get into *if we are now to become involved in boredom with the intention of explicating the three metaphysical questions above.*

For what remains obscure to us is precisely the extent to which boredom is supposed to be our fundamental attunement, and evidently an essential fundamental attunement. Perhaps nothing at all rings a bell with us, and nothing is conjured up. Where might the reason lie for this? Perhaps we are not acquainted with *this* boredom because we do not at all understand boredom *in its essence.* Perhaps we do not understand its essence because it *has never yet become essential* for us. And in the end it cannot become essential for us, because it not only belongs at first and for the most part to those attunements that we shake off in our everyday lives, but to those attunements that we do not allow to attune us as attunements even when they are there. Perhaps that very boredom which often merely flashes past us, as it were, is more essential than *that* boredom with which we are explicitly concerned whenever this or that particular thing bores us by making us feel ill at ease. Perhaps that boredom is more essential which attunes us neither favourably nor unfavourably, and yet does attune us, but attunes us in such a way that it seems as though we were not attuned at all.

This *superficial boredom* is even meant to lead us into *profound* boredom, or, to put it more appropriately, the superficial boredom is supposed to manifest itself as the profound boredom and to attune us through and through in the ground of Dasein. This fleeting, cursory, *inessential* boredom must become *essential.* How are we to bring this about? Are we explicitly and intentionally to produce boredom in ourselves? Not at all. We do not need to undertake anything in this respect. On the contrary, we are always already undertaking too much. This boredom becomes essential of its own accord, if only we are not opposed to it, if we do not always immediately react to protect ourselves, if instead we make room for it. This is what we must first learn: *not to resist straightaway* but *to let resonate.* Yet how are we to make room for this initially inessential, ungraspable boredom? Only by not being opposed to it, but letting it approach us and tell us what it wants, what is going on with it. Yet even to do this, it is necessary in the first place that we remove from indeterminacy whatever we thus name and apparently know as boredom. We must do this, however, not in the sense of dissecting some psychological experience, but in such a way that we thereby approach ourselves. Whom? Ourselves—*ourselves as a Da-sein.* (Ambiguity!)

> *§21. The interpretation of boredom starting from that which is boring. That which is boring as that which holds us in limbo and leaves us empty. The questionableness of the three conventional schemata of interpretation: the cause-effect relation, something psychological, and transference.*

Boredom: if we gather together all our analyses hitherto, then we have now said a number of things about it, and yet we are certain of this: We have not yet understood it as *attunement.* We already know, and do not now wish to forget, that it is not in the first place a matter of interpreting this or that attunement, but that the understanding of attunement ultimately demands of us a transformation in our fundamental conception of man. Attunement, correctly understood, first gives us the possibility of grasping the Da-sein of man as such. Attunements are not a class of lived experience, such that the realm and order of experiences would themselves remain untouched. Thus, from the very beginning we are intentionally not starting out from boredom, if only because it would then look all too much as though we wanted to subject to analysis some spiritual experience in our consciousness. We are not really starting from boredom, but from *boringness.* Put formally, boringness is what makes something *boring* what it is whenever it is *boring* us.

Something *boring*—a thing, a book, a play, a ceremony, yet also a person, a group of people, indeed even an environment or a place—such boring things are not boredom itself. Or can even boredom be boring in the end? We shall leave these questions open and postpone them until we are led to them ourselves. We are acquainted with such boring things because in and through their boringness they cause boredom in us. We become bored by boring things, so that we are thereby bored. This already presents us with several aspects: [1.] *that which is boring in its boringness;* [2.] *becoming bored by* this *boring thing* and *being bored with* such a thing; [3.] *boredom* itself. Are these three pieces which belong together? Or is it merely [1.] and [2.] which belong together? Or are they in general one and the same, in each case seen from a different perspective? Presumably they are not simply ranged alongside one another. Yet how do they relate to one another? Is what is named in third place merely a combination? All this remains questionable. In any case we can already see one thing: boredom is not simply an inner spiritual experience, rather something about it, namely *that which bores* and which lets being bored arise, comes toward us precisely *from out of things themselves.* It is much rather the case that boredom is outside, seated in what is boring, and creeps into us from the outside. Strange—ungraspable though this is at first, we must follow what *everyday* speaking, comportment, and judgment actually expresses: that things themselves, people themselves, events and places themselves are *boring.*

Yet—it will at once be retorted—of what help is it to us to attempt to begin our interpretation of boredom by characterizing what is boring? For as soon as we start with what is boring, we will find ourselves saying: it is whatever bores us and thus causes boredom. After all, only out of boredom can we understand what that which is boring is in its boringness, and not the other way around. Therefore we must indeed begin with boredom itself. This is a plausible consideration. And yet it rests on an illusion that conceals the entire problem. For what does it mean to say that certain things and people cause boredom in us? Why precisely these things and that person, this place and not another? Furthermore, why this thing now and not at another time, and why does what bored us earlier suddenly not do so at all? There must, after all, be something that bores us in all these things. What is it? Where does it come from? That which bores us, we say, causes boredom. What is this *causation?* Does it correspond to some process like the onset of cold which causes the column of mercury in a thermometer to sink? Cause—effect! Marvellous! Is it some kind of process, as when one billiard ball strikes another and thereby causes movement in the second?

We will not get anywhere at all on this track, quite apart from the fact that even this cause-effect relation, as we have illustrated it with reference to two bodies making contact and striking one another, is already entirely problematic. How does boredom bore—how is such a thing possible? I emphasize time and again that we may not turn away from the fact that we find *things themselves* boring and say of them that *they themselves* are boring. We cannot escape at all from the task of first, albeit not definitively, saying what that which is boring and which influences us is in its boringness. This is why we are asking with respect to the boringness of whatever is boring: what is this? We are asking: what does boring mean?, and are simultaneously asking: what kind of a property is this?

We find something boring. We find it so and say: it *is* boring. Yet—when we say and mean that this or that 'is boring', then at first we no longer think at all of the fact that it causes boredom or has caused it in us, that it bores us. The expression 'boring' is an *objective* characteristic. A book, for example, is badly written, tastelessly printed and presented; it is *boring*. The book itself—in itself—is boring, not only boring for us to read and while reading it, but it itself, the intrinsic construction of the book, is boring. Perhaps it is not necessary at all that in reading this boring book we are bored, just as on the other hand it is possible for us to be bored while reading a book which is nevertheless interesting. We say such things as a matter of course.

Boring—by this we mean wearisome, tedious; it does not stimulate and excite, it does not give anything, has nothing to say to us, does not concern us in any way. This is not yet a determination of its essence, however, but merely an explanation that initially suggests itself. Yet if we explain whatever is boring in this way, we have indeed unexpectedly proceeded to interpret the initially objective character of the book's boringness as something which *concerns us in such and such a way* and therefore stands in such and such a relation to us as subjects, to our subjectivity, influences us in such and such a way, determines our attunement [*uns . . . be-stimmt*]. Then boringness is not some exclusively objective property of the book after all, such as its bad cover, for instance. The characteristic of 'boring' thus *belongs to the object* and is at the same time *related to the subject*.

Yet if we look more closely, this is valid only for boringness and not for the property of the book, the fact that it has been badly bound. 'Bad' can here mean: tasteless, and this already indicates that even this objective characteristic is related to the subject. That which does not arouse any pleasure in us, but rather the opposite, is tasteless. But 'bad cover' can certainly also mean: not finished in fine, genuine, and above all durable material. Yet even here, where a characteristic of the material itself is meant, the subject-relatedness is not absent. For what does 'non-durable', 'non-lasting' mean? It means in and during the use we make of it, which may last a long time and thus be demanding. Thus this characteristic too is relative to our dealings with the book and its cover. Therefore even those properties of things which are apparently most objective are related to the subject. It is thus nothing exceptional for the property 'boring' to belong to the object and be related to the subject; rather it is like this with every property. Nonetheless, we somehow sense that the character of the boringness of a book is something quite different from the fact that it is badly written and suchlike.

Naturally—the reply will be—this is, after all, an old truth which all idealist philosophy has always maintained, namely that properties do not accrue to things themselves, but are representations, ideas that we as subjects transfer onto objects. This is surely quite evident precisely in our case, concerning the characteristic of boringness. This case is merely one example of a generally recognized fact. All such properties—boring, cheerful, sad (event), funny (game)—these properties which have to do with attunement are related to the subject in a special sense; not only that, they stem directly from the subject and its situation. We *transfer* subsequently those attunements which things cause in us onto the the things themselves. Ever since Aristotle's *Poetics* we have had the expression 'metaphor' (μεταφορά) for this. Even in Aristotle's *Poetics* it was seen that in language and poetic depiction there are particular statements and coinages in which we transfer (μεταφέρειν) these attunements that things cause in us—sadness, cheerfulness, boringness—out of ourselves and onto things. After all, we know from school that the language of poets, and everyday linguistic usage, are permeated by such metaphors. We speak of a 'laughing meadow' and do not mean that the meadow itself is laughing, we speak of a 'cheerful room', of a 'melancholy landscape'. The landscape is not itself melancholy [*schwermütig*], but merely attunes us in such a way, causes this attunement in us. And similarly with the 'boring book'.

Certainly, this is the general view and conclusive explanation. However, does it explain anything? Even if we admit for the moment that we transfer onto things the effect of an attunement caused in us, *why* do we transfer such characteristics of attunements onto things? After all, this does not happen by chance or arbitrarily, but evidently because we find something *about things* which demands of its own accord, as it were, that we address and name them in this way and not otherwise. We may not explain away this fact lightly, before we have become clear in general about what lies in the fact that we find the landscape melancholy, the room cheerful, the book boring. Even if we admit for the moment that we do 'transfer' something here, then we do so in the opinion that what is transferred somehow pertains to the thing itself. Surely it may at least be asked and even must be asked: *What* is it, then, that here causes the attunement or *gives rise to transference?* If it already lies in the things themselves, can we then simply speak of a transference? All this is not so self-evident after all. In that case, we are no longer transferring something, but in some way *apprehending* it *from the things themselves.*

What have we gained from this appraisal? Nothing at all—with respect to a definition of what is boring as such. Perhaps we have unexpectedly hit upon a more general problem, namely what kind of property we are dealing with in general. Right now we see only this much—initially in a rough and ready characterization coming from the outside: these characteristics are on the one hand objective ones, taken from the objects themselves, from out of them, yet at the same time subjective ones, and according to the common explanation transferred from subjects onto objects. Characteristics such as 'boring' therefore *belong to the object* and yet are *taken from the subject.* Yet these are contradictory, incompatible determinations. In any case we are unable to see how they are possible in their unity. Nor has it been decided whether this twofold characterization actually fits the facts of the matter at all, or whether it does not rather distort them from the outset, no matter how self-evident it may appear. Yet if we are thus unclear about the general characteristic of the boringness of a thing taken as a property, may we then hope to explain this particular property in the right way? Do we then not simply lack any purchase on the problem? Indeed. This tells us only one thing: If we are thus surrounded by difficulties, then it is all the more important to keep our eyes open. Hence we do not want to explain the facts of the matter by rash theories—no matter how current or acknowledged they may be.

Let us return to our first characterization of boringness and of that which is boring. We shall repeat what we mean by it, and how we can explicate boringness in its meaningful context. We can take two points from this:

[1.] We say that the book is 'wearisome', 'tedious'. What we address as *boring* we draw *from the thing itself,* and also mean it as belonging to this thing.

[2.] At the same time we say that the book is not stimulating or exciting, it does not offer anything, does not affect us. If we paraphrase and explain this quite spontaneously, then we are speaking unexpectedly of a characteristic which does not have any content of its own. Rather what is essential about it lies precisely *in its relation to us,* in the way in which we are *affected* or not affected.

Hitherto we have emphasized only the relation to the subject. We were surprised by it and perhaps also even led astray. Yet we have completely overlooked the way in which we here explain this characteristic of boringness by direct paraphrase. This is precisely what is important. We did not say that what is boring is that which *causes* boredom in us. Nor did we merely avoid *saying* this in order, for instance, not to have to explain the same by way of the same (tautology); for there is no tautology here. Nor did we even *think* that the *boringness* of what is boring consists in *causing* boredom. We did not think of this—of this interpretation—because we have no such experience at all. For, as already mentioned, it is certainly possible that in reading we have not bored at all, that we did not 'have the feeling' that boredom was being induced in us. And yet we call the book boring, and this without saying anything untrue and without lying. We call the book boring straightaway, because *straightaway* we do not at all understand 'boring' as though it were synonymous with inducing boredom. We straightaway take 'boring' as meaning *wearisome, tedious,* which is not to say indifferent. For if something is wearisome and tedious, then this entails that it has not left us completely indifferent, but on the contrary: we are present while reading, given over to it, but not taken [*hingenommen*] by it. Wearisome means: it does not rivet us; we are given over to it, yet not taken by it, but merely held in limbo [*hingehalten*] by it. Tedious means: it does not engross us, we are left empty [*leer gelassen*]. If we can see these moments together in their unity somewhat more clearly, then perhaps we have made an *initial* gain, or—to put it more cautiously—are moving in the proximity of a proper interpretation: that which bores, which is boring, is *that which holds us in limbo and yet leaves us empty.*

Let us note that the whole view that something is induced in us, that the state of boredom is aroused, has now vanished. We are not saying that boredom has been induced in us. Maybe not—yet surely we are merely paraphrasing this and mean in effect that boredom is caused. Not at all. Do we wish to say instead that we were affected in such and such a way and in this find ourselves disposed in such and such a way? We do not mean this either; for we do not first and foremost merely wish to say what sort of effect the book had on us, but rather what character the book itself has. Hence when we say: the book is thus, this means that it can affect someone in such and such a way and in so doing can let someone find themselves disposed in such and such a way. Yet even this is not what we wish to express, but rather that the book is such that it brings us into an attunement that we would like to see suppressed.

We are speaking *from out of* an attunement which factically is not 'provoked' at all, and not with respect to some possible effect that might be caused in us. For this reason we cannot transfer it onto the thing that supposedly causes it either. Nor are we speaking from out of an attunement that could be evoked merely in its pure possibility, but from out of an attunement which we know *could arise at any time,* but which we suppress, which we do not wish to let arise. Is there a difference here? We say: from out of an attunement, but *not* out of a *caused effect;* from out of a possible attunement, one that may possibly befall us. It is from out of an attunement that we find something thus and thus and address it thus. This does *not* mean *transferring* an *effect* and its characteristics *onto the inducing cause.*

Yet have we advanced even a single step with all these discussions? Not at all! On the contrary, now everything really has become confused. The simple state of affairs—we call a book boring, i.e., it causes boredom in us—is completely muddled and interpreted in a contrived and incomprehensible way. And yet—we do not wish to force ourselves to arrive at a bare definition of boringness and boredom in our first attempt, but to understand the problem. However little consolation the result may be at first sight, we have nevertheless experienced something essential: [1.] What is boring is not so called simply because it effects boredom in us. The book is not the outer cause, nor is the resulting boredom the inner effect. [2.] Therefore, in elucidating the facts of the matter, we must disregard the cause-effect relation. [3.] The book must nonetheless make itself felt, not, however, as an inducing cause, but rather as that which *attunes* us. This is where the question lies. [4.] If the book is boring, then this thing outside the soul has in itself something of the possible, perhaps even suppressed attunement that is in us. Thus, although it is inside, *the attunement plays around* the thing outside at the same time, and indeed without our transferring any induced attunement from within us outside onto the thing. [5.] The thing can ultimately be boring only because the attunement already plays around it. It does not cause the boredom, yet nor does it receive it merely as something attributed by the subject. In short: boredom—and thus ultimately every attunement—is a hybrid, partly objective, partly subjective.

§22. Methodological directive for the interpretation of becoming bored: avoiding the approach of an analysis of consciousness, and maintaining the immediacy of everyday Dasein: interpretation of boredom in terms of passing the time as our immediate relation to boredom.

It is not this result that interests us, however, but the question: *Why* is attunement such a hybrid? Has this something to do with attunement itself, or with the way in which we explain it and attempt to explain it? Is attunement ultimately something totally different and free from any hybrid characteristics?

We may be permitted to ask these questions, yet then reminded of what we really sought to do, and have now achieved. We wanted, after all, to deal with the boringness of what is boring and specifically not with boredom, and yet we have been led to boredom after all. Certainly, we see that boredom is connected with becoming bored and with being bored. Yet we can see with equal clarity that if we now consider becoming bored and being bored, we may no longer consider them as some subjective state occurring in a subject. Instead we must from the outset and in principle take into account what is boring as well—each specific thing.

What does all this tell us? We cannot characterize what is boring as such at all, unless we clearly see what it is in general, namely something that attunes us in such and such a way. This means that we are already encountering an essential question: *What does it mean to attune?* We cannot simply say that to attune means to cause an attunement. We have thus discovered this *question*—a possible problem, one which is unavoidable and far more essential than any seemingly plausible explanation of this questionable characteristic, 'boring'.

With great laboriousness we have thus merely arrived at a negative result. Yet do we need to go to such lengths just to see this? Can we not achieve this result much more directly, and indeed with a positive content at the same time? Becoming bored obviously means becoming bored *by* something, being bored obviously means being bored *with* and *in doing* something. Conversely, something boring is '*related*' to becoming bored, or at least to a potential for becoming bored. That is clear. If we put it like this, then it seems as though we might have gained a new basis. And yet this clarity reveals itself as an illusion as soon as we recall that this relating of a subjective state of attunement to an objective thing, and vice-versa, is entirely questionable. This is precisely what led us astray in a mistaken direction of questioning.

If we now investigate becoming bored and being bored, then it is initially of little help to say that being bored is being bored with . . . and in. . . . It is especially of no help if we proceed in such a way as to understand what is boring as an object to which we relate, though in a different way than in knowing or willing. For the *problem* is precisely this *relatedness, its fundamental character.* To put it in general terms: determining our attunement is here to be grasped as something attuning us in such and such a way, and this *being attuned* is to be grasped as the *fundamental nature of our Dasein.* To ask this concretely once again: Whenever we love something, a thing or indeed a human being, is what or who we love merely the cause arising somewhere of a state arising in us, a state we transfer onto what we call our beloved? Of course not, it will be said, for the beloved is simply the object of our loving. Yet what does 'object' mean here? Something our love stumbles across and clings to? Or is all this not merely stated in a superficial way, but fundamentally wrong? Is it not the case that in love we do not stumble upon an object at all, yet nonetheless love something? This may stand merely as an indication that if we leave aside the cause-effect relation, we have not taken any positive step forward. Indeed the problem has become more acute.

On the other hand, there does now seem to be more prospect of getting behind the riddle of boredom if we examine the state of becoming bored and being bored. But we have been warned. Not only that in so doing we are not to neglect what is boring and that which bores us, but that this becoming bored and being bored is not some state that merely arises, one that we lay before us for investigation like some laboratory preparation. Yet how else are we to proceed? We must after all bring ourselves into some *relationship* to this state if we wish to make any assertions about it. Which is the appropriate relationship? Surely we can regard as valid the general rule of placing an object under the best conditions of observability. This rule is valid in the sciences. And thus in philosophy too. No—it is the other way around: It is not because this rule is valid in the sciences that it is valid for us, but it is valid in the sciences because this rule is grounded in an originary, essential connection. In accordance with this, the *substantive content* and *kind of being* of a *being* pre*scribe* the *possible manifestness* (truth) *belonging* to it. The various regions of beings and the individual things there are, each according to their substantive content and kind of being, are dependent upon a particular kind of truth, of unconcealment. This openness, which pertains to every being in accordance with its substantive content and in accordance with its way of being, in each case *prefigures* in turn the specific possible and appropriate *ways of access to the being that is itself to be grasped.* Through the respective kind of truth, which is tied up with being, the way, the possibility, and the means of appropriating or warding off beings, of possessing beings or losing them, are prefigured. This is not to say in any way that such access is one of theoretical interrogation and observation—in the scientific sense—but only to say that if scientific knowledge is to be gained, then in accordance with its intention and its possibilities it must satisfy that essential connection between being and truth. For this reason explicit rules become necessary for the sciences. The necessity of having to proceed methodologically, i.e., of investigating a being according to its kind, does not exist because science demands such a thing, but is called for by science on the basis of the essential belonging together of being and truth.

We, however, do not wish to observe boredom. Perhaps such a thing is altogether impossible. Yet we do want to experience something about boredom, about its essence, about the way in which its essence unfolds. Can we do this in any other way than by *transposing* ourselves into an attunement of boredom and then observing it, or by *imagining* a certain boredom and then asking what belongs to it? For surely it is all the same whether we are investigating an actual case of boredom or an imagined, i.e., merely possible case. After all, we are not interested in this particular boredom that we have right now, but boredom itself as such and what belongs to it, i.e., to every *possible* case. Thus an imagined case of boredom will fulfil the same function for us.

So it seems, indeed. If we transpose ourselves into boredom or imagine we are doing so and then get to work on it and observe it, we shall satisfy the fundamental rule of investigation. And yet, precise though this assignment of tasks may seem, it misses our task. It makes the lived experience of attunement into an object swimming in the stream of consciousness which we as observers gaze after. In this way we *precisely do not enter our originary relationship to boredom,* nor its relationship to us. When we make it into an object in this way then we refuse it precisely the role it is supposed to have in keeping with the most proper intention of our questioning. We refuse it the possibility of unfolding its essence as such, as the boredom in which we are bored, so that we may thereby experience its essence.

If what is boring and that which bores us, and together with this, boredom itself, is something which is uncomfortable for us, something that we do *not* wish to let arise, something that we immediately try to drive away when it arises—if boredom is something that we are fundamentally *opposed to* from the very beginning, then it will originally manifest itself as that to which we are opposed *wherever* we are opposed to it, *wherever* we drive it away—whether we do so consciously or unconsciously. This occurs wherever we create a diversion from boredom for ourselves, where we in each case *pass the time* in such and such a way and with this intent. Precisely wherever we are opposed to *it,* boredom *itself* must want to assert itself, and wherever it presses to the fore in such a way, it must *impress itself upon us* in its essence.

Thus it is precisely in *passing the time* that we first gain the correct *orientation* in which we can *encounter* boredom *undisguised*. Consequently we may not make boredom into an object of contemplation as some state that arises on its own, but must consider it in the way that we move within it, i.e., in the way that we seek to drive it away.

However—it will be objected—boredom is now indeed not being isolated as some lived experience, free-floating, the naked object of some observation, and we are indeed now letting it emerge; we first have it precisely when we are involved in driving it away. Yet the state of affairs has essentially not altered. How do things stand with our passing the time? Are we not now making this, instead of boredom, into the object of some observation—only in such a way that boredom is, as it were, simultaneously hidden within our passing the time as that which we drive away? In that case we do not have a pure, isolated action of boredom, but our reaction against it, the reaction *and* that which it reacts against, not *one* lived experience, but two which are coupled together. It does indeed seem like this, and yet things are otherwise. We have not merely pushed a second lived experience in front of it—if only for the reason that we do not first need to connect our passing the time as a particular lived experience, as it were, but constantly maintain ourselves within it, and indeed in such a way that in so doing we know nothing, strictly speaking, of lived experiences in the soul and suchlike.

Now we can see for the first time what is decisive in all our methodological considerations. It is not a matter of concocting a region of lived experiences, of working our way into a stratum of interrelations of consciousness. We must precisely avoid losing ourselves in some particular sphere which has been artificially prepared or forced upon us by traditional perspectives that have ossified, instead of preserving and maintaining the immediacy of everyday Dasein. What is required is not the effort of working ourselves into a particular attitude, but the reverse: what is required is the *releasement* [Gelassenheit] *of our free, everyday perspective*—free from psychological and other theories of consciousness, of the stream of lived experience and suchlike. Because, however, we are permeated by such theories—often understood in their most obvious sense and in keeping with an elucidation of the meaning of the words—it is indeed much more difficult to plant such releasement in oneself than to learn and memorize one or more theories. It is from this perspective that we must comprehend the apparent laboriousness with which we are attempting to work our way toward such a trivial phenomenon as boredom. Working our way toward it in this manner means dispelling all those attitudes that tend to impose themselves upon us.

Our task now is not the interpretation of what is boring as such, but becoming bored by such a thing, being bored with. . . . Here we must heed the fact that becoming bored by . . . and being bored with . . . do not simply coincide. It indeed seems as though they are both caused by something boring and do not, for instance, represent two different kinds of attunement, but one and the same: on the one hand insofar as the attunement is seen from the perspective of its cause, from that which is having an active effect, so that the attunement may thus be characterized passively as becoming bored; on the other hand, however, the same attunement may be characterized as being bored insofar as we have it within us, insofar as it is something everyone finds within them. And yet there is a distinction between the two which must be pointed out at this stage and which, in accordance with the very nature of this distinction, is important for the path our appraisal is to take.

In becoming bored by something we are precisely still held fast by that which is boring, we do not yet let it go, or we are compelled by it, bound to it for whatever reason, even though we have previously freely given ourselves over to it. In being bored with . . . , on the other hand, a certain detachment from that which is boring has already occurred. That which is boring is indeed at hand, yet we are bored without that which is boring specifically or explicitly boring us; we are bored—almost as though the boredom came from us and as though the boredom continued to propagate itself, without needing to be caused by or bound to what is boring any more. In becoming bored by this book, however, we are still concentrating on the thing at issue, indeed precisely on this. In being bored with . . . the boredom is no longer nailed fast to something, but is already beginning to diffuse. Boredom has then not arisen from this particular boring thing, on the contrary it radiates out over other things. It, boredom itself, now gives our Dasein a strange horizon over and beyond the particular boring thing. It does not merely relate to the particular thing that is boring us, but settles over several things, over other things: everything becomes boring.

We cannot even ask yet what this distinction in attunement properly is and what underlies it, let alone give an answer at this stage, since we have not yet seriously clarified what kind of attunement in general lies in becoming bored and in being bored.

For the purposes of showing this we shall therefore initially discard once more the distinction we have indicated, in order to take up the question concerning it at a later stage in a more incisive form. What is common to both phenomena is that we are bored by and with something specific, albeit in a different way.

§23. Becoming bored and passing the time.

We shall not consider *becoming bored* and being bored in themselves, but shall consider this boredom as that which we drive away [*vertreiben*], or seek to drive away, namely by *passing the time* [Zeitvertreib]. This is not something that we resort to of our own accord, as it were, without any boredom having set in, but a passing the time which lays claim upon us specifically out of and in opposition to a particular boredom.

a) Passing the time as a driving away of boredom that drives time on.

We are sitting, for example, in the tasteless station of some lonely minor railway. It is four hours until the next train arrives. The district is uninspiring. We do have a book in our rucksack, though—shall we read? No. Or think through a problem, some question? We are unable to. We read the timetables or study the table giving the various distances from this station to other places we are not otherwise acquainted with at all. We look at the clock—only a quarter of an hour has gone by. Then we go out onto the local road. We walk up and down, just to have something to do. But it is no use. Then we count the trees along the road, look at our watch again—exactly five minutes since we last looked at it. Fed up with walking back and forth, we sit down on a stone, draw all kinds of figures in the sand, and in so doing catch ourselves looking at our watch yet again—half an hour—and so on.

An everyday situation with well-known, banal, yet quite spontaneous forms of passing the time. What are we really passing here? This question is strangely ambivalent. As the phrase says, we pass the time. Yet what does it mean here to pass the time? We cannot, after all, shake time off. To pass here means to make it pass by, to propel it, drive it on so that it passes. Our passing the time, however, is in itself really a passing of boredom, where passing now means: driving away, shaking off. Passing the time is *a driving away of boredom that drives time on.*[1]

What are we trying to chase away here in wanting to kill time—i.e., *what is time?* In passing the time we do not chase time away. Not only because this is ultimately altogether impossible, but because the whole attitude of passing the time—as we shall see later—is *not* really directed toward *time,* even though in doing so we constantly look at the clock. What do we really want in constantly looking at the clock? We merely want to see time passed. What time? The time until the train arrives. We constantly look at the clock because we are waiting for that point in time. We are fed up waiting, we want to have done with this waiting. We shake off boredom. Is the boredom that springs from this looking at the clock some kind of waiting, then? By no means. Being bored with something, after all, is not a waiting for something. In our example the most

---

1. 'Zeitvertreib ist *ein Zeit antreibendes Wegtreiben der Langeweile.*' [The German for passing the time, *Zeitvertreib,* literally means a 'driving away of time'.—Tr]

we can say is that it is waiting itself that is boring and that bores us, but boredom is not itself a waiting. Furthermore, not every waiting is necessarily boring. On the contrary, waiting can be full of suspense. In which case there is then no room for boredom at all. We thought we were already on the trail of boredom with the phenomenon of passing the time, yet once again it has disappeared.

To what extent, however, is the *waiting* in our example *boring?* What constitutes its boringness? Perhaps it is because it is a having to wait, i.e., because we are forced, coerced into a particular situation. This is why we become impatient. Thus what really oppresses us is more this impatience. We want to escape from our impatience. Is boredom then this impatience? Is boredom therefore not some waiting, but this being impatient, not wanting or being able to wait, and for this reason being ill-humoured? Yet is boredom really an attunement of ill humour or even an impatience? Certainly impatience can arise in connection with boredom. Nevertheless, it is neither identical with boredom, nor even a property of it. There is neither a patient nor an impatient boredom. The impatience rather has to do with the manner and way in which we want to get boredom under control and are often unable to get it under control. Our passing the time has this peculiar character of a fluttering unease that brings this impatience with it. For what happens in becoming bored is that our unease while having to wait does not allow us to find anything that could grip us, satisfy us or let us be patient.

Being bored is neither a waiting nor a being impatient. This having to wait and our impatience may be present and surround boredom, but they never constitute boredom itself.

Before we continue with our interpretation of boredom, we shall recall once more the steps we have taken hitherto. We carried out a provisional examination of boredom from various angles. These considerations led us to see: [1.] That an interpretation of boredom is evidently necessary; for boredom is indeed known to us, yet we do not really know it intimately. Indeed, when we look more closely we find the essence of this attunement quite ungraspable: it disappears. [2.] We saw that when we attempt such an interpretation of boredom it is initially not at all clear *where* we should begin, in what direction we should inquire and guide the interpretation, or *how* we are to make this known phenomenon thematic. A general methodological maxim could indeed provide the guideline that all investigation must see to it that each object is brought under the best conditions of observability. We soon saw, however, that this apparently quite universal and self-evident maxim is something that science merely applies, something that goes back to a fundamental relation between being and truth. This universal directive therefore has nothing to tell us so long as it remains unclear in what way whatever we are investigating—namely this attunement—is, and what kind of truth belongs to it; whether this relation, and the way in which the attunement is, are in each case such that they can be made the object of scientific observation. We then also saw that this maxim not only tells us nothing, but fundamentally leads us astray, that whenever we follow it, it misleads us into bringing such a lived experience, called boredom, before us as an observable object, with apparently legitimate, yet fundamentally exaggerated and mistaken precision. It is rather a matter of seeing boredom *as it bores us,* and of grasping it as it occupies us. It always *shows itself* in such a way that we immediately turn *against* it. Whenever we make boredom an object—if we may say such a thing—we must from the outset let it emerge as something that we turn against, not in an arbitrary manner, but—to put it crudely—in this peculiar reaction that is provoked of its own accord by the emergent boredom, and which we call *passing the time.* We must approach this peculiar *unity* of a *boredom* and a *passing the time* in which a confrontation with boredom somehow occurs. Finally, we saw that we have thereby extended our field of appraisal beyond an isolated lived experience to its unity with passing the time. We saw, however—this will emerge more clearly at a later stage—that although we are also making present to ourselves an example of passing the time, it is immediately closer to us than this and that we constantly reside within it. What is at issue, then, is precisely transposing ourselves back into this immediacy of everyday comportment, away from all the theories and methodological efforts that seem necessary. Our investigation must nonetheless show that this does not mean we can proceed in an arbitrary manner. In passing the time we rescue ourselves from boredom. To show this we provided a simple depiction of one particular boring situation. We are beginning with the phenomenon of passing the time and asking initially what is really being passed here. It is not time that is being passed, although in a way it does make sense to say so, as we shall see. Boredom is passed off or driven off by our driving time on in a certain sense. When we say that *passing the time is a driving away of boredom that drives time on,* this seems to be a very precise definition of *passing the time.* Yet upon closer investigation we see that this definition is incorrect. For in this driving time on and driving boredom away something has already been said about *boredom,* namely this moment of driving time on, driving it by. We can then no longer say that in doing so we are driving boredom away. In other words, when we take the definition in this formal way, we may no longer speak of boredom itself. This is mentioned only as an aside, so that you do not become set on this definition. More important is the concrete question: What does all this mean? Toward the end I pointed to what *oppresses* us [*uns* bedrängt] in this boring situation. It is the peculiar *waiting* that we want to have done with, so that the suggestion is that perhaps boredom is this waiting. Finally, we saw that waiting and boredom are not identical. Rather waiting itself can have the character of boringness, yet need not do so.

b) Passing the time and looking at our watch. Becoming bored as being affected in a paralysing way by time as it drags.

Strange: in this way we experience many kinds of things, yet it is precisely boredom itself that we cannot manage to grasp—almost as though we were looking for something that does not exist at all. It is *not* all the things we thought it was. It vanishes and flutters away from us. And yet—this impatient waiting, the walking up and down, counting trees, and all the other abandoned activities attest precisely to the fact that the boredom is there. We confirm and reinforce this evidence when we say that we are *almost dying of boredom*. Perhaps against our intentions and against our will we are betraying something mysterious in saying this: namely that boredom ultimately *grasps at the roots of Dasein,* i.e., prevails in the ownmost ground of Dasein. Or is it instead merely an exaggerated and exaggerating way of putting things when we talk of a consuming, deadly boredom? We shall leave open how much it may be just cliché and habit to say such things on particular occasions. In any case, these expressions are not accidental. Boredom is there, is something specific, and yet is nevertheless always surrounded by these extraneous circumstances in which we become sidetracked time and again in our ongoing investigations.

Thus it will ultimately not be of any help to us either if we approach boredom from the perspective of passing the time, in order to see what we are struggling against in passing the time. Or perhaps we have not yet sufficiently transposed ourselves into such passing the time and repeatedly let ourselves be distracted too readily by things that boredom could ultimately be—impatience, waiting, things that persuade us that they might be what we are looking for. Why so? The phenomenon has many aspects. What do we need? We need a secure guideline, a *reliable measure.* If we start from our general characterization once more, then boredom and our passing the time which is opposed to it now become clearer to us: What is at issue in boredom [*Langeweile*] is a while [*Weile*], tarrying a while [*Verweilen*], a peculiar remaining, enduring. And thus time, after all. And as opposed to that, passing the time. In such passing the time we see the peculiar comportment of continually pulling out our watch, the watch by which we measure time. Thus what is decisive in passing the time, and indeed in *what* it shakes off, namely boredom, is, after all, *time.* Passing the time is therefore a shortening of time that drives time on, namely the time that seeks to become long [*lang*]. It is thus an intervention into time as a *confrontation with time.* We must therefore begin here and ask what is happening to time in this context, how we relate to time, and so on.

If by way of the phenomenon of passing the time we indeed wish to catch sight of what is shaken off in it, namely boredom, it will be a good idea to focus on that occurrence within our passing the time which we have already mentioned on several occasions: this continual *looking at our watch.*

In doing so, however, we must take careful note of the fact that this looking at our watch is not itself a passing the time. It does not belong on the same level as counting trees or walking back and forth. It is not a way or means of passing the time, but only a sign that we want to pass the time, or more precisely that our passing the time is not really succeeding, that the boredom is still tormenting us, and is doing so increasingly. Looking at our watch already indicates, by its helpless gesture, our failure to pass the time, and thus indicates that we are becoming increasingly bored. This is why we look repeatedly at our watch—yet this is not some purely mechanical action. *What* do we wish to ascertain? Just what time it is in general? No, in itself this does not interest us at all. Rather we wish to ascertain how much time is left until the train departs, or whether the time until the train arrives will soon have elapsed, i.e., whether we must continue to struggle against the emergent boredom by this unsuccessful killing of time, strangely lacking in any goal. It is not a matter of simply spending time, but of killing it, of making it pass *more quickly.* This means that it is going *slowly.* Does being bored then mean grasping the fact that time is going slowly? Yet in boredom we do not ascertain anything, nor do we grasp anything, nor do we make time the object of investigation. On the contrary, in boredom we are *bound* precisely by—nothing. Not even by time, the slowness of time. And where does this slowness stem from? In what does this slowness consist? Is it because time is *too long?* Does this long while of boredom arise because we have four hours to wait? Can we not also be bored with something that perhaps only lasts a quarter of an hour? Perhaps we are not bored at all with a party that continues an entire night. Thus the length of time plays no role, not because time is too long, i.e., not because the measurable stretch of time which we objectively plot on our watch is too great—not because the progress of time is slow, but because it is *too* slow. We fight *against* the progress of time which is slowing down and is *too* slow for us, and which in boredom *holds us in limbo.* We fight against this peculiar vacillating and dragging of time. This vacillating and dragging of time contains whatever it is that is burdensome and paralysing.

Yet ought time to pass more quickly, then? And if so, how quickly? What speed is time supposed to have? Does it have a speed at all? Time evidently takes its regular course, unfurls almost like the regular pulse of some unassailable monster: sixty seconds in every minute, and sixty minutes in every hour. Yet does time consist of hours, minutes, and seconds? Or are these not merely measures in which *we* entrap it, something we do because, as inhabitants of the earth, we move upon this planet in a particular relation to the sun? Do we need these measures and a commensurate regularity only for the purpose of measuring time? Can we say how quickly or slowly time itself passes, whether it has a speed at all and whether it allows this speed to change? Does time really take an unwavering, regular course? Or is it not rather of a highly temperamental essence? Are there not hours that are like a moment? Are there not minutes that are like an eternity? Does it merely seem like this to us, or is time really sometimes short, sometimes long, sometimes fleeting, sometimes crawling and never regular? Is it really like this? Or is time really as shown by our watches, as it presses upon us daily and hourly? Or are we here merely deceived, persuaded of something by a measuring instrument that is perhaps indispensable? Are we merely persuaded of this calculable time in the face of which that time which cannot be calculated sinks to the level of an illusion and is merely subjective, as our banal cleverness is able to tell us? Precisely that time which, in our supreme bliss, is as fleeting as the glance of some profound eye, yet in our deepest need is as burdening and inert as a slow-moving, almost stagnant river—this very time is merely subjective and not properly real! What is reality here, and where does illusion begin? Or may we not ask in this way at all? With the apparently trivial observation that in boredom, time passes too slowly, we see that we have already entered the greatest obscurity and difficulty.

However things may stand in this respect, from the perspective of passing the time and according to its ownmost intention we can say that what is at issue in passing the time is *wanting to overcome the vacillation of time.* To be slow and to drag are not the same thing; that which drags is indeed necessarily slow in a certain sense—but not everything that is slow necessarily drags. The time that drags must be coerced into passing more quickly, so that its being paralysed does not paralyse us, so that the boredom disappears. The result for our *guiding problem* of what *becoming bored* properly is then reads: Becoming bored is a peculiar *being affected in a paralysing way by time as it drags and by time in general,* a being affected which oppresses us in its own way. Thus we must further inquire as to *how* time oppresses us here in becoming bored. Time—yet we saw precisely in our attempt to grasp the slowness, the dragging of time, that time has become altogether enigmatic for us. Not only is *our relationship to time in our becoming bored* now obscure, but *time itself* is obscure. What can this mean: becoming bored is a being affected by time, by time as it drags, and in a paralysing way? Is it only in boredom that we are affected by time? Are we not constantly bound to time, pressed and oppressed by time, even when we believe and say that our time is entirely at our own disposal?

This being affected by time in boredom, however, is evidently a *peculiar impressing* [Andrängen] *of the power of that time* to which we are bound. This entails that time can oppress us or leave us in peace, sometimes in this way, sometimes in that. This is ultimately bound up with its own capacity for transformation. *Becoming bored* and *boredom* in general are then evidently entirely *rooted in this enigmatic essence of time.* What is more—if boredom is an attunement, then time and the way in which it is as time, i.e., the way in which it *temporalizes itself,* plays a peculiar part in Da-sein's being attuned in general.

We are increasingly tempted to pose the whole problem of boredom simply in terms of the problem of time. And yet we ought not to give in to this temptation, even if it were to simplify our investigation to a certain extent. We must stick with boredom, so that *precisely through its essence we may take a look into the concealed essence of time* and thereby into the connection between the two.

c) Being held in limbo by time as it drags.

Accordingly, we shall consider anew the way the question is posed and our orientation in questioning. We shall attempt *to let becoming bored be seen from the perspective of passing the time, as that to which the latter is opposed.* Passing the time is a way of taking action against the dragging of time that oppresses us. Yet it is equally clear that in driving time on so that it passes by, we are not *directed toward time.* In passing the time we are not specifically occupied with time. Nor do we see how such a thing could be possible at all. We do not, after all, stare at the seconds flowing by, in order to drive them on. On the contrary, even though we often look at the clock, we look away again just as quickly. Toward what? Toward nothing in particular. Yet how so? We do not look at anything in particular because nothing in particular offers itself to us. Indeed the inherent predicament of becoming bored is precisely that we cannot find anything in particular. We indeed look for something. Yet we are looking for something that will divert our attention. Divert it from what? From being oppressed by time as it drags. We are seeking to pass the time, i.e., precisely not to be occupied with time, not to dwell upon time or to ponder it. Passing the time: strangely, this means an occupation that diverts our attention away from time as it drags and from its oppressing us.

What is this oppression? It is not time assailing us, not some sudden onslaught of time, but a *specific kind of oppressing:* the dragging of time. Yet surely something that drags precisely holds back, keeps itself distant, and does not oppress. How can it oppress? This is why we speak of a specific kind of oppressing. We also came across it on our first approach. We already know this oppression. We found it in that very thing which is boring, that which bores us: *that which holds us in limbo.* Yet how is a holding in limbo supposed to be oppressive? When we are held in limbo we have, after all, some leeway to move; something opens before us; there is nothing there at all that could oppress us. Yet this is precisely what is at issue: in becoming bored we are held in limbo, and indeed by time as it drags. To where are we held, then? To where does time hold us, and what is it that we dwell upon? We find the answer to this question if we pay attention to *where* we wish to arrive through passing the time. For passing the time betrays to us where we want to get away from, and this is precisely that place to which time in its slowness holds us. In passing the time we seek something to occupy us, something we can dwell upon. What happens when we do so? Does time pass more quickly whenever we have found such a thing? To what extent does it then pass more quickly? Do we observe the course of time in the occupation that we have found in order to pass the time? Do we ascertain that it is passing more quickly? No. What is characteristic is that we do not pay attention to time at all. Time goes more quickly because its dragging is no longer there. Its dragging has disappeared, because in a certain way we forget time altogether. It is now impossible for time to tarry [*verweilen*] for too long, because it cannot tarry at all. Where have we passed time away to when we have forgotten it? We do not as yet have an answer to this. Why can we not find an answer to this question? We have not said *which* time we are passing here. We are not simply passing time in general. We saw, furthermore, that within certain limits it remains irrelevant how great the stretch of time is. Yet it is after all a *particular* time which is at issue, namely this interval of time until the train departs. *Being held in limbo* does not happen over any course of time whatsoever, but over this particular interval of time that drags between our arrival and the departure of the train. It holds us, and in doing so holds us up. But *to where* does it hold us, and *alongside what* does it hold us up? After all, it does not bind us to itself. We are held by factical time and yet do not pay attention to it. Could we not be happy that it 'holds us up'? After all, what we are looking for is precisely something with which to occupy ourselves.

Earlier we arrived at the insight that both *boredom—whiling* [Weilen], *enduring, dragging*—as well as our associated *passing the time,* have to do with *time.* Accordingly we have now intentionally pursued the phenomenon of passing the time in *that* direction which lets us see how we thereby attempt to subvert time, i.e., to eliminate time as it *drags* over an interval of time that oppresses us. The dragging of time proved to be that which holds us in limbo. Accordingly, becoming bored is a *being held in limbo by time as it drags over an interval of time.* We do not yet in any way see through what is really happening here, however, how time in general relates to us such that, as dragging, it can hold us in limbo in such a way; nor how time in general stands at our command, such that we can try to speed up or eliminate its dragging. For what is at issue is evidently not our mere assessment of time, which would be purely subjective.

The question now is whether, via an increasingly penetrating interpretation of being held in limbo by time as it drags, we can catch sight of the full essential import of this particular form of boredom. In so doing, and with regard to what we have said in general about time, we shall leave entirely open the extent to which we succeed in solving this real and strange enigma concerning time, its speed, and suchlike, and shall remain for now within this particular form of boredom: becoming bored by. . . . We shall try to clarify *how* this dragging of time *holds us in limbo,* and how this becoming bored is thereby made possible.

d) Being left empty by the refusal of things, and an insight into its possible connection with being held in limbo by time as it drags.

Just as we will hardly dispute altogether that this being held in limbo belongs to becoming bored, we will certainly insist that being held in limbo does not alone constitute boredom. For in passing the time we simultaneously seek to occupy ourselves with something. Yet how do we go about this? Is it by forcing ourselves to go to work despite there being a pleasant snowfall on the hills? No, in passing the time we seek for something to occupy us; though certainly not as though we were busy at a cottage where someone is chopping wood and another is fetching the milk, and we, in order to help out, then go and draw some water. In the activity we have sought in passing the time we are not interested in what occupies us, nor even whether anything comes of it and we thereby help others. We are interested neither in the object nor in the result of the activity, but in *being occupied as such* and in this alone. We are seeking to be occupied in any way. Why? Merely so as not to fall into this *being left empty* that is emerging in boredom. Is it therefore *being left empty* that we wish to escape from, rather than being held in limbo? Is *being left empty* then what is essential in boredom? It is something other than being held in limbo, and yet like the latter belongs to becoming bored.

   Yet what is this being left empty? *What* is left empty here? And in what sense? We seek to eliminate being left empty by being occupied with something. Such being occupied with something is a specific manner and way in which, for example, we *deal* with things. There are various possibilities here: We can let things sit there as they are or work on them, we can set them out ready or write with them. Being occupied gives our dealings with things a certain manifoldness, direction, fullness. But not only that: we are also *taken* [hingenommen] by things, if not altogether *lost* in them, and often even *captivated* [benommen] by them. Our activities and exploits *become immersed* [aufgehen] *in something.* When we get hold of something that occupies us, we scarcely have time for anything else. We are entirely tied up with it, and in such a way that even the very time that we use for it and waste on it is no longer there at all, and all that is at hand is whatever satisfies us. *Being left empty* and *being satisfied* are associated with our *dealings* with things. Being left empty is eliminated when things are at hand, at our disposal.

   Yet let us recall the boring situation which we depicted as an example. Are there not things at hand here, for instance: the station, the timetable, the rural street, the trees and indeed the whole area, which we know very little about and where we can ascertain things for days on end? All the same we are bored, i.e., we are left empty. Accordingly, this being left empty cannot mean that in boredom we are transformed in such a way that all things disappear entirely, as it were, so that nothing remains before us or around us. That is altogether impossible. Insofar as we indeed exist factically, insofar as we *are there,* we are transposed into the midst of other beings. These things that are, after all, are at hand for us at all times—in whatever scope and with whatever transparency. That nothing is at hand any more and all things slip away from us—how can this happen? Yet perhaps there are ways of our Dasein in which such a thing is possible. However this is not the case in boredom. It cannot be the case. For how can we become bored by *something,* i.e., be left empty by *something,* if nothing at all is at hand? What is boring, after all, must precisely be at hand in order to bore us, i.e., to leave us empty. In coming to be left empty, things are not carried away from us or annihilated. Indeed, is there anyone who could see to such a thing? Certainly not we ourselves, we who in boredom and out of pure boredom are precisely seeking to be occupied. Although the things are at hand, they leave us empty. We must even say that they leave us empty precisely because they are at hand.

And yet—are we bored because a railway station with timetables is present here, and a road running along in front of it with rows of trees on either side? Evidently not, for if that were the case we would necessarily constantly become bored everywhere, since we constantly encounter things everywhere. Thus it is not because these things are at hand in general, but because they are precisely at hand *in such and such a way* that they bore us. How so? What is it about them? After all, they do nothing at all to us, they *leave us completely in peace.* Certainly—and this is precisely the reason why they bore us.

Yet what else can these things do than to peacefully satisfy that which they themselves are? Nor do we demand anything else of them, neither in boredom nor otherwise. Can the trees outside that we enumerate in our boredom do anything other than stand alongside the street and grow toward the sky? *What is it that suddenly happens,* then, so that all these things bore us, so that a boredom befalls us *from out of them?* We cannot now say in turn that they bore us because they leave us empty. Rather the question is: *What does it mean to leave empty, to come to be left empty?* To leave empty does not at all mean: to be absent, not to be present at hand; rather things must be at hand in order to leave us empty. Does it mean being present at hand, then? But being present at hand does not leave us empty either. What is important is not what is at hand in general, but these specific things that are at hand. Which ones? Those things that belong to the environing world of the *boring situation* that we depicted. A boring thing is one which belongs to a boring situation. What an exemplary explanation! We said that things leave us in peace, and this leaving us in peace is a leaving us empty that proceeds from things. Thus, becoming bored is this being left in peace. Yet when we are left in peace by something, do we then also automatically become bored by it? Is it not the other way around, that someone who does not leave us in peace at all and is constantly running after us ultimately becomes boring and grows wearisome for us? Things leave us in peace, do not disturb us. Yet they do not help us either, they do not take our comportment upon themselves. They *abandon us to ourselves*. It is because they have nothing to offer that they leave us empty. To leave empty means to be something at hand that *offers nothing*. Being left empty means to be offered nothing by what is at hand.

Yet what can the miserable and deserted railway station offer us, what more can it offer us than its function as this public building—to give us access to tickets and provide shelter and a place to wait? And this is precisely what it offers. Indeed, this is precisely what we demand of it also, since we are in the middle of a journey or trip. That is the sole legitimate use that we can make of it—the claim that it expects of us. How can we say that it offers nothing? How can it leave us empty, i.e., bore us here? Or does the station bore us precisely because it offers us what we expect of it, and yet in so doing fails to offer it, so that we take refuge in the street? What do we expect of the station? That it be a station in general? No—but rather that we can use it as a station, i.e., that at this station we can immediately enter the train and depart as quickly as possible. It is a proper station precisely whenever it does not force us to wait. The station at hand refuses itself to us as a station and leaves us empty because the train that belongs to it has not yet arrived, so that there is such a long time that drags on until the arrival of the train. Thus it does not yet offer us what it properly ought to. To do so, however, it must be precisely a railway station and as such be at hand, in order to allow us to wait. Why else does it have a waiting room?

And yet—it may be objected—the fact that the station does not offer this immediate possibility of our departing without a wait, the fact that it refuses itself to us in this way is not, after all, the fault of the poor station, but simply our fault for arriving too early, because we were mistaken about the timetable. This may be correct. Yet we are not asking about what causes or is responsible for boredom. We are asking what the essence of that which bores us as such, or the essence of becoming bored by something, consists in, quite irrespective of how such becoming bored may have been factically caused in each case. Though we may be to blame for arriving too early, and though the state railway may be responsible for the fact that there are so few trains running, this does not tell us anything about what it means to say that the station bores us. We are merely asking what it is about it as something boring which makes it bore us. We are not asking about the causes from which precisely this boredom has arisen.

We have now indeed received an answer to our question, and done so via a closer characterization of being left empty. What is at hand (the station) does not offer that which we expect of it in the particular situation. The station accordingly does not fulfil our expectations of it. We say that it disappoints us. Becoming disappointed, however, does not mean becoming bored. This offering nothing that leaves us empty is not our being disappointed. Where we become disappointed we have nothing more to seek and we withdraw. But here we precisely stay; not only that, but we are *held in limbo*. And yet it is not only the station that now refuses itself, but first and foremost its *surroundings,* and together with these surroundings *as a whole* the station now manifests itself entirely as this station which refuses itself.

We do not yet see clearly what is really happening here when the boring station also brings its surroundings to the point of boring us. The result in any case is that leaving empty as refusal indeed presupposes something *at hand,* but what is at hand must precisely be something *particular* and something *expected* in a particular situation, so that we *can come to be left empty by something,* in the sense of *becoming bored by. . . .*

The station in itself is not boring. Yet what does this mean: in itself? Is there then nothing boring in itself? Or are there not indeed things which are boring in themselves, to which precisely stations belong? Is not every station boring, even though trains constantly arrive and depart and crowds of people throng? Perhaps it is not only all stations that are boring for us. Perhaps, even though trains constantly enter and leave, bringing people with them, there is still a peculiar sense of something more in these stations which anyone who passes tenement blocks in large cities has experienced. One could say that, while it may be like this for us, some peasant from the Black Forest will take enormous pleasure in it, and therefore boredom is a matter of taste. Whether we can reduce it to taste is another question. Certainly—here once more we are faced with something we cannot penetrate and which at first leads beyond our problem. Yet precisely in this interpretation of being left empty we inevitably discovered that being left empty in itself can never make boredom comprehensible. Yet unexpectedly this points us back to the first moment we mentioned. This can now initially be expressed concretely in the following way: the fact that the station leaves us empty, its refusal, is somehow connected with the fact that time drags. Ultimately the dragging, oppressive time that holds us in limbo is what permits the station not to offer what it ought to.

We have achieved what we were seeking: [1.] an elucidation of coming to be left empty by things; [2.] an insight into the possible connection of this second characteristic of boredom with the first, namely being held in limbo by time as it drags.

Over and above this, the only thing we can see is that there is some connection here. Perhaps it has also become clear that these two moments are not simply pieced together, but are structurally interwoven. What is more: it looks in our case as though even the first moment, being held in limbo, were the all-embracing and primarily determinative one. For the time that drags and holds us in limbo does not yet let the station come into its own. The station cannot properly be what it is supposed to be for us as long as the moment of the train's arrival is not there. The dragging of time as it were refuses the station the possibility of offering us anything. It forces it to leave us empty. The station refuses *itself*, because time refuses *it* something. It excludes it, and yet cannot eliminate it, with the result that now, precisely in this not yet offering anything, this self-refusal, in the fact that it lets us wait—precisely in this way the station becomes more obtrusive, more boring in its leaving us empty.

How much time is capable of here! It has power over railway stations and can bring it about that stations bore us. On the other hand it becomes apparent that time of itself, the mere course of time, does not bore us. Rather becoming bored is this *essential being held in limbo in coming to be left empty.* Becoming bored is thus the fact that particular things, in what they offer us or do not offer us and in the way that they do so, are in each case *co-determined* by a *particular time,* in each case have *their* particular time. Things can leave us empty only along with that being held in limbo that proceeds from time. On the other hand, this time that drags can hold us in limbo only if things having the characterized possibility of refusal stand at the disposal of time, if they are bound to time. To put it crudely: what is at issue here in the possibility of boredom is an as yet obscure relation of the dragging along of time to the things that refuse themselves. But this means that what is at issue is the question of *what time itself is,* such that it can have this relation to things, and furthermore such that from out of such a relation something like boredom is possible as an *attunement* that attunes *us* through and through.

At the same time we saw from our concrete example that the station in itself does not bore us or leave us standing, but does so only insofar as the train is not yet there; that it is therefore lacking a particular connection with a particular point in time. To put it positively: In order for the station not to bore us in this particular form of boredom, it is necessary that we come across it in its *specific* time, which in a certain way is the ideal time of a railway station: namely before the train departs. If things evidently have *their* time in each specific case, and if we precisely come across things in *their* specific time, then perhaps boredom will fail to appear. Conversely: boredom is only possible at all because each thing, as we say, has *its* time. If each thing did not have *its* time, then there would be no boredom.

This thesis must now be clarified, not in the sense of a discussion of this proposition, but rather in a decisive and increasingly focussed continuation of our interpretation of these fundamental moments of becoming bored that are structurally interwoven in a peculiar way: being held in limbo and being left empty. Yet all this is to be taken neither as psychology, nor as an answer or solution.

Chapter Three

The Second Form of Boredom: Being Bored with
Something and the Passing of Time Belonging to It

*§24. Being bored with something and the kind of
passing the time pertaining to it.*

**a) The need for a more original grasp of boredom in order
to understand the structural link between being held in
limbo and being left empty.**

We are involved in a discussion of boredom, and indeed a particular form of
boredom which we grasp terminologically as becoming bored by something.
We have attempted to extract *two structural moments* of this form and to
interpret them in greater detail: firstly *being held in limbo* by time as it drags
along, and then this *coming to be left empty* by things and in general by the
individual beings surrounding us in this specific boring situation. We asked
what this leaving empty consists in, and in so doing saw that in order for beings
to be able to leave us empty in this characteristic way in the sense of boring
us, they must themselves be at hand. Leaving empty does not mean something
being absent, but is a particular kind of being present at hand in accordance
with which things refuse us something—not in general or universally or indeterminately, but refuse something that we spontaneously *expect* within this
particular situation under these specific circumstances. This now yields the
characterization of what leaves us empty as something that is itself connected
in some way with the first moment: with that which holds us in limbo. For this
boring railway station in whose surroundings we are bored while waiting for
the train does not in fact bore us as a station in general, but as a station only
under these *particular* circumstances, when the moment of the train's arrival
is not yet there. Here, there becomes manifest, albeit in an as yet quite rough
and indeterminate way, a peculiar *connection* between leaving empty and holding in limbo. From this we can see that *holding in limbo itself determines and
sustains leaving empty.* Insofar as that which holds us is time in some particular
form, time evidently also plays a role in this peculiar leaving empty, in this
leaving us standing that proceeds from things. We thereby see once more the
strange and enigmatic power of time, which is now evidently not restricted to
one structural moment of becoming bored, namely being held in limbo, but
also extends into the second moment: leaving empty, being left empty. Now
that we have clarified the two structural moments to this extent, the decisive

question of the *intrinsic* connection between these two moments imposes itself. This connection evidently cannot be an external bond. If holding in limbo and leaving empty are structural moments of boredom and of becoming bored, then these two structural moments must in themselves accord with one another from out of the essence of boredom. There must be manifest between them a peculiar structural *link* [Fuge] which is determined in advance from the whole and original essence of boredom. We take from this the *methodological guideline* that we shall grasp the *intrinsic unity* of these two structural moments, and thereby the *whole structure* of becoming bored, only if we now succeed in seeing this original link between these two moments.

Accordingly, if we wish to examine boredom more closely we must attempt to let emerge more clearly *this structural link between being held in limbo and being left empty* in becoming bored. Structural link here means initially that they are not simply stuck together, but tailored to one another, structurally interlinked. But by what? Where does this being tailored to one another come from? Evidently from the essence of boredom, of becoming bored. The two cannot belong together by accident, but together—with respect to one another—both have *sprung from* the essence of boredom. Therefore we shall understand the unity of the two, the kind of linkage, only by grasping *boredom more originally* than hitherto. Yet how are we to grasp becoming bored more originally?

Thus far we have considered boredom with respect to our becoming bored by something in a particular situation. But this kind of boredom is not the only one. If we are seeking a more original conception of boredom then we must also correspondingly endeavour to envisage a *more original form* of boredom, thus presumably a boredom in which we become *more* bored than in the situation we have characterized. A boredom in which we become more bored, in which our boredom grows? In which it thus endures longer? Yet we already know from what has been said earlier that the duration of boredom decides nothing about its extent; that we can indeed be more bored in someone's company for five minutes than during the whole four hours we are waiting at the station. The objective span of time is not decisive for the extent and degree or, as we must also say more clearly and definitively, for the *depth* of boredom. If we seek to envisage a more original boredom, we must inquire in a direction in which there manifests itself to us a boredom which—as we have already said—is more deadly, grasps more at the roots of our Dasein: a *more profound* boredom. In doing so we do not yet know what this peculiar dimension of depth is supposed to mean here. In any case, it points in the direction of our very own essence, the essence of ourselves, which becomes bored; it points in the direction of the ground of our essence, from which the possibility of every form of boredom will evidently spring in some sense. We will find the more original unity of the two structural moments of boredom, being held in limbo and being left empty, via the interpretation of a more profound boredom.

Is there such a boredom? We recall that at the beginning of our analysis proper we established a distinction which at first looked merely like a linguistic distinction. We distinguished between becoming bored by something and being bored with something. In introducing this distinction we also indicated—albeit only in a rough and ready way—how it is to be determined more closely. Perhaps the distinction between these two forms of boredom lies precisely in boredom's becoming more profound. Perhaps it is to be found in this second form, in being bored with. . . . If by interpreting being bored with . . . we succeed in demonstrating this form of boredom to be a more profound one, then we have thereby not merely found a type of boredom, for instance, which we can add to the first so that we would have two types—we are not interested in that. Rather when looking back at the first form and considering a boredom that is becoming more profound we are at the same time dealing with the peculiar *direction* of becoming more profound and thereby with its *pointing to the proper depth* of boredom as such. Accordingly, the interpretation of a second form of boredom, being bored with . . . , with respect to the first is now of decisive methodological significance in the context of our overall task.

b) Being bored with something and the transformed manner of passing the time: passing the time as that with which we are bored.

In order now to contrast retrospectively the second form of boredom with the first, we must recall the first form more clearly in a particular respect. In the *first form* of boredom, becoming bored by . . . in the situation depicted, we are bound in a peculiar form to the specific surroundings of the railway station in question where we are waiting. Yet this being bound to the situation is only *one* moment of the characteristic determinacy of this boredom. *Within* this situation to which we are bound it is something *quite determinate*, the station, the street, or the region, that bores us. What bores us and is boring is quite specific, something with which we are acquainted. We know that this thing or that is boring us. We are acquainted with it, without being in a position to say from within boredom what it really is. Within this situation to which we are bound, that which bores us is characteristically *quite specific*.

This, however, does not yet allow us to adequately grasp the determinacy of this situation. One essential and characteristic moment consists in the fact that in this becoming bored by . . . within this situation, we are as it were firmly stuck. We cannot get away from this environment, not merely because we are forced to wait and are held to this waiting. Rather, within such having to wait we become increasingly stuck with having to wait, which becomes less and less interesting and increasingly burdensome for us. This peculiar *becoming firmly stuck with the situation* itself also belongs to this quite specific and determinate becoming bored by particular things within this particular situation. Now what is characteristic here is that the corresponding way we pass the time has a peculiar leeway. Here we can make all sorts of attempts to occupy ourselves in a specific way, in which neither the object nor our success in doing so concerns us in any way.

How does all this now compare to the *second form of boredom,* which we grasp terminologically as *being bored with . . .* ? It will first be necessary to consider an *example* again. Here, however, it is conspicuous at the same time that if we attempt to consider an example of this second form of boredom, then this is not so easy or clear cut, for the very reason that the limit of this second form, as opposed to the first, fundamentally cannot be drawn precisely at all, because the limits merge together. This is not accidental, but is tied in with the inner essence of boredom in general. Yet in order to see a distinction at all, we must envisage an emphatic and extreme, or relatively extreme, con-trast to the first form of boredom. We shall attempt to find such a case, and indeed once again, as in the first instance, to find one that is distinctly everyday, accessible to everybody and almost inconspicuous.

We have been invited out somewhere for the evening. We do not need to go along. Still, we have been tense all day, and we have time in the evening. So we go along. There we find the usual food and the usual table conversation, everything is not only very tasty, but tasteful as well. Afterward people sit together having a lively discussion, as they say, perhaps listening to music, having a chat, and things are witty and amusing. And already it is time to leave. The ladies assure us, not merely when leaving, but downstairs and outside too as we gather to leave, that it really was very nice, or that it was terribly charming. Indeed. There is nothing at all to be found that might have been boring about this evening, neither the conversation, nor the people, nor the rooms. Thus we come home quite satisfied. We cast a quick glance at the work we interrupted that evening, make a rough assessment of things and look ahead to the next day—and then it comes: I was bored after all this evening, on the occasion of this invitation.

Yet how so? With the best will in the world we can find nothing that could have bored us there. And yet I myself was bored. With what, then? I *myself—* did I then bore *myself?* Was *I what was boring for myself?* Yet we recall quite clearly that not only was there nothing boring, but I was not at all occupied with myself either, not for a moment. I was not occupied with myself in any kind of pensive reflection that would have been the precondition for such boredom. On the contrary, I was totally involved, involved in and part of the conversation and everything else. Indeed, we do not even say that I was bored with *myself,* but that I was bored with the evening. Or is perhaps all this subsequent talk that I was really bored after all merely an illusion that arises from an ensuing bad mood over the fact that I have now sacrificed and lost this evening? No: it is quite clear that we were bored, even though it was all so pleasant. Or perhaps it was precisely the pleasantness of this evening with which we were bored?

Yet when we talk in this way, have we not made an unfair judgement? Is this not ultimately the kind of conduct which only a very blasé person could indulge in, someone who is used to seeing everything in advance in this peculiar light of being fundamentally bored, someone who, due to this peculiar way of being bored in the face of everything, has in advance a dissatisfied, disapproving attitude toward everything everywhere? Yet, we are not now asking whether it was justified or unjustified for us to be bored, nor whether the boredom now at issue can be traced back, in its factical development and whatever provoked it, to a tired, blasé attitude or to something else. We are asking what properly belongs to this *having been bored with the evening* as we have depicted it, and how this form of being bored with . . . is to be *distinguished* from the first form, from becoming bored by . . . in the specific situation of the railway station.

It is a matter of interpreting this second form of boredom in itself and from out of itself, and in so doing of bringing it closer to ourselves. In attempting this, we recall the generally established *guideline* of our procedure, according to which we are not investigating some free-floating boredom in itself, but always investigating boredom within that *passing the time* that is specifically associated with this boredom, that passing the time in which boredom is warded off or repressed as the case may be.

We shall take a look at the aforementioned situation of being bored with . . . , and everyone must do so for themselves. The specific situations are different. We shall take as a common starting point the evening of the invitation as we outlined it. It has now become completely clear to us—albeit in retro-spect—that we were bored after all with the evening. We now quite clearly remember a repeated, though suppressed yawning. This was not some reactive symptom of being tired or relaxed. We were bored. And passing the time? We search in vain. However clearly there stands before us the whole evening and the course it took, we can ascertain nothing of any passing the time. Did we let boredom take its course, then, so that it completely dominated us? That was evidently not the case either. For otherwise it would have come over us more clearly. Was there merely an inkling of this being bored discernible during the evening, so that we paid no further attention to it? Or does not this absence of our passing the time prove the absence of our having been bored, something of which we merely persuade ourselves after the event?

Yet assuming that we have not deluded ourselves, we were bored with the evening. Is it so surprising then that at first sight we find nothing of any passing the time? We must even have the good sense to say that in this respect we are searching in vain, if indeed we behaved correctly in other people's company. We even had to hide our yawning; and it was inappropriate to drum our fingers on the tabletop, as we were tempted to do for a moment. Thus there was a boredom after all, and merely no passing the time opposing it. In itself—one might think—this must indeed be possible. In accordance with its essence, any passing the time is indeed always related to boredom, but not the reverse. It is not necessary that boredom encounter resistance immediately. In the end, it is precisely what is characteristic of this second form of boredom, of being bored with . . . as distinct from becoming bored, that passing the time is absent in it. Here we would, as it were, have a free-floating, unimpeded boredom. Yet even if this were the case, we would now merely have discerned the consequence of this boredom in accordance with its proper essence: the absence of any passing the time, but nothing would be clarified about this proper essence itself. It is its proper essence, however, that we wanted to bring to light.

It is only with difficulty, however, that we can bring ourselves to say that there is no passing the time at work here. It is difficult, for one thing, on the basis of our general knowledge of boredom, which always somehow paralyses and therefore provokes a counter-movement. And then again when we recall our yawning and the temptation to drum our fingers. This tells us merely that the kind of passing the time here evidently does not have the same character as in the first instance, where we were able to move freely, to attempt and to 'get into' all kinds of things without being hindered. There we could abandon ourselves to the fluttering unease of passing the time, in looking for something to occupy us. Accordingly, in the second instance passing the time would be 'repressed' ['verdrängt'], and the reason for this repression would be our necessary adherence to the rules of politeness. To this it would have to be retorted that this being bored with . . . after all does not always and not only appear on the occasion of invitations, being as it were not essentially bound up with the latter. These are all excuses, stemming from the fact that here we cannot find the same form of passing the time straightaway—something that we are now trying to explain, instead of looking more closely and interpreting in terms of the situation.

Passing the time is not lacking in this boredom either. Nor is it hidden or repressed, but presumably *transformed* in a particular way. How can we catch sight of this, without distorting the situation in any way? The yawning and the wanting to drum our fingers were a flaring up, as it were, of the kind of passing the time that we are acquainted with, in which we somehow seek to occupy ourselves. It is merely a matter of correctly seeing this flaring up of passing the time—*not* of viewing it in terms of isolated incidents, but of understanding it in the context of the whole situation of the evening, of sitting together, of making conversation. We resort to these attempts from time to time. Just as we are on the verge of playing with our watchchain or a button, cigars are passed around again. We have already let them pass by once, but now we take a cigar. We are not getting sleepy, and yet—we smoke, not to become more sleepy, nor to be stimulated by the nicotine, but because smoking itself is a socially ideal way of passing the time, which is not to say that everyone who smokes is passing the time in so doing, i.e., is bored. Socially ideal—this is intended to mean that smoking is part of it all, one is encouraged to do so, and in this way—without our knowing it—an inconspicuous possibility of passing the time plays right into our hands. Passing the time is thus there in this situation too, though admittedly hard to find, and this precisely because it presents itself in such a public manner.

We said, however, that in this second form of boredom, passing the time is transformed compared to the first form. Surely that means something other than that it is merely hard to find. Yet what is supposed to be transformed in this being occupied—instead of counting trees and drawing figures in the sand, we have this rolling a cigar between our fingers, inhaling, watching the smoke formations, then keeping an eye on how long the ash lasts and other such things. In addition, we have also heard that the object and outcome are completely irrelevant as regards our being occupied in passing the time. Thus with this interpretation we are on a false trail, we have strayed off the right path, the path we indicated in saying that it is a matter of seeing these possibilities of passing the time as they flare up in the unfolding of the situation. Thus we must regard this smoking in the same way, and not compare it with earlier forms of passing the time and being occupied. We then see that we do not now sit there lost in thought and immersed in ourselves, occupying ourselves with the cigar, but that while smoking we precisely participate in the conversation and are in strangely high spirits the whole evening. Smoking itself does not appear specifically as a deliberate way of being occupied, of passing the time against boredom. Boredom—has it been driven away, blown away with the cigar smoke? Or is it precisely there while we smoke and make conversation— since boredom after all is evidently not something like a fly that we can chase away or kill? Passing the time is not like some device, installed to drive away boredom. Rather, in accordance with its meaning, however much our passing the time fights against boredom, it also firmly captures it at the same time. This being bored is precisely there while we are smoking, and smoking, as an occupation, itself becomes entirely part of the course of the conversation and the other activities. This sheds some initial light on the situation. It is not smoking as an isolated occupation, but our *entire comportment and behaviour* that is our *passing the time*—the whole evening of the invitation itself. This is why our passing the time was so difficult to find.

Yet if the evening itself is now supposed to have become our passing the time, then what is it that is boring, what is that by which we become bored?

We noticed, after all, that there was nothing boring about the whole evening. Indeed. And from the very outset we are not speaking of boredom in the sense of a *becoming bored by* . . . , but what is at issue is our *being bored with* the evening. In any case, however, we must then note this much: The evening is that with which we are bored, and *simultaneously, what* we are bored *with* here is *passing the time*. In this boring situation, *boredom and passing the time become intertwined* in a peculiar way. Passing the time creeps into our becoming bored and, diffused throughout the whole situation, achieves peculiar proportions that it is never able to assume in the first form in our discontinued and restless attempts. We find nothing boring, and yet passing the time takes on such proportions that it lays claim to the whole situation for itself. Strange! What does all this point to: nothing boring—neither this nor that—in the whole situation, and yet this situation is offered as a counter to boredom? This strange intertwining of our passing the time and becoming bored itself—does this point to the fact that this boredom is 'more profound'? But what does this mean? What can we conclude from these indications? Boredom becomes more and more concentrated on us, on our situation as such, whereby the individual details of the situation are of no consequence; they are only coincidentally that *with* which we *ourselves* are bored, they are not *that which* bores us.

§25. Contrasting the second form of boredom with the first with respect to the essential moments of being held in limbo and being left empty.

Being bored with. . . . Perhaps what we have accomplished thus far has brought the second form of boredom close enough for us to now attempt to contrast it with the first, to discern their differences, and thus to grasp the *direction in which it becomes more profound*. In this way we may discern the path leading to *originary* boredom.

Contrasting the two forms of boredom with one another is of course meaningful and justified only if it does not degenerate into an indiscriminate comparison. Such contrasting must instead keep to the essential moments that have been worked out thus far, if only in one of their particular transformations: *being held in limbo* and *being left empty*. Our investigation indeed began to falter here at the decisive point: the question of the *structural linking* and *unity* of the two. Yet even without having decided this question, we can still ask whether these two moments are also to be found in the second form of boredom and, if so, how they have been transformed. Yet before setting to work on a comparative interpretation with respect to these two structural moments, we shall attempt a general contrasting of the two forms of boredom with one another. The perspective of the comparison here is that moment which has occupied us continually from the beginning, and repeatedly gives us cause for concern, namely *that which is boring.*

a) General contrasting of the two forms of boredom with one another from the point of view of that which is boring: determinate and indeterminate boring things. The apparent absence of being held in limbo and being left empty in the second form of boredom.

In the *first instance* of boredom, what is boring is evidently *this or that,* this railway station, the street, the region. It is not to be disputed that this is what is boring in such boredom, even though we do not yet correctly understand how this is possible. Bored by . . . means left standing and held in limbo by. . . .

In the *second instance* we find *nothing that is boring.* What does this mean? We do not say that we become bored by this or that; on the contrary, we even find that there is really nothing boring around us. More accurately, we are *not* able to say *what* is boring us. Accordingly, in the second instance it is *not* that there is nothing boring *at all,* rather what is boring us has this character of '*I know not what*'. In such boredom we also have quite clearly before us whatever is boring us as this 'I know not what', without any explicit reflection or looking for it. Because we are sure of this, we can be equally assured in answering the question of what bores us here: *not this* room, *not these* people, *not* all *these* things. Yet in this situation the very question does not in fact arise at all. It is posed neither by others nor by us ourselves; rather in this situation we *ourselves* are bored. We let ourselves slip into this strange *casualness* regarding this '*I know not what*'.

If therefore we say that in the second instance there is nothing boring to be found, this then means: there is *no being we can determinately name,* or no determinate context of such beings, that bores us directly. It does not at all mean, on the other hand, that nothing boring is to be found here at all. The comparison of the two forms of boredom shows that in the first form we have a *determinate boring thing,* whereas in the second form we have *something indeterminate that bores us.*

That determinacy of the whole situation in accordance with which we are forced into it in a peculiar way is bound up with the determinacy of whatever is boring in the first form. This in turn goes together with the character of the specific time; it is an interval of time during which we are forced to wait. Yet in these respects there is evidently a sameness or similarity between the two situations. For even during the evening of the invitation we are stuck, indeed given the whole situation we are almost more restricted by social rules and circumstances. Likewise, such an evening also has its normal timespan. And yet this similarity between the two situations is merely superficial. Assuming the evening lasted only two hours, it would thus be shorter by half than our wait at the railway station, yet the boredom in the second case would not on account of this be less than in the first. On the contrary. We can already see that such differences in time play virtually no role.

Something else is essential, however. In accepting the invitation in the second case we have *given ourselves time; we have* time for it and *leave* ourselves time for it, whereas in the first case we do not wish to *lose* any time and are ill at ease due to time's passing too slowly. Thus this boredom is not at all of such a kind that here—on the evening of the invitation—we are waiting impatiently for when it is time to leave. We do not look—not even furtively—at the clock, we do not think of doing so at all, and yet we are bored with the evening. Accordingly, we here find a boredom in which time is not pressing, in which time does not at all play the role it did in the first. We must ultimately say that the interpretation of boredom arrived at previously, according to which *being held in limbo* by time as it drags belongs to boredom, fits only the first form. Yet did we say with respect to this first form that here time is pressing? We found precisely the opposite: that it drags, and that such dragging was not something that presses us [*das Drängende*], but something that oppresses us [*das Bedrängende*]. In the second case, on the other hand, time is neither pressing, nor does it drag; thus we are not oppressed by it either. And yet we are bored. *It*—we know not what—bores us. In the second case we evidently do not find any being held in limbo by a dragging of time.

How do things stand concerning the second of the structural moments of becoming bored by . . . that we explicated, i.e., our *being left empty* by beings refusing themselves in a particular way? Things and people at this evening do not leave us standing, after all. We are quite taken by everything and the evening is full. And yet we move and maintain ourselves in a passing the time which encompasses everything, the whole evening, within it, so that the evening satisfies us and constitutes, as it were, that which occupies us. Indeed this is all the more the case since in fact we do not even expect or demand any result or any use from it. But *what,* then, is this passing the time summoned up *against?* What is it supposed to satisfy or fill? Which emptiness? *What leaves us empty* is *whatever is boring us.* We saw that what is boring us here is that '*I know not what*', that unknown in the whole situation in response to which the evening itself—which comprises the situation—is organised. The emptiness is, roughly speaking, at least as great as the fullness. Yet then the emptiness is filled and is no longer there. In this second form of boredom, then, we find absent both being held in limbo by the dragging of time and being left empty by those beings surrounding us in the situation, those beings we might expect to refuse themselves, yet which in this situation do not even think of doing so.

b) Obstructive casualness as the deepening manner in which we are left empty by what is boring us. Being left empty in a self-forming emptiness.

What is the result of our contrasting the two forms of boredom with one another? The result is evidently that we are not at all able to grasp the second form with the aid of the structure which we found in the first form. Thus a comparison becomes altogether impracticable. Stated positively, this means that we must interpret the second form of boredom purely on its own terms, without glancing sideways at the structure of the first, and must do so by using our selected guideline: the relation between our attendant passing the time and the boredom which is to be passed away in it. For after all, this result provides the following comparison: if initially it seemed as though there were no passing of time in the second form of boredom, such passing the time unexpectedly manifested itself to a strange degree. It is not any particular being occupied within the situation, but the situation itself as a whole which functions as that which occupies us. With this *expansion* of passing time there is linked a further characteristic of it which we must now explicitly emphasize: the *inconspicuousness* of passing the time as such—not inconspicuousness merely or in the first instance for others, but insofar as passing the time does not specifically occupy us ourselves as such passing the time. We allow ourselves to slip into it, just as though it were already lying in wait. For this reason, such passing the time also lacks that fluttering unease of searching for something with which to occupy ourselves. It is peculiarly casual and assured.

All these moments pertaining to passing the time in this second case could easily mislead us into *concluding* that if passing the time is so inconspicuous here, then the second form of boredom accompanying it is merely one that is dawning quite faintly, one that does not fully unfold and is not any more profound at all, as we had thought.

That might perhaps be very perceptive, but it contributes nothing toward explaining the *phenomenon*. We may not simply start from the features of passing the time viewed superficially and then draw "conclusions" about the supposed features of the boredom accompanying it. Instead we have the task of accentuating how *in* this passing the time and *for* it, the boredom specific to it *announces* itself. We must ask: What does that *against which* such passing the time is directed look like? What does that which attempts to rise up against such passing the time look like? Yet have we not already cut ourselves off from any answer to this question? We found, after all, that what bores us in this boredom is that 'I know not what', that indeterminate unknown. Good—it will be said—it is now a matter of eliminating the indeterminacy and rectifying the unfamiliarity. Then we will get behind whatever this passing the time turns against. Will we get behind it? No. At most what we will achieve is that we ourselves will overlook the initial result of our interpretation of the second case. For this 'I know not what', the indeterminate unfamiliarity, characterizes what is boring. We may not eliminate it, but must precisely hold on to this indeterminate and unfamiliar phenomenon in its indeterminacy and unfamiliarity, not replace it with a determinacy and familiarity. It is a matter of seeing how *this* boring thing bores us, and what this *being bored with* actually is.

What is boring us: not this and not that, but an 'I know not what'. However, this indeterminate, unfamiliar thing could after all be precisely that which must leave us empty. In that case, precisely in this respect, we would find a *being left empty* in this boredom. Yet let us look more closely. Are we attuned in such a way, do we feel ourselves left standing by those beings within the situation? Not really. For this to be the case and to be possible, we would actually have to set out and seek to become satisfied by things in the sense indicated. But what is missing here is precisely the unease of being on the lookout for . . . , we are not doing any seeking at all; on the contrary, in fact: we are involved in all that is going on, we are in there chatting away. Yet this is after all a peculiar form of comportment and perhaps characteristic of the whole situation of the evening: this *being in there chatting away,* a letting oneself be swept along by whatever is transpiring there. What is it about this *casualness?* How does it relate to being left empty in the first case we looked at? Can we say that, in contrast to being left empty, the casualness of joining in is a being satisfied, because we let ourselves be swept along? Or must we say that this casualness [*Lässigkeit*] is a being left empty [*Leergelassenheit*] that is *becoming more profound?* To what extent? Because—as this [German] term is meant to indicate—in this casualness we abandon ourselves [*uns überlassen*] to our being there alongside and part of things.[1] This entails that any seeking to be satisfied by beings is absent in advance. Being left empty does not now first ensue in and through the absence of fullness, the refusal of this or that being, rather it *grows from the depths,* because its own precondition, namely seeking to be satisfied by beings, is already obstructed in such casualness. It now no longer even arises. Here too what bores us has the character of leaving us empty, but of a leaving empty that attacks more profoundly; it is a preventing of that seeking, and the diffusion of casualness. For this reason, our being satisfied, in being there and part of things, manifests itself, if only faintly and indeterminately, as an illusion (a peculiar dissatisfaction!)—as a passing the time

---

1. [Tr: Heidegger here employs several cognates deriving from the root *lassen: Leergelassenheit,* "being left empty," which is a primary element of boredom; *Lässigkeit,* "casualness," and *sich überlassen,* to "abandon oneself to." Later in this section he will speak of our "leaving ourselves behind" (*Sichzurücklassen*) in abandoning ourselves. *Lassen* has the sense of both *leaving* and *letting.* In the term *seinlassen,* "letting be," which will occur later in the text, the *lassen* is undecidable with respect to being transitive or intransitive: in this case it has the sense of both *leaving* something to be and *making* something be.]

which does not so much drive off boredom as precisely *attest* to it and let it *be-there* [da-sein].

Here it also becomes manifest that what is boring can bore us without directly coming toward us from particular boring things. What is boring is that which thwarts us and spreads this peculiar casualness—where does it come from? In such casualness there arises a *slipping away, away from ourselves* toward whatever is happening. We shall see later what this means. If that which is boring us thwarts our comportment, brings about casualness, does this mean it is already in us? Yet we know that this 'in us' and this interior, all these kinds of things are questionable, and we actually want the converse, namely we seek to grasp ourselves in the ground of our essence via the interpretation of attunement. *Obstructive casualness* as a more profound way of leaving empty is a moment of *that* boredom which we rightly call a *being bored with*. We are bored with. . . . This indicates that the boredom in this being there alongside beings as part of a situation comes *from us*. Yet this 'comes from us' is still obscure and must remain so, above all until we have decided how things stand concerning the first structural moment of being held in limbo.

Before we inquire about the second essential moment of being bored with, namely being held in limbo, we shall summarize in a more incisive way the comparison thus far between the second form of boredom and the first. We are at the stage of interpreting the second form of boredom, being bored with. . . . What is important is that we bear in mind the overall thrust of the investigation, so that we can then catch sight, if only indirectly, of what distinguishes the second from the first form of boredom, without going into it in detail. In this situation of being bored with, there is nothing boring to be found among the beings surrounding us. For this reason we speak of *ourselves* being bored with. . . . Nor do we initially find any passing the time in this situation, but rather a peculiar unease in which we are concerned about such passing the time. What seems to ensue from this at first is the absence of boredom. This absence of boredom seems, furthermore, to be fully confirmed by the impossibility of immediately finding those particular structural moments of boredom, being left empty and being held in limbo, in this second form. For how can we speak of a being left empty here, when we are, after all, right there and part of the conversation? We are not delayed either, for we are there alongside and part of things of our own accord. Thus what is also missing in this situation is our being held in limbo by the dragging of time. We are not tensely looking forward to the end, we are not looking at the clock, time is going neither too slowly nor too quickly for us; after all, we have left ourselves time for the evening. And still there is this boredom.

What we have said about the situation hitherto is certainly completely accurate. We do not find any of these aforementioned moments, we do *not* find them *in that way* in which we did in the previously described form of boredom.

The only consequence to be drawn from this is that perhaps these structural moments of being left empty and being held in limbo have become *transformed*. The form of boredom in this second case is not accidental, but in accordance with its essence is perhaps more inconspicuous, more concealed. Precisely from this we may not conclude—as it seems reasonable to do—that because the boredom is more inconspicuous it is perhaps faint, superficial, fleeting. Quite the contrary. The question is: What bores us in this being bored with . . . , in which we can find no determinate boring thing? We do not know what bores us. Or to put it more incisively, we know quite clearly that what bores us is indeed this 'I know not what', this thing that is indeterminate and unfamiliar. The question is: What does it mean to say that this thing which is indeterminate and unfamiliar bores us?

In the *previous* case the result was quite clear: What is boring, the particular things with which we try to occupy ourselves, as it were, somehow leave us empty. *Here* however we are taken not with this or that, but with everything, and therefore satisfied. Are we really satisfied? What would that mean? It would mean that our entire activity would be fulfilled by this evening. Yet that is evidently not the case. Nor can it rightly be demanded, even of the most splendid event, that it be in a position to satisfy the *resolute openness* [Entschlossenheit] *of our whole Dasein* in such a way that we could rest our existence on such an occasion. There can be no question, however much such a thing satisfies us, of its determining us in such a way that our being and non-being would depend upon it. The evening does not correspond to what we, without clearly knowing it, properly seek for our own selves. To put it more accurately, we seek nothing further at all from this invitation. We went along just to spend the evening. We cannot and do not wish to be properly satisfied at all, yet do not wish to be left empty either. We go along with things, we *chat* away, perhaps for some restful relaxation. Yet precisely our seeking nothing more from the evening is what is decisive about our comportment. With this 'seeking nothing more' something is *obstructed* in us. In this chatting along with whatever is happening we have, not wrongly or to our detriment, but legitimately, left our proper self behind in a certain way. In this seeking nothing further here, which is self-evident for us, we *slip away* from ourselves in a certain manner.

There is a peculiar *casualness* to be found here, and indeed in a twofold sense: *first,* in the sense of abandoning ourselves to whatever there is going on; and *second,* in the sense of leaving ourselves behind [*Sichzurücklassen*]: ourselves namely, our proper self. In this casualness of *leaving ourselves behind in abandoning ourselves* to whatever there is going on, *an emptiness can form.* Becoming bored or being bored is determined by this emptiness forming itself in our apparently satisfied going along with whatever there is going on. Thus here too, in this form of boredom, we find a being left empty, and indeed an essentially *more profound* form thereof in contrast to the previous case. There, the being left empty consisted merely in the absence of fullness. It consisted in the fact that particular things with which we were seeking to entertain and occupy ourselves refused themselves to us. Here, however, there is not simply an emptiness that remains unfilled, rather an emptiness precisely first *forms* itself. This emptiness is a being left behind of our proper self. This self-forming emptiness is this 'I know not what'—that which weighs upon us to a greater or lesser extent.

c) Not being released from our time as being held in limbo to time in its standing.

However little prospect there seemed at first glance of specifically finding the moment of being left empty in the second form, it leapt out clearly as soon as we resisted adopting it from the first form as a fixed structure and imposing it on the second form, but sought to understand in terms of the situation what is properly boring in this being bored with. . . . We found a more originary manner of being left empty—and must now expect to do the same with respect to *being held in limbo*. Here too we must beware of simply asking: Is this moment also to be found in the second form in the way that we encounter it in the first? We must rather pose the problem in the following way: what, in the second form of boredom, *corresponds* to that *first mode* of being held in limbo in the first form? Is a transformation also manifest here in the sense of a deepening?

In the *first form* we spoke of being held in limbo by time as it drags. This became relatively clear, although we at once encountered obscurity as soon as we asked where we are held to in this being held in limbo. For it is not enough to say that we are detained alongside those beings that offer themselves in the specific situation, and that we must hold out there and wait. For precisely this being detained alongside particular beings that refuse themselves receives its intensity only from the fact that in so doing, we are held in limbo by the dragging of the time that we must here squander in vain in our fruitless waiting.

In the *second form,* on the other hand, we have in advance *left* ourselves time for the evening. We *have* time. It is not pressing, and for this reason cannot go too slowly either, i.e., it cannot hold us in limbo as the dragging of time. Commensurate with this we do not look at the clock at all in such being bored, we give no thought at all to the end of the evening. Yet what does this mean? How do things stand in *this form of boredom concerning our relationship to time?*

The answer must be found via the path we have outlined, i.e., from the perspective of *passing the time.* We have already characterized the latter in its transformed guise. Passing the time is not one particular, isolated occupation

within the situation, but is the situation itself, permeating everything inconspicuously. It takes place in this casual being alongside and part of all that is
going on. This is grounded in casualness, which is the originary way in which
we are left empty. Passing the time resides in whatever belongs to being bored
with . . . itself. We are bored with the evening. The evening itself is our passing
the time.

What is happening to time here? After all, we have already in advance *left*
ourselves time for things—we *have* time. We do not need to take account of
it; we can, as it were, without looking around us, *spend* it and *lose* it during
the evening. We have time to such an extent that during the evening this *during*
[Während] does not even occur to us. We pay no attention to *enduring*
[Währen], i.e., to the lasting flowing away and dissipating of time. Accordingly,
we are here not *held in limbo* by time, but rather the converse: time does not
bind us to itself. It *abandons us* entirely *to ourselves,* i.e., it leaves us free and
lets us be entirely there, alongside and part of things.

Yet if time has thus become indifferent, indeed has virtually disappeared,
can we then still speak of a boredom or even of a supposedly more profound
boredom? Evidently not. That time is indeed somehow involved here is manifest in the fact that the situation is determined in advance in such a way that
it, and we in it, precisely *have time.* What does it mean that we *leave* time for
ourselves, that time does not bind us to itself? *We* leave time for *ourselves,* and
the time that has been left in this way leaves *us* free to *be there, alongside and
part of things.* We have time for the evening; yet we are bored with the evening.
We do not at all take time specifically in order to be bored, on the contrary.
In this having time for . . . there lies the possibility that the time that we take
for things will be filled; and precisely here there arises this being bored. In
boredom, therefore, nothing happens through the fact that we have taken time,
rather it is ultimately the very fact that we have taken time that gives time the
possibility of *holding us in limbo* and indeed *in a more profound way.*

We see nothing particular that is boring in the situation, and yet we are
bored by this 'I know not what', by that which is indeterminate and unfamiliar.
Although we are there and part of things and satisfied, there persists an
emptiness. This indicates that all the things we are now chattering away about
do not properly satisfy us after all. Not properly—why not?

Let us consider this evening. Although we are entirely immersed in it, we
have given ourselves this time only, not time as a whole. What whole? That
to which we ourselves are entrusted, and which is apportioned to us. We take
time for ourselves. Yet in so doing we have not cut a piece out of this whole
like a piece of cake. Instead we take this time for ourselves. What happens
here? How does *our whole time become transformed* through this taking time?
We bring it to a *stand*—yet do not cause it to vanish. On the contrary. We
leave time for ourselves. Yet time does not leave us. It does not release us—

indeed it releases us so little that, as standing, it now spreads a *stillness* into Dasein, a stillness within which Dasein diffuses itself, yet at the same time becomes hidden as such, precisely by our joining in with things during the time that we have taken. It is, after all, only this evening that we have left ourselves time for—and only for this time. The time that we leave ourselves announces itself inconspicuously enough as regards its length. Time does not bind us, it withdraws, as it were, and yet—by *abandoning* us only for a period to our *being there and part of things, it does not release us* entirely. On the contrary, in this way it manifests precisely our being bound to it. But in what way does this happen? What is time doing when it grants us this period? It does not drag. Nor does it announce itself by forcing or imposing itself among things as it flows away. For precisely this obtrusiveness would disturb us in our being there and part of things during the evening. It cannot therefore impose itself in its passing and rushing by. Does it then hide itself? This is not possible either, for otherwise it could not show itself at all—even if inconspicuously—in its periodic nature as it grants itself. It does not show itself as flowing away or as pressing and yet it nevertheless shows itself—but how? In such a way that it seems as though it were not there. It shows itself yet does not flow—it *stands*. Yet this does not at all mean that it has vanished, rather this *standing of time* is a *more originary holding in limbo,* which is to say, *oppressing.*

In general, time is almost constantly familiar to us as passing and determinate, but standing time is indeterminate and unfamiliar. In this indeterminate unfamiliarity, standing time stands into the situation, and precisely this specific chattering and having time for whatever is going on lets time stand and leaves it standing. It does not tarry too long a while [*verweilt*] in its course, it does not drag, but simply *whiles* [weilt] and *endures.* During this enduring it merely abandons us to this being there and part of things—abandons us but does not release us. This *not releasing* us, however, announces itself as a *more originary being held in limbo* than that of a protracted being detained through mere dragging, which finds its end with the advent of a point in time. Now, however, something of the power of time is manifesting itself, of that time which stands there only so as *to bind us more originarily.* This happens precisely where we believe we have time, whereas whenever we think we have no time and that we are losing it unnecessarily, our being held in limbo is merely protracted.

Yet our own self is after all familiar to us. We can determine it in such and such a way without question at any time. What could be closer to us than our own self? To what extent is our self *left behind* and *left standing* in being bored with something, and, as *standing, indeterminate* and *unfamiliar,* so that it oppresses us as something strange and ungraspable? Hitherto we have seen only this: Even the second form of boredom has the structural moment of *being left empty,* albeit in a *transformed* form and not so conspicuously as the first.

It is thus to be expected that the second structural moment, *being held in limbo,* will not be absent either, though it too will certainly be *transformed* and difficult to make visible.

Here we must recall that what it is difficult to make visible in the interpretation of boredom, namely the *essence* of what is boring, is immediately and without question there in the boredom of being bored, and is so in its way of being boring. But the difficulty is precisely to take explicitly into its essence whatever is immediately there. This hint will have to suffice here in order to prevent our confusing the two.

Being held in limbo by time as it drags is manifestly not to be found in the second case of boredom. Here indeed it seems as though time were not essential to the whole situation at all. Nor can it be otherwise, if we recall how the whole situation is determined in advance. We have *left* ourselves *time* for this invitation. We have *taken time* for the evening. What does it mean to take time? *What* time have we taken for ourselves here? Some span of time that is freely lying around and belongs to no one? Or does the time that we take *belong* to someone? *It belongs to us.* We take time from *that* time which is apportioned to us; from the time to which our whole Dasein is given over; from the time of whose scale, moreover, we are not at all certain. From this time we simply take time. How so? Do we cut a piece out of time as we cut a piece out of the cake during the course of the evening? Evidently not. Yet however this occurs—it is already strange that we take time from our time, from the time that belongs to us. After all we do not first need to take such things from ourselves. And furthermore—what do we take this time for? So as to *leave* it for ourselves. Where do we leave it? To where do we take [*bringen*] this time we have taken? We spend it, get through it [*bringen sie durch*], *waste it.* We take time in such a way that we do not have to reckon with it. We thus undertake something with our time. We transform time in a certain way. We spend [*verbringen*] it—i.e., in and during our spending it we constantly remove it [*bringen sie weg*], but in such a way that in and during this removal it precisely does not appear. We remove the time *during* our spending of it, i.e., we remove precisely this *during* within which the invitation and the evening endure, this 'during' in its enduring. Enduring—this means lasting, namely lasting in the sense of the constant flowing away of time, that is, the 'now' and 'now' and 'now'. We close ourselves off from this unsettling and paralysing sound of the sequence of nows ticking away which can be stretched to a greater or lesser extent. We take this time so as to leave it for ourselves, i.e., *to give it up as flowing away.*

Yet what happens in this giving up of time, in this closing ourselves off before the flow of enduring? After all, we cannot step out of time. Nor do we wish to do so at all, but want to have this time for ourselves. If we spend it and give it up, then this can only mean that *we* relate to it in a particular way. How? We make time *stand*. We let the time we have taken for the evening—our taking consists precisely in this—endure in such a way during the evening that in being there alongside and part of whatever is going on we take no note of its flow or its moments. The enduring of the 'during' swallows up, as it were, the flowing sequence of nows and becomes a *single stretched 'now'* which itself does not flow, but stands. The 'now' is stretched and made to stand and held in this stretched standing in such a way that we are entirely there alongside and part of whatever is going on around us, i.e., in such a way that we are *entirely present* [ganz Gegenwart] *for* what is present [*das Anwesende*]. Entirely present [*gegenwärtig*] to the situation, we bring our time to a stand.

What does this entail? What does the *standing of time* have to do with *being bored,* or even with the indeterminate, unfamiliar thing that is boring us here? Nothing initially—just as we are not necessarily bored in every situation we have left ourselves time for. It is merely *possible* that we will be bored in such a situation. If such being bored actually occurs—as we assume—then what is the connection between this standing of time and our being bored? Is the specific moment of boredom that we are now seeking, *being held in limbo,* connected to this standing of time, except that being held in limbo would now happen not through time as it drags, but *through time as it stands?*

We bring time to a stand, but—and we must take careful note of this—we do not make it vanish. On the contrary, it is precisely a matter of seeing what is meant by the fact that standing time during the situation stands, as standing, into our Dasein. Letting time stand happens in our being there alongside and part of whatever is going on or happening around us. This chattering and letting oneself go with whatever is happening is possible only if, from the outset, we constantly let whatever is going on come toward us, come *up against us,* just as it is given. It is possible only if we *are entirely present* [ganz Gegenwart] in the face of whatever is happening around us, or, as we say, only if we simply *make present* [gegenwärtigen]—here understood in the transitive sense—that is, if we let whatever is given round about us be specifically and solely present [*anwesend*] as such, so that we go along with it at all times.

Yet what does it mean to say that we are entirely present in this situation? This entails that we do not turn to whatever, however, or wherever we have been, it entails that we have forgotten it. Entirely present, we have no time either for what we have perhaps planned for tomorrow or for some other time, for whatever we have resolved or not resolved to do, whatever task we turn ourselves to, whatever stands before us, whatever we shirk. Entirely present for whatever is happening, we are cut off from our having-been and from our future. This *being cut off* from our *own having-been* and our *own future* does not mean that the latter are factically removed or taken away, but means a peculiar dissolution of the future and having-been into the mere present, a *modification* of having-been and future. Having-been and future do not become lost, it is not that they are not there at all, but they become modified in the peculiar manner of becoming enchained within the mere present, i.e., in a joining in that merely makes present. The time during which we are thus present thereby comes precisely to a stand—not any time at all, but *that which endures* during the presence of the evening. The enduring of the 'now' is henceforth sealed off from the past. The 'now' can no longer show itself as that which was earlier; with the forgetting of having-been, the possible *horizon for every earlier* is closed off. The 'now' can only remain 'now'. Yet the 'now' cannot show itself as that which is later either, as that which is yet to come. Nothing can come because the *horizon of the future* has been unbound. *Sealing off* the past and *unbinding* the future do not eliminate the 'now', but they take away its possibility of a transition from not-yet to no-longer, its flowing. Sealed off and unbound on both sides, it becomes stuck in its abiding standing, and in its being stuck *it stretches itself* [dehnt sich]. Without the possibility of transition, only persisting remains for it—it must remain *standing.*

By being cut off on both sides in the direction of having-been and future, the present becomes compressed [*gedrängt*] into itself, and the peculiar time which is there in the present, namely the 'now', stretches itself by itself as it were. By the fact that the horizon in the direction of past and future remains closed off to it, the 'now' no longer receives the possibility of showing itself as the earlier and the later. The 'now' has no possibility other than that of being the 'now' of nows at that particular time. Through the 'now' becoming compressed into being in the 'now', the 'now' stretches itself. It is not that individual now-points are heaped upon one another; rather insofar as the 'now' becomes what is now, and gives and expends itself as that which is now, the 'now' itself stretches itself. There are not several nows, but fewer and fewer, indeed merely one, a stretched one which stands in this peculiar being stretched. This standing of the 'now' and of enduring is no mere being at a standstill, as though nothing further would now happen any more, as though this stretched 'now' would as it were stand around abandoned somewhere. Rather this stretched 'now' stands into our Dasein.

It is this time in its standing during the evening that we have taken and take for ourselves through being entirely present. We said that the time we take for ourselves is *our* time. This time in its standing—this is our sealed off having-been and our unbound future, i.e., our whole time of our Dasein in a peculiar transformation. In this transformed form our whole time is compressed into this *standing 'now'* of the duration of the evening. This standing time—this is *we ourselves;* it is *our self* as that which *has been left behind* with respect to its *provenance* and *future.* This standing 'now' can, in its standing, precisely tell us that we have left it standing, which means, however, that it precisely is not releasing us, but that our being bound to it is impressing itself upon us [*uns aufdrängt*]. The standing 'now', the "during" of the evening in which the invitation endures, can manifest to us as such precisely this being held in limbo, being bound to our time. This *not being released* from our time, from our time which impresses itself upon us from the direction of the standing 'now', is our *being held in limbo to time in its standing,* and is thus the sought-after structural moment of being bored with. . . . Not only does time in its standing not release us, it precisely summons us, it sets us in place. When, letting ourselves go along with being there and part of things, we are thus set in place by the standing 'now' that is our own, albeit relinquished and empty self, then we are bored.

§26. *The structural unity of the two structural moments of being bored, grounded in a making-present that brings the time taken to a stand. Boredom as springing from the self-temporalizing temporality of Dasein.*

This standing 'now' which thus sets us in place (summons us) is what bores us. Yet we said that what bores us in this boredom is the 'I know not what', that which is indeterminate and unfamiliar. Is this standing time indeterminate and unfamiliar? Indeed. For in the realm of the everyday we know time precisely as that which passes, that which flows. Time is virtually the prime example of what passes and does not remain standing. It is the time that flows that is familiar to us. This familiar phenomenon is also always determinate and determinable for us, either by the clock or else through any event at any time: now as this car is driving past, now as I am speaking here. The *standing 'now'* however, in the above situation, is something *unfamiliar,* and it is simultaneously *indeterminate,* indeed indeterminate in an emphatic sense. We do not wish to have it determined at all. In being there alongside and part of things, we all the while pay no attention to the respective nows during the evening. This indeterminate, unfamiliar standing 'now' can weigh upon us in the manner of simultaneously summoning us before it as we slip away, *setting* us in place, albeit in such a way that its standing becomes more standing, as it were, more constant.

   With reference to the first structural moment, being left empty, we saw that it consists in a self-forming *emptiness;* this self-forming emptiness is what is *boring.* It must therefore be identical with the indeterminate, unfamiliar *standing 'now'* we have discovered here. In our leaving ourselves time for the evening, time can take form as this standing 'now', and in its self-forming indeterminacy and self-forming unfamiliarity, i.e., in its self-forming emptiness, it can *leave* us *empty,* and in leaving us empty simultaneously *hold us in limbo.*

   Yet we have thereby expressed a decisive insight that we have been seeking all along: an insight into the *unity of the two structural moments* of being left empty and being held in limbo. These are not two pieces arbitrarily stuck together; rather, letting ourselves go in this peculiar chattering away is a making present of whatever is taking place. Wholly present, we bring time to a stand. The time that has come to a stand forms an emptiness that irrupts against the background of everything that is happening. At the same time, however, it is this self-forming emptiness that sets us in place, binds us to itself, holds us in limbo in this way as our own proper self that we ourselves have left standing and from which we slip away.

The structural unity of the two structural moments is grounded in a making-present that brings the time taken to a stand. The unitary essence of boredom in the sense of the unitary structure of the two moments must therefore be sought in time after all. Not merely in time in general and universally, however, not only in time as we know it, but in the manner and way in which we stand with respect to the time that is familiar, in the manner and way in which this time stands into our Dasein and in which our Dasein itself is temporal. *Boredom springs from the temporality of Dasein.* Boredom therefore, we may say in anticipation, arises from a quite determinate way and manner in which our own temporality *temporalizes itself.* This tallies with the thesis that we announced earlier, namely that boredom is possible only because every thing, and more fundamentally every Dasein as such, has its time.

§27. Concluding characterization of being bored with something: the peculiarity of that passing the time which belongs to it as the way in which whatever is boring arises out of Dasein itself.

We wish to keep to our *path,* however, and thus precisely to illuminate for the first time, through our *ever-deepening interpretation of boredom,* the temporality of Dasein and thereby Dasein itself in its ground.

The present interpretation has been made possible via a comparison and contrasting of two forms of boredom, namely becoming bored by . . . and being bored with. . . . We described being bored with . . . as the *more profound* of the two. We also arrived at a transformed version of the two structural moments of being left empty and being held in limbo.

On the basis of the interpretation we have given of being bored with . . . we can now first understand correctly the peculiarity of that passing the time which belongs to and is associated with this boredom. We said that our passing the time in being bored with . . . does not have the halting and uneasy character of the first form, but is identical with our entire participation in the evening, and is accordingly peculiarly inconspicuous. Our passing the time as such struggles against boredom. This boredom, however, spreads out beyond what has been characterized as boring: the standing 'now' that sets us in place and at the same time lets us go. This standing 'now' stands during the evening, it is this 'during' itself. What is boring as such is accordingly diffused in its strange ungraspability throughout the whole enduring of the evening. Our passing the time must correspond to this. We do indeed pass time, we pass away the standing 'now'. We drive it on—not the 'now' that drags, in order to make it pass more quickly, but the standing 'now'. We pass it away, pass away this standing time, the *during* within which we are immersed in this evening. Our passing the time drives away whatever is boring. Because the 'during' is what is boring, the whole evening must be organized as a way of passing the time. Yet because what is boring is here diffused throughout the particular situation as a whole, it is far more oppressive—despite its ungraspability. It oppresses precisely in and during the inconspicuous way in which we are held at a distance in our passing the time.

If we thus summarize our characterization of the second form of boredom, we see that in the first case what is boring comes from outside, as it were, so that we become bored by. . . . A *particular* situation with *its* circumstances *transposes us* into boredom. Here on the other hand, in the second case, what is boring does not come from outside: *it arises from out of Dasein itself.* This means that precisely because the boredom is dissipated throughout the whole situation in this creeping way, it cannot be bound to this situation as such. The second form of boredom is less situation-bound than the first. What surrounds us in the second situation, those beings that hold us captive—even though we let ourselves go in their direction and are entirely there alongside and part of things—are, as regards the boredom itself and its arising, only what accompanies it, only the occasion on which it comes to arise. Boredom here means *oneself* being bored—and indeed bored with. . . . In this second boredom we are held *more toward ourselves,* somehow enticed back into the specific gravity of Dasein, even though, indeed precisely because in so doing we leave our own proper self standing and unfamiliar. In the first form, by contrast, we are also somehow alongside ourselves and oppressed—for otherwise there would be no boredom as an attunement at all—yet nonetheless that first form is an uneasy fidgeting that is directed outward.

§28. The second form of boredom as becoming more profound in contrast to the first.

We have thus already indicated in what sense we must address the second form of boredom as the more profound boredom in contrast to the first. We are asking about how this boredom becomes more profound, however, so that from the *direction* in which it becomes more profound we may obtain a preliminary indication and prefiguring of the *originary depth of the full essence of boredom.* In order to clarify this direction we must now explicitly characterize and sum up how *the second form of boredom becomes more profound* with respect to the first.

In our provisional contrasting of the two forms of boredom we pointed on several occasions to a distinction readily visible at first sight, namely their *different relationship to time.* In the second form we leave ourselves time. The whole situation is determined by this. In the first, on the other hand, we are oppressed by the dragging of time, i.e., here we have no time, here we do not want to lose time unnecessarily. The initial result of this is that this first situation is indeed basically the more serious; we do not wish to lose any time, i.e., we wish to lose none of our time. The boring situation is also provoked by the fact that we are concerned and worried about our time and thereby about ourselves. In the second form, by contrast, we ultimately waste time and leave our self standing. The first situation is therefore of greater intensity and more serious in contrast to the second, less serious, frivolous one. The more profound boredom must accordingly correspond to the more intense situation. For only where the intensity is higher is there depth, and vice-versa. Therefore it will not do to take the second form of boredom as the more profound form without further ado—especially since the distinction now noted is a distinction with respect to their relationship to time, and time itself somehow constitutes the concealed essence of boredom.

In the face of this difficulty, which imposes itself of its own accord, we must indeed initially hold fast to the fact that the distinction exposed earlier between the two forms of boredom (with respect to the second form of boredom being essentially anchored in Dasein as such) resulted from boredom and its structure. In the face of this distinction which lies in the matter itself it can be of no consequence that the situation in the first form, as a situation, is perhaps of greater intensity than that in the second form. Certainly—in both cases the kind of situation is not accidental to the character of the boredom involved. Thus we cannot pass by an explicit question and decision: How do things stand concerning the two situations and their relationship to time? Does our not having any time and not wanting to take time in the first form point to a more serious situation and one of greater intensity in contrast to having time and wasting time in the second? With respect to the first form the question is surely: Why do we have no time? To what extent do we not wish to lose any time? Because we need it and wish to use it. For what? For our everyday occupations, to which we have long since become enslaved. We have no time because we ourselves cannot keep from joining in everything that is going on. This *not having any time* is ultimately a *greater being lost of the self* than that wasting time which leaves itself time. Perhaps there lies in this having time a far greater balance and thereby security of Dasein—a being-alongside-oneself [*Bei-sich-*

selbst] that at least *has an intimation* that what is essential in Dasein cannot be forcibly brought about by any busyness or mad rush—which certainly does not exclude, but perhaps precisely necessitates that we are nonetheless bored with things in this very situation where we leave ourselves time. This having time and having no time is essentially ambiguous. The 'having no time' that looks like the most rigorous seriousness is perhaps the way in which we are most lost in the banalities of Dasein.

It thereby becomes manifest that it is not at all so easy to contrast these forms of boredom with one another, and that strangely interwoven perspectives open up here which we shall not pursue any further at this point. For us, only this much is clear: it is impossible to infer straightforwardly a more serious, more profound Dasein from not having time, or to infer a less serious, superficial Dasein from leaving oneself time. It remains that the way in which boredom becomes more profound can be read off only from the specific constitution of boredom itself in each case.

We shall now attempt to record provisionally these moments of *distinction with respect to depth* in a list of specific points; provisionally because we are not at all sure whether what we have achieved hitherto has as yet made the full essence of boredom transparent for us.

The investigation thus far has provided us with seven points by which to characterize, by way of comparison, the distinctions with respect to depth, and in listing these points we shall simultaneously provide a summary of our interpretation thus far. (In what follows, the two forms of boredom, becoming bored by . . . and being bored with . . . , are designated by I and II respectively in the list of seven points).

[1.] With respect to the structural moment of *being left empty:*
   In I, we have merely the absence of any fullness for an emptiness that is at hand;
   in II, the emptiness first forming itself.

[2.] With respect to the structural moment of *being held in limbo:*
   In I, we have a being detained by whatever is dragging in a time we somehow need;
   in II, not being released and being set in place by standing time as our self that has been left behind.

[3.] With reference to boredom *in relation to the situation:*
   In I, we have a being bound and stuck fast to the particular situation which is limited by extrinsic circumstances;
   in II, not being bound to the particular happenings unfolding in the situation.

   This third, general distinction is explained in greater detail by the next two points, 4 and 5.

[4.] In I, in the person who is bored there is the attempt, conspicuous to oneself, to pass the time in seeking to be occupied in a particular way with something arbitrary;

in II, there is the inconspicuous occurrence of a passing the time, hidden from the self that is bored, in our entire comportment during the situation.

[5.] In I, we have a fluttering *unease* of passing the time, a running up against boredom that somehow easily becomes confused, and accordingly a *being driven around within* boredom itself. (For our unease in passing the time precisely makes the boredom itself to some extent more pressing and more unsettling.)

In II, passing the time is rather more of an *evasion in the face of* boredom, and boredom itself is more a *letting oneself be bored.*

[6.] The distinction with respect to the *range of resonance* of boredom:

In I, we have a being forced in *between* particular boring things, and correspondingly a sticking fast to them;

in II, the floating dissipation of boredom *throughout* the whole situation.

Finally, looking back over the six previous points and summarizing everything once more:

[7.] In I, we have, as it were, the *extrinsic* arrival and advent of boredom *from out of* a particular environment;

in II, the arising of boredom *within* and *from out of* Dasein on the occasion of a specific situation.

Accordingly, in I, we have a fidgeting directed outward in accordance with the contingency of boredom;

in II, a being drawn into the specific gravity of boredom.

Through this summary the *designations* which we gave the two forms of boredom, becoming bored by . . . and being bored with . . . , have now also been clarified and have shown themselves to be appropriate and legitimate.

It would, however, be a *misunderstanding* if we were merely to take what is summarized in these seven points as a result, instead of demonstrating all this to ourselves in a living manner by now retracing the various interwoven paths taken by our investigation hitherto. For, to point it out once more, in case you have not yet noticed: it is not a matter of taking a definition of boredom home with you, but of learning and understanding how to move in the depths of Dasein.

Chapter Four

The Third Form of Boredom: Profound Boredom
as 'It Is Boring for One'

*§29. Prerequisites for penetrating into the essence of
boredom and of time: questioning the conception of man
as consciousness, and the way in which the essence of boredom
opens itself up in its depth.*

Following our vacation, we shall now attempt to give a concise account of the
overall context of our investigation. We wish to work our way into a particular
philosophizing that moves in the realm of the essential, i.e., necessary questions
for us today. We determined philosophizing as comprehensive questioning
arising out of Dasein's being gripped in its essence. Such being gripped however
is possible only from out of and within a fundamental attunement of Dasein.
This fundamental attunement itself cannot be some arbitrary one, but must
permeate our Dasein in the ground of its essence. Such a fundamental attunement cannot be ascertained as something present at hand that we can appeal
to, or as something firm upon which we might stand, but must be awakened—
awakened in the sense that we must let it become awake. This fundamental
attunement properly attunes us only if we do not oppose it, but rather give it
space and freedom. We give it freedom whenever we await it in the correct
sense, by letting this attunement arrive and approach us, as it were, just as all
proper awaiting, as in a human relationship between two people, is not something remote, but a possibility in which we can be nearer to the other who is
awaiting us than if he or she were immediately in our proximity. A fundamental
attunement of our Dasein must come nearer to us in this kind of awaiting.
For this reason we can only ever encounter such a fundamental attunement
of our Dasein in a question, in a questioning attitude. This is why we asked
whether perhaps contemporary man has become bored with himself, and
whether a *profound boredom* is a fundamental attunement of contemporary
Dasein. To be able to maintain a transparency in this question, and to await
in this question that fundamental attunement which does not first need to be
produced, we must have the corresponding horizon for being open in this way,
i.e., the essence of boredom must be clear to us.

   To this end we attempted to bring the essence of boredom nearer to us
through an interpretation of two of its forms, which in themselves stand in
a relationship of becoming more profound and being more profound. Lastly,
with regard to this we noted the distinctions between these two forms of

boredom and tried to grasp them under seven points. In the first and second points we characterized the structural moments of boredom: being left empty and being held in limbo. In the third, we determined the specific situation-relatedness of boredom. In the fourth and fifth, we characterized the specific kinds of passing the time that accompany boredom in each case, and how they relate to one another. In the sixth point, we tried to establish a distinction in the range of oscillation of the two forms of boredom. Finally, we specified the provenance and specific proximity of boredom to the ground of Dasein in each case. In this final, decisive, all-embracing respect we saw that the *first* form of becoming bored by something comes to meet us from the outside as it were, while the *second* points to the fact that boredom arises out of Dasein itself.

By establishing a distinction in depth we have also already indicated the *direction* in which boredom *becomes more profound,* though this is all we have done. We have not yet penetrated into the depths of its very essence.

Must we stop at this mere *preliminary indication* of the depth of its essence? In other words, can we now merely draw an indirect conclusion and infer further what the *concealed depths of boredom* might look like? Evidently we have certain possibilities of doing so. For we can see that the more profound it becomes, the more completely boredom is rooted in time—in the time that we ourselves are. Accordingly, we must as it were be able to construct profound boredom out of the essence of time conceived more profoundly. This is a clear task and one which can be performed—provided that we understand time itself in its essential depths. Yet we know precisely nothing concerning this. What we wish to do is the converse of this—as already emphasized repeatedly— namely *to press forward to the essence of time through our interpretation of the essence of boredom.* We do not wish to do so on account of any particular obstinacy on our part, but because the essence of time *cannot be illuminated at all in any other way,* i.e., it cannot be illuminated by our simply speculating about time and thinking up another concept of time. This is certainly not to say that the interpretation of boredom is the *only* way toward understanding original temporality. Presumably, however, it is *one* way, such as it must be, i.e., *such a way* as does not regard time as something we find within our consciousness or as a subjective form. It is a path on which, even *before* setting out and going along it, we have already comprehended that precisely the *essence* of consciousness and the *essence* of subjectivity must be put into question *in advance* in order to remove the chief obstacle preventing our access to original time. We must therefore take careful note that the conception of man as consciousness, as subject, as person, as a rational being, and our *concept* of each of these: of consciousness, subject, I, and person, must be put in question. And what must be put in question is *not* merely our *access* to consciousness in the Cartesian sense of the *method* of grasping consciousness, but the *initial positing* of man as consciousness in general, or as a nexus of lived experience or the like—all this must be put into question if a path is to be cleared for us to penetrate into the essence of boredom, and together with it into the essence of time.

If we choose a path through boredom, then it must be a path that leads into the depths of boredom itself. Calculating these depths indirectly by way of inference will not help us in any way. Yet can we tear these *closed depths* of boredom from out of concealment? If this is to be possible, then it can happen only *if these very depths of the essence of boredom open themselves up.* This in turn is possible only if profound boredom *bores as such,* if this profound boredom attunes us through and through and thus puts us in a position to measure the extent of this boredom itself in its depths.

§30. No longer permitting any passing the time as understanding the overpowering nature of profound boredom. Being compelled to listen to what profound boredom gives us to understand.

Are we familiar with this profound boredom? Perhaps we are familiar with it. Yet we now know from what has already been said that the more profound the boredom, the more silent, the less public, the quieter, the more inconspicuous and wide-ranging it is. Correspondingly, our accompanying passing the time is less recognizable as such. Perhaps indeed there is no passing the time at all for this profound boredom. Perhaps this absence of any passing the time is distinctive of it.

The forms of boredom we have dealt with hitherto have already been characterized and designated as becoming bored by something in a particular situation, and as being bored with something on the occasion of a particular situation. And profound boredom? How are we to designate this? We shall try to do so, and shall say that profound boredom bores whenever we say, or better, whenever we silently know, that *it is boring for one.*

It is boring for one. What is this 'it'? The 'it' that we mean whenever we say that it is thundering and lightening, that it is raining. It—this is the title for whatever is indeterminate, unfamiliar. Yet we are familiar with this, after all, and familiar with it as belonging to the more profound form of boredom: *that which bores.* It—one's own self that has been left standing, the self that everyone himself or herself is, and each with this particular history, of this particular standing and age, with this name and vocation and fate; the self, one's own beloved ego of which we say that *I myself,* you yourself, we ourselves are bored. Yet we are now no longer speaking of *ourselves* being bored with . . . , but are saying: It is boring for one. It—for one—not for me as me, not for you as you,

not for us as us, but *for one*. Name, standing, vocation, role, age and fate as mine and yours disappear. To put it more clearly, precisely this 'it is boring for one' makes all these things disappear. What remains? A universal ego in general? Not by any means. For this 'it is boring for one', this boredom, does not comprise some *abstraction* or generalization in which a universal concept 'I in general' would be thought. Rather *it is boring*. This is what is decisive: that here we become an undifferentiated no one. The question is: what is happening here, what is happening in this 'it is boring for one'?

If, however, in accordance with our earlier procedure, we look for an example, then we see that there is none to be found. Yet not because this boredom does not happen, but because when it happens it is not at all relative to a particular situation or particular occasion and the like, as in the first and second forms of boredom. The fact that it is boring for one can occur out of the blue, and precisely whenever we do not expect it at all; certainly there can also be situations in which this fundamental attunement irrupts, situations which are personally quite different with respect to personal experience, occasion, and fate. To cite one possible, but entirely non-binding occasion which has perhaps already been encountered by one or other of us, without our having explicitly noticed the emergence of this boredom and without our explicitly being annoyed of our own accord: 'it is boring for one' to walk through the streets of a large city on a Sunday afternoon.

Evidently this profound boredom, if we follow our *methodological principle,* must in turn be temporalized in terms of *passing the time,* as something *against which* our passing the time can turn. Yet already in the more profound form of boredom, in being bored with, we met a relationship between passing the time and boredom in which this passing the time is limited to an evasion in the face of . . . , and in which struggling against . . . is given up. In the second form, boredom is accordingly that in the face of which we take evasive action. Now, however, in this 'it is boring for one', we no longer even attain this evasion in the face of boredom. Passing the time *is missing* in this boredom. Yet in what sense is it missing? What does this missing mean here? Missing in the sense that it simply does not happen, that we forget it, as it were, that we do not think of bringing it to bear against the emergent boredom? None of these. If no passing the time emerges here with respect to this boredom, then this must tie in with the character of *this* boredom. The absence of passing the time must be determined in part by boredom itself. Passing the time is missing, and yet we may very well think of it, but in such a way that we have already understood that all passing the time is powerless against this boredom, against this 'it is boring for one'. We understand this from out of the boredom itself. In this 'it is boring for one' lies the fact that this boredom wishes to tell us something, and indeed not something arbitrary or contingent. This attunement to which we give expression in 'it is boring for one' has already *transformed*

Dasein in such a way that in our being transformed we also understand that not only would it be hopeless to want to struggle against this attunement with some form of passing the time, but that it would almost be something presumptuous to close ourselves off from what this attunement wishes to tell us. The passing the time corresponding to this boredom is not simply missing, but is *no longer permitted* by us *at all* with regard to this boredom in which we are already attuned. This no longer permitting any passing the time at all is demanded by the particular boredom itself. Thus here too, indeed precisely here, the manner and way in which passing the time *responds* to the boredom manifests the character of the boredom itself. To no longer permit any passing the time means to let this boredom be overpowering. This entails already understanding this boredom in its *overpowering nature*. This understanding of boredom, however, is not attached to this boredom from the outside, as though—before we cease all passing the time—we were observing it psychologically. Rather the 'it is boring for one'—this 'it is thus for one'—has in itself *this* character of *manifesting how things stand concerning us*. This attunement brings us ourselves into the possibility of an *exceptional understanding*. Attuning and being attuned have the intrinsic character of a making manifest, though this does not exhaust the essence of attunement. Generally we are not in a position to give this boredom a hearing, and this because we are indeed familiar with it as boredom, but generally identify it in one form or another with the more common, superficial kind of boredom. More accurately, in this attunement one is in such a way as to know that something is to be 'said' in and through such being attuned.

Whereas in the first case of boredom we are concerned to shout down the boredom by passing the time so that we *do not need to listen to it;* and whereas in the second case what is distinctive is a *not wanting to listen,* we now have a *being compelled to listen,* being compelled in the sense of that kind of compelling force which everything *properly authentic* about Dasein possesses, and which accordingly is related to Dasein's *innermost freedom.* The 'it is boring for one' has already transposed us into a realm of power over which the individual person, the public individual subject, no longer has any power.

§31. Concrete interpretation of profound boredom along the guiding thread of being left empty and being held in limbo.

Thus here too, where—at a rough glance—passing the time is factically entirely absent, a look into the essence of this form of boredom is already possible from this perspective. Yet this is now to be taken only as preparation for the concrete interpretation of this third form of boredom along the guiding thread of the two structural moments and their unity: *being left empty* and *being held in limbo*. We now know from our interpretation of the first and second forms of boredom that these structural moments are in each case transformed, that they are not rigid standards, not a fixed framework that we can lay at the basis of every form of boredom, but merely directives for catching sight of its proper essence in each specific case and determining it on its own terms, while running the risk that the form of being left empty and being held in limbo will now become transformed anew in this third case.

a) Being left empty as Dasein's being delivered over to beings' telling refusal of themselves as a whole.

In this 'it is boring for one' we are not seeking to fill a particular emptiness—one that is at hand and that has arisen through a particular situation—by means of a particular being that is accessible in a particular situation. We are not concerned with filling a particular emptiness that arises for us out of particular circumstances; for instance, out of our arriving too early at the station. Here the emptiness is not the lack of any particular fulfilment. Nor is this emptiness a self-forming of that emptiness in which one's own proper self is left standing, in a being left behind which is accompanied by letting oneself go, and which, in itself, is indeed a letting oneself go with whatever offers itself. In this 'it is boring for one' we find no such letting oneself go with the particular beings in a particular situation, and yet in this 'it is boring for one' precisely the *emptiness* and *being left empty* are quite unambiguous and straightforward. But *what emptiness is this*, when we are not explicitly seeking any particular fulfilment and do not even leave our own self behind in this being left empty? What emptiness is it, when we do not become bored by particular beings, and are not bored ourselves either, as this particular person? It is an emptiness precisely where, as this person in each case, we want nothing from the particular beings in the contingent situation as these very beings. Yet the fact that precisely here we want nothing is already due to the boredom. For with this 'it is boring for one' we are not merely *relieved* of our *everyday personality,* somehow distant and alien to it, but simultaneously also *elevated beyond* the particular situation in each case and beyond the *specific beings* surrounding us there. The whole situation and we ourselves as this individual subject are thereby indifferent, indeed this boredom does not even let it get to the point where such things are of any particular worth to us. Instead it makes *everything of equally great and equally little worth.* What is this 'everything', and to what extent does it become the same for us? This boredom *takes us precisely back to the point* where we do not in the first place seek out this or that being for ourselves in this particular situation; it takes us back to the point where all and everything appears indifferent to us.

Yet this does not happen in such a way that we first run through individual things including ourselves, and then evaluate them in accordance with whether they are still of any worth to us. That is absolutely impossible. It is in itself impossible to accomplish such a thing, quite apart from the fact that it is factically not the case. This *indifference of things and of ourselves with them* is not the result of a sum total of evaluations; rather each and every thing at once becomes indifferent, each and every thing moves together at one and the same time into an indifference. This indifference does not first leap from one thing over onto another like a fire, so as to consume each thing; rather all of a sudden everything is enveloped and embraced by this indifference. Beings have—as we say—become indifferent *as a whole,* and we ourselves as these people are not excepted. We no longer stand as subjects and suchlike opposite these beings and excluded from them, but find ourselves in the midst of beings as a whole, i.e., in the whole of this indifference. Beings as a whole do not disappear however, but *show themselves precisely as such* in their indifference. The *emptiness* accordingly here consists in the *indifference* enveloping beings *as a whole.*

Before we ask how we must grasp this emptiness more closely and how, correspondingly, being left empty is to be determined, we shall summarize our interpretation of profound boredom thus far. We are considering a *third* boredom which is meant to bring us closer to the depths of the essence of boredom, not by way of a construction of boredom in terms of time (which must be possible in principle) but in the same way as with the previous forms. From the outside this looks as though we have simply compiled an arbitrary list of the variations of boredom in general. And yet we have already seen a certain criterion for connecting these forms: their becoming more profound. Continuing in the same direction, as it were, we are now attempting to consider a third form, which we encapsulate in the designation 'it is boring for one'. 'It', 'for one'—this already expresses the fact that in this instance there is not some particular boring thing there, but also the fact that we ourselves in a particular comportment familiar to us in our everydayness are not at issue either. It expresses the fact that what is individual about us ourselves and familiar to us recedes, and is made to recede in this way by boredom itself. This already means that in this boredom we do not carry out some abstraction, for instance, on the basis of which we generalize ourselves from a particular individual ego to a universal ego in general. Boredom in the form of 'it is boring for one' already approaches us more closely if we note that passing the time is missing from it. This being missing is no mere absence or forgetting of passing the time, but emerges from boredom itself by way of our here no longer permitting any passing the time in general. This means that we abandon ourselves to this boredom as something that becomes overpowering in us and which we understand in a certain way in this overpowering, without being able to explain it while we are bored, or even wanting to explain it. Accordingly, we are not opposed to this boredom in any passing the time that seeks to drive it away, nor do we really evade it, but we experience a peculiar compulsion in it, a compulsion to listen to what it has to tell us. We experience our being compelled to enter the peculiar truth or manifestness that lies in this attunement as in every attunement in general. Yet from this association of passing the time with boredom, important though it may be in each case, we do not yet penetrate into the inner essence of the third form. We can succeed in this only if we consider the structural moments of being left empty and being held in limbo. Certainly, at the outset of the investigation these moments must be taken as completely non-binding, at the risk of their becoming transformed. Being left empty is here no longer the absence of a particular satisfaction through being occupied with something—we do not seek such a thing at all. Nor is it leaving one's own self standing, in the face of which we let ourselves go with something in which we become immersed. And yet all beings, not just this one or that one, stand in a strange indifference, not as though all beings were lined up in sequence, but all at once.

Yet, can we then still speak of a *being left empty* when we ourselves after all belong to these things that have become indifferent? If we ourselves belong to these things that have become indifferent, then it is surely a matter of indifference whether we are satisfied or left empty. After all, being left empty is always possible only where there is some claim to being fulfilled, where the necessity of a fullness exists; it is not the indifference of emptiness. Yet if beings as a whole stand in an indifference, then *everything* indeed, even this being left empty, is indifferent, i.e., impossible. Certainly, and it is for precisely this reason that we say: it is boring *for one;* not for me as me, but for one, and that means for one as this particular Da-sein. Yet this determinacy of Dasein is not connected to the petty I-ness that is familiar to us. The indifference of beings as a whole manifests itself for Da-sein, but for Da-sein as such. This means that through this boredom Dasein finds itself set in place precisely before beings as a whole, to the extent that in this boredom the beings that surround us offer us no further possibility of acting and no further possibility of our doing anything. There is a telling refusal on the part of beings as a whole with respect to these possibilities. There is a telling refusal on the part of beings for a Dasein that, as such, in the midst of these beings as a whole, comports itself toward them—toward them, toward those beings as a whole and their now telling refusal—and must comport itself toward them, if it is indeed to be what it is. Dasein thus finds itself delivered over to beings' telling refusal of themselves as a whole.

Being left empty in this *third form* of boredom is *Dasein's being delivered over to beings' telling refusal of themselves as a whole.* In this 'it is boring for one' we find ourselves—as Dasein—somehow left entirely in the lurch, not only not occupied with this or that being, not only left standing by ourselves in this or that respect, but as a whole. Dasein is now merely suspended among beings and their telling refusal of themselves as a whole. The emptiness is not a hole between things that are filled, but concerns beings as a whole and yet is *not* the *Nothing*.

b) Being held in limbo as being impelled toward what originally makes Dasein possible as such. The structural unity of being left empty and being held in limbo as a unity of the expanse of beings' telling refusal of themselves as a whole, and of the singular extremity of what makes Dasein possible.

And yet, this 'it is boring for one'—from whatever depths it may arise—does not have the character of despair. This being left empty as being delivered over to beings' telling refusal as a whole does not singularly dominate Dasein, it alone does not constitute boredom, but in itself it is *associated with* something else, as we know formally: with a *being held in limbo,* together with which it first constitutes boredom. Without an essential transformation of itself, in which it leaps over into another attunement, this profound boredom never leads to despair.

It is now a matter of seeing how, in boredom, being left empty is associated with this other structural moment. Yet once again we may not simply presuppose this association on the basis of what has gone before. It is rather a matter of seeing this association of being left empty and being held in limbo anew and from out of the essence of this boredom itself. Therefore—almost as though we knew nothing at all of the second structural moment—we must ask: To what extent is the specific being left empty of this third form of boredom in itself associated in general with something else? Boredom and its being left empty here consist in being delivered over to beings' telling refusal of themselves as a whole. What lies in the fact that there is a telling refusal on the part of beings as a whole with respect to the possibilities of doing and acting for a Da-sein in their midst? All telling *refusal* [Ver*sagen*] is in itself a *telling* [Sagen], i.e., a making manifest. What do beings in this telling refusal of themselves as a whole tell us in such refusal? What do they tell us in refusing to tell? It is a telling refusal of that which somehow could and was to be granted to Dasein. And what is that? The very *possibilities* of its doing and acting. The telling refusal tells of these possibilities of Dasein. This telling refusal does not speak about them, does not lead directly to dealings with them, but in its telling refusal it *points to them* and makes them known in refusing them. Accordingly this telling refusal on the part of beings as a whole merely indicates indeterminately the possibilities of Dasein, of its doing and acting, it merely tells of them indirectly and in general. This indeed corresponds to that which is indeterminate and which moves us whenever we know that it is boring for one. Beings as a whole have become indifferent. Yet not only that, but simultaneously something else shows itself: there occurs the dawning of the possibilities that Dasein could have, but which are left unexploited precisely in this 'it is boring for one', and as unexploited leave us in the lurch. In any case, we see that in telling refusal there lies a reference to something else. This reference is the *telling announcement* [Ansagen] *of possibilities left unexploited*. If the emptiness of this third form of boredom consists in this telling refusal on the part of beings as a whole and if, correspondingly, being left empty consists in being delivered over to this, then being left empty nonetheless has in itself a structured relation to something else on account of the reference contained in such telling refusal. In accordance with what has gone before, we may here presume that this *telling, this pointing to the possibilities left unexploited* which lies in such a refusal itself, is ultimately the *being held in limbo* that belongs to such being left empty.

Yet what does the *telling announcement* of unexploited possibilities of Dasein which is contained in this telling refusal have to do with being held in limbo? Above all, however, let us recall that while interpreting the *two* previously discussed forms of boredom we in each case discovered a specific *time-relatedness* in the structural moment of being held in limbo; not only that, but precisely the moment of being held in limbo in each case opened up a perspective upon the time-like essence of boredom. In the first form, it was being held up by the dragging of time, in the second, being set in place by standing time. And here in the third form? Even though the telling announcement of refused possibilities has to do with the specific being held in limbo of this third form, there is nothing to be found here of time. Just as in general this third form of boredom has nothing of an explicit time-relatedness in itself—neither a dragging of time nor the spending of a determinate time that we leave ourselves. One is rather almost tempted to say that in this 'it is boring for one' one feels timeless, one feels removed from the flow of time.

It indeed seems like this, and it would be wrong to cover over somehow this aspect of remoteness from time in this boredom, or rashly to misinterpret it for the sake of a particular theory. Yet we must certainly recall what has gone before, and only if we do so will the meaning of our previous discussions fully take effect.

We recall that each time we attempted to penetrate into the time-structure of boredom, we were forced to recognize the fact that we cannot get by with the ordinary conception of time as a flowing away of now-points. At the same time, however, we saw that the closer we come to the essence of boredom, the more obtrusive its rootedness in time becomes, which must reinforce us in the conviction that boredom can only be comprehended in terms of originary temporality. Now that we are attempting to work our way forward into the essential depths of boredom, there is nothing at all to be seen of time—just as though we were blinded by the nearness of the essence of boredom. It is indeed so, and not merely here in this particular attunement of boredom. In all interpretation of what is essential in every field and area of Dasein, there comes the point at which all knowledge and in particular all learned wisdom is of no further assistance. No matter how avidly we scrape together what people before us have said, it is of no avail if we cannot summon the energy for simply seeing what is essential—precisely at the point where it seems as if there is nothing more to see or to grasp. And so it is now. On the one side, we have a certain insight into the character of profound boredom, yet nothing of time or the time-structure of this boredom. On the other side, we have some knowledge of the temporal essence of boredom as such and thus an expectation that the time-character of precisely this profound boredom will leap out and confront us in a major way.

Given this state of affairs, there remains only one option: to continue along its own lines the interpretation we have begun, without regard to the initially concealed temporal essence of this—and precisely this—third form of boredom, instead of giving up our interpretation and forcibly dragging in the time-structure externally corresponding to those forms of boredom discussed earlier.

We grasped being left empty in this third form as being delivered over to beings' telling refusal of themselves as a whole. This telling refusal is in itself—not by chance, but corresponding to its essence as telling refusal—a telling announcement of the unexploited possibilities of Dasein, which finds itself there in such being delivered over in the midst of beings. In such telling announcement of refused possibilities there lies something like an indication of something else, of the possibilities as such, of the unexploited possibilities *as* possibilities of Dasein. This telling announcement which points toward . . . thus goes together with such telling refusal. It is now a matter of determining this more closely. For only in this way will we bring to light the specific being held in limbo of the third form, and indeed in its relation to being left empty. Now if this telling announcement which points toward the possibilities of Dasein goes together with such telling refusal, then the specific character of this telling announcement, and thus of the being held in limbo which we are seeking, will also be determined by the specific character of the telling refusal of beings as a whole. Wherein does what is peculiar to this telling refusal consist?

It is boring for one. It is not *this* or *that* being that we are bored by. It is not we who, on the occasion of this particular situation, are *ourselves* bored— rather: *it* is boring *for one*. It is not this or that being within easy reach in this particular situation which tellingly refuses itself, but rather all those beings which precisely envelop us in the situation recede into an indifference.

Yet not only all beings in whatever specific situation we happen to be in, wherever this 'it is boring for one' arises, but rather the 'it is boring for one' itself explodes the situation and places us in the *full expanse* of whatever is in each case manifest *as a whole* to this specific Dasein as such, in each case has been manifest, and in each case could be. There is a telling refusal on the part of beings as a whole, and this in turn not merely in one particular respect, in our looking retrospectively at something particular, or in the prospect of something particular that we wish to undertake with these beings. Rather these beings refuse themselves as a whole in the said *expanse* in every *respect,* altogether in *prospect* and in *retrospect.* In this fashion beings become indifferent as a whole.

For whom then? Not for me as me, not for me with these particular prospective intentions and so on. For the nameless and undetermined I, then? No, but presumably for the self whose name, status and the like have become irrelevant, and which is itself drawn into indifference. Yet the self of Dasein that is becoming irrelevant in all this does not thereby lose its determinacy, but rather the reverse, for this peculiar impoverishment which sets in with respect to ourselves in this 'it is boring for one' first *brings* the *self* in all its nakedness *to itself* as the self that *is there* and has taken over the being-there of its Da-sein. For what purpose? *To be that Da-sein.* Beings as a whole refuse themselves tellingly, not to me as me, but to the Dasein in me whenever I know that 'it is boring for one'.

Dasein as such, i.e., whatever belongs to its potentiality for being as such, whatever concerns the possibility as such of Dasein, is affected by the telling refusal of beings as a whole. What concerns a possibility as such, however, is whatever *makes it possible,* that which lends it possi*bility* as this very thing which is possible. Whatever is utmost and primary in making possible all possibilities of Dasein as possibilities, whatever it is that sustains Dasein's potentiality for being, its possibilities, is affected by this telling refusal of beings as a whole. This means, however, that those beings refusing themselves as a whole do not make a telling announcement concerning arbitrary possibilities of myself, they do not report on them, rather this telling announcement in such telling refusal is a *calling* [Anrufen], is that which properly makes possible the Dasein in me. This calling of possibilities as such, which goes together with the telling refusal, is not some indeterminate pointing to arbitrary, changing possibilities of Dasein, but an utterly unambiguous pointing to *whatever it is* that makes possible, sustains, and guides all essential possibilities of Dasein, that for which we apparently have no content, so that we cannot say what it is in the way that we point out things present at hand and determine them as this or that. This strange lack of content to whatever properly makes Dasein possible should not disturb us, or rather we may not eliminate what is disturbing about the lack of content belonging to this 'it is boring for one', if we are at all in a position to let this attunement 'it is boring for one' oscillate in us over the entire expanse of its oscillation. The telling announcement that points toward that which properly makes Dasein possible in its possibility *impels us toward the singular extremity* [Spitze] *of whatever originarily makes possible.* It is boring for one. Being held in limbo is rendered more extreme in a singular manner in the direction of whatever originarily makes Dasein possible in the midst of those beings thus manifest as a whole, and this corresponds to the full expanse of beings in their telling refusal of themselves as a whole, those beings in whose midst we find ourselves disposed. It is boring for one. To such coming to be left in the lurch by beings' telling refusal of themselves as a whole there simultaneously belongs our being impelled toward this utmost extremity that properly makes possible Dasein as such. We have thereby determined the *specific being held in limbo of the third form: being impelled toward the originary making-possible of Dasein as such.*

Both, this complete *expanse* of beings in their telling refusal as a whole, and the singular *extremity* of whatever makes Dasein as such possible—both at the same time in their own unity become manifest as what is at work in Dasein whenever it must tell itself: It is boring for one. Expanding into the enveloping limit of beings as a whole in the manner of intensifying the extremity of Dasein in the direction of what is originarily singular in whatever makes Dasein itself possible—this is the being bored, the boredom that we mean when we say that it is boring for one. This *leaving empty that takes us into an expanse* together with a *holding us in limbo that intensifies extremity* is the originary manner in which the attunement that we call boredom attunes us.

§32. The temporal character of profound boredom.

We have now elaborated both structural moments of the third form of boredom and made them visible in their structural unity. We were able to accomplish this without reference to time. Neither time as it drags nor the standing time we leave ourselves in being bored plays any role here. Above all, it is quite evident in this 'it is boring for one' that the clock does not play any part. Looking at the clock here loses all meaning. Yet even taking time or having no time are without any significance here. And yet, however far removed we remain in this boredom from using the clock at all, it is also a matter of indifference whether precisely now when it is boring for one we have time or have no time. However unconcerned we are about time in whatever way—we are just as close to it, and in this 'it is boring for one' we move just as deeply within the essence of time. For reasons that will shortly come to light, we must restrict ourselves for now merely to indicating what is time-like in this third form of boredom. Certainly it is necessary here that we direct all our powers of concentration toward the whole phenomenon, in order to catch sight of the temporal character of this profound form of boredom.

a) Being entranced by the single threefold horizon of time as the temporal character of being left empty.

There is a telling refusal on the part of beings as a whole. They recede into an indifference. Everything is worth equally much and equally little. Beings withdraw from us, yet remain as the beings that they are. All beings withdraw from us without exception in every respect [Hinsicht], everything we look at and the way in which we look at it; everything in retrospect [Rücksicht], all beings that we look back upon as having been and having become and as past, and the way we look back at them; all beings in every prospect [Absicht], everything we look at prospectively as futural, and the way we have thus regarded them prospectively. Everything—in every respect, in retrospect and prospect, beings simultaneously withdraw. The *three perspectives* [Sichten] of respect, retrospect, and prospect do not belong to mere perception, nor even to theoretical or some other contemplative apprehending, but are the perspectives of all *doing and activity* of Dasein. This simultaneous totality of perspective in which Dasein constantly moves—even if one perspective is obscured or clouded, even if another is one-sidedly favoured—the simultaneity of these three perspectives proceeds to distribute itself into *present, having-been,* and *future.* These three perspectives are not lined up alongside one another, but originarily simply united in the horizon of time as such. Originarily, there is the *single* and *unitary universal horizon of time.* There is a telling refusal of all beings simultaneously in 'what' and 'how' they are: *as a whole,* as we put it. This now means: *in one originarily unifying horizon of time.* This 'as a whole' is evidently possible only insofar as beings are enveloped by the single yet simultaneously threefold horizon of time. This horizon of the whole of time which is fully disclosed in this way must be at work if it is to be possible for there to be a telling refusal of beings *as a whole.*

Yet from this it merely becomes clear that time ultimately participates in making possible the manifestness of beings as a whole, but not in the telling refusal of beings as a whole. In such a way time in the end participates everywhere that beings as a whole manifest themselves—which after all does not necessarily have to happen by way of a telling refusal. We gain nothing from this indication concerning the horizon of time. In other words: an essential relatedness of this third form of boredom to time is by no means manifest via this route. At most we have a long since familiar piece of self-evidence in accordance with which, whenever we wish to unite all beings, past, present, and future in one, we require precisely the horizon of time in all three directions.

Never yet, however, has the case been heard of in philosophy where a bland triviality did not conceal behind it the abyssal difficulty of the problem. In the present instance there is not merely *one* problem, but an entire dimension of such problems.

Let us concede for a moment—in as rough and approximate a fashion as we now understand it—that the full horizon of time is the condition of possibility for the manifestness of beings as a whole, quite irrespective of how beings as a whole behave and announce themselves here, whether they are given in telling refusal or in some other way. What does it mean here to say that time is a horizon? One can relatively easily indicate such a thing, and yet it is hard to say what horizon means here, or how this—namely functioning as a horizon—is possible in terms of the essence of time.

Yet even if these questions are posed and worked out in a legitimate manner—which is by no means the case—even then we are not finished with our problem but only at the very beginning. For this does not yet decide whether the temporal horizon participates only in the manifestness of beings as a whole, or also in the fact that there can be a telling refusal of beings as a whole. If the latter is the case, then this means that the temporal horizon is in each case playing a role in every manifestation of beings as a whole, not only in general, but precisely with respect to each specific kind. Yet this then entails that the temporal horizon can play a role in manifold ways which are still entirely unfamiliar to us, and that we do not have the slightest intimation of the abysses of the essence of time.

How do things stand concerning this *horizon of time,* which as it were surrounds beings as a whole? Past, present, future—are they like the arrangement of scenery on a stage, the scenery that stands around beings and thus forms the space in which beings can play their roles? Horizon—is a horizon like the wall of some vessel whose walls have nothing to do with the contents, cannot and do not want to do anything to the contents other than embrace and enclose them? How do things stand concerning this horizon of time? *How does time come to have a horizon?* Does it run up against it, as against a shell that has been placed over it, or does the horizon belong to time itself? Yet what is this thing for, then, that delimits (ὁρίζειν) time itself? How and for what does time give itself and form such a limit for itself? And if the horizon is not fixed, to what is it held in its changing? These are central questions, yet—as we can easily see—ones that concern the essence of time in general, which essence we cannot and do not wish to discuss now off the cuff. Nonetheless, however, we ought now to provide some indication concerning the extent to which the telling refusal of beings as a whole and all that belongs to them in the essence of the third kind of boredom, *the extent to which* the *being left empty* and *being held in limbo* of this form of boredom are bound up with *time.* We cannot escape this task; we must show that and how this specific being left empty as such and thereby the being held in limbo pertaining to it are possible in terms of the essence of time and it alone.

It is boring for one. This entails being left empty and being delivered over to beings' telling refusal of themselves as a whole. In such an attunement, Dasein is in no way able to obtain anything from beings as a whole. Beings as a whole withdraw, yet not at all in such a way that Dasein is left alone. Beings as a whole withdraw, this means: Dasein is indeed there in the midst of beings as a whole, has them around, above, and within itself, yet cannot give way to this withdrawal. It cannot—the attunement attunes in such a way that the Dasein which is thus attuned can no longer bring itself to expect anything from beings as a whole in any respect, because there is not even anything enticing about beings any more. They withdraw as a whole. Yet this *withdrawal* [Entzug] of beings which announces itself in them is possible only if Dasein as such can no longer go along with them, only if it is entranced as Da-sein, and indeed as a whole. Precisely this temporal horizon, therefore, which holds beings as a whole open and makes them accessible in general as such, must simultaneously bind Dasein to itself and entrance it. It is boring for one. This attunement in which Dasein is everywhere and yet may be nowhere has its own peculiar feature of entrancement. *What entrances* is nothing other than the *temporal horizon*. Time entrances [*bannt*] Dasein, not as the time which has remained standing as distinct from flowing, but rather the *time beyond such flowing and its standing,* the time which in each case *Dasein itself as a whole* is. This whole time entrances as a horizon. Entranced by time, Dasein cannot find its way to those beings that *announce* themselves *in the telling refusal of themselves* as a whole precisely within this horizon of entrancing time.

It is boring for one. Entranced, and yet accustomed to being acquainted and concerned only with beings and indeed with this or that being in each case, Dasein finds nothing, in the telling refusal of these beings as a whole, which could "explain" this entrancement to it. It is from here that there stirs what is enigmatic and concealed in the power that envelops us in this 'it is boring for one'. For in this attunement, after all, we do not usually philosophize about boredom or in boredom, rather—it is boring for one. Instead, we leave this concealed entrancement its power.

It thus becomes apparent that *being left empty* is possible only as our *being entranced by the temporal horizon as such,* in which entrancement of Dasein beings can withdraw from Dasein and refuse themselves to Dasein. For the Dasein that is entranced, the emptiness of this telling refusal as a whole arises on the side of beings. This entrancement of Dasein must—and this is the peculiar sense of this attunement—precisely leave such emptiness its undiminished leeway and space in which to play. What is entrancing in this attunement is not the determinate time-point at which the specific boredom arises; for this determinate 'now' sinks at a stroke; the sign of this is that we do not worry at all about the clock and suchlike. Nor is that which entrances, however, a more stretched 'now', such as the span of time during which this boredom persists. This boredom does not need such things at all, it can take hold of us in an instant like a flash of lightning, and yet precisely in this instant the whole expanse of the entire time of Dasein is there and not at all specifically articulated or delimited according to past and future. Neither merely the present nor merely the past nor merely the future, nor indeed all these reckoned together—but rather their *unarticulated unity* in the simplicity of this unity of their horizon all at once.

b) Being impelled through the entrancement of time toward the moment of vision as the temporal character of being held in limbo. The temporal unity of being left empty and being held in limbo.

It is boring for one. What we thus—and indeed not by accident—explicitly attempt to clarify with great effort and elaborateness is there in the attunement in a straightforward simplicity, yet in such a way that if this boredom were to arise and we were to let ourselves be attuned through and through by it, we could give it a more animated oscillation if we really understood it. Yet from what has been said we do not yet understand it, not yet entirely—because thus far we have brought only the temporal nature of one moment, that of being left empty, closer to us. We know, however, that in this telling refusal of beings as a whole there lies our being impelled toward the extremity of that which makes Dasein possible as such.

Time is that which, in this boredom, strikes Dasein into time's entrancement. Through such entrancement it gives beings as a whole the possibility of a telling refusal of themselves to the Dasein that is entranced, i.e., the possibility of holding before Dasein as it were, as unexploited, the possibilities of its doing and acting in the midst of these beings and with reference to them. This entrancing power of time is thus that which is properly telling in refusal. This means however at the same time, according to what we said earlier, it is that which also calls and tells of what is properly refused, i.e., what is uncircumventable if Dasein, in keeping with its possibilities, is to be what it can be and as it can be. What entrances in telling refusal must at the same time be that which gives [something] to be free in its telling announcing and which fundamentally makes possible the possibility of Dasein. What entrances at the same time disposes over that which properly makes possible, indeed this *entrancing time* is itself this *extremity* that essentially makes Dasein possible. The time that thus entrances Dasein, and announces itself as thus entrancing in boredom, simultaneously announces and tells of itself as that which properly makes possible. Yet whatever that which entrances as such, namely time, announces and tells of as something in fact refused; what it precisely holds before us as something that has apparently vanished; what it gives to be known and properly makes possible as *something possible* and only as this, as something that *can be given to be free;* what it *gives to be free* in its telling announcing—is nothing less than the *freedom of Dasein* as such. For this freedom of Dasein only is in Dasein's *freeing itself.* The self-liberation of Dasein, however, only happens in each case if Dasein *resolutely discloses* [sich entschließt] itself *to itself,* i.e., discloses itself [*sich erschließt*] for itself as Da-sein. To the extent, however, that Dasein finds itself disposed in the midst of beings, as in each case this Dasein with this its time in the unity of its threefold perspective, Dasein can resolutely disclose itself only if it brings these beings together into an extremity, only if it resolutely discloses itself for action here and now in this essential respect and in this chosen and essential possibility of its self. This *resolute self-disclosure* of Dasein to itself, however, namely in each case to be in the midst of beings what it is given to be in its determinateness—this resolute self-disclosure is the *moment of vision* [Augenblick]. Why? Dasein is not something present at hand alongside other things, but is set in the midst of beings through the manifestness of the full temporal horizon. As Dasein it always already maintains itself in this three-fold perspective. As that which rests in time it only is what it can be if in each case at its time—and that simultaneously means in each case here and now, with reference to these beings that are precisely thus manifest—it is *there* [da], that is, opens itself up [*sich aufschließt*] in its manifestness, that is, resolutely discloses itself. Only in the resolute self-disclosure of Dasein to itself, in the moment of vision, does it make use of that which properly makes it possible, namely time as the moment of vision itself. The moment of vision is nothing other than the *look of resolute disclosedness* [Blick der Entschlossenheit] in which the full situation of an action opens itself and keeps itself open. What time as entrancing accordingly keeps to itself, and in keeping it to itself simultaneously announces and tells of as something that can be given to be free, giving it to be known as possibility, is something of that time itself; it is that which makes possible, which that time itself and it alone can be: the moment of vision. *Dasein's being impelled into the extremity of that which properly makes possible* is a being impelled *through entrancing time into that time itself,* into its proper essence, i.e., *toward the moment of vision* as the fundamental possibility of Dasein's existence proper.

It is boring for one. In this, the time that entrances as a whole announces and tells of itself as that which is to be ruptured and can be ruptured solely in the *moment of vision* in which time itself, as that which properly makes Dasein possible in its actions, is at work. Thus we see, albeit only roughly, that on the basis of this entrancement of the temporal horizon as such and of the moment of vision that is also announced in this telling refusal, precisely this *unity* of *being left empty* and *being held in limbo* in the third form of boredom is *determined* through and through by the *essence of time*.

What we here designate as 'moment of vision' is what was really comprehended for the first time in philosophy by Kierkegaard—a comprehending with which the *possibility* of a completely new epoch of philosophy has begun for the first time since antiquity. I say this is a possibility; for today when Kierkegaard has become fashionable, for whatever reasons, we have reached the stage where the literature about Kierkegaard, and everything connected with it, has ensured in all kinds of ways that this decisive point of Kierkegaard's philosophy has not been comprehended.

We have attempted to explicate the *temporal character of the third form of boredom*. We can conclude from all that has been said hitherto that here we encounter a limit to this investigation, and that therefore the investigation necessarily has a peculiar difficulty compared to all our earlier ones. There are two reasons for this difficulty. The first lies in the essence of this boredom itself, insofar as this boredom conceals its temporal character in a distinct sense, or in any case conceals it to all appearances; secondly, the reason for the difficulty in carrying out the demonstration we have set ourselves lies in the way in which we pose our question and in the nature of our path, which leads via boredom to time, without our having in advance adequately assured ourselves of the essence of time; in other words, the path leads straight into the dark, without our having a light that could illuminate the path before us. Despite this we must, in following the inner necessity of our approach, attempt to follow this path to the point where we reach a limit.

We attempted to explicate the character of time along the guiding thread of the structural moments already familiar to us with reference to this 'it is boring for one'. The outcome here was that being left empty is related to the telling refusal of beings as a whole. Beings can only refuse themselves as a whole if they are somehow manifest as such, i.e., as a whole. The possibility of the manifestness of beings as a whole lies in the temporal horizon itself opening itself in accordance with all its dimensions. Yet the temporal horizon is not simply some neutral container that envelops these beings as a whole, rather it itself participates in the telling refusal of beings by the fact that as such, namely as the time of Dasein, as its whole time, it entrances Dasein, entrances it namely insofar as Dasein is attuned through and through by this boredom, this 'it is boring for one'. The temporal horizon entrances Dasein so that it can no longer pursue those beings in whose midst it finds itself disposed at all times, so that it neither sees nor seeks any further possibility at all of concretely reflecting about itself within these beings in whose midst it is set in place. It is not beings that properly refuse, but time, which itself makes possible the manifestness of these beings as a whole. What properly refuses is simultaneously that which announces merely itself in turn, as that which gives

Dasein the possibility of making itself concretely possible as this Dasein in each case within and in the midst of beings as a whole. The temporal entrancement that becomes manifest in this 'it is boring for one' can be ruptured only through time. Only if the temporal entrancement is ruptured do beings as a whole no longer refuse themselves, i.e., only then do they give up their own possibilities, make themselves graspable for each specific Dasein and give this Dasein itself the possibility of existing in the midst of beings in one particular respect, in one particular possibility in each case. The temporal entrancement can be ruptured only through time itself, through that which is of the proper essence of time and which, following Kierkegaard, we call the moment of vision. The moment of vision ruptures the entrancement of time, and is able to rupture it, insofar as it is a specific possibility of time itself. It is not some now-point that we simply ascertain, but is the look of Dasein in the three perspectival directions we are already acquainted with, namely present, future, and past. The moment of vision is a look of a unique kind, which we call the look of resolute disclosedness for action in the specific situation in which Dasein finds itself disposed in each case.

I have attempted to determine the essence of the moment of vision and its rootedness in the essence of temporality, in the essence of Dasein itself, in *Being and Time*, §65. Certainly you cannot understand these paragraphs in isolation, without appropriating the whole work in its inner construction. I refer to it, however, as an external aid for dealing with this problem, which is not solved there but merely grasped in its nucleus as it were.

It is boring for one. *Entranced in the expanse of the temporal horizon* and yet thereby *impelled into the extremity of the moment of vision* as that which properly makes possible, that which can announce itself as such only if it imposes itself compellingly as something possible—this is what occurs in such boredom. It happens in accordance with its essence neither in such a way that we are merely blindly abandoned to this entrancement, nor such that we can grasp the moment of vision, but in such a way that we are told of *both*—simultaneously in telling refusal and telling announcement. Both—which are not two, but one—this is *the one* unitary phenomenon in which we, or rather the Dasein in us, oscillates out into the expanse of the temporal horizon of its temporality and thus is able only to oscillate into the moment of vision pertaining to essential action. This oscillating in between such expanse and such extremity is our being attuned, this boredom as attunement. The expanse of the entrancing temporal horizon is neither recognized as such, nor specifically grasped at all, yet nonetheless it manifests itself in this entrancement that remains indecipherable. The extremity of the moment of vision is neither chosen as such, nor reflected upon and known. It manifests itself to us as that which properly makes possible, that which is thereby intimated as such only in being entranced in the direction of the temporal horizon and from there, intimated as what *could* and ought to be given to be free in Dasein's proper essence as that which makes it most intrinsically possible, yet now in the entrancement of Dasein is not thus given.

To this extent, and only to this extent, the temporal character of this third form of boredom may be illuminated on the path on which we have set out. This means that a limit to our path does now indeed become manifest here; our path becomes more and more difficult because our view ahead is more obscure. Here 'temporal character' does not simply mean that boredom is among other things also determined by time, but means that the *full structure of this boredom is made possible through time itself;* time itself—which has now become more enigmatic for us when we think of the horizon of time, its expanse, its horizonal function—among other things as entrancement—and finally when we think of the way in which this horizon is connected to what we call moment of vision.

§33. The essential meaning of the word 'boredom' or 'Langeweile': *the lengthening of the while in profound boredom as the expansion of the temporal horizon and the vanishing of the extremity of a moment of vision.*

And yet—precisely now, starting from our interpretation of this third form of boredom, we can *give the word boredom, 'Langeweile', a more essential meaning.* In boredom, *Langeweile,* the *while* [Weile] becomes *long* [lang]. Which while? Any short while? No, but rather that while whilst Dasein is as such, the while that measures out that tarrying awhile [*Verweilen*] which is allotted to Dasein as such, i.e., the while whilst it is to be in the midst of these beings, in confrontation with them and thus with itself. It is this whole while—and yet a short while; and so every Dasein in turn is a short while. This while of Dasein, i.e., its own time, is at first and for the most part concealed from Dasein, as what it simply uses up as it were, or else makes itself aware of in an inappropriate manner when it reckons with this while, calculates it in advance for itself, just as though Dasein itself were a business. In boredom, and indeed especially in this form when 'one is bored', this while of Dasein becomes long. This does not mean that the short time of Dasein appears longer. Human Dasein can become essential in terms of the brevity of objective time, and it can remain inessential even if it reaches seventy years old or more. With this time what is at issue is not the time of the clock or chronology, but the *lengthening* or *shortening* of *time proper.* For what is at issue is fundamentally not the quantitative measure of the shortness or length of endurance in which a Dasein is. That the while becomes long means that the horizon of whiling—which at first and for the most part shows itself to us, if at all, as that of a present, and even then more as what is now and today—*expands itself into the entire expanse of the temporality of Dasein.* This *lengthening of the while* manifests the while of Dasein in its indeterminacy that is never absolutely determinable. This indeterminacy takes Dasein captive, yet in such a way that in the whole expansive and expanded expanse it can grasp nothing except the mere fact that it remains *entranced* by and toward this expanse. The lengthening of the while is the *expansion of the temporal horizon,* whose expansion does not bring Dasein liberation or unburden it, but precisely the converse in *oppressing* it with its expanse. In this expanse of time it oppresses Dasein and thus includes in itself a peculiar indication of its *shortness.*

The lengthening is a *vanishing of the shortness of the while.* Yet just as with length, we are not thinking shortness as quantitatively short duration, rather the *vanishing* of shortness is the vanishing of the sharpness and *extremity of a moment of vision pertaining to action and existence that is in each case determinate.* This vanishing of this shortness, of the extreme nature of a moment of vision, in the lengthening of the while precisely does not make the moment of vision vanish, however; rather only the possibility vanishes here, whereby the possibility of whatever is possible is precisely intensified. In vanishing, the *moment of vision* still presses itself upon us as *that which is properly and tellingly refused in time's entrancing,* as the properly authentic possibility of that which makes possible the existence of Dasein. We thereby see how in boredom this expanse and shortness, both rooted in time, spring in turn in their peculiar connectedness from the specific way in which the temporality of Dasein is, or rather temporalizes itself.

§34. Summary 'definition' of profound boredom as a more incisive directive for interpreting boredom and as preparation for the question concerning a particular profound boredom in our contemporary Dasein.

Thus we may say, in summarizing our whole analysis at the stage we have now arrived at: *Boredom is the entrancement of the temporal horizon, an entrancement which lets the moment of vision belonging to temporality vanish. In thus letting it vanish, boredom impels entranced Dasein into the moment of vision as the properly authentic possibility of its existence, an existence only possible in the midst of beings as a whole, and within the horizon of entrancement, their telling refusal of themselves as a whole.*

This intrinsic structure of the 'it is boring for one' can thus be formally expressed in a definition. Yet even this definition, which has arisen from a more penetrating interpretation, does not tell us much if it is taken as an assertion in which something is supposed to be established, instead of as a *more incisive directive for interpretation,* i.e., one more laden with questions, namely for an interpretation which unexpectedly has left itself behind and brought the Dasein it has interpreted to the verge of the attunement to be interpreted, yet has never directly transposed it into this attunement itself. What we have always explicated one-sidedly in this interpretation—the two structural moments and their structural articulation—now proves not to be false, but presumably to be over-emphasised. It proves to be something that we will correctly understand only if we comprehend boredom in terms of the *unity of its essence,* if we comprehend that which is structurally linked in terms of the *linkage belonging to this structural link.* We may not piece together or produce the attunement out of what has been said, but on the contrary must, in being attuned, create the full transparency for our being attuned, so that when we are attuned in this way, such transparency will radiate out of the unity of the attunement in its structure while remaining within it.

Yet even if we were to admit this definition of boredom as a definition in the usual sense, it would still have to be said that it was read off too one-sidedly from the third form of boredom, and thus is by no means universal enough to fit all forms, such as the two discussed initially. This is how it seems. We must concede that we have borrowed this definition from the third form of boredom. Yet at the same time we must recall that the third form of boredom is not an arbitrary form of boredom, but with respect to the first and second form is the more profound, i.e., at the same time the more essential. Only where we succeed in grasping the *essentiality* of something do we come close to its essence, but never if we concern ourselves in the first place with finding the most universal possible essence that fits all forms, i.e., the emptiest, as the sole and proper essence. If *philosophy* is *knowledge of the essence*—and this is what it is in the correctly understood sense—then its possibility is grounded in the first instance, and decisively where everything is concerned, in the essentiality of its questioning and in the power of its questioning to be essential. This is not a matter of method, but one of engagement [*Einsatz*] and of the *possibility of engagement pertaining to a philosophizing existence.* The dimension of decidability in these questions, whether they are essential or not, lies in philosophizing itself. This means that we can neither decide about the essentiality of questioning and thus about the outlook and scope of essential knowledge of the essence in some prior methodological recommendation, nor in some belated philosophy about philosophy, but only in philosophizing itself. Commensurate with the innermost relatedness of all essential action as a whole—be it art, philosophy or religion—what is true for the poet is true of philosophy: the poet should create, not talk.

Thus here once again we have already—as everywhere—talked too much *about* philosophy. We are never sparing enough with such talk about philosophy, never active enough *in* philosophizing. Only if we experience its essence from out of philosophizing itself will we become intimate with the essence of philosophy. Yet we will not experience this by reading or reviewing philosophical literature, but only by making the effort to philosophize. This must bring us to the point where we can understand a philosopher better than he understood himself. This does not mean, however, that we should rebuke him and point out to him which precursors he is dependent upon, but that we are in a position to concede him more than he himself was in possession of. If someone does not summon up the inner freedom as a philosopher to be such a person to whose essence it necessarily belongs to be better understood than he understands himself—then philosophy has passed that person by, in spite of all philosophical erudition. Philosophy is only there to be overcome. Yet it can only be overcome if it stands in the first place, and can be overcome all the more essentially the more profound the resistance is that it summons up through its being there [Dasein]. Overcoming, however, does not occur through refutation in the sense of demonstrating mistakes and things that are incorrect. Whether we regain this intrinsic freedom of philosophical confrontation and discussion, to what extent it can ever be realized at all in any given era: this no one can say objectively. Yet that does not release us from the effort of comprehending this and drawing attention to it in the correct way, i.e., always indirectly.

Yet why are we pointing precisely now to such a thing, i.e., to the problem of the essentiality of philosophical questioning, at this stage where we have apparently more or less reached a conclusion in our interpretation of the essence of boredom? We do so in order to prevent it appearing as though we had now—absolutely, as it were—illuminated boredom in itself; and in order at the same time to indicate in a positive manner and in advance that the *characterization of the essentiality of the third form of boredom itself depends upon a hitherto inexplicit philosophical engagement* that we may not evade. For this reason we may not take this interpretation to be a piece of knowledge that we now have at our disposal, with whose aid we can perhaps more or less skilfully answer the question of what boredom is, but must take it merely as preparation for the fact that the analysis of this attunement gives us the readiness to ask after a *particular* boredom *of our* Dasein. We are not to initiate any speculation about boredom, but must guide our interpretation of boredom hitherto into a readiness to see a profound boredom of our Dasein, or not to oppose it, insofar as it is. It was therefore necessary to recall this character of philosophizing which we mentioned in our introductory lectures in another respect.

The fact that we orient our definition of the essence of boredom toward its essential form is not a narrowing of this definition, but the converse—it creates the very possibility of comprehending the genuine context for these transformations of boredom, for a transformation that is not some arbitrary, free-floating changing of forms, but bound to the occurrence of Dasein in which boredom in each case arises in such and such a way and thereby clings to the surface or finds its way back into the depths. Thus we cannot, for instance, simply apply the acquired definition to the first or second form, as though these were two special cases of the third as the universal instance. Accordingly, if such an illegitimate attempt to apply the third form to the first and second should fail, we may not conclude from this either that the definition of the third form is therefore wrong. Yet even if we avoid such an external coupling of the three forms discussed, it is still difficult enough to bring the definition we have attained of the third form into any sort of context at all.

However the main obstacle which prevents our being able to see at first the original and essential context of the three forms is a *prejudice,* and indeed one that is implied and constantly reinforced by our own discussions of the three forms hitherto. It is a matter of identifying this prejudice.

In our interpretation of boredom we set out from a superficial boredom, as we put it, from becoming bored by something. From this boredom we allowed ourselves to be drawn back to more and more profound forms. Becoming more profound was characterized according to various moments. All this made it seem as though the more profound boredom developed factically in this way— as though the first were the cause of the second and as though the second passed into the third, as though ultimately the third form arose from the first. Yet precisely this is not the case. So little does the first form of boredom pass over into the third, by passing through the second for instance, that on the contrary the first form precisely holds the others down and keeps them at bay, in particular the third. The characteristic unease of the first form of boredom and the peculiar passing the time that accompanies it is not some mere psychological side-effect of this boredom, but belongs to its essence. This entails that in such becoming bored by something the human being who is bored— without explicitly knowing it—wants to escape from the 'it is boring for one', i.e. (as we now see more clearly), to remove him- or herself from the possibility that the Dasein in him or her will become manifest and begin to oscillate in the third form of boredom as characterized, i.e., in its expanse and in its becoming more extreme. To put it another way: in the first form of boredom there is still a faint reflection, although not recognized as such, of the possibility of profound boredom that is not understood. The first form of boredom as such can indeed never pass over into the third, yet conversely, the first is itself presumably still rooted in the possibility of the third, and comes from the third form of boredom with respect to its possibility in general. The first form is neither the cause, nor the reason or point of departure for the development of boredom into the second and third forms, but vice-versa: the third form is the condition of the possibility of the first and thereby also of the second. *Only because this constant possibility—the 'it is boring for one'—lurks*

*in the ground of Dasein can man be bored or become bored by the things and
people around him.* Only because *every* form of boredom comes to arise *out of
this depth* of Dasein, although we *initially do not know* this depth and *even less
pay attention* to it—only for this reason does it seem as though boredom came
from nowhere at all. For this reason the forms of boredom are themselves
fluid: there are manifold intermediate forms in accordance with the depth from
which the boredom arises, more accurately: according to the depth which man
grants his own Dasein. For this reason the second form of boredom has a
peculiar *intermediate position.* Being bored with . . . can become a becoming
bored by . . . , it can become an 'it is boring for one'. Yet this does not at all
mean that the second form of boredom causes the others as such. If it seems
as though this form passes over into one of the others, then it indeed only
seems so. In truth and fundamentally a corresponding transposition of man's
existence always occurs in advance here—either toward the surface and into
the realm of his busy activities, or into the dimension of Dasein as such, that
of existing proper. We cannot in this context discuss the more precise relationship pertaining to the origin of these three forms, nor does this task belong to
this lecture course.

Hitherto we have dealt with boredom in various forms. We have even dealt
with a profound boredom, with one form thereof, but we have not at all dealt
with what is decisive, *with the boredom that today perhaps determines our Dasein
here and now.* Everything up to now can only be the opening of the tunnel, as
it were, which we must enter in order to see what is occurring in our Dasein
today and in order to comprehend this meaning as the *fundamental meaning
of our Dasein*—not because we are intent upon an anthropology or philosophy
of culture, but as that which opens up the proper questioning of philosophizing
for us. Our next question is thus faced with the task of taking this step from
the provisional elucidation of the essence of boredom to the peculiar kind of
demonstration of the possibility of the fundamental attunement of a profound
boredom in *our* Dasein.

§35. Temporality in a particular way of its temporalizing as that which properly bores us in boredom.

Because, however, the origin of boredom and the original relationship between
the various forms of boredom remain and must remain completely concealed
from our everyday understanding of this attunement, our everyday consciousness is also governed by uncertainty as to what properly bores us, as to what
that which is originarily boring is. At first it seems that what bores us are boring
things and people and suchlike. It would be wrong and at the same time
unfruitful to want to eliminate this strange illusion. In the second form of

boredom, that which bores us manifests itself as time in its standing. It is now no longer the things surrounding us, nor one's own person that bores us. What bores us is time. It is what specifically leaves us empty and holds us in limbo. Certainly it is the time that we have left ourselves, the time which still remains fixed in the form in which we think we know it in the everyday, the time with which we reckon. Yet now in the third form of boredom what leaves us empty in the manner of entrancing us is the time of Dasein as such, and what holds us in limbo and impels us is this time in its possibility as moment of vision, the temporality of Dasein itself with reference to that which is essentially proper to it, and indeed in the sense of the making possible of Dasein in general: *horizon and moment of vision. What bores* us in profound boredom, and thus—in accordance with what we have said earlier—what is solely and properly boring, is *temporality in a particular way of its temporalizing.*

What is boring is neither beings nor things as such—whether individually or in a context—nor human beings as people we find before us and can ascertain, neither objects nor subjects, but *temporality as such.* Yet this temporality does not stand alongside 'objects' and 'subjects', but constitutes the ground of the possibility of the subjectivity of subjects, and indeed in such a way that the *essence of subjects* consists precisely in *having Dasein,* i.e., in always already enveloping beings as a whole in advance. Because things and people are enveloped by temporality and permeated by it, even though it is temporality in itself which properly and singularly bores us, the legitimate illusion can arise that things are boring, and that it is people themselves who are bored.

How this illusion comes about, why it is necessary and legitimate, to what extent things and people can thus occasion and evoke boredom—all this can only be made transparent once we stand within those central questions that are to arise for us as fundamental metaphysical questions by way of a fundamental attunement of boredom.

§36. The ordinary assessment of boredom and its suppression of profound boredom.

How unfamiliar the essence of boredom and its origin remains and must remain to our everyday understanding is attested by the *ordinary assessment of boredom.* Boredom in the ordinary sense is disturbing, unpleasant, and unbearable. For the ordinary understanding all such things are also of little value, they are unworthy and to be condemned. Becoming bored is a sign of shallowness and superficiality. Whoever sets a proper task for his or her life and gives it content does not need to fear boredom and is secure in the face of it.

Yet it is hard to tell which is the greater in this morality—its hypocritical self-assuredness or its banality. However none of this—the fact that ordinary understanding makes such judgements about boredom—is accidental, but has its reasons. One decisive reason for misunderstanding boredom is the *failure to appreciate the essence of attunement in general,* not merely of boredom as a particular attunement, and this in turn goes back to an apparently self-evident and absolute conception of Dasein. Moods are something that awaken pleasure or displeasure in us, something to which we have to react accordingly. Boredom is unpleasant once and for all, a condition to be eliminated.

Here we fail to appreciate two things: [1.] that attunement in itself makes manifest, namely makes manifest Dasein itself in the way that it is and finds itself disposed alongside itself and alongside things; [2.] that it can do this only if it arises from the ground of the essence of Dasein, in a way that is for the most part withdrawn from Dasein's freedom.

Yet if such a thing as boredom is understood in the ordinary sense, then it is precisely the *dominance of this understanding* that *suppresses profound boredom* and itself constantly contributes to keeping boredom where we like to see it, so that one can pounce upon it within the field of the busy activity of Dasein in its superficiality. Here we see that a certain conception of feelings and suchlike is not as harmless as we think, but has a decisive and essential say in their possibility, their scope, and their depth.

Chapter Five

The Question Concerning a Particular Profound Boredom as the
Fundamental Attunement of Our Contemporary Dasein

*§37. Reconsideration of the question concerning a profound
boredom as the fundamental attunement of our Dasein.*

Through this interpretation we have entered into a peculiar kind of knowing.
We cannot ever reproduce the essential contents of this knowing in a formula,
because it does not consist in the kind of accumulated knowledge which a
lecture course on zoology or modern history may have given us over the same
two months. In the sciences our listening takes us a step forward every hour;
each day gives us a further cluster of notes and a few more sheets. Yet *we* have
less each day, each hour we make less progress and have instead increasingly
approached a standstill. Not only that, but we have perhaps worn through the
ground we were standing on to begin with, we have perhaps reached a place
that is groundless, and begun to float, entered an *attunement*. A mere attunement—and after so much effort. Indeed perhaps not even an attunement, but
only the more transparent *possibility* of one, i.e., a receptivity for it, a receptivity that has grown, that has laid down roots in Dasein, so that Dasein can
summon up the possibility of making this attunement possible, of being attuned. Indeed, if we have attained this and precisely this, namely a *more
transparent receptivity for this attunement*—in whatever form—then this is
already enough. It is something that we can never simply count as a result,
something about which I could never, and should never, examine any of you.

We have only a more transparent receptivity for this attunement that we
call boredom, and with this transparency we perhaps have an understanding
of the fact that while it is easy to master boredom by busily passing the time,
and thus perhaps to put on a show of a sound and worthy ability to cope
with and master life, it is difficult *not to be opposed to a profound boredom,
difficult to let oneself be attuned through and through by it, so as to hear
something essential from it.* Yet if we understand this then we will certainly
no longer believe that such a profound boredom could be ascertained or could
be there simply through the fact that we talk about it, or could be there simply
for us to talk about. This profound boredom only becomes *awake* if we do
not counteract it.

Yet this very *demand* which measures up to the essence of the boredom
originally arising in Dasein and results directly from understanding it—this
demand meets with *mistrust* precisely from us today. Not to counteract our

Dasein, when everything is pressing for decision and decision is on everyone's lips? Not to take counteraction when the needs of Dasein are piling up on all sides? Not to counteract—is that not a call for a paralysing lack of courage, for resignation, for a feeling of doom and despair? Is this not to spread darkness and gloom over Dasein, instead of ensuring a bright noonday for Dasein with all the means that can be thought up?

Such mistrust with respect to the demand not to take counteraction easily agrees with the verdict of sound human understanding. Yet the question is whether not taking counteraction means standing at a loss, doing nothing and allowing oneself to be overcome by some attunement or other. It means neither this, nor that, bustling activity, it means neither this passivity nor that activity, but something this side of the two: *Dasein's keeping to itself,* which is a *waiting.* This waiting is not indeterminate, but is *directed out toward an essential questioning of Dasein itself.* We have already asked this question (cf. p. 77ff. above). Yet we did not pose this question to those who run around in public and give themselves credit for their own achievements, those servants of culture who ape their own inventions; we did not ask where these people stand in the course of world history, or how far they have come hitherto and what is to be the outcome in this respect. We did not ask *where* man stands, but *how* things stand concerning man, concerning the Da-sein in man. We posed this question more definitively by asking: *Has man in the end become boring to himself?*

We must now reconsider this question as that question which announces a waiting of Dasein that keeps to itself, i.e., which provides a hold for this keeping to itself. For this is what common understanding and the so-called praxis of life and all programmaticism never understands or can understand, namely that a *question* is able to provide a hold. According to reason, after all, this is achieved only by the *answer.* The answer is a fixed proposition, a dogma, a conviction.

We have now to take up this question again—Has man today in the end become boring to himself?—as the question in which we ready ourselves for a fundamental attunement of our Dasein. *Now, again*—having attempted to clarify the essence of boredom and accordingly now being in a position *to repeat the question more transparently.* More transparently—for we now see more clearly: [1.] on the one hand what the structure and structural moments of boredom, being left empty, and being held in limbo and their original unity are; [2.] that this unity in its origin springs from that temporality in which the essence of boredom oscillates; [3.] various fundamental forms of boredom.

Concerning our reconsideration of the question: Has man in the end become boring to himself?, we now see at once that we cannot ask whether contemporary people become bored by particular things or become more bored than in other epochs. It can neither be a matter of people becoming bored by particular things, circumstances or events, nor of being bored with particular occasions. For here too boredom takes place in a particular passing the time, or more accurately in situations which are taken on more or less explicitly and consciously as a passing the time in order to ward off our possibly being bored. *Our question*—has man today become boring for himself?—*can only mean: Is it ultimately boring for the Dasein in contemporary man as such?* We are asking concerning one profound boredom, concerning *one*—i.e., one *in particular,* i.e., one of *our* Dasein, not just about profound boredom in general or universally. If we asked in this way before, and if it seemed as though in the foregoing interpretation of boredom we had as it were an objective recipe for boredom before us, then this, as is now apparent, was an illusion. We only understand profound boredom as such from out of a particular, i.e., essential boredom, and accordingly all interpretation of its superficial forms takes its lead and derives its illumination from there. Essential knowledge is possible only from out of and in an originary questioning.

§38. The question concerning a particular profound boredom in the direction of a specific being left empty and a specific being held in limbo.

We are questioning concerning a *particular* profound boredom of our Dasein. We are *questioning* concerning it. For this questioning we now have guidelines from the essential structure of profound boredom as indicated above. We are questioning in the direction of the structural moments of being left empty and being held in limbo and their unity, i.e., we are questioning in the direction of the *specific being left empty* of profound boredom, the *specific being held in limbo* of profound boredom, and concerning the *specific ground of their unity.*

a) The essential need as a whole and the absence (telling refusal) of any essential oppressiveness in our contemporary Dasein as being left empty in this particular profound boredom.

We are questioning in these particular directions and are intentionally doing so in an almost schematic way. Profound boredom, its being left empty, means being delivered over to beings' telling refusal of themselves as a whole. It is thus an emptiness as a whole. We ask: Is *our* Dasein attuned through and through by such *emptiness as a whole?* Emptiness—in accordance with everything that has been said hitherto, this does not mean a pure Nothing, but rather emptiness in the sense of telling refusal, self-withdrawal, thus emptiness as lack, deprivation, *need* [Not]. Are we affected by a need, does any such need concern us? More than one, we will retort: everywhere there are disruptions, crises, catastrophes, needs: the contemporary social misery, political confusion, the powerlessness of science, the erosion of art, the groundlessness of philosophy, the impotence of religion. Certainly, there are needs everywhere. Yet it will be said that it is, after all, one-sided to see nothing but needs. For the renewed attempts and efforts which are constantly made to control these needs, to put an end to them, to convert them directly into order and satisfaction are just as intense and clamorous. In keeping with this, it is not only individuals that are at work everywhere, but groups, associations, circles, classes, parties—everyone and everything is organised to meet such needs and every organisation has its program.

Precisely this contemporary reaction to the needs of Dasein surely confirms these needs, though at the same time and prior to this it also confirms something else. This bustling self-defense against these needs *precisely does not allow any need to emerge as a whole.* These needs are therefore no proof of the emptiness as a whole that we are asking about. They cannot announce any *being left empty as a whole,* if indeed this 'as a whole' does not mean merely adding together individual needs and miseries. We look in vain for such a *need as a whole.* Thus our questioning concerning a profound boredom in our Dasein, concerning a corresponding being left empty, despite all individual needs, remains without grounds, without any evidence that would even be adequate to answer it. The question is without any hold and is arbitrary, it does not stick to what is there before us, indeed it is unwilling to be satisfied with what is there.

Perhaps, however, our question concerning this need as a whole has not yet been pointed in the right direction. If we thus find no answer to our question concerning a need as a whole, do we then have to relinquish this question out of hand? Or has it to do with the way in which we ask that our attention is not drawn toward a possible answer? We are questioning concerning an emptiness as a whole, concerning a need, therefore, which cannot possibly have the character of those needs we have enumerated. Not this social misery, not that political confusion, not this powerlessness of science, not that erosion of art, not this groundlessness of philosophy, not that impotence of religion—the need in question is not the fact that this or that need oppresses [*bedrängt*] in such or such a way. Rather what oppresses us most profoundly and in a concealed manner is the very *absence of any essential oppressiveness* [Bedrängnis] *in our Dasein as a whole.*

The absence of an essential oppressiveness in Dasein is the *emptiness as a whole,* so that no one stands with anyone else and no community stands with any other in the rooted unity of essential action. Each and every one of us are servants of slogans, adherents to a program, but none is the custodian of the inner greatness of Dasein and its necessities. This *being left empty* ultimately resonates in our Dasein, its emptiness is the absence of any essential oppressiveness. The *mystery* [Geheimnis] is lacking in our Dasein, and thereby the inner terror that every mystery carries with it and that gives Dasein its greatness remains absent. The absence of oppressiveness is what fundamentally oppresses and leaves us most profoundly empty, i.e., the *fundamental emptiness that bores us.* This absence of oppressiveness is only apparently hidden; it is rather attested by the very activities with which we busy ourselves in our contemporary restlessness. For in all the organizing and program-making and trial and error there is ultimately a universal smug contentment in not being endangered. This contentment in the ground of our Dasein, despite all the many needs, makes us believe that we no longer need to be strong in the ground of our essence. We concern ourselves only with learned competencies that can be instilled. The present is full of pedagogical problems and questions. Strength and power, however, can never be replaced by the accumulation of learned competencies, rather if anything is achieved by the latter it is the suffocation of all such things.

b) The most extreme demand on Dasein as such, simultaneously announced in the telling absence of any oppressiveness (the moment of vision that is simultaneously announced) as the being held in limbo of this particular profound boredom.

The deepest, essential need in Dasein is not that a particular actual need oppresses us, but that an essential oppressiveness refuses itself, that we scarcely apprehend and are scarcely able to apprehend this telling refusal of any oppressiveness as a whole. And this for the reason that what *announces and tells of itself* in such telling refusal remains inaudible. Because it is not heard we can merely inquire about it in the first instance. Yet just as with regard to the being left empty of our Dasein, we must inquire about the *being held in limbo* that is in unity with it, in order to first attain a *complete questioning* concerning a profound boredom as the fundamental attunement of our Dasein.

All telling refusal has its incisiveness only in the fact that what is refused in it is also announced as such in all its harshness, i.e., announced and displayed in its necessity in such telling refusal. If, however, we today do not understand this essential need of our Dasein, the absence of any oppressiveness, then it must be partly due to the fact that we are unable to hear and to understand in advance what is also announced in this telling refusal. Whoever makes no demand upon themselves can never know of a refusal or of being refused, but sways in a contentment that has what it wants and wants only what it can have. Yet just as we were unable to ascertain what we indicated as the profound being left empty of our Dasein as something present at hand, but were only allowed to draw attention to it by way of questioning, so too we are now allowed only to ask: What is simultaneously announced in this absence of oppressiveness, in *this* telling refusal of beings as a whole? *Which particular being held in limbo* can belong to this particular being left empty? We became acquainted with the specific being held in limbo of profound boredom as our being impelled toward the extremity of that which makes Dasein possible as such, toward the moment of vision. We therefore ask: *Which moment of vision* can and must be simultaneously announced as that which properly makes possible in this telling refusal of any oppressiveness? *To what* must Dasein *resolutely disclose itself* as such, so as to rupture the entrancement of that need—the need of the absence of any oppressiveness as a whole—i.e., so as first to be at all equal to that profound need and to be open for it, so as to truly experience it as oppressive? Commensurate with that emptiness as a whole, the most extreme demand [*Zumutung*] must be announced to man, not some arbitrary demand, not this or that one, but the demand pure and simple made upon man. And what is that? *It is that Dasein as such is demanded of man, that it is given to him—to be there.*

Yet do we not all know this? Yes and no. We do not know it to the extent that we have forgotten that man, if he is to become what he *is*, in each case has to throw Dasein upon his shoulders; that he precisely is not when he merely lets himself set about things in the general fray, however "spirited" this may be; that Dasein is not something that one takes for a drive in the car as it were, but something that man must specifically take upon himself. Yet because we are of the opinion that we no longer need to be strong or to expect to throw ourselves open to danger, all of us together have also already slipped out of the danger-zone of Dasein within which, in taking our Dasein upon ourselves, we may perhaps overreach ourselves. That any oppressiveness as a whole is absent today is perhaps most pointedly manifest in the fact that today presumably no one overreaches themselves in their Dasein, but that we at most manage to complain about the misery of life. Man must first resolutely open himself again to this demand. The necessity of this disclosive resolution is what is contained in the telling refusal and simultaneous telling announcement of the moment of vision of our Dasein.

To what therefore does Dasein have to resolutely disclose itself? To first *creating* for itself once again a *genuine knowing concerning that wherein whatever properly makes Dasein itself possible consists.* And what is that? The fact that the *moment of vision* in which Dasein brings itself before itself as that which is properly binding must time and again stand before Dasein as such. Before itself—not as a fixed ideal or rigidly erected archetype, but before itself as that which must first precisely wrest its own possibility from itself again and take itself upon itself in such a possibility.

What, therefore, is demanded by the moment of vision simultaneously announced in this absence of any oppressiveness as a whole? That the moment of vision itself be understood, and that means seized upon, as the *innermost necessity* [Notwendigkeit] *of the freedom of Dasein.* What is simultaneously announced is the necessity of understanding the fact that Dasein must first of all bring itself into the realm of what is free again, must comprehend itself as Da-sein.

With the absence of any essential oppressiveness—if this absence of oppressiveness really oppressed us—there would have to go together a hunger for the most extreme and primary possibility of this moment of vision. Yet we cannot ever objectively assert or ascertain in itself that this emptiness leaves us empty and in so doing impels us toward the extremity of this moment of vision. We cannot ascertain the *oscillation between the expanse of this emptiness* and the *extremity of this moment of vision,* i.e., we cannot register this profound boredom of our Dasein as though it were a matter of fact. We can only ask whether in the end this profound boredom attunes our Dasein through and through, i.e., we can ask whether our contemporary everyday human traits, our being human, is not such that in everything—in all its doing and acting and being blinded by this—it acts counter to the possibility of that profound boredom arising. We can only ask whether contemporary man narrows down that *expanse of his concealed and most profound need* to those needs for which he immediately finds some self-defense, so as to satisfy and appease himself in this. We can only ask whether contemporary man has always already broken off and twisted and blunted that *extremity of the most incisive moment of vision* and keeps it blunt through his haste to react, through the abruptness of his programs, a haste and abruptness which he confuses with the resolute disclosedness of the moment of vision. We cannot ascertain that profound boredom in the Dasein of contemporary man. We can only ask whether contemporary man precisely in and through all his contemporary human traits does not suppress that profound boredom, and that means: whether he does not conceal his Dasein as such from himself—in spite of all his psychology and psychoanalysis, indeed precisely *through* psychology, which today even presents itself as depth psychology. We can only understand that profound boredom, create room for it, in such questioning. Yet to question concerning *this fundamental attunement* does not mean to further justify and continue the contemporary human traits of man, but to liberate the humanity in man, to liberate the humanity of man, i.e., the *essence* of man, *to let the Dasein in him become essential.* This liberation of the Dasein in man does not mean placing him in some arbitrary position, but loading Dasein upon man as his ownmost burden. Only those who can truly give themselves a burden are free. Questioning concerning this fundamental attunement—this means: questioning concerning *what fundamental attunement as such gives us to question.* Only in such questioning are we able to bring ourselves to the point where it can be decided whether we can summon the courage of mood [*Mut*] for what this fundamental attunement gives us to know. We must therefore *really* question what this attunement gives us to question, we must question concerning what *oppresses* us in this fundamental attunement and perhaps simultaneously *vanishes* as a decisive *possibility.* This is what we are to understand, namely to *help bring to word* that which Dasein wishes to speak about in this fundamental attunement—bring it to that word which is not simply a matter of gossip, but the word that addresses us and summons us to action and to being. We are to understand this word, i.e., *to project the truth of fundamental attunement upon this essential content.*

PART TWO

Really Asking the Metaphysical Questions to Be
Developed from the Fundamental Attunement of
Profound Boredom. The Question: What Is World?

Chapter One

The Metaphysical Questions to Be Developed from
the Fundamental Attunement of Profound Boredom

*§39. The questions concerning world, individuation,
and finitude as what is given to questioning through
the fundamental attunement of profound boredom in
our contemporary Dasein. The essence of time
as the root of the three questions.*

What we ought to find oppressive, then, is the absence of any oppressiveness
as a whole, the very expanse of this emptiness as a whole. What do we mean
by this expression '*as a whole*'? How can Dasein find itself placed in this way
among beings as a whole? And what is at work here when this 'as a whole'
presses in upon us on every side? We shall designate the expanse of this 'as a
whole', which manifests itself in profound boredom, as *world*. In accordance
with what this fundamental attunement confronts us with, we must ask: *what
is world?*

The moment of vision which properly makes Dasein possible is simultaneously announced in this telling refusal of beings as a whole. This moment
is the look of resolute disclosedness of Dasein for its Da-sein, a Da-sein that
in each case is as existing in the situation it has unreservedly seized upon, an
existing which is always singular and unique. We are asking about what this
fundamental attunement announces to us as possibility whenever we ask what
this moment of vision is, whenever we ask what it is that occurs in and through
this moment, whenever we ask concerning the *individuation* of Dasein with
respect to itself.

We are not asking about *world* and *individuation* here as some arbitrary pair
of questions, but rather as something which manifests itself precisely in the
fundamental attunement of profound boredom in an *original unity* and *structural link,* something which only as this unity is capable of attuning us through

and through in this telling refusal that announces, this telling announcement that refuses.

We are thus asking about what it is that this fundamental attunement of profound boredom properly and really gives us to question whenever we ask: Whence the necessity of this relation between 'expanse' and 'extremity', between horizon and moment of vision, between world and individuation, and why does it arise? What kind of 'and' is it that links these terms? Why must that expanse of the entrancing horizon ultimately be ruptured by the moment of vision? And why can it be ruptured only by this moment of vision, so that Dasein attains its existence proper precisely in this rupture? Is the essence of the unity and structural linking of both terms ultimately a *rupture?* What is the meaning of this *rupture within Dasein itself?* We call this the finitude of Dasein and ask: *What does finitude mean?* Only with this question have we attained the question that fully gains a purchase upon what it is that is trying to voice itself in that fundamental attunement. *Is it not the finitude of Dasein that resonates in the fundamental attunement of profound boredom and attunes us through and through?*

At the very beginning of our lecture course we simply posed, in a rather arbitrary and violent fashion, those three questions which the fundamental attunement of profound boredom leads us to ask: what is world?, what is finitude?, what is individuation? But now the matter is somewhat clearer. These questions do not arise from books, they have not been culled by adaptation from a variety of philosophical schools, nor have they merely been repeated in obeisance to a trivialized metaphysical tradition. On the contrary, they now betray their possibility, i.e., their *necessity in the need of our Dasein.* Only when these questions are rooted in the place from which we now see them arising, and only when they remain rooted there, do they represent genuine questions. Yet if they really are genuine in this way, then they are not new. However, if they are not new, they are not old either. Neither new nor old, these questions are essential questions. In what is essential, however, everything associated with mere striving after originality or—what amounts to the same but is even more suspect—everything that seeks to contest an originality that was never attempted in the first place, has also become a matter of irrelevance. The question which continues to face us is simply whether or not we are capable of experiencing, or at least releasing, the liberating power harbored within these questions as questions.

Our three questions were posed in the following order: [1.] What is world? [2.] What is finitude? [3.] What is individuation? We have developed them in such a way, however, that finitude has emerged as the third and pressing question. Yet third in what sense? *As the unifying and original root of the other two.* Because this question is the most originary, the one which holds together the other two, we place it in the *middle* of the series. This is intended to indicate its originary character. In the order in which we proceed to address our three questions, however, we shall only be able to engage with this one in third place. And this is also to say that in addressing the first and second questions, we shall in each case already find ourselves pressed to deal with the third.

We have attempted to unfold these three questions—What is world? What is individuation? What is finitude?—from out of a fundamental attunement of our Dasein, to unfold them in *such a way* that in the very process the *fundamental attunement* of that profound boredom should become *ever more acute* as *possibility.* We are not now leaving this fundamental attunement behind us as a supposedly ascertained fact that is finished and done with. On the contrary, the *elaboration of these questions* is nothing other than an *accentuation of the possibility of that fundamental attunement.* Yet this profound boredom, and boredom as such, is rooted in the *temporality* of Dasein. Thus in their origin, our three questions themselves reach back into the *question concerning the essence of time.* But the question concerning the essence of time is the *origin of all the questions of metaphysics* and of their potential unfolding. Whether in fact the problematic of metaphysics must always be developed on the basis of the temporality of Dasein, however, cannot be objectively decided for the whole of world history, as it were. The possibility of a different kind of necessary grounding for metaphysics must remain open. However this possibility is not some empty, formal or logical possibility; rather what is possible regarding this possibility depends entirely upon the fate of man.

Let us now look back once more over the path we have followed. Taking as our guideline the elucidated phenomenon of boredom in its relative clarity, and especially that of profound boredom, we have attempted to clarify *one* fundamental attunement of our Dasein, *one* experience of profound boredom in our Dasein. This elucidation proceeded as a form of questioning. In this connection we took as our point of departure one structural moment of profound boredom, namely *being left empty* in the sense of the telling refusal of beings as a whole. In the profound boredom with which we are concerned, this corresponds to the absence of any oppressiveness and the lack of mystery in our Dasein—a Dasein which knows only neediness and the necessary acts of self-defense encountered in this attunement or perhaps on an even more superficial level of our Dasein. To this inner trait of being left empty, the absence of any oppressiveness, there corresponds a unique *being held in limbo* in the sense of the moment of vision which indirectly announces itself at the same time. Corresponding to the absence of oppressiveness as a whole, the necessity of responding to this situation is simultaneously announced, the necessity of the ultimate demand [*Zumutung*] upon man. This is the demand that he necessarily shoulder once more his very Dasein, that he explicitly and properly take this Dasein upon himself. Man must first resolutely open himself up to this demand again, or learn how to do so—not indeed because someone tells him to do so in the course of some lecture or other, but solely to the extent that such a demand transpires from out of an actual oppressiveness of Dasein as a whole. The only thing we can try to accomplish in our questioning way is to develop a readiness for this oppressiveness and for the moment of vision which belongs to it—for that moment of vision which contemporary man misinterprets as the speed of his reactions and the sudden haste of his pro-grams. This demand has nothing to do with some human ideal in one or other domain of possible action. It is the *liberation of the Dasein in man* that is at issue here. At the same time this liberation is the task laid upon us to assume once more our very Dasein as an actual *burden*. The liberation of the Dasein in man is one which human beings can only ever accomplish in and for themselves in each case from out of the ground of their essence. This does not mean that the challenge in question demands that we withdraw from contem-porary reality, that we despise or attack it. But similarly—and this would merely be the correlative reaction—it does not demand that we adopt emer-gency measures for the protection of culture in a kind of spurious instant response. In attempting to understand the challenge to contemporary man to assume his Dasein once again, we must from the outset guard against the misunderstanding that we can ever hope to approach what is essential through some general collective enthusiasm for what is in fact inessential. What is at issue in this challenge is rather that each and every Dasein should comprehend this necessity for itself out of the ground of its essence. And if, in spite of all our neediness, the oppressiveness of our Dasein still remains absent today and the mystery still lacking, then we must principally concern ourselves with preparing for man the very basis and dimension upon which and within which something like a mystery of his Dasein could once again be encountered. We should not be at all surprised if the contemporary man in the street feels disturbed or perhaps sometimes dazed and clutches all the more stubbornly at his idols when confronted with this challenge and with the effort required to approach this mystery. It would be a mistake to expect anything else. We must first call for someone capable of instilling terror into our Dasein again. For how do things stand with our Dasein when an event like the Great War can to all extents and purposes pass us by without leaving a trace? Is this not perhaps a sign that no event, however momentous it may be, is capable of assuming this task if man has not prepared himself for awakening in the first place? The fundamental attunement of a profound boredom, once awakened, *can* manifest to us the absence of such oppressiveness and this moment of vision at the same time. We have attempted briefly to develop our three ques-tions—What is world? What is finitude? What is individuation?—from out of this fundamental attunement as one possibility for which we here have a sign. We have done so in order to make it quite clear that these are not merely bookish or literary questions, nor questions that belong to some movement or school of philosophy, but rather questions posed by the essential need of Dasein itself, if indeed it is a matter of Dasein first becoming transparent to itself again and thus allowing itself to be touched by something different. At the same time this is to say that the whole problematic, insofar as it emerges from this fundamental attunement, is directed toward a dimension of questioning which is already indicated through this fundamental attunement itself. Our claim is that the fundamental attunement of boredom is rooted in the temporality of Dasein. The *temporality of Dasein* and thus the *essence of time* itself is the *root of these three questions* which in themselves, in their own peculiar unity and connection, express the *fundamental question of metaphysics*. This is what we have called the *question concerning being: Being and Time.*

§40. The way in which the three questions are to be asked.

It thus seems as if we know *what* it is we now have to ask about in our questioning. Yet precisely if we were to cling rigidly to this knowledge we should easily forget what is of equal urgency here, namely clarity concerning *how* these three questions are to be asked, *how* we must orient ourselves toward the possible answers, and *how* alone we should interpret such answers.

By answering these questions we do not intend to erect a worldview as an edifice in which one is invited to dwell. Perhaps contemporary man is not even really, i.e., responsibly prepared for what is specifically described as a worldview. Nor will we be tempted to believe that these questions and the answers we give to them will eliminate the need of contemporary Dasein. Such need will at best merely be rendered more acute, more acute in the sole possible sense that this questioning will bring us to the *brink* of possibility, the *possibility* of restoring to Dasein its *actuality*, that is, its *existence*. Yet between this uttermost brink of possibility and the actuality of Dasein there lies a very fine line. This is a line which one can never merely glide across, but one which man can only leap over in dislodging his Dasein. Only individual action itself can dislodge us from this brink of possibility into actuality, and this is the *moment of vision*. Philosophizing, on the other hand, can only lead us to the brink and always remains something penultimate in this respect. Yet it can only ever lead us this far if it actually runs ahead into this penultimate domain and thus grasps its entirely precursory character and finitude. This means comprehending that it must not abandon itself in a gullible and vacuous fashion to a host of different and possibly legitimate investigations, while leaving whatever remains to chance and God alike. For what remains here is the essential, and this consists in actually leading us to the brink of our possibilities and preparing in advance the possibility of such leadership and the specific path for it to take.

All this suggests *how* we are to ask our three questions. This questioning can only ever serve to make us attentive to that fundamental attunement, i.e., to manifest the Dasein in contemporary man once more, so that he can in general perceive the possibility in which he must stand if he is successfully to respond to what presses upon him as a necessity, namely not acting counter to what is essential in Dasein. Not acting counter to the essential here means *being held to oneself.* Being held to oneself, however, can occur only by virtue of that truth in which Dasein manifests itself. All this must be said lest we lose ourselves unawares in these very questions, lest these questions degenerate into a kind of free-floating speculation that turns entirely upon itself. More essential by far than the acumen and rigor of conceptual incisiveness (which we may also need and which has a special character of its own compared to scientific thought) is the seriousness with which we strive to keep these questions on the right path. This is necessary if they are to serve the task which is given over to philosophizing: *not to describe the consciousness of man but to evoke the Dasein in man.* This evocation cannot come about through some kind of enchantment or mystical contemplation but only through sober conceptual questioning. It is certainly true that this questioning, in contrast to all scientific investigation, can never be accommodated within a determinate domain or activated within such an enclosed sphere. This questioning *must first form its own interrogative space* in the act of questioning, and only in the act of questioning is it capable of *keeping* this interrogative space *open.*

§41. The beleaguering of the three questions by tradition and by sound common sense.

If we take them as they initially presented themselves to us, then surely our three questions—What is *world?* What is *finitude?* What is *individuation?*—simply ask about something with which we are all already familiar. Certainly all the questions of philosophy are of a such a kind that we could almost say that the more philosophy concerns itself with a problem completely unfamiliar to everyday awareness, then the more philosophy is avoiding the central issues and concerning itself with the inessential. The more familiar and self-evident the object of its questioning is, the more essential is the question involved. But precisely because of this we must also say that the ambiguity involved is all the more pressing. As common sense usually sees the matter, philosophy does not merely inquire after what is already quite familiar to common sense, that which common sense itself no longer really feels the need to ask about anyway. Rather it seems as though philosophy also asks its questions in just the same way as sound common sense tends to do, or would do, *if* common sense were ever to inquire further into what is self-evident. This is indeed how the matter looks, but in fact it is nothing like this. All great and genuine philosophy moves within the limited sphere of a few questions which appear to common sense as perennially the same, although in fact they are necessarily different in every instance of philosophizing. *Different* not in any merely external sense, but rather in such a way that the *self-same* is in each case essentially *transformed* once more. Only in such *transformation* does philosophy possess its genuine self-sameness. This transformation lends a *properly primordial historicity* to the *occurrence* of the history of philosophizing, a historicity which makes its own demands (sacrifice, being overcome). We cannot comprehend this historicity and will never be able to get a grasp of it if, for instance, we associate it with the notion of history derived from the sensational historical accounts we find in the newspapers. The *historicity of the history of philosophy,* and correspondingly, albeit in quite a different way, the historicity of the history of *art* and of *religion* are intrinsically and wholly divergent. Yet on the basis of this divergence they are nevertheless entirely connected with one another in a way which still remains entirely obscure to us. Yet what we have called *transformation* does not mean what the vanity of the literati understands by the word, namely striving always and at any price to say the opposite of what has been said before or, should they always arrive too late to participate in this enterprise, explaining in hindsight that this is what they have said long ago. The *self-sameness* of philosophy does not, however, consist in the fact that everyone thinks the same thing and says yes to everything. Since ordinary understanding with its self-complacent ideal looks for just such a self-sameness in philosophy and then factically fails to find it, the only alternative remaining to it is to regard the history of philosophy as a kind of madhouse in which everyone attempts to obliterate his opponent and produce some new opinion of his own. For this reason the very idea of the *philosophia perennis* is merely a means by which ordinary understanding organizes the history of philosophy from a standpoint outside of philosophy itself. For this history remains utterly unintelligible and inaccessible to such an understanding if it cannot perceive identical problems eternally handled in identical ways throughout the history of spirit—just as everyday life always deals with identical problems in identical ways.

Thus the three questions are not only familiar with respect to *what* they deal with, they are also familiar *as questions* or themes within the history of philosophy. These questions find themselves beleaguered by the tradition and sound common sense alike. Yet both these forces serve only to level down such questioning, to rob our questioning of its edge and thus to prevent an insight into the necessary exertion of thought in which alone these questions can come to fruition.

Chapter Two

The Beginning of Metaphysical Questioning with the Question
of World. The Path of the Investigation and Its Difficulties

*§42. The path of a comparative examination of
three guiding theses: the stone is worldless,
the animal is poor in world, man is world-forming.*

We begin with the first of our three questions: *What is world?* Even now we tend
to take this explicit question as a free-floating question asked along the way just
like any other. Initially we do not know where we should look for an answer to
it. Indeed, if we consider the matter more closely, we do not even know what we
are asking about, or in what direction our questioning is moving. The *first path*
toward an initial clarification entails, as in all such cases, that we pay close
attention to the word and pursue the *history of the word* 'world' and the historical
development of the concept it contains. I have attempted to pursue this path in
my essay *On the Essence of Ground.*[1] It is true that the exposition offered there
of the concept of κόσμος, *mundus,* 'world' merely indicates the characteristic
stages of this history and above all remains wholly within the parameters set by
the theme of the essay. The exposition given there can, however, serve as a
preliminary orientation as far as the concept of the term is concerned. Yet the
theme treated there not only requires a broader and more concrete exposition,
it also needs to be supplemented, or rather founded for the first time by *that*
history of the concept of world which is not expressed in the history of the word
at all. The history of the word provides only the exterior. The inner history
involved can only be perceived in connection with the fundamental *problem* of
metaphysics and along the lines of a clarified understanding of the *problem* of
world. I shall not repeat here what I said in that context, but acquaintance with
the earlier discussion could be useful in this connection, and all of Section II of
the essay is important generally concerning this problem. Here I would just like
to give a very general indication of the context in which, from an external point
of view, the problem of world initially arises. The most familiar aspect of the
problem reveals itself in the distinction between God and world. The world is
the totality of beings outside of and other than God. Expressed in Christian
terms, such beings thus also represent the realm of created being as distinct from

1. *Vom Wesen des Grundes* (Frankfurt: Klostermann, 1973), pp. 23–37 (sixth edition). First
published in 1929. [Trans. T. Malick, *The Essence of Reasons* (Evanston, Illinois: Northwestern
University Press, 1969).]

uncreated being. And man in turn is also a part of the world understood in this sense. Yet man is not simply regarded as a part of the world within which he appears and which he makes up in part. Man also stands over against the world. This standing-over-against is a *'having'* of world as that in which man moves, with which he engages, which he both masters and serves, and to which he is exposed. Thus man is, first, a part of the world, and second, as this part he is at once both master and servant of the world.

However crude this distinction may be, it does indicate man's ambivalent position in relation to the world—as well as the ambivalent character of the concept of world itself. Initially and for some time to come we shall employ the word 'world' in this ambivalent sense. Historical reflection is capable of bringing these connections into sharper focus.

In contrast to this *historical path* toward an understanding of the concept of world, I attempted in *Being and Time* to provide a preliminary characterization of the *phenomenon of world* by interpreting the *way in which we at first and for the most part move about in our everyday world.* There I took my departure from what lies to hand in the everyday realm, from those things that we use and pursue, indeed in such a way that we do not really know of the peculiar character proper to such activity at all, and when we do try to describe it we immediately misinterpret it by applying concepts and questions that have their source elsewhere. That which is so close and intelligible to us in our everyday dealings is actually and fundamentally remote and unintelligible to us. In and through this initial characterization of the phenomenon of world the task is to press on and point out the phenomenon of world as a problem. It never occurred to me, however, to try and claim or prove with this interpretation that the essence of man consists in the fact that he knows how to handle knives and forks or use the tram. The path followed in *Being and Time* in the attempt to shed light on the phenomenon of world really requires a very broad and wide-ranging perspective which cannot even remotely be made visible here in this lecture.

Instead we have chosen to follow a *third* path at this point—the path of a *comparative examination.* As we said, man is not merely a *part of the world* but is also master and servant of the world in the sense of *"having"* world. Man has world. But then what about the other beings which, like man, are also part of the world: the animals and plants, the material things like the stone, for example? Are they merely parts of the world, as distinct from man who in addition *has* world? Or does the animal too have world, and if so, in what way? In the same way as man, or in some other way? And how would we grasp this otherness? And what about the stone? However crudely, certain distinctions immediately manifest themselves here. We can formulate these distinctions in the following three theses: [1.] the stone (material object) is *worldless;* [2.] the animal is *poor in world;* [3.] man is *world-forming.*

In attempting to uncover the essence of *worldlessness,* of *poverty in world,* and of *world-formation,* we shall also be exploring the various ways in which beings can be related to world. Through a comparative interpretation of this kind it must be possible to open up the essence of world and bring it sufficiently close to us to really begin to ask about it for the first time. For the problem of world by no means lies simply in the need to provide a more exact and more rigorous interpretation of the essence of the world. On the contrary, the real task is to bring the *worldly character* of the world into view for the first time as the possible theme of a *fundamental problem* of *metaphysics.*

In addition to the aforementioned historical path, the second path (which proceeds from man's everyday understanding of the world and remains within this understanding), and the third path (that of the comparative examination upon which we are about to embark), there are other possible paths which we shall not introduce here. Yet all of these paths necessarily have their own specific limitations and difficulties. This is because each of these paths comes from without, that is, each one brings with it the principles and perspectives that are characteristic of ordinary understanding. And whichever way we have chosen to follow, our task will be to disabuse ourselves of these initially habitual perspectives and ways of questioning, or to transform them by virtue of the force of what we come to see with ever greater clarity. This is true of *every* metaphysical problem. And this implies that in principle we can never assess metaphysics by employing the criteria of ordinary understanding, irrespective of whether metaphysics is considered to be beneficial or inimical to culture. In fact metaphysics is neither of these things, or, viewed from an external perspective, metaphysics is both at once. Metaphysics is "ambiguous" precisely because it is basically prior to such distinctions.

It is true that the third path, the path of a comparative examination, seems the most approachable because it is so adaptable and because in the process of making and grasping distinctions we can first really glimpse whatever is self-same and concordant. And yet precisely this third path presents special difficulties of its own which must be mentioned briefly at the outset, if they are not continually to impede our progress. We shall merely *state* these difficulties here, not eliminate them.

§43. The fundamental difficulty with respect to content and method in determining the essence and accessibility of life.

The comparative examination concerns material things (the stone), animals, and man. In order even to negotiate the problem we must accordingly already have at our disposal certain essential distinctions between these three realms. Or at least it must be possible for us to indicate such distinctions if required.

Yet it is difficult to determine even the distinction between man and animal. Of course, it is easy to say that one is a rational living being, while the other is a non-rational living being. But the question is precisely this: what does reason, or the lack of reason, actually mean here? Even if we succeed in clarifying this question, it is still uncertain whether this distinction does in fact represent what is most essential and what is metaphysically important here. When we ask this question concerning the relation between man and animal, we cannot therefore be concerned with deciding whether or not man is descended from the ape. For we cannot begin to pose this question, let alone answer it, until we clearly appreciate what the distinction between them is and how this distinction should be drawn. And this does not mean finding out how humans and animals are distinguished from one another in this or that particular respect. It means finding out what constitutes the *essence of the animality* of the animal and the *essence of the humanity* of man and through what sort of questions we can hope to pinpoint the essence of such beings at all. Then again, we can only determine the animality of the animal if we are clear about what constitutes the *living character of a living being,* as distinct from the non-living being which does not even have the possibility of dying. A stone cannot be dead because it is never alive.

Yet the difficulty here is not merely one of *content* with respect to *what* life as such is but is equally and almost more emphatically a *methodological* one: *by what path* can and should we gain access to the living character of the living being in its essence? In what way should life, the animality of the animal, and the plant-character of the plant be made accessible to us? It is not sufficient merely to provide a morphological description of the animal's form, its limbs, and so on; it is insufficient to explore the physiological processes and then to add on some form of animal psychology. For in all of this we have already presupposed that the animal is alive, that in its behavior the animal is also disposed in a certain manner. How are we to get to the bottom of this? The animal can perhaps neither observe itself, nor communicate any such observations to us. And even if the animal expresses itself and announces itself, as it seems to us, in a variety of expressive sounds and movements, it is we who must first interpret and analyze such forms of expression.

We are thus confronted by two fundamental difficulties: [1.] *What* are we to *determine* the essence of life in general *as?* [2.] *How* are living beings as such—the animality of the animal and the plant-character of the plant—originarily *accessible?* Or is there no possibility of any original access here at all? But what would that imply with respect to the essential character of living beings, however this character is given? In the course of our comparative considerations both of these questions must be left open, but that also means that we must always have some answer ready, however provisional and tentative, in order to guide us as we pursue our comparative considerations. On the other hand, these comparative considerations can and must ultimately make some contribution toward the clarification and possible answering of these questions.

Thus we constantly find ourselves moving in a circle. And this is an indication that we are moving within the realm of philosophy. Everywhere a kind of *circling*. This circling movement of philosophy of course is alien to ordinary understanding which only ever wants to get the job in hand over and done with as quickly as possible. But going round in circles gets us nowhere. Above all, it makes us feel dizzy, and dizziness is something uncanny. We feel as though we are suspended in the Nothing. Therefore there must be no such circling and thus no circle in philosophy! This is, after all, a universal principle of logic. That is why all scientific philosophy prides itself on getting by without this circle. Yet anyone who has never been seized by dizziness in the presence of a philosophical question has never asked the question in a philosophical way, that is, has never entered the circle in the first place. The only thing that ordinary understanding can see in this circling motion is the movement around the periphery which always returns to its original point of departure on the periphery. Thus it misses the decisive issue here, which is an insight into the *centre* of the circle as such, an insight made possible in such a circling movement and in this alone. For the centre only manifests itself as such as we circle around it. And this is why every attempt to argue away such circularity in philosophy only leads us away from philosophy itself. Likewise every objection which argues that our examination is circular already demonstrates that it is not a philosophical objection at all and is consequently quite vacuous as far as philosophy is concerned. Of course this is not to say that every circular proof is a sign of philosophical thinking (circle and turbulence).

To sum up, then, we find ourselves moving in a circle when we *presuppose* a *certain fundamental conception concerning* both *the essence of life* and *the way in which it is to be interpreted* and then proceed on the basis of this presupposition to open up a path which will lead us to a fundamental conception of life.

*§44. Summary and renewed introduction following the
vacation: metaphysics as comprehensive questioning;
awakening the fundamental attunement of profound
boredom; the metaphysical questions to be developed
from the fundamental attunement. Guidelines
for correctly understanding this talk about
the fundamental attunement of philosophizing.*

Metaphysics—metaphysical knowledge is a *comprehensive* questioning in this twofold sense: [1.] that beings as a whole are in each case conceptually included in every metaphysical question; and [2.] that whoever is involved in metaphysical questioning is in each case caught up in the question as well, and is fundamentally affected by the act of questioning and the object of questioning. Man only finds himself involved and affected at all if he is already capable of being affected in his Dasein and can find himself gripped in this ability to be affected, indeed if this possibility of *being gripped* lies in his very essence. This essential possibility of being gripped belongs to the essence of man insofar as his Da-sein always— but not exclusively—implies *being attuned*. Only a being that is intrinsically attuned in general can find itself adversely attuned. Whatever is adversely attuned can undergo a change of attunement. Where there is attunement, there is the possibility of a change of attunement, and thus also of *awakening attunement*. Consequently, in order to be able to develop such a comprehensive questioning, it was first necessary to awaken a fundamental attunement and create the pos- sibility of our being gripped. The first part of our lecture course, which consisted in a quite specific interpretation of *a profound boredom in the ground of our Dasein*, was dedicated to just this task. Yet the investigations of the first part of the course only derive their justification and import from the second part. For it is here that we hope actually to ask the metaphysical questions to be developed *out of the fundamental attunement*. We developed three such questions: [1.] What is world? [2.] What is finitude? [3.] What is individuation? Here the second question is also the most originary and most central one. We will not pursue the connection between fundamental attunement and metaphysics any further at this juncture. I should merely like to offer certain *guidelines* with respect to a few points in order to facilitate our understanding of what is to come and to prevent the immediate misunderstandings which inevitably arise from the ambiguity of philosophy itself.

[1.] When we grounded our questioning in a fundamental attunement, this particular fundamental attunement, we did not mean to imply that the three questions developed out of this attunement also exhaust its metaphysical signif- icance, as if these three particular questions were the only ones capable of being developed from this fundamental attunement. They are simply drawn *from* it.

[2.] Nor do we mean to imply that this particular fundamental attunement in itself is the only path which leads to these three questions. Precisely if they really are metaphysical questions, then we must be able to unfold them *from out of every* fundamental attunement of Dasein.

[3.] Yet which fundamental attunement we choose in order to develop and pursue these questions is not simply a matter of arbitrary decision on our part. It is true that in a certain sense we do choose, and do so freely, and yet in the deepest sense we are bound and compelled as well. This choice is certainly not merely a matter of making an arbitrary selection from what happens to lie before us. Rather:

[4.] The choice involves binding ourselves to the intrinsic character of metaphys- ics itself which compels the engagement of a particular finite Dasein, that is, compels us to assume in its entirety the conditioned nature of questioning which this finite Dasein implies. Yet when we question from out of a particular fundamental attunement in each case, this does not mean that this attunement overwhelms the others, prevents them or reduces their significance. On the contrary:

[5.] Every genuine fundamental attunement liberates and deepens, binds and releases the others. To this day we know all too little about this fundamental occurrence of attunement in Dasein. Nor will we ever come to know such things through a psychology of feelings or be able to account for them by means of reflection, however ingenious it may be. We shall only be able to experience this fundamental occurrence through Dasein itself, and then only to the extent that we actually summon up the effort to be *there* [da *zu sein*]. Consequently it is just as mistaken to ascribe an absolute status to one fundamental attunement alone as it is to relativize all the possible fundamental attunements with respect to one other. This procedure is mistaken because we are not dealing here at all with things lying on the same level that could simply be exchanged for one another. Rather:

[6.] This occurrence of a fundamental attunement itself and the very choice in question as an engagement of the philosopher's existence is rooted in the history of Dasein. But history cannot be calculated. It can only be inhibited and distorted by calculation and manipulation. If the fundamental attunement of metaphysics in a specific case, and the manner and measure of its attunement, is a matter of fate, that is, something which can change and does not remain binding for every era, then *philosophy nonetheless remains in an exceptional proximity to a particular fundamental attunement.* It does so not because it is philosophy, but because philosophy, like art in its own way, actually requires what we try clumsily and misleadingly enough to express when we say that it must be creative. 'Creative' here is not intended to suggest some special privilege or superiority with respect to the uncreative activities of menials or profiteers for example. It indicates a creativeness which possesses its own intrinsic obligations and requires an appropriate attitude to sustain it. Creative achievement is a free formative activity. Freedom is only to be found where there is a burden to be shouldered. In creative achievement this burden always represents an imperative and a need that weighs heavily upon man's overall mood, so that he comes to be in a mood of melancholy.[1] All creative action

---

1. '. . . eine Not, an der der Mensch schwer trägt im Gemüt, so daß ihm schwer zumute ist.' [The German *Mut* commonly means "courage" in contemporary usage, but has the older meaning of "cheer" or "spirits," as in the English *mood,* with which it shares the same etymological root. Heidegger is here appealing to this older sense of *Mut.* Thus we have rendered *zumute sein* (being in a certain "state of mind") as "being in a mood"; *Schwermut* (the normal word for "melancholy") as "mood of melancholy" or "melancholic mood"; and *Gemüt* (commonly translated as "the mind") as "overall mood." The root *Mut* will play an important part in the characterization of the animal's "poverty" in world, where "poverty" translates the cognate *Armut.* (See §46 for Heidegger's elaboration of this.) Other cognates of *Mut,* including *demütig* ("humiliating") and *Zumutung* (an "unreasonable demand or expectation"), also appear in the text.—Tr.]

resides in a mood of melancholy [*Schwermut*], whether we are clearly aware of the fact or not, whether we speak at length about it or not. All creative action resides in a mood of melancholy, but this is not to say that everyone in a melancholic mood is creative. Aristotle already recognized this connection between creativity and melancholia when he asked the question: Διὰ τί πάντες ὅσοι περιττοὶ γεγόνασιν ἄνδρες ἢ κατὰ φιλοσοφίαν ἢ πολιτικὴν ἢ ποίησιν ἢ τέχνας φαίνονται μελαγχολικοὶ ὄντες;[2] Why is it that all those men who have achieved exceptional things, whether in philosophy, in politics, in poetry, or in the arts, are clearly melancholics? Aristotle explicitly mentions Empedocles, Socrates, and Plato in this context. (Aristotle also distinguishes between a μελαγχολία διὰ φύσιν and a μελαγχολία διὰ νόσον).

[7.] As a creative and essential activity of human Dasein, philosophy stands in the *fundamental attunement of melancholy*. This melancholy concerns the form rather than the content of philosophizing, but it necessarily prescribes a fundamental attunement which delimits the substantive content of philosophical questioning.

It is particularly dangerous to point out these connections today, because such reflections are immediately misused in the attempt to appropriate creative products and works of all kinds by analyzing their provenance and their creative production in psychological terms. The life of spirit in our present day, with respect to itself and its history, is largely trapped in this blind alley and can move neither forward nor backward. For the false belief that something has been comprehended and appropriated once we have explained its provenance in psychological or anthropological terms is a blind alley. Because we can explain everything in this way, we seem to have acquired an objective position with respect to things. And we manage to persuade ourselves that this psychologically objective explanation and acceptance of anything and everything with regard to its psychological origin represents a form of superior freedom and tolerance. But in fact this approach fundamentally represents the most complacent and comfortable form of tyranny in which we risk nothing, not even our own viewpoint, since of course there is a psychological explanation for this too. Everything we previously said about attunement and our earlier attempt to awaken a particular fundamental attunement can be driven, or even slide of its own accord, in the direction of this innermost corruption of our era. Everything we have said can slide in that direction precisely because with these considerations we perhaps find ourselves moving at the centre of philosophizing itself and thus in the greatest possible proximity to the ambiguity of philosophizing.

We must learn to understand all the more clearly, then, that attunements only are *what they are* when they *attune us,* that is, when they determine the

---

2. Aristotle, *Problemata. Aristotelis Opera.* Ed. I. Bekker (Berlin, 1831). Vol. II. Λ1, 953a 10ff.

attunement of *actual action. Our* action in this context is a *particular kind of attuned questioning.* We began by characterizing our first question, What is world? We pointed out that there are *various paths* we can take in unfolding this question: [1.] the historical examination of the history of the concept of world [2.] the unfolding of the concept of world on the basis of our everyday understanding of world. And as a third way we have chosen the path of a *comparative examination.* The main points of our approach are encapsulated in three theses: [1.] The stone is worldless; [2.] The animal is poor in world; [3.] Man is world-forming.

Chapter Three

The Beginning of the Comparative Examination,
Taking the Intermediate Thesis That the Animal
Is Poor in World as Our Point of Departure

The path we shall follow in elaborating the question 'What is world?' will be that of a comparative examination. However, the question itself is not a rootless one. Fundamental attunement constitutes the enduring site of our question, and this is something we must constantly remember. By means of a comparative examination of our three theses (the stone is worldless, the animal is poor in world, man is world-forming) we hope to delimit in a provisional manner what we should understand by the term *world* in general, as well as the direction in which we should look for such understanding. What is world? That is our question. Yet we do not ask it in order to receive just any answer, nor one that takes the form of a "definition," but in order to actually unfold a metaphysical question. Proper metaphysical comprehension lies in the correct unfolding of the question. Or, to put it in another way, metaphysical questions do not receive an answer, if that means communicating some known fact or other. Metaphysical questions remain without an answer, not because we cannot find one on account of the supposed impossibility of metaphysics, but because the kind of answer that consists in communicating some established fact is quite inadequate for such questions. Indeed it only corrupts and stifles them.

However, in order actually to unfold the question 'What is world?' we must acquire an initial understanding of what we mean by 'world' and what it is that we reserve this term for. We are undertaking the aforementioned comparative examination of stone, animal, and man, according to which the stone is worldless, the animal poor in world, and man world-forming, in order to provide this initial understanding. The perspective from which we shall make our comparison, that in respect of which we shall do the comparing, is the *specific relation* that stone, animal, and man in each case has toward *world.* The distinctions in respect of this relation, or in the absence of such a relation, will help to set in relief what we call *world.* Initially, a comparative examination of this kind seems to proceed in an extremely naive manner, as if the three beings we have mentioned were three things of the same order, as if they were all on the same plane. We shall begin our comparative analysis by *starting from the middle,* that is, by asking what it means to say that *the animal is poor in world.* Thus we shall also constantly be looking to two sides at once, both toward the worldlessness of the stone and toward the world-forming of man, and from there in turn back toward the animal and its poverty in world. Initially, the position adopted in this comparative procedure decides nothing about the metaphysical order involved.

§45. The propositional character of this thesis and the relation between metaphysics and the positive sciences.

a) The thesis that 'the animal is poor in world' as a statement of essence and a presupposition of zoology. The circular movement of philosophy.

Our guiding thesis with reference to the animal claims that *the animal is poor in world.* What sort of proposition have we here, and similarly in the cases of the other two? A proposition about the animal. The animal is the object of investigation in zoology. Is then our proposition borrowed from zoology? For zoology is surely a suitable kind of investigation, oriented as it is to all those facts circumscribed by the term 'animal'. Our thesis is a proposition like that which states that the worker bees in the bee community communicate information about newly discovered feeding places by performing a sort of dance in the hive, or like that which states that mammals have seven cervical vertebrae. However, we see at once that in fact our thesis does not tell us something merely about insects or merely about mammals, since it also includes, for example, non-articulated creatures, unicellular animals like amoebae, infusoria, sea urchins and the like—*all* animals, *every* animal. Expressed in a rather extrinsic way we could say that our thesis is more universal than these other propositions. Yet why is it more universal, and in what respect? Because this thesis is meant to say something about animality as such, something about the essence of the animal: it is a *statement of essence.* It is not a statement of essence simply because it holds true for all animals and not merely for some of them. Rather, it is the other way around: it holds true for all animals because it is a statement of essence. Universal validity can only result from our knowledge insofar as it is essential in each case, and not the other way around.

Yet where does the essential character of a statement like that possessed by our thesis lie, if not in its universality? Where does the proposition 'the animal is poor in world' come from? We can answer once again that it derives from zoology, since this is the science that deals with animals. But precisely because zoology deals with animals this proposition cannot be a result of zoological investigation; rather, it must be its *presupposition.* For this presupposition ultimately involves an *antecedent determination* of what belongs in general to the *essence of the animal,* that is, a delimitation of the field within which any positive investigation of animals must move. Accordingly, if our thesis already contains a presupposition of all zoology, we cannot expect to derive the thesis from zoology in the first place. This seems to imply that in elucidating the proposition we will simply dispense with all the detailed wealth of acquired knowledge in this field, knowledge that can no longer be mastered even by the experts in it. So it seems. But what possible criterion do we then possess for the truth of our thesis? Where do we draw that thesis from in the first place? Is it an arbitrary one, or is it a hypothesis, the truth of which can be confirmed only by a specific investigation?

It is neither of these. The proposition does not derive from zoology, but it cannot be elucidated independently of zoology either. It requires a specific orientation toward zoology and biology in general, and yet it is not through them that its truth is to be determined. However, we cannot analyze this relationship more closely at this juncture.

Here I merely wish to point out the peculiar character of the proposition in question and the manner in which ordinary understanding approaches such propositions. We seem to take them from the relevant science (here zoology) and, at the same time, we try to use them to first secure a specific domain for the science in question and thus to secure its possibility as a science. Thus it is that we find ourselves moving in a *circle*. Ordinary understanding can only perceive and grasp what lies straight in front of it: it thus wishes to advance in a straight line, moving from the nearest point on to the next one, and so on. This is called progress. Ordinary understanding can only perceive circular movement in its own way too: that is to say, it moves along the circumference, taking its movement around the circle as a straightforward progression, until suddenly it stumbles upon its starting-point and comes to a standstill, at a loss because of its lack of progress. Since progress is the criterion employed by ordinary understanding, such understanding finds any circular movement objectionable and considers it a sign of impossibility. The fateful thing, however, is that this argument about circular movement is employed in philosophy itself, even though it is but a symptom of a tendency to reduce philosophy to the level of ordinary understanding.

The essential feature of the circular movement of philosophy does not lie in running around the periphery and returning to the point of departure. It lies in that view of the centre that this circular course alone can provide. The centre, that is, the middle and ground, reveals itself as such only in and for the movement that circles it. The circular character of philosophical thought is directly bound up with its ambiguity, an ambiguity that is not to be eliminated or, still less, levelled off by means of dialectic. It is characteristic that we repeatedly find in the history of philosophy such attempts to level off this circularity and ambiguity of philosophical thinking through the use of dialectic, and most recently in a grand and impressive form. Yet all dialectic in philosophy is only the expression of an embarrassment.

We can see that the relation between metaphysics and the positive sciences is and must be an ambiguous one if our thesis is a *metaphysical* rather than a zoological one. We must be prepared to assume the burden of this peculiar ambiguity, the disquieting circularity of our thesis, and attempt to approach its substantive content more closely. Yet in order to do so we must determine more clearly the relationship between our philosophical questioning and the science we call zoology—an elucidation that will be valid for the relationship between philosophy and all the sciences.

b) The relation of our philosophical questioning to zoology and biology.

Zoology, like every other science, is historical not simply with respect to the advances represented by its results but equally with regard to the regressions in its mode of inquiry. The regressions of a science are not generally obvious, but they are much more central than the advances, insofar as they always involve a failure of proper questioning in the science concerned. They imply a displacement of the proper metaphysical import of the science onto the outer surface of more specific areas of research, areas that may be left to support one another in mid-air. Every science is historical because the fundamental position a science adopts toward its domain and the way it conceives that domain in the first place are subject to change and transformation.

Today—and we can only ever speak of *our* Dasein as we are doing now—we find ourselves in a favorable situation. It is favorable not merely on account of the great variety and vitality of research but also because of a fundamental tendency to restore autonomy to 'life', as the *specific manner of being pertaining to animal and plant,* and to secure this autonomy for it. This suggests that within the totality of what we call natural science, contemporary biology is attempting to defend itself against the tyranny of physics and chemistry. That is not to say that within certain areas, or in the context of certain approaches within biology, questions framed in terms of physics and chemistry are never justifiable or useful. Rather, what the struggle within biology against physics and chemistry really means is that *'life' as such cannot in principle be grasped from within the perspective of these disciplines.* Yet this also implies that we cannot start by explaining 'living substance' in physico-chemical terms, only to find ourselves in the embarrassing position of having to admit some other factor later on when our calculations fail and we are left with an inexplicable residue. On the contrary, the delimitation of life must be accomplished on the basis of the fundamental character of living beings themselves as something that cannot be explained or grasped at all in physico-chemical terms. The task confronting biology as a science is to develop an entirely new projection of the objects of its inquiry. (Expressed from another point of view, which is not necessarily identical with what we have just said, the task today is to liberate ourselves from the mechanistic conception of life. Up till quite recently this negative tendency has been pursued under the slogans of 'vitalism', the 'tele-ological perspective of life', the 'struggle against mechanism' and so on. How-ever, this view of life is burdened with misunderstandings as great as those that beset the mechanistic conception of life.) What we have said already suggests that we cannot make any advances in this major task, or even com-prehend it properly, if we now merely advocate the case for animal psychology as opposed to mere morphology and physiology. For if we follow this path we shall fail to address the question from the perspective of the animality of the animal, and simply misinterpret in turn what has already been misinterpreted and distorted by the physico-chemical perspective, employing a psychology crudely adopted from the human domain.

Taking all this into consideration, we can now appreciate the magnitude of the difficulties surrounding a *metaphysical interpretation of life*. We can under-stand how hard it is for biology to assert its own essence within the domain of natural science.

However, inasmuch as the existence of every science, and thus that of biology as well, is historical, we cannot comprehend the occurrence of science or establish its relation to metaphysics by expecting biology to postpone the labors of positive research until a satisfactory metaphysical theory of life becomes available. Nor, indeed, can any purely autonomous and free-floating metaphys-ical theory, developed subsequently as a so-called synopsis, have any signifi-cance in this regard. We cannot separate metaphysics and positive research, playing them off against one another in this manner. They are not two con-secutive phases of a production process. The relation between them cannot be established in a rationalized, technical sort of way, as if science and metaphys-ics simply represented two branches of a single industrial concern, the former supplying the facts and the latter providing the fundamental concepts. On the contrary, the *inner unity of science and metaphysics* is a matter of *fate*. The significance of this fate is twofold. First, the whole possibility of a science always depends upon whether or not in a given era leading researchers emerge alongside the countless workers and technical experts who are also required. What I mean by the leadership of researchers does not consist in the startling or unusual character of their discoveries; rather, it consists in an original solidarity with the most elementary content of their respective fields. Actual and original solidarity with the most elementary content of their fields does not necessarily require explicit support from a fully developed philosophy or metaphysics. It is not the proper purpose of the latter to be instantly applied like a medicine, but rather, irrespective of any possible immediate application, to perform the incalculable task of preparing Dasein for that readiness on the basis of which such natural originality thrives. The second fundamental condition for the possibility of a genuine science as a matter of fate is that the contemporaries in question are alert enough and bold enough to sustain people such as researchers and allow them to be-there [*da-sein*]. Yet today we lack precisely the strength and confidence to let others who can accomplish something essential be there as such. This is a characteristic though dubious feature of the age. We react to the sensational because that is all we are hungry for, and we confuse what is sensational with what is great. On account of this same hunger for the sensational we are similarly lavish and indiscriminate in the praise we are ready to bestow. Yet we are equally liable to pass by what is essential, if only because we so seldom possess the capacity for genuine admiration, and so seldom manage to open one another up to what really deserves our admiration, remaining strong in such admiration. We can put this complaint more concretely with an apposite reference precisely to zoology: how many hundred competent students of natural science pass through the zoological institute of our university without being affected in the slightest by a researcher of the stature of Spemann? The effect of such influence should not express itself in a vain personality cult; it can only prove itself in the thoughtful respect which the individual shows in the world of such researchers.

The relation between metaphysics and positive research is not a matter of an organized operation or prearranged coordination. Rather, it is a matter of fate, and this means that it is always determined in turn by an inner readiness for communal cooperation. I touch upon it here because this state of affairs is decisive for our universities today. There are characteristic signs on both sides that such readiness is lacking. On the part of philosophy this is represented by that peculiar hyper-sophistication which allows us to imagine ourselves to be in a superior position merely on the basis of a second-hand philosophical knowledge of concepts and conceptual formulae that we have merely heard about or read in books, and which causes us to lecture the special sciences in a supercilious manner. Philosophical knowledge is supposed to be superior because of its more universal character. Yet this hyper-sophistication, this vacuous cleverness, is not a mature understanding that has been wrested from the matter itself. Corresponding to this hyper-sophisticated pseudo-philosophy, what we find in the field of research is a stubborn appeal to the so-called facts and an inability to understand that a fact yields nothing by itself, that every fact we can produce has always already undergone a process of interpretation. Between them, the hyper-sophistication of philosophy and the intransigence of the sciences create the hopeless situation in which both parties obstinately persist in talking past one another and foster the spurious freedom in which each eventually leaves the other to its own devices. Yet this freedom at bottom represents no more than the insecurity which belongs to everything that is inadequate and unsatisfactory. Such a state of affairs is symptomatic of contemporary science and represents its innermost danger.

And it is a danger all the more fatal because it is not properly recognized or understood. On the contrary, this situation is thought to herald an ideal state of affairs in which science becomes a self-enclosed technique and philosophy becomes another element within so-called general educational culture. It is obvious that we cannot possibly in this way prepare ourselves for any actual community between metaphysics and science as something actual. Admittedly, it seemed for a while that science itself was becoming increasingly unstable and this gave rise to the slogan 'the crisis of foundations in the sciences'. However, this crisis cannot break through in the serious and above all enduring manner that is required, because we are not sufficiently willing to let ourselves be shaken, so as to acquire the necessary range of vision for both the immensity and the elementary nature of the new tasks ahead. Science will not allow itself to enter such crisis because it is already much too preoccupied with the realm of practical and technical serviceability. This is how things have been up to now, and so matters stand: one side provides the fundamental concepts while the other delivers the facts. These are the essential existentiell reasons behind the contemporary relation between science and philosophy. These are the reasons it is so difficult to find our way when confronted by the necessity of securing the relation between philosophy and science in the requisite manner.

In what we have said so far, right from the beginning, we have avoided the erroneous idea that science is a nexus of valid propositions behind which there lies something else in turn that claims validity. Rather, we understand science as one possibility of the existence of human Dasein, one that is not necessary for the Dasein of man but represents a free possibility of existence. In this connection we can see that the fundamental character of this free possibility lies in historicity, and that the way in which it unfolds is not a matter of organization or of any dominant philosophical system, but a matter of the specific fate of Dasein in each case. Assuming that we find ourselves placed within this fate, we shall discover a proper stance with respect to the connection between living philosophy and living science only if we can sow among us the seeds of an appropriate mutual understanding. This is not the kind of thing that can be taught. It is a matter of an inner maturity of existence.

On account of this connection, we are forced to take up a certain orientation with regard to zoology. However, we must not do this in a superficial manner by merely reporting on the current state of research and by examining the sundry theories involved. Rather, we must simply bear in mind that all the disciplines that deal with life are caught up today in a remarkable transformation, the basic tendency of which is directed to restoring an autonomous status to life. This is not simply a straightforward and self-evident matter either, as the entire history of the problem demonstrates. Throughout the long history of the problem of life we can observe how the attempt has been made either to interpret life—that is, the kind of being that pertains to animals and plants—

from the perspective of man, or alternatively to explain life by means of laws adopted from the realm of material nature. Yet both of these erstwhile forms of explanation produce an inexplicable residue which in general is simply explained away. What is lacking in all this is insight into the necessary task of securing above all else *the essential nature of life in and of itself* and a resolute attempt to accomplish it. The fact that we may not take success for granted here, as the history of the problem shows, suggests that the disconcerting false trails we have followed hitherto are not the result of superficial thinking. There are essential reasons for them. On the other hand, we can see that the conception of life in terms of its intermediate position between material nature and human existence often forms the core of a general view that interprets man and everything else from the perspective of life: the biological worldview. Max Scheler recently attempted to treat this hierarchical sequence of material beings, life, and spirit in a unified manner within the context of an anthropology. He did so in the conviction that man is the being who unites within himself all the levels of beings—physical being, the being of plants and animals, and the being specific to spirit. I believe this thesis to be a fundamental error in Scheler's position, one that must inevitably deny him any access to metaphysics. The extent to which this is the case will become apparent as our considerations proceed. Nevertheless, the way in which Scheler has posed the question, however programmatic it has remained, is still an essential one in many respects and superior to anything yet attempted.

> *§46. The thesis that 'the animal is poor in world' in*
> *relation to the thesis that 'man is world-forming'.*
> *The relation between poverty in world and world-*
> *formation does not entail hierarchical assessment.*
> *Poverty in world as deprivation of world.*

If we now return from these fundamental considerations to our thesis that the animal is poor in world, we must admit that recent research in biology, provided that we are capable of interpreting it in a philosophical way, strongly suggests the possibility of illustrating this thesis directly. At the same time the thesis is framed in such a way that, like every metaphysical thesis, it is capable of compelling positive research to engage in fundamental reflection. Indeed, at first sight, our thesis seems to run directly counter to the most penetrating fundamental reflections in biology and zoology, when we consider that ever since J. von Uexküll we have all become accustomed to talking about the *environmental world of the animal.* Our thesis, on the other hand, asserts that the animal is poor in world. It would make an instructive contribution to our understanding of the problem in question if we could now enter into a detailed and philosophical interpretation of the recent theory of life. But we cannot do so at this juncture, especially since the main thrust of our considerations does not rest upon a thematic metaphysics of life (of animals and plants).

We have placed our thesis that the animal is poor in world *between* the other two, which assert that the stone is worldless and that man is world-forming. If we now consider the second thesis in relation to the third, then it immediately becomes clear why we have done so. Poor in world implies poverty as opposed to richness; poverty implies less as opposed to more. The animal is poor in world, it somehow possesses less. But less of what? Less in respect of what is accessible to it, of whatever as an animal it can deal with, of whatever it can be affected by as an animal, of whatever it can relate to as a living being. Less as against more, namely as against the richness of all those relationships that human Dasein has at its disposal. The bee, for example, has its hive, its cells, the blossoms it seeks out, and the other bees of the swarm. The bee's world is limited to a specific domain and is strictly circumscribed. And this is also true of the world of the frog, the world of the chaffinch and so on. But it is not merely the world of each particular animal that is limited in range—the extent and manner in which an animal is able to penetrate whatever is accessible to it is also limited. The worker bee is familiar with the blossoms it frequents, along with their colour and scent, but it does not know the stamens of these blossoms *as* stamens, it knows nothing about the roots of the plant and it cannot know anything about the number of stamens or leaves, for example. As against this, the world of man is a rich one, greater in range, far more extensive in its penetrability, constantly extendable not only in its range (we can always bring more and more beings into consideration) but also in respect to the manner in which we can penetrate ever more deeply in this penetrability. Consequently we can characterize the relation man possesses to the world by referring to the extendability of everything that he relates to. This is why we speak of man as world-forming.

If we now look more closely at the distinction between poverty in world and world-formation in this form, this distinction reveals itself as one of degree in terms of levels of completeness with respect to the accessibility of beings in each case. And this immediately supplies us with a concept of world: world initially signifies the sum total of beings accessible to man or animals alike, variable as it is in range and depth of penetrability. Thus 'poor in world' is inferior with respect to the greater value of 'world-forming'. This is all so obvious that there is no need to discuss it any further. We have long been familiar with such self-evident observations, so much so that we do not understand what all the commotion is about or what this distinction is supposed to contribute to determining the essence of the animality of the animal. It looks as if we are simply tampering with the problem by introducing specific terms like world and environmental world into the discussion.

Certainly the relation we have described above between the animal's poverty in world and the world-formation of man has a suspiciously self-evident clarity that actually disappears as soon as we really come to grips with the issue. Nevertheless, we must be aware of this apparent clarity if we are to understand the kind of arguments to which our supposedly most natural considerations always tend so casually to appeal. We identified a relation of difference in degree with respect to the accessibility of beings, a relation of more and less, of lower and higher, a relation of levels of completeness. Yet even a little reflection soon renders it questionable whether in fact poverty is necessarily and intrinsically of lesser significance with respect to richness. The reverse might well be true. In any case this comparison between man and animal, characterized in terms of world-formation and poverty in world respectively, allows no evaluative ranking or assessment with respect to completeness or incompleteness, quite irrespective of the fact that such evaluative ranking is factically premature and unsuitable here. For we immediately find ourselves in the greatest perplexity over the question concerning greater or lesser completeness in each case with respect to the accessibility of beings, as soon as we compare the discriminatory capacity of a falcon's eye with that of the human eye or the canine sense of smell with our own, for example. However ready we are to rank man as a higher being with respect to the animal, such an assessment is deeply questionable, especially when we consider that man can sink lower than any animal. No animal can become depraved in the same way as man. Of course in the last analysis this consideration itself reveals the necessity of speaking of a 'higher' in some sense. But we can already see from all this that the criterion according to which we talk of height and depth in this connection is obscure. May we talk of a 'higher' and a 'lower' at all in the realm of what is essential? Is the essence of man higher than the essence of the animal? All this is questionable even as a question.

This habitual assessment is not merely questionable with regard to the relation between man and animal, and is an assessment which consequently demands careful examination to determine its legitimacy, its limits, and its usefulness. The questionable character of this approach also affects the judgements we make *within* the animal realm itself. Here too we are accustomed to speaking about higher and lower animals, but it is nevertheless a fundamental mistake to suppose that amoebae or infusoria are more imperfect or incomplete animals than elephants or apes. Every animal and every species of animal as such is just as perfect and complete as any other. Thus it should be clear from everything we have said that from the outset this talk of poverty in world and world-formation must not be taken as a hierarchical evaluation. Certainly we wish to articulate a relation and a distinction here, albeit in another respect. In what respect? That is precisely what we are seeking to discover. But first of all it is necessary to determine the concept of *poverty*

[Armut] in an appropriate manner and to define its specific meaning in connection with the phenomenon of world if we wish to comprehend our thesis concerning poverty in world.

What is poor here by no means represents merely what is 'less' or 'lesser' with respect to what is 'more' or 'greater'. Being poor does not simply mean possessing nothing, or little, or less than another. Rather being poor means *being deprived* [Entbehren]. Such deprivation in turn is possible in different ways depending on *how* whatever is poor is deprived and comports itself in its deprivation, *how* it responds to the deprivation, *how* it takes this deprivation. In short: with regard to *what* such a being is deprived of and above all to *the way* in which it is deprived, namely *the way* in which it is *in a mood* [zu Mute]—*poverty in mood* [Ar-mut]. It is true that we rarely employ or under-stand the idea of poverty in this proper sense which relates to the characteristic way in which man is poor. We tend to employ it in the more extended and weaker sense of 'poor' or 'meagre', in talking of the poor or meagre flow of water in a stream, for example. Yet even here it is not merely a case of comparing what is less at one moment with what is more at another. In this context 'poor' implies having a lack or insufficiency. Here too poverty repre-sents a lacking or absence of something which could be present and generally ought to be present. This weaker sense of 'poor' must be distinguished from the other sense of being poor which is a kind of *being in a mood* [Zumuteseins], one that we must characterize by the term '*in a mood of poverty*' [armmütig], by analogy with 'in a mood of melancholy' [*schwermütig*] or 'in a mood of humility' [*demütig*]. This is meant to indicate that poverty is not merely a characteristic property, but the very way in which man comports and bears himself. *Poverty in this proper sense* of human *existence* is also a kind of deprivation and necessarily so. Yet from such deprivation we can draw our own peculiar power of procuring transparency and inner freedom for Dasein. Poverty in the sense of *being in a mood of poverty* [Armmütigkeit] does not simply imply indifference with respect to what we possess. On the contrary, it represents that preeminent kind of having in which we seem not to have. 'Poverty' as a noun in its weaker usage implies both these senses, including the 'poor' flow of water in the river, even though in this case the river in its being deprived cannot be in any kind of mood.

What then is the significance of the word 'poverty' in the expression 'world-poverty'? How is the 'poverty in world' of the animal to be understood? In what sense is the animal domain to be described as poor? At the moment all this remains obscure. It cannot be decided by reflections on language but only by taking a look at animality itself. In any case the poverty in question does not express a purely quantitative difference. Yet this is already to say that in the expressions 'poverty in world' and 'world-formation' the term 'world' itself cannot express quantity, sum total, or degree with respect to the accessibility of beings.

§47. The thesis that 'the animal is poor in world' in
relation to the thesis that 'the stone is worldless'.
Worldlessness as not having access to beings. Provisional
characterization of world as the accessibility of beings.

Now that we have defined the concept of poverty more precisely as a kind of deprivation in some sense, we can begin to take another step toward understanding what the poverty in world of the animal signifies. If poverty implies deprivation then the thesis that 'the animal is poor in world' means something like 'the animal is deprived of world', 'the animal has no world'. This step also helps to define our second thesis in relation to the third, according to which man is world-forming. For man does have a world.

But then the relation between the second thesis and the first, according to which the stone is worldless, instantly becomes problematic because there no longer seems to be any distinction between them. The stone is worldless, it is without world, it has no world. Neither the stone nor the animal has world. But this not-having of world is not to be understood in the same sense in each case. The different expressions world*lessness* and *poverty* in world already indicate that there is indeed a distinction here. But if the animal is thus brought into such proximity to the stone, then we immediately find ourselves confronted by the decisive question as to the distinction between the way in which the stone has no world and the way in which the animal does not have a world. Being worldless and being poor in world both represent a kind of not-having of world. Poverty in world implies a deprivation of world. Worldlessness on the other hand is constitutive of the stone in the sense that the stone *cannot even be deprived* of something like world. Merely not having world is insufficient here. The possibility of being deprived of world requires further conditions. What do we mean, then, when we say that the stone cannot even be deprived of world? We must initially clarify this point at the present stage of our investigation.

Let us provisionally define world as those beings which are in each case accessible and may be dealt with, accessible in such a way that dealing with such beings is possible or necessary for the kind of being pertaining to a particular being. The stone is without world. The stone is lying on the path, for example. We can say that the stone is exerting a certain pressure upon the surface of the earth. It is 'touching' the earth. But what we call 'touching' here is not a form of touching at all in the stronger sense of the word. It is not at all like *that* relationship which the lizard has to the stone on which it lies basking in the sun. And the touching implied in both these cases is above all not the same as *that* touch which we experience when we rest our hand upon the head of another human being. The lying upon . . . , the touching involved in our three examples is fundamentally different in each case. Returning to the stone: it lies upon the earth but does not touch it. The earth is *not given* for the stone as an underlying support which bears it, let alone given as earth. Nor of course can the stone ever sense this earth as such, even as it lies upon it. The stone lies on the path. If we throw it into the meadow then it will lie wherever it falls. We can cast it into a ditch filled with water. It sinks and ends up lying on the bottom. In each case according to circumstance the stone crops up here or there, amongst and amidst a host of other things, but always in such a way that everything present around it remains essentially *inaccessible* to the stone itself. Because in its being a stone it has no possible access to anything else around it, anything that it might attain or possess as such, it cannot possibly be said to be deprived of anything either. The stone is, i.e., it is such and such, and as such turns up here or there or is simply not present. It is—but is essentially *without access* to those beings amongst which it is in its own way (presence at hand), and this belongs to its being. The stone is worldless. The *worldlessness* of a being can now be defined as its having no access to those beings (*as* beings) amongst which this particular being with this specific manner of being is. Having no access belongs to and characterizes the specific manner of being of the particular being in question. It is beside the point to regard the fact that the stone has no access as some kind of lack. For having no access is precisely what makes possible its specific kind of being, i.e., the realm of being of physical and material nature and the laws governing it.

The lizard basking in the sun on its warm stone does not merely crop up in the world. It has sought out this stone and is accustomed to doing so. If we now remove the lizard from its stone, it does not simply lie wherever we have put it but starts looking for its stone again, irrespective of whether or not it actually finds it. The lizard basks in the sun. At least this is how we describe what it is doing, although it is doubtful whether it really comports itself in the same way as we do when we lie out in the sun, i.e., whether the sun is accessible to it *as* sun, whether the lizard is capable of experiencing the rock *as* rock. Yet the lizard's relation to the sun and to warmth is different from that of the warm stone simply lying present at hand in the sun. Even if we avoid every misleading and premature psychological interpretation of the specific manner of being pertaining to the lizard and prevent ourselves from 'empathetically' projecting our own feelings onto this animal, we can still perceive a distinction between the *specific manner of being* pertaining to the lizard and to *animals,* and the *specific manner of being* pertaining to a *material thing*. It is true that the rock on which the lizard lies is not given for the lizard *as* rock, in such a way that it could inquire into its mineralogical constitution for example. It is true that the sun in which it is basking is not given for the lizard *as* sun, in such a way that it could ask questions of astrophysics about it and expect to find the answers. But it is not true to say that the lizard merely crops up as present at hand *beside* the rock, *amongst* other things such as the sun for example, in the same way as the stone lying nearby is simply present at hand amongst other things. On the contrary, the lizard has its *own relation* to the rock, to the sun, and to a host of other things. One is tempted to suggest that what we identify as the rock and the sun are just lizard-things for the lizard, so to speak. When we say that the lizard is lying on the rock, we ought to cross out the word 'rock' in order to indicate that whatever the lizard is lying on is certainly given *in some way* for the lizard, and yet is not known to the lizard *as* a rock. If we cross out the word we do not simply mean to imply that something else is in question here or is taken as something else. Rather we imply that whatever it is is not accessible to it *as a being*. The blade of grass that the beetle crawls up, for example, is not a blade of grass for it at all; it is not something possibly destined to become part of the bundle of hay with which the peasant will feed his cow. The blade of grass is simply a beetle-path on which the beetle specifically seeks beetle-nourishment, and not just any edible matter in general. Every animal as animal has a specific set of relationships to its sources of nourishment, its prey, its enemies, its sexual mates, and so on. These relationships, which are infinitely difficult for us to grasp and require a high degree of cautious methodological foresight on our part, have a peculiar fundamental character of their own, the metaphysical significance of which has never properly been perceived or understood before. We shall learn more about this fundamental character when we come to our concluding interpretation later on. The animal has a specific relationship to a circumscribed domain with respect to its sources of nourishment, its prey, its enemies and its sexual mates. But throughout the course of its life the animal also maintains itself in a specific element, whether it is water or air or both, in such a way that the element belonging to it goes unnoticed by that animal, although as soon as the animal is removed from its appropriate element and placed in an alien environment it instantly reacts by attempting to escape from the new element and striving to return to its original one. Thus certain things are accessible to the animal in a way which is not arbitrary and within limits which are not arbitrary either. The animal's *way of being,* which we call '*life*', is *not without access* to what is around it and about it, to that amongst which it appears as a living being. It is because of this that the claim arises that the animal has an environmental world of its own within which it moves. Throughout the course of its life the animal is confined to its environmental world, immured as it were within a fixed sphere that is incapable of further expansion or contraction.

Yet if we understand *world* as the *accessibility of beings,* how can we possibly claim that the animal is poor in world—especially if poverty implies being deprived—when it is obvious that the animal does have access of some kind?

Even if the animal has access to beings in a different way from ourselves and within more narrowly circumscribed limits, it is still not entirely deprived of world. The animal has world. Thus absolute deprivation of world does not belong to the animal after all.

§48. The sense in which the animal has and does not have world: attaining a place from which to begin the elucidation of the concept of world.

The preceding comparative examination has already succeeded in clarifying the significance of our three theses, but that only means that our guiding problem, the question concerning the concept of world, has become more acute. Our perplexity about what we should understand by world and the relationship to world has increased. If by world we understand beings in their accessibility in each case, if such accessibility of beings is a fundamental character of the concept of world, and if being a living being means having access to other beings, then the animal stands on the side of man. Man and animals alike *have world.* On the other hand, if the intermediate thesis concerning the animal's poverty in world is justified and poverty represents deprivation and deprivation in turn means not having something, then the animal stands on the side of the stone. The animal thus reveals itself as a being which *both has and does not have world.* This is contradictory and thus logically impossible. But metaphysics and everything essential has a logic quite different from that of sound common understanding. If these propositions concerning the having and not-having of world in relation to the animal are legitimate, then we must be employing the ideas of world and accessibility of beings in a different sense in each case. In other words, the concept of world has still not been clarified. We cannot as yet see our way forward on account of the obscurity of this concept. Nevertheless we have found the place where such elucidation must begin and have identified the knot which we must first strive to undo. We shall only be able to do so if we pursue its intricate entanglements and the convolution of the propositions that the animal has and does not have world. For this is where the two extremes of worldlessness and world-formation are, as it were, intertwined with one another. Only in solving this problem in an original fashion will we be able to see what world means and, even more importantly, see whether we really understand the concept and the phenomenon of world or whether all this simply remains an empty phrase for us. This intertwining is expressed in the intermediate position occupied by the thesis concerning the animal. Consequently we must attempt once again to acquire further insight into the essence of the animal and its animality. But we will now no longer be able to proceed with the same naivety as we did before. For we have already seen that the world of the animal, if we may express ourselves in this way, is not simply a degree or species of the world of man. Nor is the animal a being that is simply present at hand. On the contrary, its specific manner of being is defined by the fact that it has access of some kind. The question which now concerns us more precisely is this: What does the animal relate to, and what sort of relationship does it have to whatever it seeks as nourishment, seizes as prey, or attacks as hostile?

Chapter Four

Clarification of the Essence of the Animal's Poverty in World by Way of the Question Concerning the Essence of Animality, the Essence of Life in General, and the Essence of the Organism

§49. The methodological question concerning the ability to transpose oneself into other beings (animal, stone, and man) as a substantive question concerning the specific manner of being that belongs to such beings.

We have, then, to specify how the animal stands in relation to all of this, and how whatever it is that the animal stands in relation to is given for the animal. But how are we to do so? How else than by transposing ourselves into the animal? But do we not then run the danger of interpreting the being of the animal from our own perspective? Perhaps we could ultimately obviate any misinterpretation that might arise. However, there is another much more important and quite fundamental question here: *Can we transpose ourselves into an animal at all?* For we are hardly able to transpose ourselves into another being of our own kind, into another human being. And what then of the stone—can we transpose ourselves into a stone?

Thus once again we find ourselves immediately confronted by a *methodological* question, but one which is *quite unique in kind*. Basically, every methodological question, that is, every question which concerns how we should *initially* approach and *subsequently* pursue a given subject matter, is directly connected with the question concerning the *substantive character* of the subject matter itself. But here this is the case in a quite exceptional sense. For the *substantive problem* with which we are concerned is precisely that of *accessibility itself,* the question concerning the potential access that man and animal characteristically have to other beings. Strictly speaking, therefore, this methodological question is a *substantive one.* Thus when we ask about transposing ourselves, about the possibility of man's transposing himself into another human being, into an animal, or into a stone, we are simultaneously asking this question as well: what is the kind of being which belongs to these beings insofar as they permit, resist, or possibly forbid as entirely inappropriate any such self-transposition into them in each case?

What are we to say, then, concerning the possibility of man's transposing himself into another being, whether it is a being like himself or one which is quite different in kind? We cannot hope to unfold this question in all its breadth here, for it must be kept within *those* limits prescribed by the problem at issue.

First of all we must clarify our thesis that the animal is poor in world. We shall attempt to elucidate the question concerning the possibility of man's transposing himself into another human being, into an animal, or into a stone, precisely *through* these *three* questions: Can we transpose ourselves into an animal? Can we transpose ourselves into a stone? Can we transpose ourselves into another human being? In asking these questions we are less concerned with the problem of the possibility of grasping these beings ourselves than we are with what we can hereby learn about those very beings that are to be grasped. Our discussion of this question of self-transposition serves simply to clarify the position of stone, animal, and man in relation to the problem of world. The specific task of the following discussion is to eliminate that initial naive approach to the question which assumes that we are dealing with three beings all present at hand in exactly the same way.

In general the question at issue concerns the possibility of man's transposing himself into another being that he himself is not. In this connection self-transposition does not mean the factical transference of one existing human being into the interior of another being. Nor does it mean the factical substitution of oneself for another being so as to take its place. On the contrary, the other being is precisely supposed to remain *what* it is and *how* it is. Transposing oneself into this being means going along with what it is and with how it is. Such going-along-with means directly learning how it is with this being, discovering what it is like to be this being *with* which we are going along *in this way*. Perhaps in doing so we may even see right into the nature of the other being more essentially and more incisively than that being could possibly do by itself. Going along with the other being can also mean helping to bring it to itself—or possibly letting it be mistaken about itself. Consequently, this self-transposition does not mean actually putting oneself in the place of the other being and displacing it in the process. However clear this *negative* injunction may seem, the positive interpretation of self-transposition that is frequently offered is nonetheless misleading. It is said that of course there is no question of *any actual* transporting oneself into another being, as if we could somehow vacate our own position and directly fill out and occupy the place of that being. The transposition is not an actual process but rather one that *merely transpires in thought*. And this in turn is easily understood to mean not an actual transposition, but an *'as if,'* one in which we *merely act as if* we were the other being.

This conception of self-transposition, one which is also widespread within philosophy, contains a fundamental error precisely because it overlooks the decisive *positive* moment of self-transposition. This moment does not consist in our simply forgetting ourselves as it were and trying our utmost to act as if we were the other being. On the contrary, it consists precisely in we ourselves being precisely ourselves, and only in this way first bringing about the possibility of ourselves being able to go along with the other being while remaining *other* with respect to it. There can be no going-along-with if the one who wishes and is meant to go along with the other relinquishes himself in advance. 'Transposing oneself into . . .' means neither an actual transference nor a mere thought-experiment that supposes such transference has been achieved.

Yet the question remains: What does it mean to say here that we bring about the possibility of going along with the other by our being ourselves? What does 'going-along-with' mean? *What* is it that we are going along *with* and *how* do we do so? If we understand self-transposition into another being as a way of going along with this being, then it is obvious that the expression 'self-transposition' is still liable to be misunderstood in certain respects and indeed is quite inadequate with respect to the decisive aspect of the issue. The same is true of the term 'empathy' which suggests that we must first 'feel our way into' the other being in order to reach it. And this implies that we are 'outside' in the first place. The term 'empathy' has provided a guiding thread for a whole range of fundamentally mistaken theories concerning man's relationship to other human beings and to other beings in general, theories that we are only gradually beginning to overcome today. Yet just as the coining of a new word and its elevation to a key expression indicates the emergence of a new insight, so too the disappearance of such expressions from our language often marks a change in understanding and the renunciation of a former error. It is no mere willfulness or eccentricity if in philosophy today we no longer speak of 'lived experiences', 'lived experiences of consciousness' or 'consciousness' itself. On the contrary, *we find ourselves forced to adopt another language because of a fundamental transformation of existence.* Or to put it more precisely, this change transpires along with this new language. If today we give up using the term 'empathy', if we regard this talk of self-transposition into another being in a purely provisional and conditional manner and prefer a different way of talking instead, then it is not simply a matter of choosing a better expression to express the same opinion or the same thing. On the contrary, *both the opinion and the matter in question have changed into something else.* On the other hand, it is no accident either that expressions like 'self-transposition' and 'empathy' have come to play such a dominant role in describing man's fundamental relationships to beings. We cannot pursue the reasons for this here. Instead, after this provisional elucidation of what we properly mean by 'self-transposition', namely a going-along-with, we will proceed to elucidate the three questions: Can we transpose ourselves into an *animal?* Can we transpose ourselves into a *stone?* Can we transpose ourselves into *another human being?*

When we pose this *first question:* Can we transpose ourselves into an animal?, what is it that is actually in question here? Nothing other than this: whether or not we can succeed in going along with the animal in the way in which it sees and hears, the way in which it seizes its prey or evades its predators, the way in which it builds its nest and so forth. For we do not question the fact that the being into which we wish to transpose ourselves does relate to other beings, that it has access to its prey and to its predators and deals with them accordingly. The question as to whether we can transpose ourselves into the animal assumes without question that in relation to the animal something like a going-along-with, a *going along with it in its access to and in its dealings with its world* is possible *in the first place* and does not represent an intrinsically nonsensical undertaking. We do not question that the animal as such carries around with it, as it were, a sphere offering the possibility of transposition. The only question concerns our factical success in transposing ourselves into this particular sphere. The only question concerns the steps we have factically to take in order to accomplish this self-transposition and the factical limits to such an undertaking.

When we pose the *second question:* Can we transpose ourselves into a stone?, we find ourselves involved in a completely different kind of question, in spite of the fact that it has the same linguistic form as the first. Here we do not ask ourselves whether we factically possess ways and means of going along with the stone in its way of being and kind of being. We ask rather whether the stone as a stone offers us, or could ever offer us, any possibility of transposing ourselves into it at all, whether something like a going-along-with still has any sense at all in this case. Now we generally have a quick and ready answer to this question: No, we reply, we cannot transpose ourselves into a stone. And this is impossible for us not because we lack the appropriate means to accomplish something that is possible in principle. It is impossible because the stone as such does not admit of this possibility at all, offers no sphere intrinsically belonging to its being such that we could transpose ourselves into the stone. I say emphatically that we *usually* answer in this way because in fact there are ways and means belonging to human Dasein in which man never simply regards purely material things, or indeed technical things, as such but rather 'animates' them, as we might somewhat misleadingly put it. There are two fundamental ways in which this can happen: first when human Dasein is determined in its existence by *myth,* and second in the case of *art.* But it would be a fundamental mistake to try and dismiss such animation as an exception or even as a purely metaphorical procedure which does not really correspond to the facts, as something phantastical based upon the imagination, or as mere illusion. What is at issue here is not the opposition between actual reality and illusory appearance, but the distinction between quite different *kinds* of possible *truth.* But for the moment, in accordance with the subject under consideration, we shall remain within that dimension of truth pertaining to scientific and metaphysical knowledge, which have together long since determined the way in which we conceive of truth in our everyday reflection and judgement, in our 'natural' way of knowing.

If we now pose the *third question:* Can we as human beings transpose ourselves into another human being?, we find ourselves in a different situation again compared to the first two questions. It is true that we seem to be confronting the same question as in the case of the animal. Indeed it appears much less questionable to us, indeed as not questionable at all, that in certain contexts and situations other human beings on average comport themselves to things exactly as we do ourselves; and furthermore, that a number of human beings not only have the same comportment toward the same things, but can also *share* one and the same comportment *with one another,* without this shared experience being fragmented in the process; it appears that it is possible, accordingly, to go along [*Mitgang*] with others in their access [*Zugang*] to things and in their dealings [*Umgang*] with those things. This is a *fundamental feature* of man's own immediate experience of existence. Once again the only questionable thing concerns the factical extent of this ability to go along with others and the means to facilitate it in particular cases. For we know from the everyday experience of our Dasein, and often enough seem to lament the fact, that we find it so difficult to transpose ourselves into other human beings and so seldom find ourselves really able to go along with them.

Nevertheless, this third question as to whether we can transpose ourselves into another human being is not the same as the question as to whether we can transpose ourselves into an animal. In the latter case we tacitly assume that this possibility of self-transposition and a certain going-along-with exists in principle, that the very idea makes sense as we say. Yet here where man is concerned we cannot even make such an assumption concerning the intrinsic possibility of one human being transposing him- or herself into another human being. The reason we cannot make this assumption is not because other human beings forbid the possibility of our transposing ourselves into them by their very essence, as was the case with the stone. Rather, it is because this possibility already and originally belongs to man's own essence. Insofar as human beings exist at all, they already find themselves transposed in their existence into other human beings, even if there are factically no other human beings in the vicinity. Consequently the Da-sein of man, the Da-sein in man means, not exclusively but amongst other things, being transposed into other human beings. The ability to transpose oneself into others and go along with them, with the Dasein in them, always already happens on the basis of man's Dasein, and happens as Dasein. For the being-there of Da-sein means *being with others,* precisely in the manner of Dasein, i.e., existing with others. The question concerning whether we human beings can transpose ourselves into other human beings does not ask anything, because it is not a possible question in the first place. It is a meaningless, indeed a nonsensical question because it is fundamentally redundant. If we really think the concept and essence of man in asking whether or not we can transpose ourselves into another human being, then we soon realize that we cannot think this question through to the end. Being-with belongs to the essence of man's existence, i.e., to the existence of every unique individual in each case.

And yet how often we feel burdened by our inability to go along with the other. And do we not experience a new sense of elation in our Dasein each time we accomplish such going-along-with in some essential relationship with other human beings? Thus the ability to go along with . . . , the ability to transpose oneself, is also questionable where other human beings are concerned, but it is questionable *even though, indeed precisely because,* in accordance with the essence of his being man always already finds that he is with others. For it is part of the essential constitution of human Dasein that it intrinsically means being with others, that the factically existing human being always already and necessarily moves factically in a particular way of being with . . . , i.e., a particular way of going along with. Now for several reasons, and to some extent essential ones, this going along with one another is a going apart from one another and a going against one another, or rather, at first and for the most part a going alongside one another. It is precisely this inconspicuous and self-evident going alongside one another, as a particular way of being with one another and being transposed into one another, that creates the illusion that in this being alongside one another there is initially a gap which needs to be bridged, as though human beings were not transposed into one another at all here, as though one human being would first have to empathize their way into the other in order to reach them. For a long time now this illusion has also led philosophy astray and has done so to an extent one would hardly credit. Philosophy has reinforced this illusion even further by propounding the dogma that the individual human being exists for him- or herself as an individual and that it is the individual ego with its ego-sphere which is initially and primarily given to itself as what is most certain. This has merely given philosophical sanction to the view that some kind of being with one another must first be produced out of this solipsistic isolation.

You can see from this context how crucial it is to grasp this fundamental relationship between human beings and thus the essential character of human Dasein in an adequate manner. Crucial, that is, if we are successfully to pose the further question of how man, to whose essence such being with others belongs, can transpose himself as man into an animal. It is somehow self-evident that the animal for its part bears with it a peculiar sphere of its own that makes possible a transposition into it in accordance with its own animality.

Let us now summarize once more what we have said so far. The question we are confronting concerns the essence of the animality of the animal. The task in this connection is to develop this question as a question. For us the development of the question itself is far more essential and important than finding some quick and ready answer to it. For any answer, if it is a true one, is conditional and thus changing and changeable. But what remains as a permanent and recurrent task of philosophy is precisely to develop the fundamental difficulty of this question properly, to grasp the question concerning *the essence of animality* and thus *the essence of life in general* in all its questionableness. It is only in this way that we shall succeed in coming to grips with the substantive content of the problem involved here.

That is why in the investigation so far we have deliberately and repeatedly attempted to clarify the difficulty of the problem from quite different points of view, in the last resort by seeking to orient the possibility of human beings transposing themselves into other human beings, into an animal, or into a stone. The specific intention of this particular discussion was to free us completely from the naive view from which we originally started, namely that the beings in question—stone, animal, man, and indeed plants—are all given to us on the same level in exactly the same way. This apparently natural and immediate point of departure from a manifold of apparently homogeneous givens is in fact an illusion. And it is an illusion that is instantly revealed for what it is as soon as we begin to pursue the question: Can we transpose ourselves into an animal, a stone, or a human being? In this connection we have merely adumbrated the idea of self-transposition by talking about going along with. And we immediately discovered that the expression 'self-transposition' is fundamentally inappropriate, at least where we are concerned with one human being going along with another. This expression and the way of questioning associated with it is especially inappropriate if the term 'empathy' is invoked. In addressing these three questions: Can we transpose ourselves into an animal, into a stone, or into a human being?, we saw with respect to the first that transposing oneself into an animal is in principle a possibility for man, i.e., one that is not meaningfully in question for him. The only thing that is questionable concerns the factical realization of this possibility of transposing oneself into the animal. With respect to the stone, the question: Can we transpose ourselves into a stone?, is impossible in principle, and the question about how we might go about factically transposing ourselves is consequently quite meaningless here. With respect to man and the human potential for self-transposition into another human being, it transpired that the question is superfluous because in a sense it does not know what it is asking. For if the question is really directed toward man in his essence, it becomes redundant to the extent that being human means being transposed into the other, means being with the other. The question concerning the factical realization of such being-with-one-another is not a problem of empathy, nor a theoretical problem of self-transposition, but is a question of factical existence. From our discussion of this question, and especially of this latter one, we also saw how the erroneous theory of empathy and everything associated with it could possibly arise in the first place. For this theory emerges from the

208 Fundamental Concepts of Metaphysics [304–306]

view that in his relationship to other human beings, man is first of all an isolated being existing for himself. We would therefore in principle initially have to seek a bridge from one human being to another and vice-versa. But the illusion of such isolation arises from the circumstance that human beings factically move around in a peculiar form of being transposed into one another, one which is characterized by an indifferent going alongside one another. This illusion of a prior separation between one human being and another is reinforced by the philosophical dogma that man is initially to be understood as subject and as consciousness, that he is primarily and most indubitably given to himself as consciousness for a subject.

The theory according to which man is initially subject and consciousness, and is given to himself primarily and most indubitably as consciousness, basically arose from quite different intentions and perspectives in connection with Descartes and his attempt to lay the foundations of metaphysics. It is a theory which has come to pervade all philosophy in the modern age and was subjected by Kant to a peculiar, although not an essential, transformation. This led finally to the Hegelian attempt to absolutize the approach which takes the isolated ego-subject as its point of departure, which is why we describe this philosophy as absolute idealism. If we understand man in this sense as subject and consciousness, as modern idealism since Descartes has done as a matter of course, then the fundamental possibility of penetrating into the originary essence of man, i.e., of comprehending the Dasein in him, escapes our grasp from the start. All subsequent attempts to correct this situation have proved useless and have merely forced us into such a position as has been developed in Hegel's absolute idealism. I cannot pursue these historical connections any further here. I would merely like to indicate that the problem of the relationship of human being to human being does not concern a question of epistemology or the question of how one human being understands another. It concerns rather a problem of being itself, i.e., a problem of metaphysics. On the basis of a fundamentally inadequate metaphysical conception of man (as ego) and of human personality, Kant and his successors appeal to the notion of *absolute person* or *absolute spirit,* and then attempt to determine the essence of man in turn on the basis of this inadequate concept of spirit. The self-contained character of this absolute systematicity only conceals the questionableness of its initial approach and its point of departure, since here the problem of man, of human Dasein in general, has not been properly recognized as a problem. But Hegel's step from Kant to absolute idealism is the sole consequence of the development of Western philosophy. It became *possible* and *necessary* through Kant because the problem of human Dasein, the problem of finitude, did not properly become a problem for Kant himself. That is to say, this did not become a central problem of philosophy because Kant himself, as the second edition of the *Critique of Pure Reason* reveals, helped to prepare the turn away from an uncomprehended finitude toward a comforting infinitude. I cannot go into these matters in greater detail here but they are discussed in my book *Kant and the Problem of Metaphysics,* where I have attempted to develop the necessity of the problem of finitude in relation to metaphysics. In that book I was not concerned with providing a better interpretation of Kant. What the neo-Kantians and the older Kantians like to think about Kant is a matter of complete indifference to me. The consequence I have pointed out is a necessary one, and, in the manner in which Hegel accomplished it, is worthy of our admiration. Yet this very consequence is already a sign of overconfidence in attempting to grasp the infinite. In-consequentiality belongs to finitude, not as a deficiency or an embarrassment but as an effective power. Finitude renders dialectic impossible and reveals its illusory character. For in-consequence, ground-lessness and fundamental concealment belong to finitude.

This question concerning the ego and consciousness (Dasein) therefore is not a question of epistemology. But neither is it a question of metaphysics as a particular discipline. Rather it is the question which reveals how all *metaphysics* is possible, i.e., is necessary.

§50. Having and not having world as the potentiality
for granting transposedness and as necessarily being
refused any going along with. Poverty (deprivation)
as not having, yet being able to have.

What have we learned with regard to the problem of clarifying the essence of the animal's poverty in world from our discussion concerning the possibility of self-transposition in relation to the stone, the animal, and the human being? Being transposed into others belongs to the essence of human Dasein. As long as we keep this insight in view then we already possess an essential point of orientation with respect to the particular problem concerning the possibility of human self-transposition into the animal. But how does this really help us? Have we thereby dispelled the difficulty which besets us when we attempt to transpose ourselves into an animal in any given case? Initially we do not seem to have gained anything directly from our discussion at all. We have however gained something with respect to the other problem which we introduced, in noting that we quite self-evidently presuppose the possibility of somehow transposing ourselves into animals, and that this presupposition has a certain self-evident legitimacy. Does the fact that this presupposition is self-evident now mean in the last analysis that it is not only transposedness into other human beings which belongs to the essence of man but transposedness into animals as well, into living beings generally? For what else can it mean when we say that we make the self-evident presupposition that such self-transposition into animals is possible? This cannot mean that we tacitly come to concur with one another about this possibility, or even that we somehow come to agree that this assumption is justified. On the contrary, we already comport ourselves in this way. In our existence as a whole we comport ourselves toward animals, and in a certain manner toward plants too, in such a way that we are already aware of being transposed in a certain sense—in such a way that a certain ability to go along with the beings concerned is already an unquestioned possibility for us from the start.

Let us consider the case of domestic animals as a striking example. We do not describe them as such simply because they turn up in the house but because they belong to the house, i.e., they serve the house in a certain sense. Yet they do not belong to the house in the way in which the roof belongs to the house as protection against storms. We keep domestic pets in the house with us, they *'live' with us.* But we do not live with them if living means: *being* in an animal kind of way. Yet we *are with* them nonetheless. But this being-with is not an *existing-with,* because a dog does not exist but merely lives. Through this being with animals we enable them to move within our world. We say that the dog is lying underneath the table or is running up the stairs and so on. Yet when we consider the dog itself—does it comport itself toward the table as table, toward the stairs as stairs? All the same, it does go up the stairs with us. It feeds with us—and yet, we do not really 'feed'. It eats with us—and yet, it does not really 'eat'. Nevertheless, it is with us! A going along with . . . , a transposedness, and yet not.

However, if an original transposedness on man's part in relation to the animal is possible, this surely implies that the animal also has its world. Or is this going too far? Is it precisely this 'going too far' that we constantly misunderstand? And why do we do so? Transposedness into the animal can belong to the essence of man without this necessarily meaning that we transpose ourselves into an animal's world or that the animal in general has a world. And now our question becomes more incisive: In this transposedness into the animal, where is it that we are transposed to? What is it we are going along with, and what does this 'with' mean? What sort of going is involved here? Or, from the perspective of the animal, what is it about the animal which allows and invites human transposedness into it, even while refusing man the possibility of going along with the animal? From the side of the animal, what is it that *grants the possibility of transposedness* and *necessarily refuses any going along with?* What is this *having* and yet *not having?* The possibility of not having, of refusing, is only present when in a certain sense a having and a potentiality for having and for granting is possible. Earlier we expressed this situation in a purely formalistic way when we claimed that in a certain sense the animal has and yet does not have world. This now reveals itself as a

potentiality for granting, indeed essentially a potentiality for granting transposedness, connected in turn with the necessary refusal of any going along
with. Only where there is a having do we find a not-having. And not-having
in being able to have is precisely *deprivation, is poverty.* Thus the transposability
of man into the animal, which again is not a going along with, is grounded in
the essence of the animal. And it is this essence which we have attempted to
capture with our thesis concerning the animal's poverty in world. To summarize: the animal intrinsically displays a sphere of transposability, and does so
in such a way that man (to whose Dasein a being transposed belongs) already
finds himself transposed into the animal in a certain manner. The animal
displays a sphere of transposability or, more precisely, the animal itself is this
sphere, one which nonetheless refuses any going along with. The animal has
a sphere of potential transposability and yet it does not necessarily have what
we call world. In contrast with the stone, the animal in any case does possess
the possibility of transposability, but it does not allow the possibility of self-
transposition in the sense in which this transpires between one human being
and another. The animal both has something and does not have something,
i.e., it is deprived of something. We express this by saying that the animal is
poor in world and that it is fundamentally deprived of world.

What is this poverty in world of the animal? Even after carefully determining
what it means to be deprived of something, we still do not possess an adequate
answer. Why not? Because we cannot simply conjure up the essence of poverty
in world from out of the formal concept of deprivation. We can grasp this
poverty only if we first know what world is. Only then are we in a position to
say *what* it is that the animal is deprived of, and thus to say what this poverty
in world implies. First of all we must pursue the concept of world by examining
the essence of man and the world-forming character we have claimed for him:
we must first examine the positive moment, then the negative moment and
finally the lack.

This path of approach is so natural and obvious that we might well wonder
why we did not adopt it at the very beginning. In fact, we shall not adopt it
even now. This is not through any willfulness on our part but rather because
we are attempting *to approach the essence of poverty in world by clarifying
animality itself.* We shall leave aside the question as to whether our tacit
orientation toward man still plays a role here and what sort of role that is.

A properly primordial insight into the kind of essence pertaining to the
animal is quite indispensable if we are to accomplish our task, and this for
the following reason. Assuming that we could clarify the essence of world
with regard to the world-formation of man, assuming that we could then
satisfy ourselves as to what it means to be deprived of world simply by
inferring this—none of this could help us reach our goal unless we have
already shown with regard to the essence of animality that the animal is

deprived of something like world and how this is so. We may not evade precisely this rigorous attempt to characterize animality in a *properly primordial way.* Yet this means that we must take up the task of defining the essence of the living being, *of characterizing the essence of life,* if only *with particular reference to the animal.* Have we already accomplished this or even attempted to do so in the foregoing discussion? Obviously not. That much is clear from the fact that we have not yet addressed any of the results, insights or conceptions of zoology. Even if we cannot pursue any specialist questions here, we must nevertheless seek assistance from *the fundamental theses of zoology* concerning animality and life in general.

§51. Initial clarification of the essence of the organism.

a) The questionable character of that conception which understands the organ as an instrument and the organism as a machine. A cursory elucidation of the essential distinctions between equipment, instrument, and machine.

The most common way of characterizing the living being as such is to define it in terms of the organic as opposed to the inorganic. Of course this distinction immediately appears questionable and quite misleading as soon as we think about organic and inorganic chemistry and recall that organic chemistry is anything but a science of the organic in the sense of the living being as such. It is called organic chemistry precisely because the organic in the sense of the living being remains inaccessible to it in principle. What we mean by describing the character of the living being as 'organic' is much better expressed by the term 'organismic' (although the word is not a particularly attractive one). The fundamental thesis here is that everything that lives is an *organism.* Everything that lives is a living being in each case, and this is an organism. And this also implies that the concept of a 'living substance', a vital mass or 'life-stuff', is a meaningless one. For the idea of 'stuff' or 'substance' in this sense specifically denies the character of the living being as an organism. The living being is always an organism. Its organismic character is what determines the unity of this particular living being in each case. The unit of life is not the cell. The multicellular living being is not, as has been suggested, a community of cells. On the contrary, both unicellular and multicellular living beings alike possess a *unity* of their own in each case, i.e., they have a specific *essential wholeness* by virtue of the fact that they are *organisms.*

　　Yet *what precisely is an organism?* Is this characteristic feature actually sufficient to grasp the essence of the living being? And that means for us: does the organismic character of the animal help us to understand that essential moment which we have ascribed to the animal under the term 'poverty in world'? Or is it rather the other way around, so that the animal's poverty in world is the condition of the possibility of its organismic character? Or is it the case that we cannot bring the organismic character and the animal's poverty in world into either of these relationships with one another?

An organism is something which possesses organs. The word 'organ' derives from the Greek ὄργανον or 'instrument'. The Greek word ἔργον is the same as the German word *Werk* [work]. The organ is a *Werkzeug,* a working instrument. Thus Wilhelm Roux, one of the leading biologists of recent times, has defined the organism as a complex of instruments. So we could say that the organism itself is a 'complicated' instrument, complicated insofar as the various parts are all interwoven with one another in such a way as to produce a unified performance as a whole. But in that case how is the organism to be distinguished from a machine? And then again, how is the machine to be distinguished from an instrument, unless we are going to regard every instrument as a machine? And is every piece of equipment [*Zeug*] an instrument [*Werkzeug*]? What is it that distinguishes any piece of matter or substance from a thing which possesses the character of equipment? As soon as we attempt to clarify the essence of the organism, we immediately find ourselves confronting a whole range of different kinds of beings: purely material things, equipment, instrument, apparatus, device, machine, organ, organism, animality—how are all these to be distinguished from one another?

Is this not the same question we have been striving to elucidate all along, except that we can now insert beings having another specific manner of being—namely equipment, instruments, machines—between the piece of material substance (the stone) and the animal? It is all the more imperative to elucidate these connections precisely, because we so readily and enthusiastically resort to such ideas and concepts as those of the instrument or the machine when we attempt to explain life, even though we eliminate distinctions in the process and fail to recognize their significance. To put the question more precisely, how are we to conceive the relationship of these new kinds of beings—equipment, instruments, and machines—to what we call world? They are neither simply worldless, like the stone, nor are they ever poor in world. Yet presumably we must say that equipment, articles of use in the broadest sense, are worldless, yet as worldless *belong to world.* In general this means that all equipment [*Zeug*]—vehicles, instruments, and especially machines—is what it is and in the way that it is only insofar as it is a *product* [Erzeugnis] of human activity. And this implies that such production of equipment is only possible on the basis of what we have called *world-formation.* The equipmental character of beings and their connection with world in general cannot be elucidated any further here. I have discussed this issue in a particular respect dictated by the overall context in *Being and Time*, §15ff.

If this is the case, then it is questionable whether we should attempt to grasp organisms as instruments or machines. And if this approach is excluded in principle, then it is also impossible to endorse that procedure in biology which begins by treating the living being as a machine and then goes on to introduce supra-mechanical functions as well. This procedure certainly does greater justice to the manifestations of life than any purely mechanistic theory. Yet it still misrepresents the central problem which we repeatedly find ourselves forced to confront: that of grasping the original and essential character proper to the living being and determining whether the thesis 'the animal is poor in world' helps us to accomplish this task, at least insofar as it actually opens up the way toward a concrete interpretation of the essence of life in general.

Even if the organism cannot be grasped either as an instrument or as a machine, *characterizing the essence of equipment and machines* will allow us to define the organism more precisely in relation to these other kinds of beings. From which perspective and in what manner the organism is to be determined positively is of course a further question. Without having recourse to a detailed interpretation, let us try and elucidate these connections with some simple examples which you can develop further yourselves.

The hammer is an instrument, i.e., an item of equipment in general. It belongs to the essence of equipment to serve some purpose. In its proper ontological character it is 'something for . . .' and in this case something for producing, repairing, or improving something. The hammer can also serve to destroy certain works such as the material works of craftsmanship. Yet not every piece of equipment [*Zeug*] is an instrument [*Werkzeug*] in the proper and narrower sense. For example, the fountain pen is a piece of equipment for writing [*Schreibzeug*], the sledge is a piece of equipment for transport, a vehicle [*Fahrzeug*]—yet neither is a machine. Not every piece of equipment is an instrument, and even less is it the case that every instrument and every piece of equipment is a machine. On the other hand, a vehicle certainly *can* be a machine, like a motorbike or an aeroplane [*Flugzeug*], but it need not be. Equipment for writing can certainly be a machine (a typewriter, for example) but again it need not be. Generally speaking this means that every machine is a piece of equipment although not every piece of equipment is a machine.

Yet if every machine is a piece of equipment, that does not mean in turn that every machine is an instrument. Thus a machine is not identical with an instrument, nor is an instrument identical with a piece of equipment. Consequently it is already impossible to understand the machine as a complex of instruments or as a complicated kind of instrument. And if the organism is as different from a machine as the machine is from a piece of equipment, then the definition of the organism as a complex of instruments must certainly collapse altogether (and this is the definition of such a highly regarded researcher as Roux with his 'developmental mechanisms'[1]). Yet as long as we grasp the organism as constitutive of living beings as such, it is also impossible for us to follow von Uexküll—one of the most perceptive of contemporary biologists—in describing the machine as nothing but an 'imperfect organism'.

The machine is a piece of equipment and as such it serves some purpose. All equipment [*Zeug*] is a product [*Erzeugnis*] in some sense. The production [*Erzeugen*] of machines is described as machine construction. Analogously we can talk of the construction of instruments (equipment, kinds of apparatus, musical instruments, etc.). The construction proceeds according to a plan, and not merely as construction but as the whole productive process. Not every plan represents a construction plan (we have timetable plans, plans of military operations, reparations plans, and so on). Now in the production of equipment the plan is determined in advance by the serviceability [*Dienlichkeit*] of the equipment. This serviceability is regulated by anticipating what purpose the piece of equipment or indeed the machine are to serve. All equipment is what it is and the way it is only within a particular context. This context is determined by a totality of involvements [*Bewandtnisganzheit*] in each case. Even behind the simple context of hammer and nail there lies a context of involvements which is taken into account in any plan and which is first inaugurated by way of a certain planning. We generally employ the term 'plan' in the sense of the projection of a complex context. The construction plan of a machine already contains the articulated and ordered structure in which the individual components of the functioning machine move in concert with one another. Does this mean that the machine is a complicated piece of equipment? It is not the complexity of the structure which is decisive for the machine-like character of a piece of equipment, but rather the autonomous functioning of a structure designed for specific dynamic operations. The possibility of a particular mechanical power-source belongs to the autonomous functioning of the structure. The specifically structured processes are brought together into a single functional nexus, and the unity of this nexus is prescribed by the purpose which the machine-like equipment is meant to perform. We talk about machine construction, but not everything which can and must be constructed is a machine. Thus it is

---

1. W. Roux, *Collected Essays on the Developmental Mechanism of Organisms.* Vol. 1: Essays I–XII, mainly on functional adaptation. Vol. 2: Essays XIII–XXXIII, on the developmental mechanism of the embryo. [*Gesammelte Abhandlungen über Entwickelungsmechanik der Organismen* (Leipzig, 1895).] W. Roux, *Lectures and Essays on the Developmental Mechanism of Organisms.* Book 1: Developmental Mechanism, a New Branch of Biological Science. [*Vorträge und Aufsätze über Entwickelungsmechanik der Organismen* (Leipzig, 1905).]

only a further sign of the prevailing groundlessness of thought and understanding today when we are asked to regard the house as a machine for living and the chair as a machine for sitting. There are people who even see this deluded approach as a great discovery ushering in a new culture.

This first rough and ready elucidation of the essential distinctions between equipment, instruments and machines (leaving aside the intermediate cases of the apparatus and the instrument in the narrow sense) already allows us to ask more precisely: are the organs of the living being 'instruments' and is the living being as organism a machine? Even if the first proposition were correct, the second would not necessarily follow. Now it is certainly true that we encounter both these views in the field of biology, sometimes as an explicit theory and sometimes as one of those general notions which are so casually adopted as the basis for a particular approach, notions which are regarded as simply there for the having. Thus we talk about sense-organs as instruments of sense-perception or instruments of digestion and so on, as if these concepts were the most obvious things in the world and the most appropriate in the present context, simply because we can anatomically identify the eyes, ears, and tongue with which the animal sees, hears, and tastes. These identifiable instruments of sense-perception surely prove that the animal relates to other beings through its senses and has a particular realm of experience into which we can transpose ourselves. Thus the zoologist might well object that although we can construe all kinds of supposedly abstract and logical distinctions between equipment, instrument, apparatus, machine etc., this does not help him in any way and does nothing to change the decisive fact that animals do exhibit sense organs and instruments of sense-perception. Certainly—yet the question remains whether an organ is the same as an instrument; whether, in spite of all appeal to the facts, it is not precisely the zoologist who is falling victim to verbal confusion here; whether this unclarified and undifferentiated understanding of organ and instrument is really so irrelevant to the investigation of the facts or whether in the last analysis it is quite decisive.

b) The questionable character of the mechanistic conception of vital movement.

In biology the talk of *vital process* provides us with an analogous case to this ambivalent conception of sense organs and instruments of sense-perception. Just as with the presence of such instruments of sense-perception, so too it is a fact that the living being (the animal) has a dynamic character, that there are processes taking place within the living being. The vital process is itself a structure of unfolding processes, the most basic of which is recognized as the reflex action. Thus we can set ourselves the task of investigating in detail the reflex arcs and their relationship with one another. And in this connection the organism reveals itself as a bundle of reflex arcs. The living being certainly presents itself as something in motion; its movements can certainly be grasped and examined in mechanical terms; copious and possibly very important results can certainly be obtained in this way. Yet the possibility of understanding vital movement mechanically does not at all prove that we have thereby grasped the specific motility of life as the perspective from which to determine every concrete question concerning vital movement. The fact that the animal can be represented as a bundle of reflex arcs does nothing to prove that we have thereby thoroughly investigated the organism as such, or even grasped it as an organism at all. And here we must fundamentally emphasize once again: even if they are guided by *unclarified* and *inadequate* theories, all factual investigations of this kind will always and inevitably produce something. Results are results. Certainly, if we are simply concerned with getting a successful result— as is often the case today—then science has performed its task. But the question at issue is this: what do these results imply for our understanding of the relevant subject-area as such, and what do they contribute to our knowledge of the elementary simplicity of the *substantive essence* of animals, plants, and matter? It was necessary to recall this once again because in our present and forthcoming investigations it is not easy to avoid crude misunderstandings and steer the discussion and appraisal between the over-sophistication of philosophy already mentioned and the tendency of science to become entangled in its facts.

In summary we can say that the organism possesses organs. Certainly, but are they instruments? The organism is a process. Certainly, but can the fundamental character of motility be grasped by means of the mechanistic concept of motion? And what does this suggest as our immediate task? We must attempt to make biology and zoology recognize that organs are not merely instruments and that the organism is not merely a machine. This implies that the organism is something more, something over and above the machine. Yet the task is surely redundant because, either explicitly or implicitly, this is already recognized in the field of biology. But the fact *that* this is the case, and the *manner* in which it is the case, is precisely what is so fateful. Why? Because this recognition of a supra-mechanical moment actually appears to do justice to the proper essence of the living being. However, it does so in such a way that the initial approach is thereby sanctioned rather than overcome and is taken up into the fundamental determination of life. Here it returns in an even more virulent form to distort the original theory of the essence of life even further or to tempt it into introducing certain supra-mechanical forces (as in vitalism).

§52. *The question concerning the essence of the organ
as a question concerning the character of the animal's
potentiality as possibility. The serviceability of equipment
as readiness for something, the serviceability of
the organ as capacity for something.*

However, to put our question in a *concrete* way, to what extent is the organ not an instrument? Why can we not say that it is an instrument and something else as well, something else in the sense that the organism brings something more to the instrument and thus stamps it as an organ, so that the organism would be a structure which goes beyond the machine? The organ, the eye for example, is surely for seeing with. This *'for seeing'* is not some arbitrary property which happens to apply to the eye but is the *essence* of the eye. The eye, the organ of sight, is for seeing. But we have already identified service-ability for . . . as the character of equipment. Is the eye then some kind of equipment, equipment for seeing with, even though it does not seem to be an instrument since it does not help to produce anything? Or is it not indeed true that it does produce something? Can we not say that the eye produces the retina and along with it what is visible and seen? The eye is for seeing. Is seeing produced by the eye? We must frame our question more precisely if we wish to decide about the instrumental character of the eye: *Can the animal see because it has eyes, or does it have eyes because it can see?* Why does the animal have eyes? Why can it have such things? Only because it can see. Possessing eyes and being able to see are not the same thing. It is the *potentiality for seeing* which first makes the possession of eyes possible, makes the possession of eyes necessary in a specific way. Yet in what sense can the animal see and upon what basis can it do so? Where can we find that which makes possible this *possibility,* this *potentiality?* The potentiality for seeing—what sort of possibility is this in the first place? What is the character of this possibility? To pose the question in a fundamental way: *How* must a being *be* in the first place, such that this *possibility of the potentiality for seeing* can belong to its *specific manner of being?*

The potentiality for seeing is an essential possibility of the animal. It does not follow from this that every animal must in fact have eyes. It merely means that the potentiality for seeing as a possibility is grounded as such in animality. But animality does not necessarily have to unfold into this particular possibility and allow eyes to develop in the animal. Yet animality must be so constituted in its specific manner of being in general that the potentiality for such possibilities as seeing, hearing, smelling, and touching, belongs to it. How are we to grasp the character of this 'potentiality' as possibility?

In this connection we must begin from what lies immediately before us, from the organ which clearly belongs to this potentiality and itself serves us, as we say, for seeing or for hearing, the organ which 'makes possible' these activities (ambiguous!). It is on the basis of *this* serviceability that the organ comes into its closest proximity to equipment, to an instrument in general, and is usually identified with it. But we must recognize a *decisive distinction* precisely here where both the organ and the instrument stand in closest proximity to one another with respect to their serviceable character. The organ, the eye for example, serves for seeing. The pen, a piece of writing equipment, serves for writing. In both cases we have a serving for something, certainly, but a serving for the different activities of seeing and writing. But if they are different, they are also alike in that both are cases of human activity. And yet we were supposed to be dealing with animality and with animal organs. Unawares we have found ourselves talking of human beings where it is indeed questionable whether what we call human seeing is the same as animal seeing. Seeing and seeing are not the same thing, although human beings and animals both possess eyes and even the anatomical structure of the eye is alike in both cases. Yet even if we stay with animal seeing, respecting its entirely enigmatic character, and attempt to compare the animal organ of sight (the eye) with a piece of writing equipment, we can easily see a distinction that does not simply lie in what the organ and the equipment serve *for* in each case, but lies rather in something else. The pen is an *independent* being, something that is to hand for use by *various different* human beings. The eye, on the contrary, as an organ is *never* present at hand in *this* way for those beings that need and use it. Rather, every living being can only ever see with *its* eyes. These eyes, like all organs, are not present at hand independently in the way in which an object of use or a piece of equipment is present, for they are incorporated into the being that makes use of them. Thus we can recognize an *initial distinction* by saying that the organ is an instrument which is incorporated into the user.

Yet what does incorporated [*eingebaut*] mean here? Incorporated into what? Into the organism? But the essence of the organism is precisely what we are seeking to discover by first clarifying the distinction between organ and equipment. We must therefore ask our preliminary question in another way: Does the organ lose its instrumental character simply by virtue of being incorporated into the user, or does it never, indeed essentially never have the character of an instrument at all? This question can only be decided if once again we bring out the distinction already noted in the serviceability of organ and equipment, of eye and pen. As we can see, it is not enough to point out a difference in what the organ and the equipment serve for in each case. Nor is it enough to specify the way and manner in which, roughly speaking, organ and equipment present themselves: as incorporated and as independent. Rather, if the distinction is supposed to be one between equipment as such and the organ as such, then this distinction must lie in the character of the *serviceability itself* and not merely in what the equipment or the organ serves for. When something is in such a way as to serve for . . . , then it bestows the possibility of something else. That which is serviceable can only *bestow possibility* in this sense if, as something serviceable, it *has a possibility*. Having a possibility here cannot mean being equipped with a property. Rather it means being in such a way in accordance with its own essence that having possibility lies in its being in this way. It means that the latter, its being in such a way, is nothing other than the former, its having possibility. In the case of organ and equipment alike, serving for something is not merely an identifiable feature which is present and enables us to recognize them as organ and equipment. Nor is this some additional or incidental property which they also happen to have amongst others. Rather both the organism and equipment have and find their *essence* in *serviceability*. Being a pen means being for writing in a particular way. The pen has been made or produced as this particular piece of equipment with this in view. The pen is finished and ready [*fertig*] only when it has acquired this particular serviceability, this particular range of possibility, in the course of its production. The finished production of the equipment makes it *ready* in a twofold sense. The equipment is ready insofar as it is *finished*. But this finished state consists precisely in its being ready. And 'ready' here also implies that it *has* a certain *readiness* [Fertigkeit] which makes it *suitable* and usable for something. It is precisely the fact that it has been made ready in this particular way which gives the finished equipment its *readiness*, its suitability for writing. It is true that we talk of 'readiness' in this second sense as a skill, like ready manual dexterity for example, precisely when we are talking not about things and equipment, but about the activity of human beings, and perhaps even about the specific manner of being which animals have. Nevertheless, I shall not shy away from forcing language somewhat, and shall adopt the expression *readiness* for the *specific manner and way in which equipment can be serviceable.* I do so because such readiness can also imply the process of making something ready in and through production and preparation, a preparation or making-ready [*Verfertigen*] which procures and produces the ready-made product [*das Fertige*] as something independently present at hand and present to hand for use. Equipment offers the possibility of serving for . . . , it always has a particular readiness for . . . which is grounded in the way it has been made ready. The pen and every other piece of equipment is—wherever it is—essentially something ready, and that here means ready for writing. Readiness in this specific and well-defined sense belongs to equipment. As equipment the pen is ready for writing, but it has no capacity [*Fähigkeit*] for writing. As a pen it is not *capable* [fähig] of writing. It is a matter of distinguishing *readiness*, as a *particular kind of potentiality* which we ascribe to equipment, from *capacity*.

The possibilities of serving for . . . are, as possibilities, quite varied in their character of possibility. The possibility possessed and offered by equipment is qualitatively different as a possibility from that possibility, i.e., that potentiality [*Können*], which we ascribe to a *capacity. Equipment has a certain readiness.* The *organ,* we now claim, in each case *has a capacity.* We shall see later whether this way of speaking is wholly appropriate. First we must elucidate this *second way of having and offering possibility* more precisely and thus begin to approach the *essence of the organ and the organism.* Then we shall also be able to distinguish the organ from a piece of equipment, from an instrument, and from a machine.

Equipment always has a particular readiness, while the organ always has a capacity. Yet the eye, for example, which we have hitherto distinguished from the pen as a particular organ, no more possesses an independent capacity for seeing than the pen has a capacity for writing, especially as we pointed out that the possibility of seeing is itself the condition of the possibility of the eye as an organ. We must hold fast to the fact that the organ in itself does not have the capacity for seeing either, and must not force facts for the sake of the distinction we wished to identify between readiness and capacity. But are we holding fast to the facts when we say that the eye, taken independently, no more possesses a capacity than does the pen? When we consider it independently in this way, are we treating the eye as an eye? Or have we not already committed a crucial mistake which is precisely what allows us to equate the eye as an organ with an independent piece of equipment present to hand? An eye taken independently is not an eye at all. This implies that it is never first an instrument which subsequently also gets incorporated into something else. Rather, the eye belongs to the organism and emerges from the organism, which of course is not the same as saying that the organism makes ready or produces organs.

Organs have capacities, but they have them precisely *as organs,* i.e., as something *belonging to the organism.* The instrument, by contrast, essentially excludes that kind of belonging to something else through which the character of a capability [*Fähigsein*] is acquired. If on the other hand the organ as organ (i.e., as something belonging to and growing out of the organism) has capacities for something, then we must put it more rigorously and say: It is not the organ which has a capacity but the *organism which has capacities.* It is the *organism* which can see, hear, and so forth. The organs are 'only' for seeing, but they are not instruments. The organs are not subsequently incorporated into this capacity *in addition,* rather they grow from it and are absorbed into it, they remain within it and come to an end with it.

How are we to understand this relationship between the organ and the capacity? One thing is clear: we cannot say that the organ has capacities, but must say that *the capacity has organs.* Earlier on we said that equipment *is* of a certain readiness, while the organ *has* a capacity. Now we can see that it is more appropriate to put it the other way round: in being made ready, the equipment *has acquired* a particular *readiness for something* and *possesses* this readiness. *The organ,* on the other hand, *is in the possession of a capacity.* It is the capacity which possesses here rather than the organ. It is the capability which procures organs for itself, rather than organs coming to be equipped with capacities, let alone with forms of readiness.

§53. The concrete connection between capability
and the organ which belongs to it as subservience,
as distinct from the serviceability of equipment.

Yet what does it mean to say that capability procures organs for itself? *Capacity* as a particular kind of potentiality for being, for having and offering possibilities, is obviously not merely distinguished from the readiness for something through its character as a *kind of potentiality.* Rather, *being capable* and *being ready for . . .* announce a *fundamentally different manner of being* in each case. In accordance with our overall perspective we must therefore attempt to bring out more concretely the *connection between the capability* to see, to smell, to grasp, to feed, or to digest on the one hand, *and the organs which belong to this capability* on the other (and more precisely the way in which they belong to it). Perhaps the decisive problem lies precisely in the way and manner of this belonging.

At first sight one is tempted, and rightly so, to say that the organism itself produces its organs and thus also produces itself, in contrast to equipment which must always be produced through another. And this is precisely why the organism is distinguished from the machine, for example, which requires something other than itself, namely the builder who has that manner of being that is specific to man. The machine not only requires a builder in order to be a machine at all, it also has to be operated. The machine cannot stop or change its operation by itself, whereas the organism initiates, regulates and changes its own motility. Finally, if the machine is damaged, for example, then it requires repair or maintenance by others, and this can only be done by the specific manner of being belonging to a being which is also capable of producing a machine. The organism, on the other hand, repairs and renews itself within certain limits. *Self-production* in general, *self-regulation* and *self-renewal* are obviously aspects which characterize the organism over against the machine and which also illuminate the peculiar ways in which its capacity and capability as an organism are directed.

The facts clearly do not allow us to doubt what has been said. What we have said also gives us a pointer to the peculiarity proper to the organism as against the machine, and thus also to the way in which organs belong to the organism as against the way in which machine components belong to the machine. And yet this pointer is still dangerous because it can, and repeatedly does, lead to the following conclusion: If the organism possesses this capacity for self-production, self-regulation and self-renewal, then the organism must contain an effective agency and power of its own, an entelechy and a vital agent which effects all this (a *'natural factor'*). But this conception simply eliminates the problem, i.e., it no longer allows one to arise. Thus the real problem which is involved in determining the essence of life cannot even be seen because life is now handed over to some causal factor. We shall leave aside the fact that the appeal to some such force or entelechy actually explains nothing. By contrast to these attempts to elucidate the essence of the organism as taken up principally by the so-called vitalists in opposition to the mechanists, the task is to keep open the question of whether or to what extent the *essential connection between the capacity of the organism and its organs* can be clarified by reference to the facts we have already mentioned concerning self-production, self-regulation, and self-renewal. If we can do this, then it will also inevitably reveal with greater clarity the essence of capability in general as distinct from readiness.

Yet if we really wish to be preserved from such a naive explanation of the organism on the basis of facts which are certainly relevant in themselves, then obviously we must examine the structure of the organism and the manifold character of its organs *more concretely*. Above all we must study the connection between the individual organs and the central direction of the organism, everything that we understand by terms like central nervous system, neural transmission, stimulus, excitation, and all that this involves, namely the observation of the anatomical structure of the organs—for example, the sense-organs and the organs of nutrition. We can do this most easily by looking at those organisms which display the greatest possible variety in the unity of their organs as a whole. Certainly, we must be circumspect here, especially if we wish to prevent our investigation from turning into a purely abstract reflection with nothing but concepts. And yet we may, indeed for our fundamental purpose perhaps we must, choose *another path*. This path is by no means easier than the preceding one, but it is certainly one that brings out the essential facts and thus the essential problems in a more basic and penetrating fashion. It is precisely not the higher, more complex and more firmly structured animals, but rather the lower and tiny so-called *unicellular* protoplasmic creatures like amoebae and infusoria—creatures which apparently have no organs—which are philosophically speaking the most suitable for affording us some insight into the essence of the organ. I shall not go into the problem of protoplasm here, but merely assume a rough idea of what it is as a matter of general knowledge.

It is no accident that the concept of protoplasm, and the name itself, arose in the field of botany rather than in that of zoology. The so-called lower animals, the amoebae and infusoria, only have the protoplasm of a single cell at their disposal. We distinguish between ectoplasm and endoplasm. The tiny protoplasmic creatures are structureless and formless. They display no firm animal shape at all and that is why we describe them as polymorphic creatures. They have to form their necessary organs individually in each case, only to destroy them again in turn. Their organs are therefore temporary organs. This is the case with the amoebae. With the infusoria certain organs do remain in place, indeed all of those organs involved in propulsion and grasping, whereas the vegetative organs which serve the process of nutrition are not firmly fixed (paramaecium). The other organs by contrast are dependent upon the protoplasm. Around the food in each case there forms "an aperture which first becomes a mouth, then a stomach, then an intestine and finally an anal tract."[1] We are thus confronted by a determinate sequence of organs which replace one another in this specific sequence. This conclusively shows that the *capacities* for feeding and for digesting are *prior to the organs in each case*. Yet at the same time this capacity, a complete dynamic process which we could also roughly describe as 'assimilation', is itself a regulated one. Indeed it is a form of regularity in relation to a determinate sequence of processes. For it is the mouth which emerges first and then the intestine, not the intestine first and then the mouth.

Yet, one might well object, is not this very evidence drawn from the case of unicellular animals the most striking proof that the organism produces and then destroys its organs, i.e., makes them ready? Thus the organ is a piece of equipment, and insofar as the organ itself serves in turn to produce something it is an instrument (an instrument of digestion). The fact that in these cases the ready-made organ is only present for a short time is inadequate to ground any essential distinction between organ and equipment, especially since there are animals which permanently retain their ready-made organs. Certainly it is to some extent a matter of indifference how long a ready-made hammer actually lasts as such before it is destroyed. It still remains a hammer. In the case of organs it is not in fact a matter of indifference how long they last or when they emerge. In the nutrition process of the tiny protoplasmic creature the stomach that has been formed must actually disappear to make way for the intestine. The organs as established features, as in the case of the higher animals, are bound to the lifespan of the animal, i.e., not merely in the first place to time as an objectively definable period during which the animal lives. Rather the organs are bound into and are bound up with the temporal span which the animal is capable of sustaining as a living being. Even if we cannot pursue here the problem concerning this relationship of the organism and its

---

1. J. von Uexküll, *Theoretische Biologie*. Second, completely revised edition (Berlin, 1928), p. 98. [Trans. D. L. Mackinnon, *Theoretical Biology* (New York: Harcourt, Brace & Co., 1926).]

organs to time, it is already clear from such general reflections that *organ and equipment relate precisely to time in fundamentally different ways.* And it is this which first grounds an essential distinction in their respective manners of being, if we accept that the temporal aspect is metaphysically central for each manner of being.

With regard to our specific question of whether or not the protoplasmic creatures actually demonstrate the equipmental character of organs, we could now emphasize above all that organs are precisely not like things that are fabricated and made ready. For this reason they can never be set out or set aside somewhere. With respect to what they are and how they are, the organs remain bound up with the vital process of the animal. In addition we must point out that protoplasmic creatures, like pseudopodia for example, do produce something in order to propel themselves and then dissolve the product back into the remaining protoplasm, and so 'resolve themselves' back into it as it were. Yet when one of these apparent limbs of the animal comes into contact with that of another animal consisting of the same substance, it never flows over into the other or combines with the cellular content of the other. This means that the *organ is retained within the capacity* of touch and movement and indeed can only be superseded or replaced through this capacity.

Yet what about those cases where the emergent organs have been established and where a enduring animal form presents itself? Here, with all the higher animals, this unchanging and enduring aspect could mislead us—and factically does mislead us repeatedly—into considering the organs independently and considering them as instruments. We say that the unchanging and enduring nature of the established organs misleads us into doing this, i.e., these aspects create the illusion that the organs are something present at hand which remain throughout the changing life of the animal as a whole, especially when we compare the organs with the relative variety of what the animal is able to accomplish by means of them. The observer can thus be misled into ascribing this particular kind of presence to the organs because he or she fails to consider the organ in terms of the organism. Yet every observer will deny that he or she fails to do so. What is decisive here, however, is how the organism is understood and whether it is understood in such an originary fashion that the specific manner of being proper to living beings does announce itself. This manner of being assigns a quite specific ontological character to the unchanging and permanent nature of the organ, a character which is fundamentally different from the presence to hand of an instrument or tool which is lying around. Although they seem to be permanently present at hand, organs are in fact only given in *that way of being* which we call *life.*

We claimed that the characteristic feature of the organ was that it remains bound to the capacity itself, i.e., is not something ready-made which can be set aside. Yet the organ does not merely remain bound to the capacity in this negative sense but rather the *organ belongs positively to the capacity.* We say that the *capacity takes the organ into its service.* To put it more clearly with specific reference to our guiding question: In the case of the organ, the character of the 'in order to'—which we can also observe in any kind of equipment, instrument, or machine—is fundamentally different from that of equipment. The eye is not serviceable for seeing in the way in which the pen is serviceable for writing. Rather the organ stands in service of the capacity that develops it. The finished product that has been made ready is, as such, *serviceable for* . . . , whereas the organ which arises in and through the capacity is *subservient.* *Serviceability* [Dienlichkeit] and *subservience* [Diensthaftigkeit] are not the same. The organ always belongs to the capacity which develops it in subservience to that capacity. It can never simply be serviceable for the capacity. If, therefore, the character of the 'in order to' which marks out the organ means standing in service of the capacity, then the capacity as such must first make possible this subservience. The capacity must itself possess an originarily subservient character. It is only now that we are beginning to approach the character of possibility pertaining to capacity as distinct from readiness.

To say that a finished product is ready not only means that it is [1.] completed, and [2.] serviceable for . . . , but also means that it is [3.] incapable of getting any further in its specific being as such (equipmental being). It is now completed, that is, it is and remains something that can be called upon and used precisely as something produced and only as such. In its equipmental being it indeed enables and prescribes a particular application in each case. But with regard to this application, and how it takes place or whether it takes place or not, the equipment not only has no part to play, but equipmental being shows no intrinsic urge toward such application. The equipment is simply serviceable and with that its being is complete. If it is to serve in the specific manner of its possible serviceability, a further act quite different from that of production must first come into play and thereby wrest from the equipment its possible service in the first place. The hammer is certainly ready for hammering, but the being of the hammer is *not an urge toward* hammering. As a finished product the hammer lies outside the possible act of hammering. By contrast something like the eye, for example, which belongs to a capacity and subserves the capacity of seeing, can do so only because the *capacity is itself intrinsically subservient* and as such can take something into service. The capacity itself governs and delimits the emergence of what it takes into service and the manner in which it does so. The finished product is serviceable. That which is capable in its capability as such is subservient. Capacity *diverts itself into its own wherefore and does so in advance with respect to itself.* The being of the finished product, readiness, knows nothing of this kind. The hammer in its specific being a hammer can never as it were divert itself into hammering as this specific act for which it is serviceable. The peculiarity proper to what is capable as such, on the other hand, lies in its diverting itself into itself in advance, into its wherefore. And here we see that capability forces us to open up a *wholly new context* in distinction from the ready being of all fabricated use-objects. It is only when we take this step from capability to the specific manner of being intrinsic to it that we shall succeed in comprehending the specific possibility of capacity, in defining how the organ belongs to the organism, and thereby in deciding the question of whether the organism, as we then grasp it, is the condition of the possibility of the animal's poverty in world; or whether on the contrary it is not precisely the animal's poverty in world which enables us to comprehend why a living being can and must be an organism. If the latter is the case, then we will also have shown the thesis that the animal is poor in world to be a statement of essence concerning animality in general, rather than an arbitrary assertion about a particular characteristic pertaining to the animal.

Before proceeding any further in our attempt to clarify the essence of the organ, let us summarize the insights we have gained already. Both equipment and organ display the character we have formally expressed as the 'in order to. . . .' Both have intrinsic possibilities and offer these possibilities for specific application. The fact that they both offer such possibilities is not some subsequently acquired property, as though the hammer were first of all a hammer and then also serviceable in addition. Rather the serviceability belongs precisely to its specific being. But the way and manner in which organ and equipment offer possibilities is fundamentally different. The character of possibility and the manner of being involved may be distinguished as *readiness for something* and *capacity for something*. A piece of equipment like a pen, for example, is ready for writing but it is not capable of writing. We saw that insofar as we consider it on its own, the organ too is not capable of seeing, grasping, and so on. This suggests that the specific possibility that the organ offers depends upon the organism to which it intrinsically belongs. Here it becomes apparent that the capacity that the organ itself manifests does not belong to it as an organ, but rather that the organ belongs to a capacity. The capacity creates its specific organs for itself. It is only in the sense that the capacity in each case creates its own organs that we can say that the organs are incorporated into the organism. For the capacity incorporates the organ into itself and retains the organ within itself. The organ remains an organ as long as it is retained within the organism.

The clarification of the organism depends upon whether or not we can elucidate the intrinsic connection between organ and organism. One way of doing so is by considering the characteristic potential of the organism to govern, produce, and renew itself. Here we see the self-like character of the organism. It is precisely this self-like character which has led to a premature explanation of such selfhood and encouraged talk about a force, a vital force, or an animal soul by analogy with our own selves. Irrespective of this fact that the organism displays a self-like character, we must initially disregard any such explanation and attempt to *penetrate the essence of the organism in terms of the intrinsic structure of the capacity* through which it is determined.

We have illustrated the relationship between organ and organism with reference to unicellular living beings. Here it is apparent that the capacities and the entire order of these capacities in the process of animal digestion and growth, for example, are prior to the organs themselves. This courted the objection that the organism produces organs and that they can therefore be considered as instruments. Yet we saw that the organism does not release the organs but rather retains them within it. This intrinsic retention is not a deficiency in comparison with equipment, which is independent, but represents a higher determination metaphysically speaking. The organ remains bound to the capacity, it is *subservient* in relation to the capacity. It is not something present at hand which is serviceable for the capacity but rather something which subserves along with that capacity. This is also expressed by the fact that the capacity as such has a serving character, namely in relation to the organism itself. We must now examine more closely this subservient character of the organ, or of the capacity underlying it, in comparison with the serviceability of equipment.

§54. The intrinsically regulative character of that which is capable, as distinct from the prescription governing ready-made equipment. Self-driving toward its wherefore as the instinctual character that drives capacity.

A ready-made piece of equipment is subject to some implicit or explicit *prescription* with respect to its possible use. This prescription is not given by the readiness of the equipment, but is always derived from the plan which has already determined the production of the equipment and its specific equipmental character. Something which is *capable* on the other hand is not subject to such a prescription but is *intrinsically regulative* and *regulates itself*. In a certain sense it *drives itself toward its own capability for.* . . . This self-driving and being driven toward its wherefore is only possible in that which is capable inasmuch as capability is in general *instinctually driven* [triebhaft]. Capacity is only to be found where there is drive [*Trieb*]. And only where there is drive do we also find something like capacity, however irregular or tentative that capacity may be. And again, only there do we find the possibility of training for regular behaviour. This maintaining of instinctual self-driving toward its wherefore gives to capability its accomplishing character of a traversing, of a dimension in the formal sense, whereas the readiness of equipment is precisely something finished. Dimension is not yet to be understood in a spatial sense here, although this dimensional character of drive and of everything that is subserviently capable is presumably the condition of the possibility of the animal's being able to accomplish the traversal of a spatial domain in a quite determinate manner, whether it is a flight-path or that specific space which the fish inhabits—spatial domains whose structure is utterly different from one another. The 'in order to' of equipmental reference involves no drive. In accordance with its formation and material the hammer is serviceable for hammering. The self-driving toward its own wherefore, and thus this traversing being of capacity, is already a kind of self-regulation. This regulation does not direct subsequently what the capacity achieves but directs it by driving it in advance. In this advancing driving forth the regulation directs the order of the possible driving forces which belong to the capacity in each case. This regulation is thoroughly governed by the fundamental character of the capacity for . . . , by seeing for example, i.e., by a fundamental drive which drives throughout and activates the whole sequence of driving forces. These *driving forces* [Antriebe], which arise from the instinctual capacity in each case, do not as such merely occasion the vital movements—like nutrition and propulsion—but rather as *drives* they always permeate and drive on the whole movement in advance. That is why they are never simply mechanical, even if they can be isolated in this way, i.e., by ignoring the instinctual structure of drives in which the specific potentiality for being and thus the manner of being belonging to these drives is embedded. In principle there is no mathematical expression for this instinctual structure of drives, and it is one which is incapable in principle of being mathematized.

The regulation which always lies embedded in the capacity as such is thus a structure of instinctually organized anticipatory responses in each case which prescribes the sequence of movements that arises as soon as the capacity comes into play. In its specific being, the capacity in its self-driving movement has always already *anticipated* its possible range of achievement. *In all this we must completely set aside any idea of consciousness or soul, as well as the idea of 'purposiveness'.* On the other hand, we should also note right away that we have still not uncovered the essence of capacity and drive in their ultimate and essential grounds. But we have advanced enough to attempt to render intelligible the subservient character of what we describe as an organ on account of this subservience, as distinct from the serviceability of equipment. At the same time we have already opened up the horizon in which we can move back from the organ to the organism.

*§55. Inquiring into the achievement of the organ taken
into service in terms of subservient capacity.*

On the basis of its drive-character, capacity is intrinsically characterized as something subservient rather than as something present at hand which is serviceable for. . . . For a drive is never present at hand. As something which drives, it is essentially on the way to . . . , always driving on toward . . .—it is *something that submits to itself,* something which is intrinsically service and subservient. That which the capacity as such allows to arise and brings into relation to itself, namely the organ, is thus taken into service or released from service (as in the case of atrophy). An instrument cannot atrophy because it is never subservient, because it does not have the possibility of capacity. Rather it is simply serviceable and that is why it can only be destroyed. It is only on the basis of the originally subservient character of capacity that we can grasp and investigate as achievement the possible achievement of the organ which is taken into service. For example, we can understand *what the bee's eye achieves and its character as an organ* insofar as it is determined by *the bee's specific capacity for seeing.* The capacity for seeing on the other hand is not determined by the 'eye' of the bee and cannot be understood in this way. The anatomical structure of the bee's eye is different from that of the human eye. The bee's eye has neither pupil, nor iris, nor lens. Nevertheless, there is a recurrent principle in the way the organ of vision is constructed, as in the case of other organs. The anatomical structure can only provide some support for 'inferences' concerning the character of the bee's vision if and so long as we already keep before us the essence of animality properly understood and the particular kind of animal being which belongs to the bee. Let us take another even more concrete example of an insect eye which can be approached through a most remarkable experiment. It has proved possible to observe and even to photograph the retinal image that is produced in the case of a glow worm's vision. The retinal image of a glow worm looking in the direction of a window was observed (the technical details of the experiment can be ignored here). The photograph relatively clearly reveals a view of the window and its surrounding frame together with the mullion and transom; it reveals a large letter R which had been attached to the window pane, and in rather indeterminate outline even a view of the church tower which can be seen through the window. This is the view given on the retina of the glow worm as it looks toward the window. The insect eye is capable of forming this 'view'. But can we infer from this *what* the glow worm sees? By no means. *By reference to the achievement of the organ we cannot at all determine the capacity of vision or the way in which the achievement of the organ is taken into service by the potentiality to see.* We cannot even recognize the problem of the connection between the organ and the capacity of vision unless and until we have determined the glow worm's *environment* as such. And that in turn requires elucidation of what an *environment for the animal* means in general. The kind of achievement pertaining to the insect eye, and thus to every organ and accordingly to every organic part of the organ, is determined by being put into the service of the visual capacity of the insect, i.e., as something which has no independence of its own and is inserted as it were between the environment and the seeing animal. It is something inserted not from without, but by the specific capacity by way of its instinctual and drive-like accomplishment. From all of this we can now see even more clearly how urgent and indispensable it is to penetrate the specific character of animal capacity.

The difficulty is not merely that of determining *what* it is that the insect sees but also that of determining *how* it sees. For we should not compare our own seeing with that of the animal without further ado, since the *seeing and the potentiality to see of the animal* is a *capacity,* whereas *our potentiality to see* ultimately has a *quite different character of possibility* and possesses a *quite different manner of being.*

Organs are not present at hand in the animal, but rather stand in the service of capacities. This *standing in service* must be taken in a very strict sense. In their being, i.e., in the way in which they are located, in which they grow, and in which they atrophy, the organs are wholly bound to the service which belongs to the capacity as such. What is serviceable on the other hand never serves in this sense, although it is true that something subservient can be misinterpreted as something serviceable. This misinterpretation of subservient capacity occurs whenever the organ is understood as an instrument. More precisely speaking, it is a misinterpretation that *underdetermines* that character which immediately strikes us in the case of organ and instrument alike, the character of the 'in order to'. The essence of capacity as such, however, remains unconsidered.

§56. *More penetrating clarification of the elucidated essence of capacity in order to determine the essence of the organism (the holistic character of the organism): proper being or proper peculiarity as the manner of being specific to the animal and its way of being proper to itself.*

Can we now infer any conclusions about the essence of the organism on the basis of this characterization of the organ as something which subserves and belongs to capacities? In the first place we cannot *infer* from the organ as the known term to the organism as the unknown term, especially if we have *comprehended* the organ. For in doing so we have seen precisely that *the organ belongs to the organism.* In other words, in everything we have said about the capacity of the living being we have kept the organism in view all the time, even if we did not explicitly characterize the organism itself. Any so-called inference from the organ, which is all that seems to be known, to the organism which is not known, is as superfluous as it is impossible. Thus it is all the more necessary to gain an explicit understanding of the essence of the organism which, albeit in a rather vague way, we have had in view all along. The task of properly seeing what we have had in front of us all along may appear to be very simple, yet this kind of seeing and comprehending is actually very difficult, especially since it does not involve simply gazing or staring at something. In any case it is a kind of seeing and comprehending which is alien and burdensome for the ordinary understanding. As for the latter, the realm and field of its successes and its failures is that kind of argumentation which is capable of going on indefinitely even though it has long since ceased to see anything. Nobody notices its blindness, especially since the arguing and talking then generally gets even louder.

The kind of questioning and comprehending which adopts a quite different position *before* all argumentation, intending, or speaking was brought back to life—and that always means radicalized—through Husserl. This kind of questioning and comprehending is a, perhaps *the,* decisive characteristic of *phenomenology.* It is precisely because it is *self-evident* that it has *greatness.* And that is why it is so easily and persistently overlooked in favour of what are merely the necessary external trappings.

If therefore we always already and necessarily possess a pre- and co-understanding of the organism when we interpret the essence of the organ, then we will grasp the organism properly simply by developing in the right way what has already been revealed, rather than by making so-called inferences to something else. The decisive point lay in the elucidation of capacity, its drive-character and its serving character. Accordingly the task is simply to pursue *more penetratingly* this *essence of capacity* already elucidated. The matter itself will then lead us along the right path.

If we now recall what we have previously said about capacity, then something strikes us right away or perhaps has already struck us. Capability for . . . is in a certain sense an instinctual, accomplishing *self*-proposing and self-*pro*-posing into its own wherefore, intrinsically into itself. Capability implies this 'intrinsically into itself'. We already came upon this 'self' when we discussed the peculiar character of the organism in comparison with the machine—its *self*-production, its *self*-regulation, and its *self*-renewal, all of which is also expressed in the familiar concept of *self-preservation.* And we already rejected the all too hasty interpretation of this 'self' as a hidden force, an entelechy or an I-ness. And yet already in interpreting capacity we ourselves cannot avoid confronting this 'self'. Certainly we cannot—but the question is how we are appropriately to determine what we call the 'self'.

When we say 'self' we usually think first of all of 'I myself'. We take the self as our own ego, as subject, consciousness, self-consciousness. And to that extent we find ourselves on the point of ascribing an 'I' or a 'soul' to the organism on the basis of the self-like character we have seen it to have.

And yet, there is no avoiding the self-like character of capacity, i.e., its instinctual and intrinsic self-proposing. This lies in the structure of capacity as such. What does this self-like character initially imply? The capacity diverts itself—intrinsically driving itself forward—into the accomplishment of its wherefore. At the same time, the capacity *does not leave itself behind*, it does not escape itself as it were. On the contrary: in this instinctual 'toward', the capacity as such becomes and remains *proper to itself*—and does so *without* any so-called *self-consciousness* or any *reflection* at all, without any relating back to itself. That is why we say that on account of this essential being proper to itself the capacity is *properly peculiar.* We shall reserve the expression 'self' and selfhood to characterize the *specifically human peculiarity, its* particular way of being proper to itself. Thus we shall say that every self-like being, every being that possesses the character of personality in the broadest sense (every personal being) is properly peculiar, but not everything that is properly peculiar is self-like or possessed of an ego. The way and manner in which the animal is proper to itself is not that of personality, not reflection or consciousness, but simply its *proper being* [Eigentum].[1] *Proper peculiarity* [Eigen-tümlichkeit] is a fundamental character of every capacity. This peculiarity *belongs to itself* and is absorbed [*eingenommen*] by itself. Proper peculiarity is not an isolated or particular property but rather a *specific manner of being,* namely a way of *being proper to oneself* [Sich-zu-eigen-sein]. Just as we speak of the kingdom [*Königtum*] which belongs to the king, i.e., speak of what it means to be a king, so we also speak here of the *proper being* [Eigentum] *of an animal* in the sense of its specific way of being proper to itself. It seems as if this is a purely linguistic device for distancing ourselves from the self-like character of animal being and thus obviating a source of crude misunderstandings. The proper being of the animal means that the animal, and in the first place its specific capability for . . . , is proper to itself. It does not lose itself in the sense that an instinctual impulse to something would leave it itself behind. Rather it

---

1. [Tr: the German *Eigentum* commonly means "property," in the sense of whatever one owns. Heidegger here explains that he is using the word to mean the animal's way of owning, having, or "being proper to itself" (*Sich-zu-eigen-sein*). We have rendered *Eigentum* as "proper being," and shall translate the words *eigentümlich* (normally meaning "peculiar") and *Eigentümlichkeit* (normally: "peculiarity") as "properly peculiar" and "proper peculiarity" respectively, in order to bring out this sense of ownness and the "proper." Throughout the translation, we have generally rendered the term *eigentlich* as "proper" or "properly." *Eigentlich,* together with its correlate *uneigentlich*—which is much less common in this course—is used in *Being and Time* to refer to a possibility of the selfhood of Dasein. There Macquarrie and Robinson translate it as "authentic."]

retains itself precisely in such a drive and remains 'its self', as we might say, in this drive and driving.

§57. The organism as endowed with capability articulating itself into capacities creating organs—as the manner of being specific to that proper peculiarity endowed with capability and creating organs.

The animal never merely displays a single capacity but rather several: assimilation, growth, inheritance of acquired characteristics, propulsion, struggle with its enemies etc. Similarly, the individual organ must not be regarded in isolation, either in relation to the organism, or in relation to the other organs, even though the organs of the more developed animals may seem to be independent of one another. Our emphasis upon the fact that the animal displays several capacities is not intended merely to draw attention to the multiplicity but rather to the specific nature of the *unity* in this multiplicity. The capacities are not present at hand in the organism. Rather *what* they *are,* and *how* they *are,* their *being,* can only be discovered through an examination of the *capability for.* . . . And furthermore it is only from the perspective of this manner of being that we can determine the way in which the several capacities *are* together within the unity of the organism. It is precisely this problem concerning the potential unity of the capacities which reveals the full extent to which we have had what we designate the organism in view all along when characterizing these capacities. It will also become clear that it is equally insufficient to determine the organism as a bundle of drives, in distinction from Roux's definition. This suggests that the very characterization of the living being as an organism fails us at a certain decisive point, that the *organismic character itself points back toward a more originary structure of animality.* We shall be able to pursue the individual stages of the regressive analysis back to this originary structure only if we take our point of departure from the way in which we have already characterized capability, subservience, and drive, in distinction from the serviceability of equipment.

The organ is not equipped with capacities but rather the capacities create organs for themselves. And once again, it is not the individual capacity as such which is capable of seeing, and so on, but the *organism.* Is it the latter then, the organism, which has capacities? Certainly not. Or at least not if we blithely regard capacities once again as so many supplied properties and the organism as their underlying bearer. The organism does not have capacities, i.e., it is not an organism which is then additionally supplied with organs. Rather to say that 'the animal is organized' means that the animal is *rendered capable* [befähigt]. Being organized means *being capable.* And that implies that the animal's being is potentiality, namely the potentiality to articulate itself into capacities, i.e., into those instinctual and subservient ways of remaining proper to itself. These capacities in turn possess the possibility of allowing certain organs to arise from them. *This capability articulating itself into capacities creating organs* characterizes the *organism* as such.

We discovered that capacity as such is peculiarly proper. It has the character of proper peculiarity. But it can only have this character if the *organism* as that which is capable is determined by this *proper peculiarity:* if the organism possesses the possibility of retaining itself within [*bei*] itself. For only then can that which is capable, in articulating itself into capacities, still hold these capacities themselves together in the unity of its self-retention. This *proper peculiarity* of being proper to itself without any reflection is therefore the *fundamental condition for the possibility of being rendered capable* of having capacities and thus of taking organs into service. Thus the organism is neither 'a complex of instruments', nor a union of organs, nor indeed a bundle of capacities. The term 'organism' therefore is no longer a name for this or that being at all, but rather designates a *particular and fundamental manner of being.* We can briefly characterize this *specific manner of being* as a *proper peculiarity with the capability to create organs.* But how are we to grasp the animal's being proper to itself, its kind of proper being, if we are to avoid all recourse to any effective force, to any soul or consciousness?

We encountered this proper peculiarity, the character of remaining proper to itself, when we interpreted the structure of *capacity*. In this structure there lies a certain movement 'toward . . .' and that implies an instinctual 'away from. . . .' Away from the organism—but in such a manner that in this capability for . . . and movement away from itself the organism precisely *retains* itself, and not only sustains *its specific unity* but gives this unity to itself for the first time. But, it will be objected, the organism is not this proper peculiarity that has capability, but rather a way of actually employing capacities. For it precisely does not remain with them as possibilities but actually comes to see, to hear, to seize, to hunt, to hide, to flee, to reproduce and so forth, and thus succeeds in actualizing these capacities. But it is just this actuality of the actual animal that we are trying to determine by emphasizing, as we have been doing all along, that we must must look to the animal's *specific manner of being.*

For the present we shall leave aside the question as to whether or not we can or should proceed without further ado to interpret the relation between the capacity and the execution of what the capacity is for according to the schema of possibility and actuality. In the last analysis, potentiality and possibility belong precisely to the essence of the animal in its actuality in a quite specific sense—not merely in the sense that everything actual, inasmuch as it is at all, must already be possible as such. It is not this possibility, but rather *being capable* which belongs to the animal's *being actual,* to the *essence of life.*

Only something that is capable, and remains capable, is alive. Something which is no longer capable, irrespective of whether a capacity is used or not, is no longer alive. Something which does not exist in the manner of being capable cannot be dead either. The stone is never dead because its being is not a being capable in the sense of what is instinctual or subservient. 'Dead matter' is a meaningless concept. Being capable is not the possibility of the organism as distinct from something actual, but is a constitutive moment of the way in which the animal as such *is*—of its being. We can and must investigate everything which belongs to the essence of the animal's being in accordance with its inner possibility. That is, we can and must investigate amongst other things the inner possibility of capacity as such, so that we can recognize in our investigation a peculiar range of quite different kinds of possibility. We characterized capability as a having and offering of possibilities. But now we must examine this offering of possibilities, this specific way of being possible, this potentiality, according to its own inner possibility as something that belongs to the essence of capability.

§58. The behaviour and captivation of the animal.

a) Preliminary interpretation of behaviour as the wherefore of animal capability. Animal behaviour as drive in distinction from human comportment as action.

Although we have recognized capacity as a constitutive moment of the animal's specific manner of being, there is still something missing in our observation and determination of capability and of everything to which our investigation has led, as long as we have not considered *what* the capacity in each case is *for,* and how again we are to determine this wherefore. We talk about the capacity for seeing, seizing etc. Seeing, hearing, grasping, digesting, hunting, nest-building, reproduction—what are they? They are processes in nature, processes of life. Certainly they are. And if the stone warms up in the sunshine, that too is a process, just as when a leaf is propelled by the wind. These are all 'processes', events of nature. Yet justified as this general term is here, it immediately becomes quite vacuous when we recognize that seeing, for example, is an utterly different process from the warming of a stone. In other words, the term we use is not a matter of indifference, insofar as it is supposed to tell us something about what is named by the term. Of course all naming and terminology is arbitrary in a certain sense. But whether the terminology chosen in any given case is *suitable* or not can only be decided by looking at the *things themselves* which are named and intended in each case. The terminological arbitrariness disappears immediately if, as is usually the case, the terms used claim to represent a particular *substantive* interpretation, if they already provide the point of departure and general orientation for grasping the *matter itself*. Thus in a living language it is always possible to argue over names and terminology, but not about the suitability of a name as long as we are concerned with the *substantive content* of the matter intended by the name. It is easy to see that the most decisive thing about the specific being of the animal is lost from view if we regard hunting, grasping, or seeing, for example, simply as a process understood as a series of events.

When we observe that the stone gets warm in the sun, the leaf flies about in the wind, the worm flees from the mole, the dog snaps at the fly, we can certainly say that in all these cases we are concerned with processes, with unfolding events, with a series of stages in these movements. But we can also easily see that this way of looking at the events misses the decisive thing in the case of animals: the specific character of the worm's movement as escape, the specific character of the mole's movement as pursuit. We cannot explain escaping and pursuing simply by applying theoretical mathematics or mechanics, however complex. Here a quite primordial kind of movement reveals itself. The escaping worm does not merely appear within the context of a sequence of movements which begin with the mole. Rather the worm is *escaping from* the latter. This is not simply an event, but rather the escaping worm *behaves* as fleeing in a particular way *with respect to* the mole. And the mole for its part *behaves with respect to* the worm by pursuing it. Thus we shall describe seeing, hearing, and so forth, and also assimilation and reproduction, as a form of *behaviour,* as a form of *self-like behaviour* [Sichbenehmen]. A stone cannot behave in this way. Yet the human being can—he or she can behave well or behave badly. But *our* behaviour—in this proper sense—can only be described in this way because it is a *comportment,* because the specific manner of being which belongs to man is quite different and involves not behaviour but *comporting oneself toward. . . .* The *specific manner* in which man *is* we shall call *comportment* and the *specific manner* in which the animal *is* we shall call *behaviour.* They are fundamentally different from one another. In principle it is also possible to reverse this linguistic usage and refer to *animal comportment.* The reason why we prefer the first way of describing the matter will be revealed from the substantive interpretation itself. Being capable of . . . means being capable of behaviour. Capability is instinctual, a driving forward and maintaining oneself in being driven toward that which the capacity is capable of, toward a possible form of behaviour, a drivenness toward a performance of a particular kind in each case. The behaviour of the animal is not a *doing and acting,* as in human comportment, but a *driven performing* [Treiben]. In saying this we mean to suggest that an instinctual drivenness, as it were, characterizes all such animal performance.

Yet here again, from a purely linguistic point of view, we can see that the terminology is arbitrary if we recall that we also talk about 'driving' snow when there is no question of anything organic announcing its specific manner of being. This shows that language in all this is not subject to logic, and that a certain inconsequentiality belongs rather to the essence of language and its meanings. In other words, language is something that belongs to the essence of man in his finitude. To imagine a god expressing himself in speech is utterly meaningless.

We must now attempt to grasp this *behavioural character* of the performance of the organism in its capable drivenness. Capability as the animal's potentiality to be means *being capable of behaviour.* And vice versa, if a specific manner of being shows itself as behaviour, then the particular being must be capable and have capability. Thus we could also have taken the characterization of behaviour as our point of departure and shown its dependence upon capability. We chose the first way in order to make it clear that being capable does not simply describe the animal in its mere possibility, but that the actuality of the animal is intrinsically a being capable of. . . . The drive does not vanish when the animal is busy performing something. The instinctual moment is what it is precisely in the animal's driven performing.

b) The animal's absorption in itself as captivation. Captivation (the essence of the peculiarity proper to the organism) as the inner possibility of behaviour.

This preliminary interpretation concerning *what* it is that capability is capable *of* provides us with a further context for inquiring concretely about what is in question, namely how the organism as a capable behavioural being is proper to itself. It thus enables us to concretely inquire about the essence of the *peculiarity proper to* the organism. Behaviour is intrinsically a being capable (driving, drivenness). We said that being capable implied an intrinsic self-retention, a remaining with itself on the part of the capable being, a proper peculiarity. This characteristic must accordingly also apply to behaviour. For in its behaviour—as that which the animal is capable of—in this driven performing the animal does not drive itself away from itself. Rather the animal *is* in precisely such a way that it intrinsically retains itself and is intrinsically absorbed in itself. Behaviour and its forms are not something which radiate outward and allow the animal to run ahead along certain paths. Rather *behaviour* is precisely an *intrinsic retention* and *intrinsic absorption,* although no reflection is involved.

Behaviour as a manner of being in general is only possible on the basis of the animal's *absorption* in itself [Eingenommenheit *in sich*]. We shall describe *the specific way in which the animal remains with itself*—which has nothing to do with the selfhood of the human being comporting him- or herself as a person—this way in which the animal is absorbed in itself, and which makes possible behaviour of any and every kind, as *captivation* [Benommenheit]. The animal can only behave insofar as it is essentially captivated. The possibility of behaving in the manner of animal being is grounded in this essential structure of the animal, a structure we will now elucidate as captivation. Captivation is the condition of possibility for the fact that, in accordance with its essence, the animal *behaves within an environment but never within a world.*

We usually employ the word 'captivation' to describe a particular state of mind in human beings, one which can persist for a greater or lesser period of time. We use it then to refer to that intermediate state somewhere between consciousness and unconsciousness. In this sense we can say that captivation is also a psychiatric concept. From everything we have said so far it should by now be obvious that in talking of captivation as the essential structure of the animal there can be no question of simply transferring this state known to us from our own human experience into the animal as a permanent trait of the latter. We certainly cannot think of the animal as permanently captivated, in distinction from human beings—which would mean that in principle the animal might also be free of this state. We do not understand the term captivation to mean simply an enduring state present within the animal but rather an *essential moment of animality* as such. Even if in elucidating the essence of this captivation we orient ourselves in a certain way with reference to the human state in question, we must nevertheless draw the specific content of this structure from out of animality itself. That means that we must delimit the essence of captivation with a view to animal behaviour as such. Yet behaviour itself is grasped as that specific manner of being which belongs to being capable, i.e., to instinctual and subservient intrinsic self-diverting and self-proposing.

We say that only where captivation constitutes the essential structure of a being do we find the thorough and prevalent manner of being which belongs to behaviour. This manner of being announces itself in the case of the animal in the familiar terms of seeing, hearing, seizing, hunting, fleeing, devouring, digesting, and all the other organic processes. It is not as if the beating of the animal's heart were a process different from the animal's seizing and seeing, the one analogous to the case of human beings, the other to a chemical process. Rather the entirety of its being, the being as a whole in its unity, must be comprehended as behaviour. Captivation is not some state that accompanies the animal, into which it sometimes temporarily falls, nor is it a state in which it simply finds itself permanently. It is the inner possibility of animal being itself. We now ask: to what extent does that which we understand by captivation announce itself in hearing, seizing etc., and in such a way that we describe this 'activity' as behaviour? We do not regard captivation as a state that merely accompanies behaviour, but as the inner possibility of behaviour as such.

Before we examine this problem any further, I would like to point out once again that we are pursuing it here only from one quite specific perspective and thus in a one-sided fashion. We cannot claim in any way to be offering a complete and thoroughly developed determination of the essence of animality. If it is indeed true that this interpretation of essence must be drawn independently from the phenomenon of animality, it is equally true that it remains utterly rooted in the problematic of metaphysics which must be adequately clarified.

§59. *Clarification of the structure of behaviour in a*
concrete way: the relationality of animal behaviour,
as distinct from the relationality of human action.

Our question now is: To what extent does this captivation announce itself in seeing, hearing, and so on? Captivation designates the fundamental character of the animal's *being absorbed* in itself. Seeing, seizing, catching, and so on always take place from out of the drivenness of an instinctual and subservient capacity for the same. As being capable of this or that form of behaviour in each case, capability for . . . drives through and is driven through the behaviour itself. This means that behaviour as such is a *being driven forward*—and that also means a *being driven away.* In general, seeing, hearing, and seizing are a *being related to.* . . . Not indeed in the sense that seizing something is an independent movement, or that the unfolding of this movement then additionally comes into connection with *what* is seized. But rather in the sense that the movement is intrinsically a movement toward . . . , a reaching out for. . . . Seeing is the seeing of *what is seen,* hearing is the hearing of *what is heard.*

Of course, one will say: this is fundamentally obvious. And yet everything depends upon correctly grasping the obvious here, which has not been comprehended by far, and indeed not comprehended specifically in relation to what we are calling animal behaviour. The task is to see precisely *what kind of relationality* lies in this behaviour; to see above all how the relationality of the animal's behaviour toward what it hears and what it reaches for is distinguished from human comportment toward things, which is also a relatedness of man to things. In smelling, the animal is related to what it smells, and indeed in the manner of capable reference toward. . . . At the same time this instinctual reference toward . . . is subservient as such. The act of smelling stands intrinsically in the service of further behaviour.

In order now to bring the peculiar character of behaviour into view, we must take our methodological point of departure from a consideration of those forms of behaviour which are more remote, with respect to their consistent and intrinsic character, than those forms of comportment displayed by the higher animals that seem to correspond so closely to our own comportment. We shall therefore consider the behaviour of bees, and do so also because insects have an exemplary function within the problematic of biology.

a) Concrete examples of animal behaviour drawn from experimental research.

Let us take a *concrete example*. The worker bee collecting nourishment flies from flower to flower in the meadow. But it does not fly from one flower to the next nearest one, nor does it fly from one to another arbitrarily. It flies from one clover blossom to another and passes over the forget-me-not and other blossoms. We say that the bee is intent upon a particular flower for days and weeks on end, something which indeed is only ever true of individual bees in the swarm. Other bees from the same hive frequent other kinds of blossom. It is not the case that all the worker bees seek out the same flowers at the same time. In fact different bees can seek out different blossoms, yet they always do so consistently. The flying involved is part of the bees' *behaviour*. In its consistent search for a particular flower the bee follows a particular scent in each case. Nor is the colour irrelevant, even if the significance of the colour is limited. The flying of the bee, as one of its forms of possible behaviour, is no mere flying about but is a flying directed toward one particular scent. This directedness, its drivenness in the search for food, does not merely or even principally take place because of hunger, but rather for the purpose of collecting and storing food. The drivenness also reveals the fact that the bee belongs to a swarm. The bee finds a drop of honey in a clover blossom, for example. It sucks it up, stops sucking, and flies away again.[1] Why do we relate these trivialities here? The situation is very simple—and yet thoroughly enigmatic. For we must ask ourselves: Why does the bee fly away? Because the honey is no longer present, comes the answer. Well and good. But does the bee recognize the fact that the honey is no longer present? Does it fly away because it has recognized this fact? If this is the case, then it must also have recognized the presence of the honey in the first place. Is there any evidence that the bee recognizes the presence, or the absence, of honey? Clearly there is. For, attracted by the scent of the flower, the bee stayed on the blossom, began to suck up the honey, and then stopped doing so at a certain point. But does this really prove that the bee recognized the honey *as present?* Not at all, especially if we can and indeed must interpret the bee's activity as a driven performing and as drivenness, as behaviour—as behaviour rather than comportment on the part of the bee toward the honey which is present or no longer present.

---

1. J. von Uexküll, *Theoretische Biologie,* op. cit., p. 141.

Yet what prevents us from interpreting this driven activity on the part of the bee as comportment toward the present honey, as a recognition of the same as present or no longer present? If the bee does not recognize the presence of something, if the recognition of mere presence at hand as a specific manner of being pertaining to the honey is excluded, what is it then that governs and directs its behaviour, its flight and its return to the hive, since the bee obviously stands in some specific relation to the blossom, the scent, the hive, and so forth, i.e., to its whole environment?

The situation becomes clearer if we consider *a different case* which has received particular experimental support. A bee was placed before a little bowl filled with so much honey that the bee was unable to suck up the honey all at once. It begins to suck and then after a while breaks off this driven activity of sucking and flies off, leaving the rest of the honey still present in the bowl. If we wanted to explain this activity, we would have to say that the bee recognizes that it cannot cope with all the honey present. It breaks off its driven activity because it recognizes the presence of too much honey for it. Yet, it has been observed that if its abdomen is carefully cut away while it is sucking, a bee will simply carry on regardless even while the honey runs out of the bee from behind. This shows conclusively that the bee by no means recognizes the presence of too much honey. It recognizes neither this nor even—though this would be expected to touch it more closely—the absence of its abdomen. There is no question of it recognizing any of this, it continues with its driven activity regardless precisely because it does not recognize that plenty of honey is still present. Rather, the bee is simply taken [*hingenommen*] by its food. This *being taken* is only possible where there is an *instinctual* 'toward. . . . ' Yet such a driven being taken also excludes the possibility of any recognition of presence. It is precisely being taken by its food that prevents the animal from taking up a position over and against this food.

But why does the bee break off its sucking if the abdomen is not removed? We may say that it does so because it has had enough. But why has it had enough now, and why has it not had enough when the abdomen is missing? Because its sense of satisfaction is registered as long as the abdomen remains in place, as long as the animal remains organically intact. This sense of satisfaction cannot be registered in the bee if its abdomen is missing. And what is this sense of satisfaction? It is a state of being satiated. It is this satiation which inhibits the bee's driven activity. Thus we talk about the inhibiting behavioural effect of satiation. Exactly how this takes place, whether it is a reflex action or a chemical process or something else again, is a matter of controversy. But that is not the decisive issue for us here. We must merely see that insofar as satiation inhibits this drive, it is indeed related to the animal's nourishment. But intrinsically and fundamentally it is never a recognition of the presence of nourishment or of the amount of nourishment available. Satiation is a quite

specific kind of drivenness, i.e., a specific inhibition of the same. This inhibition, however, is not related to that which the sucking activity is related to.
The driven activity and behaviour of the bee is not governed by any recognition
of the presence or absence of that which it is driven to engage with, of that
to which its sucking behaviour stands in relation. That means that in sucking
at the blossom the bee does *not comport itself* toward the blossom *as something
present or not present.* We claim that the activity here is terminated through
an inhibition (drive and disinhibition). Yet that also means that the activity
does not simply cease, rather the drivenness of the capability is redirected into
another drive. Instinctual activity is not a recognitive self-directing toward
objectively present things, but a *behaving.* Driven activity is a behaving. This
is not to deny that something like a directedness toward scent and honey, *a
relation toward . . . ,* does belong to behaviour, but there is no recognitive
self-directing toward these things. More precisely, there is *no apprehending* of
honey *as* something present, but rather a peculiar captivation which is indeed
related to the honey. The drive is captivated. In what sense? The continued
sucking tells us the answer: it is captivated by the scent and the honey. However,
when the sucking is discontinued, the captivation also ceases. Yet this is not
the case at all. The instinctual activity is simply redirected toward flying back
to the bee hive. This flight back to the hive is just as captivated as was the
sucking, it is merely another form of captivation, i.e., another case of the bee's
behaviour.

We must content ourselves here with a brief account of how the bee
redirects its instinctual sucking into an instinctual impulse to return to the
hive, how the bee finds its way back to the hive at all, how it orients itself, as
we are accustomed to saying. In the strict sense, there is orientation only
where space is disclosed as such, and thus where the possibility of distinguishing different regions and identifiable locations within these regions is also
given. We recognize of course that the bee flies through space as it returns
home to the hive from the meadow, but the question is whether in behaving
in this way the bee opens up a space *as* space and flies through it *as* its *spatial
flight-path.* Of course it does, one may say, without initially being able to
clarify any further how the bee's traversal of this spatial flight-path is different
in kind from the flight-path traversed by a bullet. The problem of *animal
space,* of whether the animal has a space as such space at all, cannot be taken
up in isolation. The problem is rather to establish the correct basis and
perspective for this question in the first place, to ask after the basis of a
universal determination of the essence of animality which will then allow us
to inquire into the possible relationship between the animal and its space.
Thus we recognize not only the traversal of space here but also the potential
to return home, the *capacity for returning home.* We must now consider this
more closely in relation to what follows.

This capacity for finding the way back, the capacity for orientation in general, never fails, we must admit, to provoke our amazement when we think of migrating birds or the canine sense of smell for example. However, if we stay with the bee and examine what its home looks like, we see that it consists of a series of bee hives. The bee keeper generally paints the individual hives in different colours so that the bees do not return to the original mother hive by mistake. So they orient themselves according to the colour, one will say. But this is true only to a limited extent since the bee cannot distinguish between blue, crimson, and violet, nor between red and black. Thus the bee can only distinguish certain colours. If the aforementioned colours are ranged indiscriminately, then the bees do go astray, although this is not invariably the case. For it has been discovered that they also direct themselves according to the scent which they themselves emit and which allows them to distinguish between different swarms, or more precisely to identify the swarm to which they belong. We can observe how the bees will often fly back and forth above the entrance of the hive with their abdomens uppermost so that they surround the entrance hole with their scent. The fact that bees still sometimes go astray is shown not merely by experiments but also by the dead bees which can frequently be found on the sill before the entrance hole where they have been killed as intruders by the hive's fighter bees.

All of this proves only that colour and scent are involved in the bee's homeward flight. But if we consider that the flight-domain of a given swarm can range over several kilometers—although not more than three or four—and that the bees can find their way home over such distances, then it is clear that it is not the sight of the painted hives or the scent around the entrance holes which are capable of bringing the bees back, as it were, on their homeward flight. It was the experiments of Bethe, first properly explained by Radl in 1905 in his *Investigations on Animal Phototropism*,[2] which showed that something else is, it seems, primarily involved in guiding the bees back.

The *experiment,* which initially illuminates the difficulties, here proceeds as follows. A bee hive is placed out in a meadow and the swarms eventually become accustomed to this location. After a certain period of time the hive is moved back by a few meters. At first we might assume that the bees can see the hive standing in the meadow and thus could find their way back accurately in spite of the slight change of position. And yet the flight of the bees remains oriented toward the now empty spot in the meadow where the hive previously stood, despite the fact that it has only been moved a few meters away. The bees now become suspicious at the empty spot and eventually find their hive after some searching about. Are the bees guided by certain orienting features

2. E. Radl, *Untersuchungen über den Phototropismus der Tiere* (Leipzig, 1905).

like trees and so on? Orienting features of this kind may well be involved, but they do not explain precisely why the bees fly back to the empty spot. Above all, however, it is true that the bees can find their way back over great barren distances with no such orienting features. What is it that guides them and keeps them, so to speak, in the right direction? Neither the colour nor the smell of the hive, neither landmarks nor other such objects by which they could take their bearings, but—what, then? The sun.

First of all, we shall simply report the experiment without providing a philosophical interpretation, offering an initial explanation of the bee's capacity to fly back home without reference to colour, scent, or landmarks. When the bee flies out of the hive to find food it registers the direction in which it stands in relation to the sun. Usually it is only a matter of minutes before the bee returns to the hive, so that the position of the sun has only changed very slightly in the intervening time. For example, if the bee has the sun behind it to the left at an angle of 30 degrees when it flies out to its feeding place, it orients itself on the return flight so that the sun is now in front of it to the right at the same angle. Is not this activity even more astounding than the supposition that the bee recognizes the presence or absence of the honey?

But perhaps it is only the explanation of these observations which is astounding, rather than the observations themselves. Perhaps this appeal to the sun is simply a last bold attempt to solve the problem because we cannot explain the homeward flight of the bee in any other way. So maybe one should really despair of this explanation. Yet an elementary experiment suffices to convince us of the correctness of the suggested explanation. If we imprison a bee which has just arrived at its feeding place inside a dark box and only release it after a few hours (during which time the position of the sun in the sky has changed significantly), the newly freed bee will seek its hive in the wrong direction. The bee does not fly disorientedly or indiscriminately in any direction whatever, but the direction in which it flies off deviates from the direction of arrival by exactly the same angle that corresponds to the changed position of the sun. That means that in relation to the new position of the sun, the bee now flies back in keeping with the original angle of approach which it had, as it were, carried along with it. Where does it fly back to? Since it cannot find the hive in this direction, we might expect it to carry on indefinitely as if caught in the same angle. But it does no such thing. After traversing a distance which corresponds to that between the hive and its feeding place, the bee stops its linear flight altogether. It then buzzes around looking for its hive which it will eventually find as long as the distance between the hive and its present position has not become too great. It is said that the bee not only notices the direction in which it stands to the sun and keeps to this angle, but also notices the distance traversed by its flight path. So we see here a quite peculiar kind of orientation and behaviour on the part of the bee in terms of its capacity for successfully finding its way back.

There is a *further experiment* which demonstrates just how much the original direction, the direction of the return flight, and the angles involved are wrapped up in the bee's captivation with respect to the sun. For example, if we now take the box in which the bee has been imprisoned back to the hive and place it some distance behind the hive, then the newly freed bee flies in the direction in which it would have to fly in order to find the hive from the feeding place, even though the hive is relatively nearby, and it does so for the appropriate distance once again. But this only happens if the hive is standing in an empty landscape. If the bee's familiar environment is populated with trees and houses, on the other hand, then the bee follows them as landmarks and does not simply rely upon its instinctual sense of direction.

b) General characterization of behaviour: Captivation as the animal's having any apprehending of something as something withheld from it, and as being taken by something. The exclusion of the animal from the manifestness of beings.

We cannot value experiments of this kind too highly and we have no intention of prematurely complaining about the proffered explanations with the usual gesture of philosophical superiority. The task lies rather in bringing the facts revealed and clarified by such experiments directly before the essential problem.

What is going on in all this animal activity, what does it tell us about the behaviour of the animal and about the captivation we have claimed for it? If we say that the bee *notices* the position of the sun, the angles, the distance traversed in flight and so on, we should bear in mind that explicitly noticing something— apart from anything else—always involves noticing something with regard to some end, with intent to something—here with intent to finding the way back to a hive located at a particular place. But the bee knows precisely nothing of all this. For on the contrary it flies back in a pre-established direction over a pre-established distance without regard to the position of the hive. It does not strike out in a given direction prescribed for it by the place in which it has found itself. Rather it is absorbed by a direction, is driven to produce this direction out of itself—without regard to the destination. The bee does not at all comport itself toward particular things, like the hive, the feeding place and so on. But one might object that the bee does comport itself toward the sun and it must therefore recognize the angle of the sun. It should be clear that here we become involved in insoluble difficulties. Nevertheless, we must not turn away and abandon the attempt to illuminate this peculiar and characteristic behaviour. For we can succeed in doing so if we clearly recognize that no advance is possible as long as we regard this behaviour as an isolated phenomenon in its own right, and then attempt to render the bee's comportment to the sun intelligible on the basis of such an isolated treatment of behaviour. Perhaps all these relationships are determined by the peculiar captivation proper to the animal itself, a captivation which is quite different in the case of each animal species. We must ask therefore what we can learn about the general characterization of behaviour from these experiments and from such study of the actual facts; and how far we can elucidate this behaviour in order to clarify for ourselves the quite specific being which belongs to the bee and thus reveal the fundamental character of all behaviour, not merely with respect to locomotion, sucking, foraging etc. , but with respect to every kind of behaviour. If we can successfully identify this fundamental character, then we shall also be able to comprehend the nature of captivation on this basis, which will enable us in turn to clarify the essence of the organism and eventually the animal's poverty in world.

The bee is *simply given over* to the sun and to the period of its flight *without being able to grasp either of these as such,* without being able to reflect upon them as something thus grasped. The bee can only be given over to things in this way because it is driven by the fundamental drive of foraging. It is precisely because of this *drivenness,* and not on account of any recognition or reflection, that the bee can *be captivated* by what the sun occasions in its behaviour. The fact that the bee is driven in a particular direction is and remains embedded within the context of the fundamental drive for going out and foraging, and that also means within the context of the instinctual drive to return home. The drive to return home has always already overridden the directional drive, as it were. That is why the latter is immediately abandoned, and does not even come into operation, as long as the possibility of returning home is assured by the familiar environment of the hive. Yet even this fundamental foraging drive, along with the associated homing drive, is not grounded in any grasp or knowledge of the hive. In all its instinctual activity the bee is related to its feeding place, to the sun, to the hive and so forth. Yet this being related to . . . is *not an apprehending* of these things *as* feeding place, *as* sun or whatever, but rather, one is tempted to say, as something else. No, it is *not* an apprehending of something *as something,* as something present at hand. There is no apprehending [*Vernehmen*], but only a *behaving* [Benehmen] here, a driven activity which we must grasp in this way because the possibility of apprehending something as something is *withheld* [genommen] from the animal. And it is withheld from it not merely here and now, but withheld in the sense that such a possibility is 'not given at all'. This possibility is taken away [*benommen*] from the animal, and that is why the animal is not simply unrelated to anything else but rather is taken [*hingenommen*], taken and captivated [*benommen*] by things.

The *captivation* of the animal therefore signifies, in the first place, essentially *having every apprehending of something as something withheld from it.* And furthermore: in having this withheld from it, the animal is precisely *taken by things.* Thus animal captivation characterizes the specific manner of being in which the animal relates itself to something else even while the possibility is withheld from it—or is taken away from the animal, as we might also say—of comporting and relating itself to something else *as* such and such at all, *as* something present at hand, *as* a being. And it is precisely because this possibility—apprehending *as* something that to which it relates—is withheld from it that the animal can find itself so utterly taken by something else. But this captivation should not be interpreted simply as a kind of rigid fixation on the part of the animal as if it were somehow spellbound. Rather this captivation makes possible and prescribes an appropriate leeway for its behaviour, i.e., a purely instinctual redirecting of the animal's driven activity in accordance with certain instincts in each case.

Of course, this driven behaviour does *not* relate itself, and as captivated activity cannot relate itself, *to what is present at hand as such.* What is present at hand as such means what is present at hand in its *being* present at hand, as a *being.* Beings are *not manifest* to the behaviour of the animal in its captivation, they are not disclosed to it and for that very reason are *not closed off* from it either. Captivation stands outside this possibility. As far as the animal is concerned we cannot say that beings are closed off from it. Beings could only be closed off if there were some possibility of disclosure at all, however slight that might be. But the captivation of the animal places the animal essentially outside of the possibility that beings could be either disclosed to it or closed off from it. To say that captivation is the essence of animality means: *The animal as such does not stand within a manifestness of beings. Neither its so-called environment nor the animal itself are manifest as beings.* The animal in principle does not possess the possibility of attending either to the being that it itself is or to beings other than itself, because the animal is directed in its manifold instinctual activities on the basis of its captivation and of the totality of its capacities. Because of this driven directedness the animal finds itself suspended, as it were, between itself and its environment, even though neither the one nor the other is experienced *as* being. Yet this not-having any manifestness of beings, this manifestness as withheld from the animal, is at the same time a being taken by. . . . We must say that the animal is related to . . . , that captivation and behaviour display an *openness* for. . . . For what precisely? How are we to describe what is encountered, as it were—in the specific openness of being taken—with respect to the drivenness of instinctual captivation? How shall we determine what the animal relates to in its behaviour, even though this is not manifest as a being?

Yet with this question, which must be answered if we are to characterize capacity, drive, and behaviour at all adequately, we are not merely asking about *what* the animal relates *to* and *how* the animal remains related to it. With this question—which turns away from the animal, as it were, toward that which the animal properly is not—we are asking about the *essence* of the animal's *absorption* in itself, i.e., about the *fundamental character of captivation.*

§60. The openness of behaviour and captivation,
and what it is that the animal relates itself to.

In order once again to provide a concrete support for this question concerning the *openness of behaviour,* we return to our first example of the bee which started sucking and then interrupted its sucking. In discussing such behaviour we only got as far as the question of whether or not recognizing the presence of the honey as honey plays a leading part here. Our further examination of the bee's capacity for orienting itself reinforced us in the view that the animal's *relationality* to other things consists in a kind of *being taken,* even and indeed precisely where the animal directs itself toward something in its orientation. The task is to clarify such behaviour and animal activity in general even further by bringing out its fundamental character. Yet determining this fundamental character more closely only leads us to the question concerning the *openness of captivation* and the *essence* of that *for which* the captivation of the animal is open.

a) The eliminative character of behaviour.

It is true that we do not wish to pursue the problem concerning the capacity for self-orientation any further at this point. But our attention to this problem has taught us something essential: that the drives of the animal, the particular forms of its behaviour, are not to be taken in isolation; but that on the contrary the totality of instinctual behaviour within which the animal is driven must constantly be borne in mind, even when we appear to be offering an isolated interpretation. The animal's behaviour in relation to the sun does not occur as a form of recognition which is subsequently followed by an appropriate form of action. Rather the animal's captivation by the sun only occurs in and through its instinctual foraging drive. The drives and the ways in which the animal is driven (seeking out food, lying in wait for prey) do not radiate out, as it were, in so many different directions and diverge from one another. On the contrary, each instinctual drive is intrinsically determined by its *being driven with respect to* the other drives. Instinctual drivenness as being driven from one drive to another holds and drives the animal within a *ring* which it cannot escape and within which something is open for the animal. Yet while it is certain that all instinctual behaviour is a relating to . . . , it is just as surely the case that in all its behaviour the animal is incapable of *ever properly attending to something as such.* The animal is *encircled* [umringt] by this ring [*Ring*] constituted by the reciprocal drivenness of its drives. Yet we must not determine this inability to attend to something as such in a purely negative manner. What does this inability positively imply for the phenomenon of captivation and its characteristic openness? It is not simply that behaviour never displays this character of attending to. . . . On the contrary, it actually possesses an *eliminative* character in respect of that to which it relates itself. This *fundamental trait of behaviour,* its eliminative character, can show itself as destruction—as devouring—or as avoidance of. . . .

And here too, we can point to a whole range of concrete phenomena which reveal how all animal behaviour takes place within the parameters of this fundamental eliminative character or, as we also put it, this inability to attend to. . . . The comportment of insects within that instinctual sphere we describe as the sexual drive offers us one of the most striking examples of this peculiarly eliminative character proper to all behaviour. It is well known that after copulation many female insects devour the male of the species. After copulation the sexual aspect disappears, the male acquires the character of prey and is eliminated. The one animal is never there for the other simply as a living creature, but is only there for it either as sexual partner or as prey—in either case only in some form of 'away' [*weg*]. Behaviour as such is always intrinsically a form of elimination [*Beseitigen*]. But this is also why, and indeed particularly why, the comportment of the animal always gives the impression of being purely negative. But in fact there is no question of any comportment whatsoever, not even a negative one. And because there is no comportment at all, we cannot say it is positive either. From a methodological point of view this means that in attempting to elucidate the essence of this eliminative character pertaining to all behaviour, we must in principle be just as critical about interpreting this positively as we are in interpreting it negatively in terms of the animal's inability to attend to. . . .

Yet initially one might well object, before any further theoretical discussion gets underway, that in many respects experience surely tells against this attempt to define the essence of behaviour as *eliminative.* For we can all see how animals do in fact occupy themselves with things and attend to them—in nest-building, in the care with which they attend to the construction of the nest, or in the rearing of their young, or in the way in which animals play and so on. Not only do we see no eliminative behaviour here, but there are other forms of behaviour where the animal even seems to be seeking out something to which it can relate. We must therefore try and shed more light upon this problem in all its difficulty.

One could point out how animals in general and insects in particular relate to light. In this respect we can specifically distinguish between creatures which seek the light and those which avoid it. Certainly this latter form of behaviour, fleeing from the light, can be explained as a form of eliminative behaviour in the sense that it entails avoiding something. But surely the light-seeking behaviour cannot be regarded as eliminative behaviour. Certainly not, but we must also ask: In what instinctual context does this light-seeking behaviour belong? It definitely does not imply that light as such is being sought out for its own sake. If we are to understand the eliminative character of behaviour correctly, we must not regard the various modes of behaviour in an isolated manner. Then we see that the Camberwell Beauty, which belongs amongst the light-seeking creatures, always behaves in such a way that its behaviour represents a movement away from the shade. It is not the intensity of the light as such but rather the extent of the illuminated surface which governs its behaviour in relation to the light. But even here the movement directed toward the light does not represent a grasping of the light as such. On the contrary, the light-seeking behaviour always already serves to orient the creature and constantly to make possible such orientation. Consequently the light never has the opportunity to announce itself as such for the animal. Thus it is that Radl, to whom we owe some outstanding investigations concerning animal phototropism, discovered that "in the case of certain fresh-water crabs the incidence of light decisively affects their swimming position, for they always move in such a way that their eyes are directed toward the light-source, irrespective of where that source may be. If the light comes from below, then the crabs lie upside down in the water."[1] But the crabs' relation to the light, which impresses itself upon us as a constant one here, does not actually leave the animal free for the light as such. On the contrary, it is precisely its relation to the light which enables the animal to remain proper to itself as animal. The animal locks its behaviour and what is proper and peculiar to it [Eigen-tum] into the light as it were.

Yet perhaps it is the moth which flies into the light that provides the most striking and everyday example of animals that fundamentally seek out light. When the moth flies straight into the light and is destroyed in so doing, can we really imagine any more immediate way of attending to something than this form of behaviour? One might think that this creature in particular is not seeking an illuminated surface, but rather the intensity of the light-source itself. And yet we must say that this light-seeking creature plunges into the light precisely because it does not attend to the light or grasp it as such in its light-seeking behaviour. If we are to understand this phenomenon, we should note that all light-seeking creatures (positive phototropism) are governed by the magnitude of the illuminated field, while all light-avoiding creatures (negative phototropism) are governed by the intensity of the light. It is well-known that Darwin had already asked the question why moths should fly into candles but not toward the moon. Moths are light-seekers and thus seek out illuminated surfaces rather than the intensity of the light source. The moon shines upon large surfaces which thus exert a stronger effect than the light of the moon itself. The candle, on the other hand, is not capable of illuminating such large surfaces, which would counteract the effect of its own light, and thus the light-seeking creatures fall victim to the light source itself.

1. J. von Uexküll, *Umwelt und Innenwelt der Tiere.* Second, expanded and improved edition (Berlin, 1921), p. 207.

We have only discussed such behaviour toward the light as an example of *one* mode of behaviour. Our reference to the peculiar forms of orientation proper to the animal, and to animal behaviour within and toward the light, is simply intended to show that, just as in the case of smell and colour, light too possesses a quite peculiar significance for the animal. Yet all the same, and precisely for this reason, the behaviour of the animal, even if it does imply a certain directedness toward something, cannot be interpreted as meaning that such behaviour itself could grasp as such that to which it relates. In spite of all this, our own interpretation still gives the impression of being somewhat arbitrary. We understood the movement toward the light as a movement away from the darkness, the movement toward the darkness as a movement away from the light. But why on earth should we privilege the movement away from . . . over against the movement toward . . . , why not the reverse? Is it simply because the first alternative suits our preconceived ideas? By no means. For strictly speaking neither alternative is appropriate. We shall therefore continue to follow the injunction expressed above to maintain critical vigilance with respect to the supposedly more plausible positive interpretation of eliminative behaviour. But why does an apparently negative impression arise when we are discussing the character of behaviour as eliminative? It arises because the animal's behaviour expresses a kind of rejection on the part of the animal with respect to what it relates to in its behaviour. In this *rejecting things from itself* we see the animal's self-absorption. The latter does not imply that the organism is encapsulated within itself, cut off from any and every relation to the environment. But nor does this relational aspect belonging to behaviour represent an attentiveness to what is present at hand as present at hand within the environment. This eliminative character of all behaviour, the way in which it leaves things to one side, is an enigma which repeatedly forces us to address the question: What then is behaviour related to and what is the nature of this relation? Or we can now also ask: Where is the *ring* with which the animal is *encircled* as such, and how does it encircle the animal? What is this encircling [*Umringen*] like, if a relation to other things is not merely sustained, but constantly brought about [*errungen*] by this encircling?

In order to attempt to clarify the eliminative character of behaviour let us begin once again with an elementary observation. One could say that if behaviour is something thoroughly eliminative, then it is so constituted as behaviour that it does not let anything present at hand stand as it is, but rather obviates it so as to be rid of it as it were. Eliminative behaviour thus represents the continual production of an emptiness. Yet a relation to something like emptiness is only possible where there is a relation to beings as such. Thus in turn the very possibility of seeking an emptiness is given only where a relation to beings as such is possible. If we attempted to understand eliminative behaviour as a seeking of emptiness, then we should already have to understand the animal's behaviour fundamentally as a self-comportment toward beings as such. Yet that is precisely what is impossible. However this also implies that animals do not comport themselves indifferently with respect to beings either. For such indifference would also represent a relation to beings as such. But if behaviour is not a relation to beings, does this mean that it is a relation to nothing? Not at all. Yet if it is not a relation to nothing, it must always be a relation to something, which surely must itself *be* and actually *is*. Certainly, but the question is whether behaviour is not precisely a kind of relation to . . . in which *that to which* the behaviour relates in the manner of not attending to it is *open in a certain way* for the animal. But this certainly does not mean *manifest as a being*. There is no indication that the animal somehow does or ever could comport itself toward beings as such. Yet it is certainly true that the animal does announce itself as something that relates to other things, and does so in such a way that it is *somehow affected* by these other things. I emphasize this point precisely because this *relation to* . . . which is involved in animal behaviour, even though it essentially lacks the manifestness of beings, has either been quite overlooked in previous attempts to define the concept of the organism and the essence of the animal in general, or has merely been inserted as an afterthought. The possibility of providing an adequate definition of the organism as such depends upon the possibility of grasping this funda-mental character of behaviour in an adequate fashion. If it is the case that the animal does not comport itself toward beings as such, then behaviour involves *no letting-be* of beings as such—none at all and in no way whatsoever, not even any not letting-be. But in that case the inevitably misleading term for the fundamental character of behaviour, namely as elimination [*Be-seitigen*], must be taken in a quite fundamental sense. Behaviour is eliminative, i.e., it is certainly a relating to . . . but it is so in such a way that beings can never, and essentially never, manifest themselves as beings. It is only through this inter-pretation that we can discover the essence of behaviour and captivation. Yet behaviour is not blind either, in the sense in which we might want to say that beings are certainly there for the animal even though it cannot grasp them because it is not endowed with reason and does not think.

b) Animal behaviour as encircled by a disinhibiting ring.

Now if something resembling a *surrounding environment* is *open* for the animal and its behaviour, we must now ask whether it is possible to clarify this any further.

Instinctual and subservient capability for . . . , the totality of its self-absorbed capability, is an interrelated drivenness of the instinctual drives which encircles the animal. It does so in such a way that it is precisely this *encirclement* which makes possible the behaviour in which the animal is related to other things.

Related to other things—although *these other things are not manifest as beings.* Capability for . . . is not a matter of comportment toward beings. Capability for . . . never passes over into its correlative behaviour because beings as such announce themselves in such and such a way for the animal. But the other things in question do not stand in a mechanical relation to the animal either since, in its capability for . . . , the animal opens itself to what is other in approaching it. That is, the capability for . . . is what intrinsically makes it possible for something other to occasion anything like a capability to produce a specific form of behaviour in the first place, and to maintain the capability as driven in this behaviour. Capability for . . . and thus behaviour itself is open for such occasions, for stimuli, for that which initiates, i.e., disinhibits the capability for . . . in such and such a way in each case. That which the animal's behaviour relates to is such that this behaviour is open to it. This other is taken up into this openness of the animal in a manner that we shall describe as *disinhibition* [Enthemmung]. Since capability for . . . thoroughly governs the animal's specific manner of being, a being such as the animal, when it comes into relation with something else, can only come upon the sort of entity that '*affects*' or initiates the capability in some way. Nothing else can ever penetrate the ring around the animal. Here we are not yet concerned with any particular content whatsoever, but only with the fundamental character of that to which the animal can stand in relation at all.

Yet if the instinctual drives are precisely characterized by their uninhibitedness, then why should the instinctual drive have to be disinhibited in the first place? Should we not rather say that it is the other which the animal comes upon which inhibits the instinctual drive? We speak with a certain legitimacy of the uninhibitedness of instinctual drives when we consider the results of such activity as it were, what these drives drive toward and what they are driven to do, and especially when we also relate these things to our own possible comportment in and toward them—the question of control and so on. But if on the other hand we reflect upon the instinctual drive intrinsically as such—rather than upon the instinctual activity into which it can be released—and consider the instinctual structure itself, then we can see that the instinctual drive precisely possesses an inner tension and charge, a containment and inhibitedness that essentially must be disinhibited before it can pass over into driven activity and thus be 'uninhibited' in the usual, ordinary sense of the word.

That which behaviour as instinctual capability comes upon is always disinhibiting in some way. That which disinhibits in this way, and stands in relation to behaviour only insofar as it is disinhibiting, constantly withdraws [*entzieht sich*] from behaviour as it were and does so necessarily on account of its own manner of 'showing itself'—if we may talk in such terms at all. Since that which disinhibits behaviour essentially withdraws and eludes it, so too the relation of behaviour to that which occasions it is a *not attending to it.* No permanence as such is ever attained, nor indeed any change as such. The encirclement of the animal within the interrelated drivenness of its instinctual drives is intrinsically open for that which disinhibits it. Thus the *intrinsic self-encirclement* [Sich-Einringen] of the animal is not a kind of encapsulation. On the contrary, the encirclement is precisely *drawn about* the animal in such a way that it *opens* up a sphere within which whatever disinhibits can do so in this or that manner. The behaviour of the animal, contrary to how it might appear, does not and never can relate to *present-at-hand* things singly or collectively. Rather, the animal surrounds itself with a *disinhibiting ring* which prescribes what can affect or occasion its behaviour. Since this self-encirclement belongs to the animal, it always intrinsically bears its disinhibiting ring along with it and does so as long as it is alive. Or more precisely—the life of the animal is precisely the struggle [*Ringen*] to maintain this encircling ring or sphere within which a quite specifically articulated manifold of disinhibitions can arise. Every animal surrounds itself with this disinhibiting ring, and not merely subsequently once the animal has already been living for a certain period of time, because this encircling belongs to the innermost organization of the animal and its fundamental morphological structure. The way in which the animal is in each case taken by the whole is directed by the range of possible disinhibitions within its encirclement. Such being taken is open for manifold forms of disinhibition, but this openness is precisely not the manifestness of anything that behaviour could relate to as beings. This open being taken intrinsically involves the withholding of any possibility of apprehending beings. This self-encircling entails an open absorption in it—not in the so-called 'interior' of the animal, but in the ring of the interrelated drivenness of instinctual drives as they open themselves up.

This question now leads us toward the distinction we tried to express by talking of man's *world-forming* and the animal's *poverty in world,* a poverty which, roughly put, is nonetheless a kind of wealth. The difficulty of the problem lies in the fact that in our questioning we always and inevitably interpret the poverty in world and the peculiar encirclement proper to the animal in such a way that we end up talking as if that which the animal relates to and the manner in which it does so were some being, and as if the relation involved were an ontological relation that is manifest to the animal. The fact that this is not the case forces us to claim that the *essence of life can become accessible only if we consider it in a deconstructive* [abbauenden] *fashion.* But this does not mean that life represents something inferior or some kind of lower level in comparison with human Dasein. On the contrary, life is a domain which possesses a wealth of openness with which the human world may have nothing to compare.

In its instinctual relatedness to . . . , behaviour is open for. . . . But as instinctual activity it can at the same time only be touched or affected by something that brings the instinctual relatedness into play, i.e., by something that can disinhibit it. That which disinhibits and releases the inhibitedness of the instinctual drive, that which allows the instinctual activity to respond to the disinhibition, and thus allows the animal to move within certain instinctual drives, must always in accordance with its essence withdraw itself. It is *nothing enduring* that could *stand over against the animal as a possible object*—whether as something changed or unchanged [in the process]. The self-withdrawal of that which disinhibits corresponds to the essential *inability to attend* to it which is involved in behaviour, that is, the inability to attend to that which disinhibits as something objectively present at hand.

It is only because the animal's specific manner of being is behaviour, and because that which disinhibits correlatively belongs to such behaviour, that the animal can be affected by *stimuli*. Precisely the ability to be stimulated, or to be aroused (irritability), has been identified as the distinctive characteristic of 'living substance'. Johannes Müller, one of the most important physiologists, has investigated precisely this characteristic feature of life from various perspectives in his *Handbook of Human Physiology*.[2] Yet even to this day the essence of stimulus and of the ability to be stimulated has not yet been adequately determined either in the field of physiology or that of psychology, i.e., it has not been brought back to an examination of its structural conditions. Even to this day we have not recognized that the task is to ask: What are the conditions of the possibility of any stimulation in general? For the stimulus and the process of being stimulated is not the condition of possibility for the disinhibition of an instinctual drive. On the contrary, it is only where there is disinhibition and intrinsic encirclement that stimulation is possible. Of course one is accustomed to distinguishing the effect of a stimulus from a mechanical relation of cause and effect precisely by saying that in the case of mechanical pressure or impact there is always an immediate reaction of counter-pressure and counter-impact, whereas the stimulus is not subjected to any correlative counter-effect by whatever is stimulated. What it is that stimulates still remains unclarified here.

It is easy to see the extent to which this customary interpretation of stimulus and the various relations into which it enters is all too clearly oriented around a comparison with mechanical relations. Yet even disregarding this fact, the interpretation is false, so false that it actually covers over the decisive feature of the stimulus-relation. Certainly, that which is stimulated does not exert a counter-effect, a counter-stimulus as it were, back upon the stimulus that elicits the stimulation. But that by no means implies that what can be stimulated is not already related and indeed must be related to that which is supposed to be able to stimulate it. This relation to the potential stimulus must indeed be an instinctual one. It is only if this *prior relatedness* of *what can be stimulated* to that which can stimulate it already possesses the character of an instinctual drive which *instinctually en-counters* the stimulus, that anything like the eliciting

---

2. J. Müller, *Handbuch der Physiologie des Menschen.* 2 vols. Fourth, improved edition (Koblenz, 1844). [A translation exists of an earlier edition, by W. Baly: *Elements of Physiology* (London, 1837).]

of a stimulus is possible in general. This is the only way in which we can make the peculiar distribution and manifold forms of receptivity toward stimuli intelligible. For receptivity is always grounded in the range and directedness of the encompassing drivenness of the instinctual drives, delimited as it is in every case by the disinhibiting ring. In other words, it is only from this perspective that we can understand the peculiar fact that individual animals and species of animal are restricted to a quite specific manifold of possible stimuli, i.e., that their ring of possible disinhibition is distributed in quite specific directions with regard to receptivity or non-receptivity. However strong or intense a stimulus is, objectively speaking, a particular animal may be utterly unresponsive to particular stimuli. It is not as if some kind of barrier were erected in front of the animal. Rather the animal, in the unity of its captivation, does not have any intrinsic drives that are oriented in this direction. It is not instinctually open for this particular possibility of disinhibition.

Thus we can see that the circumscribed range of possible disinhibition or, as we put it, the disinhibiting ring, is intrinsic to the animal itself; that in its factical life amongst beings in each case the animal itself carves out a quite specific encircling ring [*Umringung*] within which it can be stimulated, i.e., a prior ring of potential disinhibition. Every animal surrounds itself with such an encircling ring, but it does not do so subsequently, as if the animal initially lived or ever could live without this encircling ring altogether, as if this encircling ring somehow grew up around the animal only at a later stage. On the contrary, every living being, however rudimentary it might appear to be, is surrounded in every moment of its life by such an encircling ring of possible disinhibition. More precisely, we must say that life *is* nothing but the animal's encircling itself and struggling [*Ringen*] with its encircling ring, a ring by way of which the animal is absorbed without its ever being with itself [*bei sich selbst*] in the proper sense.

§61. Concluding delimitation of the essential concept of the organism.

a) The organism as the capability for behaviour in the unity of captivation. The animal's being bound to its environment (self-encirclement open to disinhibition) as the essential structure of behaviour.

With this characterization of animal captivation we have already come nearer to the intrinsic organization of the organism. Only now are we in a position to conclude by delimiting a correct concept of the organism, insofar as that is necessary here. Negatively expressed, we must say that the organism is neither a complex of instruments nor a bundle of instinctual drives. Positively expressed, we can say that the organism is the capability for behaviour in the unity of captivation. Precisely when the attempt is made to grasp the organization of the organism and of the entire animal form as it were, the body of the animal in the narrow sense, one still goes fundamentally astray in trying to characterize the organism in a fundamental way. For the animal is not first an organism and as such an organism then something more that comes to bind itself to its environment. Rather its *being bound to the environment, the self-encircling which is open to disinhibition,* belongs to the inner essence of behaviour, i.e., belongs to that for which the capability is there as capability. This *self-encircling* is the *fundamental capability of the animal* into which all the other capacities are as it were integrated and from out of which they grow. The *organization of the organism* does not consist in its morphological, physiological configuration, in the formation and regulation of its forces, but first and foremost precisely in the *fundamental capability for self-encirclement,* and thus for a quite specific openness for a circumscribed range of possible disinhibition. But in accordance with what we have already said about capability, this fundamental capability is not some concealed propensity that occasionally subsequently shows itself. On the contrary, this capability for encirclement is the fundamental characteristic of the animal's actual being in every moment of its life-span. But if we consider the organism as the morphological unity of the [animal] body, which is what usually happens and especially today, then we have still failed to grasp the decisive structure of the organism. Recently many successful attempts have been made to investigate the environment of the animal considered specifically as an animal environment and to emphasize the way in which the animal is bound to its environment. And yet one has failed to take the decisive step toward a first authoritative characterization of the organism as long as one continues to regard matters as the Dutch biologist Buytendijk does in the following sentence: "Thus it is clear that in the animal world as a whole the way in which the animal is bound to its environment is almost as intimate as the unity of the body itself."[1] Against this we must say that the way in which the animal is bound to its environment is not merely almost as intimate, or even as intimate, as the unity of the body but rather that the unity of the animal's body is grounded as a unified animal body precisely in the *unity of captivation.* And that now means grounded in the unity of its *self-encirclement with a disinhibiting ring* within which an environment can first display itself for the animal in each case. Captivation is the fundamental essence of the organism.

We can briefly summarize the characteristic structural moments of *captivation* in six points:

---

1. F. J. J. Buytendijk, *Zur Untersuchung des Wesensunterschieds von Mensch und Tier.* In: *Blätter für Deutsche Philosophie.* Vol. 3 (Berlin, 1929–30), p. 47.

[1.] Captivation is withholding of the possibility of the manifestness of beings, a withholding which is essential and not merely an enduring or temporary one. An animal can only behave [*sich . . . benehmen*] but can never apprehend [*vernehmen*] something as something—which is not to deny that the animal sees or even perceives. Yet in a fundamental sense the animal does not have perception.

[2.] The captivation of such behaviour is at the same time a being taken of instinctual activity in which the animal is open in relation to other things. From the perspective of the animal we should never take these other things as beings, though for us it is only possible to approach such things by way of naming through language. But linguistic naming, and all language, always already involves an understanding of beings, although we cannot expand on this here.

[3.] As characterized under [1.] and [2.], captivation is at the same time an absorption in the totality of interacting instinctual drives. The specific selfhood of the animal (taking 'self' here in a purely formal sense) is its being-proper-to-itself, being proper [*Eigentum*] in all its driven activity. The animal is always driven in a certain way in this activity. That is why its being taken never involves an attending to beings, not even to itself as such. But this drivenness does not occur within a self-enclosed capsule; on the contrary, on the grounds of the being taken of the instinctual drives themselves it is always related to something else. Absorbed as it is into this drivenness, the animal nevertheless always pursues its instinctual activity in being open to that for which it is open.

[4.] With this openness for something else, which is involved in captivation, the animal has an intrinsic encircling ring within which it can be affected by whatever it is that in each case disinhibits its capability for . . . and occasions the redirecting of its instinctual drives.

[5.] This disinhibiting ring is not like a rigid armour plate fitted around the animal, but is something with which the animal encircles itself as long as it lives. It does so in such a way that it struggles with this encircling ring and the absorbed instinctual activity within this ring. More precisely: this struggling [*Ringen*] with the encircling ring which circumscribes the totality of its instinctual activity is an essential character of life itself. It is nothing other than what we are already acquainted with from our common experience of living beings: self-preservation and maintenance of the species, but grasped now in its structural belonging to the essence of captivation, to animality as such. It is not by accident that Darwinism emphasized the concept of self-preservation, which in this sense grew out of an economic perspective upon man. For this reason, the concept is misleading in many respects and one which has also given rise to misleading questions within biology, as the whole phenomenon of Darwinism shows.

[6.] Captivation as we have characterized it is the condition of the possibility of behaviour. Yet from a methodological point of view that also means that every concrete biological question concerning any animal capability for . . . , and thus concerning any particular organ and its structure, must bring its questioning back to the unity of animal captivation as a structural totality. For this fundamental conception of captivation is the prior basis upon which any concrete biological question can first come to rest.

In abbreviated form, the six points denote: [1.] withholding; [2.] being taken; [3.] absorption; [4.] openness for something else; [5.] the structure of encirclement thus given; and finally: [6.] the indication that captivation is the condition of the possibility of any kind of behaviour.

Certainly we do not mean to imply that this represents the definitive clarification of the *essence of animality* beyond which there is no need to ask any further for all time. Yet it does represent a *concrete characterization of that fundamental conception in relation to the essence of life* within which every consideration of the essence of life moves. It is one which was long neglected precisely in the nineteenth century, for all the energies devoted to research, and less because this fundamental conception of life was unknown than because it was suppressed by the prevailing mechanistic and physicalist approach to nature. The courage was lacking to take seriously what was intrinsically known, i.e., to unfold the essence of life in its genuine and proper content. Originality consists in nothing other than decisively seeing and thinking once again at the right moment of vision that which is essential, that which has already been repeatedly seen and thought before. Human history is such that it ensures that what is seen again in this way gets buried once again in time. It is true that one scientist of the grand style, Karl Ernst von Baer, was able to see something essential in the first half of the last century, even though it remains concealed within modern philosophical and theological perspectives. Yet initially his work and its influence was impeded and finally buried by the movement of Darwinism and the increasingly powerful, purely analytical method in morphology and physiology. In accordance with this method it was believed—and in part is still believed today—that we can build up the organism through recourse to its elementary constituents without first having grasped the building plan, i.e., the essence of the organism, in its fundamental structure and without keeping this structure in view as that which guides the construction. It is only during the last couple of generations that biology in the proper sense has worked to overcome this approach to the question—one which even today still governs concrete scientific work in many cases. The fact that such overcoming has happened through concrete investigation and experiment is all the more valuable, valuable at any rate in relation to the possibility of a transformation within positive science itself, which would prefer, largely with good reason, to keep itself free from the apron strings of philosophy. And yet it is a fundamental deception to believe that the effective power behind the transformation of contemporary biology is a matter of newly discovered facts. Fundamentally and primarily it is our approach to the question and our way of seeing that has been transformed—and in accordance with this the facts. This transformation of seeing and questioning is always the decisive thing in science. The greatness and vitality of a science is revealed in the power of its capacity for such transformation. Yet this transformation of seeing and questioning is misunderstood when it is taken as a change of standpoint or as a shift in the sociological conditions of science. It is true that this is the sort of thing which mainly or exclusively interests many people in science today—its psychologically and sociologically conditioned character—but this is just a facade. Sociology of this kind relates to real science and its philosophical comprehension in same the way in which one who clambers up a facade relates to the architect or, to take a less elevated example, to a conscientious craftsman.

b) Two essential steps in biology: Hans Driesch and Jakob Johann von Uexküll.

It would be instructive, as always, to pursue the history of biology from its beginnings up to the present, taking the problem we have developed as our guiding thread so that it would emerge even more clearly in all its concrete wealth and import. I must forego this, and shall simply mention *two decisive steps* that have been taken in biology. These indications may also serve to show the inner coherence of the exposition of the problem as I have given it, so that you will not think that these are just private opinions of my own. These two steps, which were decisive for biology during the last couple of generations, are certainly not the only ones, but they are the decisive ones with respect to our problem. The *first step* concerns the recognition of the holistic character of the organism. Wholeness has also become the fashion today, although this structural interconnection has been known in genuine research for decades. Wholeness means that the organism is not an aggregate, composed of elements or parts, but that the growth and the construction of the organism is governed by this wholeness in each and every stage. The *second step* is the insight into the essential significance of research concerned with how the animal is bound to its environment. Both of these steps, the first even more than the second, took place in the context of the still dominant mechanistic theory and investigation of life. This approach turned to the cell as the primal element of living things, but did so in such a way that it attempted from there to put together the organism which had already been misunderstood in its essence and shattered into a heap of fragments, while the cell itself was still considered in a chemico-physical fashion.

The first step grew out of the pioneering investigations of Hans Driesch into the embryos of sea-urchins, which represent an exemplary object for experimental embryology. Driesch elaborated the results from a fundamental angle in his investigation entitled *The Localisation of Morphogenetic Processes.*[2] The experiments cannot be described here. I shall merely identify the fundamental result in a way that immediately reveals its connection to our problem. The subsequent development of one cell-group of the embryo is determined in the context of the whole and in relation to this whole. Once this has occurred, the development proceeds independently of the environment in the direction that has already been laid down. Here we clearly see the breakthrough of the *idea of the whole*—wholeness as such as the determining factor. This is the principle result of Driesch's investigations, which was of decisive significance both for the problem of the organism in general and also for the problem of development. But it is a result that is no longer conclusive today, since it has been set upon a new basis through the equally outstanding investigations of Spemann which have turned the problem of animal development and the unity of the organism in a quite new direction.

Now for all its significance for the general problems of biology, this very insight of Driesch also represents a great danger. For it is only one step and, as always, a step taken within the modern problematic. For these experiments seemed to confirm the old conception of life, according to which the organism behaves in a purposive manner, and suggested that we must try and explain this purposiveness. Thus Driesch was driven by his experiments to adopt his biological theory, known as neovitalism, which is characterized by the appeal to a certain force or entelechy. This theory is repudiated in large measure by biology today. As far as biological problems are concerned, vitalism is just as dangerous as mechanism. While the latter does not allow the question of purposive behaviour to arise, vitalism tries to solve the problem too hastily. But the task is to recognize the full import of this purposive striving before appealing to some force which, moreover, explains nothing. Nevertheless, these concrete investigations, disregarding the philosophical theory which is bound up with them, have proved to be of decisive significance. The difficulties of Driesch's theory are not essential for our purposes. What is essential is simply the fact that the organism as such asserts itself at every stage of life of the living being. Its unity and wholeness is not the subsequent result of proven interconnections. Yet if we recall our definition of the essence of the organism (captivation), we can see that the organism is certainly grasped as a whole here, yet grasped in such a way that the animal's relation to the environment has not been included in the fundamental structure of the organism. The totality of the organism coincides as it were with the external surface of the animal's body. This is certainly not meant to imply that Driesch or other scientists have

2. H. Driesch, *Die Lokalisation morphogenetischer Vorgänge. Ein Beweis vitalist. Geschehens* (Leipzig, 1899).

ever overlooked the fact that the animal stands in relation to something other than itself. But from recognition of this fact it is a long way to the insight, first into its essence, and second into the essential nature of this relation for the structure of the organism as such.

As far as clarification of this connection is concerned, the *second step* was taken by the near contemporary investigations of Uexküll, almost all of which appeared in the 'Journal of Biology'.[3] Now biology has long been acquainted with the discipline called ecology. The word ecology derives from οἶκος, the Greek word for house. It signifies the investigation of where and how animals are at home in the world, of the way in which they live in relation to their environment. But in Darwinism precisely this was understood in an external manner in the light of the question concerning adaptation. In Darwinism such investigations were based upon the fundamentally misconceived idea that the animal is present at hand, and then subsequently adapts itself to a world that is present at hand, that it then comports itself accordingly and that the fittest individual gets selected. Yet the task is not simply to identify the specific conditions of life materially speaking, but rather to acquire insight into the *relational structure between the animal and its environment.* In Uexküll's investigations too, the theory and the type of theoretical-philosophical interpretation involved is less important than the astonishing sureness and abundance of his observations and his appropriate descriptions. His investigations are very highly valued today, but they have not yet acquired the fundamental significance they could have if a more radical interpretation of the organism were developed on their basis. In this connection the totality of the organism would not merely consist in the corporeal totality of the animal, but rather this corporeal totality could itself only be understood on the basis of that original totality which is circumscribed by what we called the *disinhibiting ring.* It would be foolish if we attempted to impute or ascribe philosophical inadequacy to Uexküll's interpretations, instead of recognizing that the engagement with concrete investigations like this is one of the most fruitful things that philosophy can learn from contemporary biology. Uexküll has set forth these concrete investigations in his book *The Environment and Inner World of Animals.*[4]

Even the fact that Uexküll talks of an 'environing world' [*Umwelt*], and indeed of the 'inner world' of the animal, should not initially prevent us from simply pursuing what he means here. For in fact he means nothing other than what we have characterized as the disinhibiting ring. However, the whole approach does become philosophically problematic if we proceed to talk about the human world in the same manner. It is true that amongst the biologists

3. *Zeitschrift für Biologie,* Neue Folge. Ed. W. Kühne and C. Voit (Munich and Leipzig, 1896ff.).
4. J. von Uexküll, *Umwelt und Innenwelt der Tiere,* op. cit., p. 207.

Uexküll is the one who has repeatedly pointed out with the greatest emphasis that what the animal stands in relation to is given for it in a different way than it is for the human being. Yet this is precisely the place where the decisive problem lies concealed and demands to be exposed. For it is *not* simply a question of a *qualitative otherness* of the animal world as compared with the human world, and especially not a question of quantitative distinctions in range, depth, and breadth—not a question of whether or how the animal takes what is given to it in a different way, but rather of whether the animal can apprehend something *as* something, something *as* a being, at all. If it cannot, then the animal is separated from man by an abyss. But in that case, transcending any supposedly terminological issue, it becomes a fundamental question whether we should talk of a world of the animal—of an environing world or even of an inner world—or whether we do not have to determine that which the animal stands in relation to in another way. Yet for a variety of reasons this can only be done if we take the concept of world as our guiding thread.

Let us once again consider both these steps together. The *first step* concerns the recognition of the organism as a whole—something that was already recognized by Aristotle, but here is grasped more concretely in relation to particular problems of life. It is a question of wholeness in a functional sense. This wholeness takes effect in every moment of the duration of the organism and its motility. Thus, this wholeness is not simply to be grasped as a mere result as distinct from a combination of elements. The *second step* concerns the insight into the way the organism is necessarily bound up with its environment, a phenomenon which was recognized in Darwinism under the concept of 'adaptation'. But with this formula it was taken precisely in a sense which led to misinterpretation of the problem, insofar as it was presupposed that the organism is something present at hand which in addition happens to stand in a relation to the environment. The organism is not something independent in its own right which then adapts itself. On the contrary, the organism adapts a particular environment *into* it in each case, so to speak. The organism can adapt a particular environment into itself only insofar as openness for . . . belongs to its essence, and to the extent that, upon the basis of this openness for . . . which permeates its whole behaviour, a certain leeway is created within which whatever is encountered can be encountered in such and such a way, i.e., is capable of exerting an effect upon the animal through its disinhibiting function.

c) The incompleteness of our present interpretation of the essence of the organism: the lack of any determination of the essence of motility belonging to the living being.

It will now have become clear how these two steps in contemporary biology compel us to confront the central problem of providing an adequate determination of the essence of the organism—a problem which can only assume its full significance today once the *metaphysical dimension* in which it oscillates is properly opened up and penetrated. This is a task that we are only now just beginning to comprehend. That is why we shall not for a moment exaggerate the significance of the *interpretation of the essence of the organism provided here* with respect to the captivation of the animal, above all because it is still incomplete. This interpretation is not incomplete in some external respect, but rather from a perspective which brings us once again before the decisive problem in determining the essence of life. For the sake of providing a complete orientation to the problem I shall briefly indicate the issue. All life is *not simply organism* but is *just as essentially* process, thus formally speaking *motion.* But in what sense? As a sequence of unfolding events? Not at all, although it is always possible to treat the processes of life in this way. Even in our everyday experience we are familiar with the birth, growth, maturing, aging, and death of animals. But all this reveals to us a *motility of a peculiar kind,* for here the organism as we now understand it does not simply happen to get caught up as it were in this motility. Rather, this motility determines the being of the animal as such. And that means that the drivenness of the instinctual drives, the driving of instinctual drives in the totality of captivation, the animal's struggle with its encirclement—that all this motility belongs to captivation. Captivation is not a static condition, not a structure in the sense of a rigid framework inserted within the animal, but rather an intrinsically determinate motility which continually unfolds or atrophies as the case may be. Captivation is at the same time motility, and this belongs to the essence of the organism.

Apart from the phenomena like birth, growth, and aging already mentioned, we have only to consider the fundamental fact of genetic inheritance in order to have some intimation of the rich abundance of problems that now begin to impose themselves around the question concerning the essence of the organism. Birth, maturing, aging, and death all too obviously remind us of the being of man, which we recognize as being historical. In view of these phenomena of the life process we have mentioned, some have even attempted to talk about organisms as historical beings (Boveri).[5] What kind of history do we find in the life process of the particular individual animal? What kind of history does the animal kind, the species, possess? The species is by no means simply a logical schema under which the actual and possible particular individuals are subsumed. The *species-character* is rather an essential *character of the being of living things,* and one that precisely finds expression in what we have come to know as the fundamental structure of animality: captivation, the animal's

5. T. Boveri, *Die Organismen als historische Wesen* (Würzburg, 1906).

struggle with its disinhibiting ring. Through its belonging to the species, the encirclement of the individual animal is not merely extended further than it would be if the animal were simply individuated, but the species as such is thereby better protected and better equipped in relation to its environment. What sort of history then does the species possess and what sort of history does the animal realm as a whole possess? Can we and should we speak of history at all where the being of the animal is concerned? If not, then how are we to determine this motility? You can see that one question gives rise to others, that one question is more essential than another, that each question is poorer with respect to its answer than the next. If we now think back from the domain of these essential questions and consider concrete biological research today, then we can see how everything is beginning to move here too, albeit hesitantly enough. It is not only the reliability and the import of the celebrated and notorious concept of 'development' which has become questionable, but we now have to confront quite new phenomena like those revealed above all through the investigations of Spemann, which have set the problem of the *particular kind of occurrence* involved in the organization of the organism upon a more comprehensive and more profoundly conceived basis.

In our task of determining the essence of the organism we deliberately avoided the question concerning the motile character of the living being as such. This question is not an arbitrary one and cannot possibly be dealt with by subsequently trying to insert it into the analysis as it were, for it is intimately bound up with the question concerning the essence of life. That this is the case can be seen if we consider something which belongs to the innermost essence of life, namely what we call *death*. The touchstone for the appropriateness and originary character of every question concerning the essence of life lies in whether or not this question has adequately grasped the problem of death and whether or not it is able to take it up into its own question concerning the essence of life in the correct way, and vice versa. Of course it would be just as foolish to try and explain life from death as it would be to try and explain death from life. Nevertheless, on the basis of its apparent negativity as the annihilation of life, death does initially possess the methodological function of revealing the apparent positivity in the problem of life. Just as every loss first really allows us to recognize and understand the value of something we possessed before, so too it is precisely death that illuminates the essence of life. Yet even if we ignore the question of whether death is simply or primarily something negative, death is still something which is intimately bound up with the motility of life. And the problem of the motility of life has to be unfolded in relation to death, although not death alone. The question concerning the essence of life in relation to the question concerning the essence of death is just as essential as the question concerning the essence of life in relation to the essence of the organism.

And just as it remains questionable whether we can speak of the organism as a historical or even historic being, so too it is questionable whether death and death are the same in the case of man and animal, even if we can identify a physico-chemical and physiological equivalence between the two. From what has been said already it is easy to see that in captivation, as the fundamental structure of life, certain *quite determinate possibilities of death,* of *approaching death,* are prefigured. Is the death of the animal a *dying* or a way of *coming to an end?* Because captivation belongs to the essence of the animal, the animal cannot die in the sense in which dying is ascribed to human beings but can only come to an end. Consequently the question concerning the essence of the natural physiological death with which the particular living individual intrinsically comes to die—irrespective of external injuries, illnesses, or dangers— represents a central problem. Here too there are many valuable observations to be found in contemporary biology, but they have not yet been seen in their inner connection with the fundamental problem of the essence of animality and of life in general.

This may suffice to remind us of the limited character of our approach to the question. Nevertheless, we can utilize this approach to clarify and to unfold the *guiding thesis that the animal is poor in world.* Above all we can render our reflections fruitful if we succeed in deciding, on the basis of the essential characterization of the organism we have now acquired, in what relationship this characterization stands to our thesis. Is the thesis that the animal is poor in world merely a proposition that follows from the definition of the essence of the organism, determined as it is by captivation, or on the contrary is this definition grounded in that thesis—grounded not merely to the extent to which we have unfolded it here but in general, so that *this thesis* could be said to express *one of the most originary principles concerning the essence of the organism* (of animality)?

Chapter Five

Unfolding the Guiding Thesis That 'the Animal Is Poor in
World' on the Basis of the Interpretation of the Essence
of the Organism at Which We Have Arrived

*§62. Being open in captivation as a not-having
of world in having that which disinhibits.*

For this it is necessary that we now elucidate what *poverty in world* means. We
must take up this question once again at the place where we left off to clarify
animality by determining the essence of the organism. We pursued this investigation in order to maintain a concrete connection between our problem and
biology. But that did not imply in any way, as the analysis has shown, that we
merely wished to collect and present results, but rather to discover, with reference
to these results, some fundamental questions in relation to our problem and thus
to bring ourselves closer to the essence of animality. For our perplexity with
respect to the concept of world and to the thesis that 'the animal is poor in world'
necessarily forced us to derive the essence of animality as far as possible from a
consideration of the animal itself. What did this perplexity with respect to the
concept of world consist in?[1] Are we now in a position to eliminate this perplexity
on the basis of our consideration of the structure of the organism, so that we
can now understand the thesis concerning the animal's poverty in world and
develop the problem of world in terms of it?

We articulated the problem as follows: if by world we understand beings in
their respective accessibility in each case, and if the accessibility of beings is
a fundamental characteristic of world, then the animal stands alongside man
if it does have access to something other than itself. Then we find a having of
world in the case of both man and animal. On the other hand, if our intermediate thesis concerning the animal's poverty in world is justified, and poverty
is a deprivation and deprivation a not-having, then the animal stands alongside
the stone which, as worldless, has no world. With the *animal* we find a *having
of world* and a *not-having of world*. Either this result is intrinsically contradictory and impossible, or we are employing the word 'world'—as the accessibility
of beings—in a different sense each time when we formulate the problem in
terms of the animal having world and not having world. In that case the
concept of world has not yet adequately been elucidated.

1. Cf. above pp. 176ff.

Have we now arrived at such an elucidation? Indeed we have. But it is still one which does not release us from talking about a *having* and *not-having* in the case of the animal. The question is merely whether in this connection we may still speak of a having of *world* and a not-having of *world.* We said that world means the accessibility of beings and pointed out that the animal does relate to something else, does therefore have access to something, for example when the dog leaps up the stairs. Not only that, we can even say that the animal has access to beings. The nest that is sought out, the prey that is seized, is surely a being that is, and not nothing; otherwise the bird could not settle upon the nest and the cat would never catch a mouse—if these were not beings. The animal does have access to beings.

On the basis of our interpretation of animal *captivation,* however, we can now see *where the misinterpretation lies.* The animal certainly has access to . . . and indeed to something that actually is. But this is something that *only we* are capable of experiencing and having manifest *as beings.* When we claimed by way of introduction that amongst other things world means the accessibility of beings, this characterization of the concept of world is easily misunderstood because the character of world remains underdetermined here. We must say that world does not mean the accessibility of beings but rather implies *amongst other things* the accessibility of beings *as such.* But if the accessibility of beings as such belongs to the essence of world, then in its captivation, as having the possibility for the manifestness of beings withheld, the animal essentially cannot have world at all, although that which it relates to can always be experienced as a being in *our* experience. Although the animal cannot have world, it does have an access to . . . in the sense of its instinctually driven behaviour. So in distinction from what we said earlier we must now say that it is precisely because the animal in its captivation has a relation to everything encountered within its disinhibiting ring that it precisely does *not* stand alongside man and precisely has *no* world. Yet this not-having of world does not force the animal alongside the stone—and does not do so in principle. For the instinctual capability of taken captivation, i.e., for being taken by whatever disinhibits the animal, is a way of being open for . . . , even if it has the character of not attending to. . . . The stone on the other hand does not even have this possibility. For not attending to . . . presupposes a being open. All this implies that in the worldlessness of the stone the very condition of the possibility of poverty in world is lacking. This inner possibility of poverty in world—a constitutive moment of this possibility—is the instinctual being-open of taken behaviour. The animal possesses this being-open in its essence. Being open in captivation is the *essential possession* of the animal. On the basis of this possession it can be deprived, it can be poor, it can be determined in its being by poverty. This having is certainly *not a having of world,* but rather being held captive to the disinhibiting ring—it is *a having of that which disinhibits.* But it is because this having is a being-open for that which disinhibits, it is because the very possibility of having whatever disinhibits manifest as a being is withheld from this being-open-for, that this possession of being-open is a not-having, and indeed a not-having of world—if the manifestness of beings as such does indeed belong to world. Accordingly we do not at all find in the animal a simultaneous having and not-having of world, but rather a *not-having of world in the having of openness for whatever disinhibits.* As a result, the not-having of world is not merely a case of having less of world in comparison with man, but rather a case of not having at all—but this now in the sense of a not-*having,* i.e., on the basis of a having. By contrast, we cannot even ascribe such not-having to the stone, because its specific manner of being is not determined by the being-open of behaviour, let alone by the manifesting character of comportment.

§63. An objection raised by ourselves to the thesis concerning the not-having of world as deprivation and poverty of the animal. Removing the force of this objection.

We have thus now grasped, in a more appropriate manner and with respect to the essence of animality, the unity of having and not having that we asserted earlier. And yet it is precisely here that the most serious misgivings arise in relation to our thesis that the animal is poor in world. We must entertain the following objection to our thesis: It is certainly true that in the case of the animal we find a not-having in distinction from the case of man. And it is equally certain that this not-having on the part of the animal is essentially different from that of the stone. But is this not-having on the part of the animal a *deprivation* of world, an essential *poverty* with regard to the world? For the animal could only be deprived of world if it at least knew something of world. But this is precisely what we have denied in the case of the animal—and indeed we must deny this all the more to the animal in view of the fact that man himself, to whose essence world-formation belongs, at first and for the most part does not properly know of world as such. However things may be in this regard, if the world is essentially closed to the animal then we can indeed talk of a not-having, but we are never permitted to understand this as a deprivation. Consequently the thesis concerning the animal's poverty in world goes too far. And if we nevertheless persist with the thesis, and indeed with good reason, then this characterization of animality by means of poverty in world is not a genuine one, not drawn from animality itself and maintained within the limits of animality, since the character of poverty in world is being conceived by comparison with man. It is only from the human perspective that the animal is poor with respect to world, yet animal being in itself is not a deprivation of world. Expressed more clearly and in a more far-reaching manner: if deprivation in certain forms is a kind of suffering, and poverty and deprivation of world belongs to the animal's being, then a kind of pain and suffering would have to permeate the whole animal realm and the realm of life in general. Biology knows absolutely nothing of such a phenomenon. Perhaps it is the privilege of poets to imagine this sort of thing. "This has nothing to do with science." In that case the thesis concerning the animal's poverty in world is not an interpretation which remains true to the proper essence of animality, but merely a comparative illustration. And if this is so then we have thereby already discovered the answer to the question we have already asked in various ways: Is the organismic character of the animal—in the sense of captivation already circumscribed—the condition of the possibility of poverty in world, or is it rather poverty in world that is the condition and the essential ground for the organism and its inner possibility? Obviously the first is the case: Captivation is the condition of the possibility of poverty in world. For if the essence of the organism lies in captivation, and having the possibility of the manifestness of beings as such withheld belongs as *one* essential moment to captivation, while manifestness of beings is a character of world, then we must now say: The *withholding of world* belongs as *one* essential moment to captivation. But that which simply represents one constitutive moment of the totality of the essence of the organism, of captivation, cannot be the ground of the possibility for the totality of its essence as such. Poverty in world is not the condition of the possibility of captivation, but rather the reverse, captivation is the condition of the possibility of poverty in world. Yet we must further weaken even this proposition and say more appropriately: Captivation as the essence of animality is the condition of the possibility of a merely comparative definition of animality in terms of poverty in world, insofar as the animal is viewed from the perspective of man to whom world-formation belongs. Our thesis that the animal is poor in world is accordingly far from being a, let alone *the,* fundamental metaphysical principle of the essence of animality. At best it is a proposition that follows from the essential determinations of animality, and moreover one which follows only if the animal is regarded in comparison with humanity. As such a conclusion, this proposition can be traced back to its ground and thus lead us toward the essence of animality. That was indeed its factical function in our investigations. If these considerations are unassailable, however, then in the end we must not only substantially reduce the significance of our thesis, but must repudiate it altogether. For the thesis is misleading precisely with respect to the essence of animality itself, i.e., it encourages the mistaken view that the being of the animal in itself is intrinsically deprivation and poverty.

Yet in that case why are we concerning ourselves at such length with the character of this thesis? It surely suffices that the substantive examination of the thesis has led us to our destination in a practical fashion. In spite of everything it has brought us closer to an elucidation of the concept of world. It is true that positively speaking we have still learned very little about the essence of world, and have only learned about the animal and its not-having of world, about its captivation. Consequently we have merely acquainted ourselves with the negative side of the matter. And yet we should consider the fact that we ourselves are the positive side, that we ourselves exist in the having of world. That is why, through that apparently purely negative characterization of world in our examination of the animal's not-having of world, our own proper essence has constantly emerged in contrast, even if not in any explicit interpretation. For we ourselves have also been in view all the time, whether we wanted to be or not, although not in the form of some arbitrary and contingent self-observation or in the form of some traditional definition of man. On the contrary, in all our investigations, which from an external per-spective seemed to get lost in specialist questions, we enjoyed the constant possibility of recalling the Dasein within us as brought to light in a funda-mental attunement. Or have we already forgotten this fundamental attunement in the meantime? Does it simply lie behind us like an episode, as something completely different that has not the slightest thing to do with unicellular living beings or the self-orienting behaviour of bees? Or does this fundamental attunement still attune us so that we constantly already question concerning the essence of world from out of this attunement; so that we looked into this fundamental attunement as we developed our question, i.e., in this context as we compared the animal's not-having of world with our own having of world, with that 'as a whole' which profound boredom itself manifests to us? Perhaps, then, the supposedly purely negative characterization—our examination of the not-having of world—will only begin to exercise its full effect once we prepare to bring out the essence of world with respect to the world-formation of man.

Up till now we have only learned a little about the essence of world and nothing at all about the ground of its possibility; and certainly nothing what-soever about the significance of the phenomenon of world in metaphysics. If that is the case then we have no right *now,* or at least *as yet no right to alter our thesis that the animal is poor in world or to level it down* to the indifferent statement that the animal has no world, whereby not having is taken as a mere not-having rather than as deprivation. Rather we must *leave open the possibility* that the proper and explicit metaphysical understanding of the essence of world compels us to understand the animal's not-having of world as a *depri-vation after all,* and to discover *poverty* in the animal's specific manner of being as such. The fact that biology recognizes nothing of the sort is no counter-ar-gument against metaphysics. That perhaps only poets occasionally speak in this way is an argument that dare not be allowed to cast metaphysics to the winds. In the end we do not first require the Christian faith in order to understand something of the saying of St. Paul (Romans VIII, 19) concerning the ἀποκαραδοκία τῆς κτίσεως, the yearning expectation of creatures and of creation, the paths of which, as the Book of Ezra IV, 7, 12 says, have become narrow, doleful, and weary in this aeon.[1] But nor is any pessimism required in order to develop the *animal's poverty in world as a problem intrinsic to animality itself.* For with the animal's being open for that which disinhibits, the animal in its captivation finds itself essentially exposed to something other than itself, something that can indeed never be manifest to the animal either as a being or as a non-being. Rather that which disinhibits, with all the various forms of disinhibition it entails, brings an *essential disruption* into the essence of the animal. Earlier on we emphasized that having the possibility of the manifestness of beings withheld constitutes merely *one* structural moment of captivation and cannot therefore be the essential ground of the whole as such. But we can now reply that in the last analysis we have not yet clarified the essential organization of the organism sufficiently at all, so as to be able to decide the significance of this withholding, and that we cannot clarify it until and unless we also take into account the fundamental phenomenon of the life process and thus death as well.

Thus the thesis that '*the animal is poor in world*' must remain as a problem, and one which we cannot broach now but which guides the further steps of our comparative examination, i.e., the proper exposition of the problem of world.

1. *Die Apokryphen und Pseudepigraphen des Alten Testaments.* Trans. and ed. E. Kautzsch. Vol. 2: *Die Pseudepigraphen des Alten Testaments* (Tübingen, 1900; new edition, 1921), p. 369.

Chapter Six

The Thematic Exposition of the Problem of World through an
Examination of the Thesis That 'Man Is World-forming'

*§64. The primary characteristics of the phenomenon of world:
the manifestness of beings as beings and the 'as';
the relation to beings as letting be and not letting
be (comportment toward, orientation, selfhood).*

If we proceed from the examination of the thesis that the animal is poor in world
to examine the thesis that *'man is world-forming'* and ask ourselves what we can
glean from our previous discussion in order to characterize the essence of world,
then we can arrive at the following kind of formula: The manifestness of beings
as such, of beings *as* beings, belongs to world. This implies that bound up with
world is this enigmatic 'as', beings *as* such, or formulated in a formal way:
'something *as* something', a possibility which is quite fundamentally closed to
the animal. Only where beings are manifest *as* beings *at all,* do we find the
possibility of experiencing this or that particular being as determined in this or
that particular way—experiencing in the broader sense which goes beyond mere
acquaintance with something, in the sense of having experiences with something.
Finally, only where there is the manifestness of beings as beings, do we find that
the relation to these beings necessarily possesses the character of *attending to . . .*
whatever is encountered in the sense of *letting it be* or *not letting it be.* Only where
there is such letting be do we find at the same time the possibility of not letting
be. Such a relation to something, which is thoroughly governed by this letting
be of something as a being, we are calling *comportment* [Verhalten], in distinction
from the behaviour of captivation. But all comportment is only possible in a
certain restraint [*Verhaltenheit*] and comporting [*Verhaltung*], and a stance
[*Haltung*] is only given where a being has the character of a self or, as we also
say, of a person. These are already important characteristics of the phenomenon
of world: [1.] the manifestness of beings as beings; [2.] the 'as'; [3.] the relation
to beings as letting be and not letting be, comportment toward . . . , stance, and
selfhood. Nothing of this kind is to be found in animality or in life in general.
But initially these important characteristics of the phenomenon of world only
tell us that whenever we come upon such characteristics, there we find the
phenomenon of world. Yet *what* the world is and *how* it is, whether and in what
sense we may speak of the *being* of world in general—all this remains obscure.
In order to shed some light here and thus penetrate into the *depths of the problem
of world,* we shall attempt to show what is meant by *world-formation.*

*§65. The undifferentiated manifestness of the various
kinds of beings that are present at hand. The
slumbering of the fundamental relationships of
Dasein toward beings in everydayness.*

We shall proceed from what is already familiar. Where there is world, there beings are manifest. Thus we shall first have to ask *how beings are manifest,* what it is that we 'have before us' here as beings. Now precisely the discussion of our thesis concerning animality showed us that manifold kinds of beings are manifest to us: material things, lifeless nature, living nature, history, products of human work, culture. But all of this is not merely uniformly presented to us on the world-stage as a confused manifold of juxtaposed items. On the contrary, within beings there are certain *fundamentally diverse 'kinds' of beings,* which prescribe certain contexts in respect of which we take up a fundamentally *different position,* even if we do not become conscious of this diversity as a matter of course. On the contrary, at first and for the most part in the *everydayness* of our Dasein we let beings come toward us and present themselves before us in a remarkable undifferentiatedness. It is not as though all things simply get conflated with one another for us without distinction—on the contrary, we are very sensitive to the substantive manifoldness of those beings that surround us, we can never have enough variety and eagerly look out for what is new and different. And yet here the beings that surround us are *uniformly manifest* as simply *something present at hand in the broadest sense*—the presence of land and sea, the mountains and forests, and within this the presence of animals and plants and the presence of human beings and the products of human work, and amongst all this the presence of ourselves as well. This character of beings as something simply present at hand in the broadest sense cannot be insisted upon too strongly, because this is an essential character of beings as they spread themselves before us in our everydayness and we ourselves are also drawn into this widespread presence at hand. It is the fact that beings can be manifest in this levelled out uniformity of the present at hand which gives to human everydayness its peculiar security, dependency, and almost inevitability, and which facilitates the ease with which we necessarily turn from one being to another in everydayness, and yet the specific manner of being that is in each case entirely essential to beings is never acknowledged in its importance. We board the tram, talk to other people, call the dog, look up at the stars, all in the same way—humans, vehicles, human beings, animals, heavenly bodies, everything in the same uniformity of what is present at hand. These are characteristics of our everyday Dasein that philosophy has hitherto neglected, because this all too self-evident phenomenon is what is most powerful in our Dasein, and because that which is most powerful is therefore the deadly enemy of philosophy. Consequently, the way and manner in which the undifferentiated manifoldness of beings initially and predominantly becomes *accessible* to us in each case lies in that familiar acquaintance that belongs to the undifferentiated way in which we talk about things and communicate information about them. That means that a *comportment* [Verhalten] *toward beings* transpires without first awakening any *fundamental relationship* [Grundverhältnis] of man toward beings—whether toward lifeless beings, living beings, or human beings themselves—as demanded by these beings themselves in each case. Our everyday comportment toward *all* beings does not move within those *fundamental relationships* that correspond to the peculiar character proper to the beings in question. It moves rather within a comportment which, from the perspective of those beings themselves, is uprooted and for that very reason is rampant and successful everywhere. We cannot here identify the reason why this everydayness in various forms and to a variable degree is necessary for human Dasein, and why therefore it should not be disparaged as something purely negative. We should merely learn to see that *from out of this everydayness*—although certainly not grounded or sustained by it—*fundamental relationships of human Dasein toward beings,* amongst which man himself belongs, are possible, i.e., *are capable of being awakened.* Accordingly there are *fundamental kinds of manifestness of beings,* and thus kinds of beings as such. An understanding for the fact that there are *fundamentally different specific manners of being itself,* and accordingly fundamentally different species of beings, was precisely sharpened for us through our interpretation of animality. Thus our entire preliminary investigation suddenly takes on a *new function.* The task is to reveal the significance of what we acquired there in its entire import for the question concerning the manifestness of beings as such, a manifestness which was indeed supposed to constitute one moment of the essence of world. In this connection we should remember this: animality no longer stands in view with respect to poverty in world as such, but rather *as a realm of beings* which are *manifest* and thus call for a *specific fundamental relationship* toward them on our part, one in which at least initially we do not move.

*§66. The manifestness proper to living nature, and the
transposedness of Dasein into the encircling contextual ring
of living beings as our peculiar fundamental relationship
toward them. The manifoldness of the specific manners of
being, their possible unity, and the problem of world.*

First of all we must recall the different ways in which man can be transposed into another human being, into animals, into living beings in general, and into lifeless things. With respect to the possibility of man's transposedness into the

animal, we can now see matters more clearly if we keep before us the fundamental structure of captivation and the disinhibiting ring that is given along
with it in each case. Every animal and every species of animal actively encircles
itself in its own way with this encircling ring, with which it circumscribes and
adapts itself to a certain domain. The ring that encircles the sea-urchin is quite
different from that of the bee, and that of the bee quite different again from
that of the great tit, and this different from that of the squirrel and so on. But
these encircling rings belonging to the animals, within which their contextual
behaviour and instinctual activity moves, are not simply laid down alongside
or in between one another but rather intersect with one another. The woodworm, for example, which bores into the bark of the oak tree is encircled by
its own specific ring. But the woodworm itself, and that means together with
this encircling ring of its own, finds itself in turn within the ring encircling the
woodpecker as it looks for the worm. And this woodpecker finds itself in all
this within the ring encircling the squirrel which startles it as it works. Now
this whole context of openness within the rings of captivation encircling the
animal realm is not merely characterized by an enormous wealth of contents
and relations which we can hardly imagine, but in all of this it is still fundamentally different from the manifestness of beings as encountered in the world-
forming Dasein of man.

For the everydayness of man in his busy occupation, beings appear quite
differently. In our everydayness we also think of all those beings which are
accessible to us in the undifferentiated way we have described as though they
belonged to the same realm in which animals also reside and to which they
too can relate. We then think that the particular animals and species of animal
adapt themselves in different ways to these beings that are intrinsically present
at hand, present in exactly the same way for all beings and thus for all human
beings. Thus the variations of animals and animal species are produced on the
basis of the varying adaptation of all animals to beings that are one and the
same. Whatever most successfully adapts itself survives the others. In the
process of adaptation the organization of the animal then variously develops
in each case in accordance with the various kinds of beings (variation). Taken
in the context of the survival of the best adapted animals, this variation then
leads to increasing perfection. Thus it is that the rich abundance of higher
animal species has developed out of the primeval slime.

Ignoring other intrinsic impossibilities in this developmental theory, we can
now see particularly clearly that it rests upon a quite impossible presupposition
which contradicts the essence of animality (captivation—encircling ring): the
presupposition that beings as such are given to all animals and moreover given
to them all in the same intrinsic way, so that all the animal has to do is to
adapt itself accordingly. But this view collapses once we understand animals
and animal being from out of the essence of animality. Not only is it the case

that beings are not present at hand in themselves for the animal, but animals for their part are *not something present at hand for us* in their being. The animal realm demands a quite specific kind of transposedness from us and within the animal realm the encircling rings of captivation are transposed into one another in a peculiar and prevalent way. It is the fundamental trait of this transposedness that first constitutes the specific character of the animal realm as a realm, i.e., the way and manner in which it holds sway within the totality of nature and of beings in general. The way in which these encircling animal rings mesh with one another, emerging from the encircling struggle of the animals themselves, points to a *fundamental manner of being* which is different from any kind of merely being present at hand. When we consider that in every case of such encircling struggle the living being in turn adapts something from nature itself into its own encircling ring, then we must say: *What manifests itself to us in this struggle of encircling rings is an intrinsically dominant character of living beings amongst beings in general,* an intrinsic elevation [*Erhabenheit*] of nature over itself, a sublimity that is lived in life itself.

Thus nature, whether it is lifeless nature or indeed living nature, is in no way to be regarded as the plank or lowest rung of the ladder which the human being would ascend, thus to assert his strange essence [*sein Unwesen*]. Yet nor is nature present at hand like the wall that it becomes when turned into an object of scientific-theoretical observation. Living and non-living nature is present at hand in the broadest sense for the everydayness of Dasein, and indeed so self-evidently that this conception is treated as the natural one that shows us the way to see the specific naturalness of nature itself. And yet, metaphysically speaking, man's ontological relationship toward nature is completely different. Nature does not stand there surrounding man with an abundance of objects—this much we can understand. Rather *human Dasein is intrinsically a peculiar transposedness into the encompassing contextual ring of living beings.* In this connection we should remember the following: it is not as if we were now on the same level as the animals, both them and us standing over against a wall of beings with the same shared content, as though the animals amongst themselves and we amongst them simply saw the same wall of beings in different ways, as though we were simply dealing with manifold aspects of the same. No, the encircling rings amongst themselves are not remotely comparable, and the totality of the manifest enmeshing of encircling rings in each case is not simply part of the beings that are otherwise manifest for us, but rather holds us captive in a quite specific way. That is why we say that man exists in a peculiar way *in the midst* of beings. In the midst of beings means: living nature holds us ourselves captive as human beings in a quite specific way, not on the basis of any particular influence or impression that nature exerts or makes upon us, but rather from out of our essence, whether we experience that essence in an originary relationship or not.

From this quite rough and ready characterization of the *specific manner of being that belongs to living nature* we can already see that in future we must not permit ourselves to speak of the totality of beings as if this were a collection of certain realms or other. Accordingly, the *manifoldness* of the various *specific manners of being* with respect to their possible *unity* poses a quite specific problem, one that can only be tackled as a problem once we have developed a satisfactory concept of *world.*

The characterization given here is itself only a first rough indication of a *perspective on a problem* that we can hardly imagine, but one that we may only dare to enter philosophically once we have grasped that the ineluctable presupposition for doing so is an adequate unfolding of the *problem of world* and thus of the *problem of finitude.*

§67. The question concerning the occurrence of manifestness as the point of departure for the question concerning world. Return of the question concerning world-formation and world to the direction disclosed by the interpretation of profound boredom.

We wish to develop this problem in the direction in which we began, namely with our three theses, i.e., we wish to proceed from and advance upon what we discovered in examining the second thesis. According to our investigation the *accessibility of beings,* and indeed of beings *as such,* is *one characteristic* of world. The essence of world is not exhausted by this determination. Indeed, the question is whether this characteristic announces anything of the *innermost* essence of world or is only a determination that *follows* from this essence. For now we shall leave this on one side and consider something else.

When we say that world is amongst other things the *accessibility* of beings, then we already thereby contradict the so-called *natural concept of world.* By 'world' we usually mean the *entirety of beings,* everything that there is, taken together. A human being comes into the world and catches sight of the light of the world. That means that he himself becomes a being among the other beings, and indeed in such a way that he himself as a human being finds before him these other beings and himself among them. World—this here means the sum of beings in themselves, and implicitly so, because this seems the most natural thing: all beings in the factical undifferentiatedness of everydayness.

Yet clearly the concept of world which we have indicated does not mean this, but means the accessibility of beings as such rather than beings in themselves. According to this, beings do indeed also belong to world, but only insofar as they are *accessible,* insofar as beings themselves allow and enable something of the kind. This is true only if beings as such *can become manifest.*

This implies that beings are not manifest beforehand, are *closed off* and *concealed*. Accessibility is grounded in possible manifestness. Does *world* then mean not beings in themselves but rather manifest beings? No, it means the *manifestness* of those beings that are factically manifest in each case.

Yet how do things stand concerning this manifestness of beings? Where is it and how is it? Is it like something that grows, brought forth as it were by beings themselves? Is the manifestness of beings a substantive property of the latter, just as hardness belongs to the stone, growth to living beings, and the property of right-angledness to the rectangle? If we have to provide information concerning any given being in any given domain whatsoever, then however closely we examine this being we shall never come upon the idea of taking the manifestness of this being as a property of it. We shall not only fail to come upon such an idea, we shall not come upon the manifestness either. Thus in this sense manifestness is unknown to us, because it is never to be found in beings as beings. Where is it to be found then? Above or behind beings? But can there be anything at all which is outside the realm of beings? And yet we do speak of the manifestness *of* beings. Consequently manifestness is something that *occurs* and occurs *with* beings themselves. When and how does this happen? And with which beings? Is this an arbitrary matter or, if the manifestness of beings occurs, must quite specific beings necessarily be manifest for something like the manifestness of beings to occur? Furthermore, if manifestness occurs and manifestness is characteristic of world, does something like world first arise in each case, so that precisely beings could be without world? Is world first formed in each case, so that we can talk of world-formation—*is man world-forming?*

These are all decisive questions on the way toward clarifying the essence of world, especially if we begin this clarification with the characteristic of manifestness. But at the same time they are, so it seems, questions that we cannot get a tangible grip on, 'abstract' questions as commonplace understanding puts it. Can we not and should we not be more accommodating to such an understanding? Must we not develop the problem of world in a more easily graspable way? Certainly we must, not for the convenience of common understanding, but in order to make visible the full extent of the problem. But that will surely be most successfully accomplished if we clarify the phenomenon of *world-formation* simply in terms of the essence of man, corresponding to the way in which we examined our second thesis. Just as we asked about animality before, so we now ask about humanity and its essence, and just as we drew upon biology and zoology for support before, so we can now draw upon anthropology. In this case we would be entering a large, multifarious, and indeed confused domain of problems, theses, and standpoints. We should have to wind our way through all this and would only fulfil our purpose with the greatest of effort. It would require a wearisome preparation in asking what man is. Where is the relevant knowledge set down? Initially and properly speaking precisely not in anthropology, psychology, characterology and so on, but rather in the whole history of man—not in something like biographical history, and not at all in historiography, but rather in that originary tradition handed down which lies within all human acting as such, whether this is recorded and reported or not. The Dasein of man always already intrinsically brings the truth about itself along with it. Today we are still a long way from seeing these fundamental connections in relation to the character of man's self-knowledge, and are still all too entangled in subjective reflection and the images that foster this kind of thing. Such reflection cannot be proved false in a purely theoretical way but needs to be removed by being uprooted, i.e., in such a way that its lack of any rootedness arouses our terror. Here, however, we shall pursue a different way.

Does asking after the essence of man therefore mean making man our theme instead of the animal? This state of affairs is clear enough—and yet when we ask about the essence of man we are asking about *ourselves*. But that does not simply mean that with this question we now turn back and reflect upon 'subjects' instead of directing our attention to objects (like the animal or the stone). It means rather that we ask concerning a being *which it is given over to us ourselves to be*. And this implies that we are only asking about man in the correct way when we ask about ourselves in the right way. This certainly does not mean that we take ourselves for the whole of humanity or for the idol of humanity. Quite the contrary, it simply clearly shows that all man's questioning about man is in the first and last instance a matter of the *existence* of man *in each specific case*. This question—what man is—does not allow the individual human being, nor especially the questioner, to sink back into a pacified state of indifference as just any particular case of the universal essence of man in general. Quite the reverse, this universal essence of man only becomes essential as such when the individual comprehends him- or herself in his or her Dasein. The question concerning what man is, if genuinely put, explicitly delivers the human being over into *his or her* Dasein. Being delivered over to Dasein in this way is the index of an intrinsic *finitude*.

It is necessary, especially today, to point out that the question concerning the essence of man is the question concerning us ourselves, because precisely this problematic is today exposed to widespread misinterpretation through common understanding. The latter sees only an extreme subjectivism in all this and eagerly strives to marshal so-called objective domains and forces against it, with the proud ulterior motive of thereby thinking more objectively and that means, of course, more scientifically.

The *question concerning world-formation* is the question concerning the human being that we ourselves are, and therefore the question *concerning ourselves*, indeed the question concerning how things stand with us. But this is what we have already asked and properly asked in our earlier attempt to *awaken a fundamental attunement in our Dasein.* Thus we are already prepared and can forego a discussion of anthropology.

But surely in the first part of the lecture course we said nothing about the essence of man and even less about what we are calling world-formation and world. Indeed. We *said* nothing about this. Yet in no way does that mean that we have not in fact come upon all these things already, but only that it did not strike us at the time. When something strikes us or ought to strike us, it must be capable of being set off against something else. In the end our earlier analysis of captivation as the essence of animality provides as it were a suitable background against which the essence of humanity can now be set off, and indeed precisely in respect of what concerns us here: *world* and *world-formation.* Finally, it will be seen that we did already treat those issues which we just now left standing as abstract questions: the problem of the *manifestness* of beings and the way in which this manifestness *occurs.*

Thus the inner coherence of our investigation completes itself. It becomes clearer how the *problem of world itself grows out of this fundamental attunement,* or at least initially derives quite specific directives from it. We now stand before the task of presenting to ourselves in an originary manner those moments involved in the concept of world which we recognized as provisional characteristics. To do so we shall *go back in that direction* which was disclosed to us through the interpretation of *profound boredom* as a fundamental attunement of human Dasein. It will be revealed how this fundamental attunement, and everything bound up with it, is to be set off over against what we claimed as the essence of animality, over against captivation. This contrast will become all the more decisive for us insofar as captivation, as precisely the essence of animality, apparently belongs in the closest proximity to what we identified as a characteristic feature of profound boredom and described as the *entrancement* of Dasein within beings as a whole. Certainly it will be seen that this closest proximity of both determinations of essence is merely deceptive, that an abyss lies between them which cannot be bridged by any mediation whatsoever. Yet in that case the total divergence of the two theses will reveal itself, and thereby the essence of world.

§68. Provisional delimitation of the concept of world: world
as the manifestness of beings as such as a whole. General
elucidation of world-formation.

Earlier we discussed *boredom,* as we saw, and not just any attunement. If we now claim to take this whole investigation as a fundamental orientation for determining the essence of man, then we must say first of all that in this examination of boredom we did indeed bring an attunement, perhaps even a fundamental attunement of man, closer to us but still merely as *one* possible psychological and indeed transitory lived experience which surely does not permit us to draw conclusions with regard to man as a *whole*. And yet, we already know from our introductory observations—and we have clarified this knowledge through the concrete interpretation of boredom—that attunements as such are not merely subjectively coloured experiences or epiphenomenal manifestations of psychological life but rather fundamental ways of Dasein itself, in which one is attuned in such and such a way, ways of Dasein in which Dasein becomes manifest to itself in such and such a manner. That is why we cannot possibly treat boredom as an object of psychology. And that is precisely why we cannot draw conclusions with regard to man as a whole from such an object of psychology. We do not even need to draw such conclusions, given that this attunement brings us to ourselves in a far more fundamental and essential way. In attunement we *are* in such and such a manner. And profound boredom shows us what that means. The Dasein in us manifests itself. This in turn does not mean that we receive information about something, about some eventuality that would otherwise have remained unknown to us. On the contrary, Dasein sets us ourselves before beings as a whole. In attunement we *are* in such and such a way: this therefore implies that attunement precisely makes *beings as a whole* manifest and makes us manifest to ourselves as disposed in the midst of these beings. Attunement and being attuned is in no way to be regarded as a knowledge of psychological states, but is rather a way of *being borne out* into the specific manifestness of beings as a whole in each case, and that means into the manifestness of Dasein as such, as it finds itself disposed in each case in the midst of this whole.

By way of repetition I would like to recall the essential moments of profound boredom, *being left empty* and *being held in limbo* in the specific concrete form of *our* boredom, *being entranced* and *being drawn into the moment of vision*. All of this showed us how the utter abyss of Dasein in the midst of Dasein discloses itself in this attunement. As we recall these things, we must take the measure of all this and do so thoroughly in order now to see that precisely with regard to our questions concerning world and the manifestness of beings we are not merely adequately prepared but already find ourselves transposed into a correct fundamental attitude of questioning. This 'one is attuned in such and such a manner' reveals itself as the formula for a manifestness of Dasein as such. *Fundamental* attunements are *exemplary* possibilities of such manifestness. This exemplarity consists not so much in the fact that what is manifest here is richer and more various as distinct from average attunements or even lack of attunement, but rather in the fact that this fundamental attunement distinctively reveals something that is manifest in every attunement in a particular way. What should we call this? It is this '*as a whole*'. Yet it was this peculiar 'as a whole' which remained so enigmatic for us when we brought the interpretation of profound boredom to a provisional conclusion. This 'as a whole' is not merely something initially ungraspable for conceptuality, but for our everyday experience as well. And indeed it is so ungraspable not because it lies in some remote and inaccessible realm which could only be reached by the highest speculation, but because it is so close to us that we have no distance from it that would allow us to catch sight of it. We ascribe this 'as a whole' to beings, and more precisely, to the manifestness of beings in each specific case. From this we can conclude once again that the concept of world initially introduced was completely inadequate and that it here comes to be further determined. Proceeding from the naive concept of world we can lay down a particular *sequence of steps* that will also establish how the investigation has proceeded.

The naive concept of world is understood in such a way that world basically signifies *beings,* quite undifferentiated with respect to 'life' or 'existence', but simply beings. In characterizing the way and manner in which the animal lives we then saw that if we can speak meaningfully of the world and world-formation of man, then world must signify something like the *accessibility of beings.* But we also saw in turn that with this characterization we get caught up in an essential difficulty and ambiguity. If we determine world in this way, then we can also say in a certain sense that the animal has a world, namely has access to something that we, *for our part,* experience as beings. But then we discovered that while the animal does have access to something, it does not have access to beings as such. From this it follows that world properly means *accessibility of beings as such.* Yet this accessibility is grounded upon a *manifestness of beings as such.* Finally, it was revealed that this is not a manifestness of just any kind whatsoever, but rather *manifestness of beings as such as a whole.*

Thus we are now in possession of a provisional delimitation of the concept of world which performs a methodological function in the sense that it prescribes for us the individual steps of our present interpretation of the phenomenon of world. World is not the totality of beings, is not the accessibility of beings as such, not the manifestness of beings as such that lies at the basis of this accessibility—world is rather the *manifestness of beings as such as a whole.* We now wish to begin our investigation from that aspect which already impressed itself upon us in our interpretation of fundamental attunement, namely this remarkable '*as a whole*'.

In however obscure a manner, world always has a characteristic *wholeness,* something somehow rounded out or however we initially wish to express it. This 'as a whole'—is it a property of beings in themselves, or is it only an aspect of the manifestness of beings, or is it neither of these? Let us ask more provisionally: even if it does not signify the sum-total of beings, does 'beings as a whole' mean precisely the whole of beings in the sense of the totality of everything in general that in itself is, as the naive concept of world suggests? If this is what were meant, then we could never remotely say that beings as a whole are manifest to us in a fundamental attunement. The fundamental attunement may be as essential as we like, but it will never provide information about the totality of beings in themselves. But then what does this 'as a whole' mean if it does not mean the substantial whole of beings in themselves? We may answer that it means the form of those beings that are manifest for us as such. Therefore 'as a whole' signifies 'in the form of the whole'. Yet what does 'form' mean here, and what does 'manifest for us' mean? Is form simply a frame that is subsequently mounted around beings insofar as they are precisely manifest for us? And what would this subsequent frame be there for? Are beings manifest in a different way than they are precisely for us? And if not, does that mean that they are subjectively grasped by us, so that we could say that world means the subjective form and the formal constitution of the human conception of beings in themselves? Must not everything in fact lead to this conclusion when we consider that our thesis claims that man is world-forming? For this surely means that world is nothing in itself but rather something formed by man, something subjective. That would be one possible interpretation of what we have hitherto said concerning the problem of world and the concept of world—one possible interpretation, but one which nevertheless precisely fails to grasp the decisive problem here.

We shall now describe the site of the problem in a preliminary fashion by explaining in general what we mean by *world-formation*. According to our thesis, world belongs to world-formation. The manifestness of beings as such as a whole, world, forms itself, and world only is what it is in such formation. Who forms the world? Man, according to our thesis. But what is man? Does he form the world in the way that he forms a choral society, or does he form the world as essentially man? Is this 'man' as we know him, or man as one whom for the most part we do not know? Man insofar as he himself is made possible by something in his being human? Could this making-possible precisely consist in part in what we are proposing as world-formation? For it is not the case that man first exists and then also one day decides amongst other things to form a world. Rather world-formation is something that occurs, and only on this ground can a human being exist in the first place. Man as man is world-forming. This does not mean that the human being running around in the street as it were is world-forming, but that the *Da-sein in* man is world-forming. We are deliberately employing the expression 'world-formation' in an ambiguous manner. The Dasein in man *forms* world: [1.] it brings it forth; [2.] it gives an image or view of the world, it sets it forth; [3.] it constitutes the world, contains and embraces it.

We shall have to confirm this threefold significance of the process of forming through a more precise interpretation of the phenomenon of world. Are we playing with language here when we speak of the threefold sense of world-formation? Indeed we are, although more precisely speaking we are playing along with the play of language. The play of language here is not merely playful, but arises from a lawfulness that precedes all 'logic' and demands a deeper binding character than the observance of rules for the correct formation of definitions. Of course, when our philosophizing intrinsically plays along with language, the danger of playing games and becoming entangled in such games is also perilously close. Yet nevertheless we must dare to play if, as we shall later see, we want to escape from the entrancing spell of everyday discourse and its concepts. Yet even if we were to concede that world signifies the subjective form of our human conception of beings in themselves, so that in fact there would be no beings in themselves at all but rather everything would merely transpire within the subject—even if we were to concede this, then amongst many other questions we should also have to ask: How can man even come to a subjective conception of beings, unless beings are already manifest to him beforehand? How do things stand concerning this manifestness of beings as such? If the 'as a whole' indeed already belongs to this manifestness, is it not then withdrawn from the subjectivity of man, and that means here from his momentary caprice in each case?

Yet why all these false trails through all these confusing questions that have failed to bring us a single step closer to answering our guiding question concerning the essence of world? This is how ordinary understanding thinks. And it thinks this way because from the outset it takes the answer to the question concerning the essence of world in the same sense as the answer to the question concerning how the stock markets are doing today. We may perhaps be free of this all too primitive conception and yet still be tempted to demand that the question concerning the essence of world be answered through a straightforward ascertainment, answered for example by our interpreting the already examined fundamental attunement of boredom more extensively and thereby informing everyone what the manifestness of beings as a whole means. *That* we finally do wish to inquire back into this fundamental attunement is certainly true, for otherwise our interpretation of it in the context of these lectures would have been pointless. But *whether* we are already sufficiently equipped for this inquiring back is another question. It becomes a burning question if we recall that the interpretation of the fundamental attunement did not indeed present us with a subjective psychological experience, on the firm basis of some concept of man (soul or consciousness). On the contrary, it was precisely this fundamental attunement which opened up original perspectives on human Dasein for us. Our genuine preparation for the problem of world will accordingly have to consist in orienting the questions that have now emerged with regard to the manifestness of beings or manifestness as a whole in the direction of this single perspective—lest we remain moving unawares and as a matter of course within an inappropriate attitude—however natural it may be. Precisely here, where we are first properly beginning to grasp the problem, we find ourselves in a crisis. It is uniquely characteristic of all philosophizing in comparison with every scientific orientation that at the moment when proper philosophical knowledge is to emerge, what is decisive is not so much taking hold of the matter, but appraising the standpoint of the investigation—and this has nothing to do with methodological reflections. If we now try and appraise the critical position where we now stand, this can only be accomplished in the context of a substantive unfolding of the problem.

§69. A first formal interpretation of the 'as' as a structural moment of manifestness.

a) The connection between the 'as', as the structural linking pertaining to relation and relational terms, and the propositional statement.

Yet what form of inappropriateness can have crept into the concepts employed so far? We said that world is the manifestness of beings as such as a whole. And we have already pointed out that something enigmatic emerges from such a characterization: namely this 'as such', beings as such, something as something, 'a as b'. It is this quite elementary 'as' which—and we can put it quite simply—is refused to the animal. We must think about the essence of manifestness and thus also about the more precise determinations of manifestness. The 'as a whole' ['im Ganzen'] stands in connection with this enigmatic 'as'. If we ask what this 'as' signifies, we would initially reply that it is a linguistic form of expression. Yet should we allow ourselves to approach the matter in this way? Do we not then end up philosophizing merely with words instead of with things themselves? And yet it is immediately clear to us that with this 'as', with 'a as b', with beings *as such,* we do think something to ourselves, even if we are unable at the first attempt to give a clear account of what is involved in this. Perhaps it is superfluous to point out that this 'as' is also essential in Latin—the *qua* of *ens qua ens*—and especially in Greek—the ἦ of ὄν ἦ ὄν. Thus this 'as' is no mere whim of our language, but is clearly somehow grounded in the meaning of Dasein itself. What does this linguistic expression 'as', *qua,* ἦ, then mean? Obviously we shall not be able to proceed merely by staring, as it were, at these particles, staring at them long enough to discover something behind them. Rather our task is precisely to bring to light that original connection from out of which and for which this 'as' has emerged as a specific meaningful coinage.

Yet we immediately recognize that the 'as' signifies a '*relation*' and that the 'as' is never given independently on its own. It points to *something* which stands in the '*as*', and equally it points to *some other thing, as which* it is. Involved in the 'as' there is a relation, and thus *two relational terms,* and these not just as any two, since the first is one term and the second is the other. But this *structural linking* [Gefüge] pertaining to the relation and to the relational terms is not something free-floating on its own account. Where then does it belong? We begin to approach the matter more closely when we unpack the expression 'a as b' and say 'a, insofar as it is b'. Thus the 'as' can only begin to function if beings are already given, so that the 'as' then serves to render these beings *explicit* as constituted in such and such a way. An 'a' that is 'b' is already given and the 'a' being 'b' is explicitly brought out in the 'as'. We already fundamentally know what we mean by this 'as' even before we articulate it clearly in language. We know this, for example, in the simple statement that 'a is b'. In understanding this assertion we understand 'a as b'. According to its structure, the 'as' therefore belongs to the simple *propositional statement.* The 'as' is a structural moment of the propositional structure in the sense of a simple propositional statement.

The simple propositional statement, however, is a construction which we say is *true* or *false* as the case may be. A statement is true when it *agrees* with that about which it asserts something; that is, if through the asserted agreement it informs us about what a matter is and how it is. But informing us about something means making something open or manifest. The statement is true because it contains a *manifestness of the matter itself.* The structure of the *statement that makes manifest* bears this 'as' within itself.

Yet we saw that the manifestness of beings is always the manifestness of beings as such. The 'as' belongs to this manifestness and together with the latter finds its common home in that construction which we have called the simple statement—'a is b'. Thus if we now pursue the structure of this construction called the 'statement', we shall obtain at a single stroke a proper clarification concerning the 'as' and its connection with manifestness, and thus also concerning this manifestness and thereby the essence of world as well.

b) The orientation of metaphysics toward the λόγος and toward logic as the fundamental reason why the problem of world has not been unfolded in an originary manner.

In ancient philosophy the assertion, the judgement, is called the λόγος. But the λόγος is surely the principal theme of *logic.* And thus it is that our problem of world, where world initially signifies the manifestness of beings as such as a whole, finds itself led back through the intrinsic clarification of this structure to the problem of the λόγος. The question concerning the essence of world is a fundamental question of *metaphysics*. The problem of world as a fundamental problem of metaphysics finds itself led back to logic. Logic is therefore the proper basis of metaphysics. The connection here is so insistently obvious that we would be amazed if it had not insistently forced itself upon the attention of philosophy from time immemorial. And indeed, as we have briefly shown with respect to the problem of world, this connection provides the basis and path for the whole of Western metaphysics and its questions, insofar as it is logic that prescribes the examination of all problems with respect to the λόγος and its truth as problems of metaphysics, that is, as questions concerning being. But this implies more than we can possibly imagine at first sight. The sharpest pointer to this state of affairs lies in the fact that today, without thinking about the origin of the matter at all, we quite unawares and blithely designate as categories those elements of being which we recognize as the proper ones and make into a problem of metaphysics. κατηγορία, the Greek for assertion, designates those moments which apply to the λόγος in a particular way, moments which the λόγος necessarily asserts as the κατηγορίαι which accompany it, which accompany assertion and have their determinate possibilities. The determinations of being are grasped as categories, i.e., as determinations of beings and with regard to how these beings stand in respect of the λόγος. This fundamental orientation on the part of metaphysics toward the λόγος permeates not only philosophy—the determinations of being as 'categories'— and not only scientific thought in general, but all of our explanatory and interpretive comportment toward beings. In spite of this, we must pose the question of whether this connection between logic and metaphysics, which has utterly ossified into self-evidence for us, is justified; whether there is, or must be, a *more originary problematic;* and whether or not precisely the usual way of asking metaphysical questions orients itself toward logic in the broadest sense precisely because insight into the peculiar character of the problem of world has hitherto been obstructed.

Before pursuing the structural moment of the 'as' any further, let us set out once again the connection between the 'as' and the guiding problem of world. We have formulated the problem of world with the thesis that man is world-forming. Thus we have indicated a connection between man and world. Perhaps the determination of the essence of man is identical with the unfolding of this problem of world-formation. We must not draw upon any arbitrary definition of man to elucidate the problem of world but must rather adopt as our own a perspective upon man from within which the essence of man himself at least becomes questionable. We do not wish to tie ourselves down to a definition, but rather to unfold the problem in terms of a fundamental attunement, especially given that the latter has a tendency to manifest the Dasein of man as such, that is, simultaneously to manifest beings as a whole in the midst of which man finds himself disposed. Once we have thus secured the task of the problem of world with regard to its site and basis however, we immediately confront a crucial difficulty. We recall that the interpretation of the fundamental attunement in no way represented a descriptive identification of a psychological property of human beings. The difficulty encountered there of gaining an appropriate stance for the question concerning man returns all the more acutely here. We have secured the problem by taking world as the manifestness of beings as such and as a whole. We emphasized two determinations: the moment of beings *as such,* and the moment of beings '*as a whole*'. The task now is to unfold the problem in such a way as to grasp the intrinsic connectedness of these two structural moments in terms of their ground and thus open up a breach into the phenomenon itself. If we concretely approach this task of clarifying the structural moment of the 'as something', then this task seems to be self-evident, especially since it leads us into a familiar context which has been extensively treated in the history of philosophy. The 'as' is a relation and as a relation it is related to the relational terms. The nature of this relation is illuminated for us when we describe it in this way: 'a' insofar as it is 'b', the 'as' in connection with the 'a' being 'b', where the being-b of 'a' then consists in the statement 'a is b'. Thus the grasping of 'a as b' already necessarily lies in the ground of the statement itself. We thereby come upon a connection between the 'as' and the statement, the λόγος, the judgement. This phenomenon of the λόγος is not only familiar in philosophy in general, and especially in logic, but λόγος in the broadest sense as reason, as *ratio,* is the dimension from within which the problematic of being comes to be developed. That is why for Hegel—the last great metaphysician in Western metaphysics—metaphysics coincides with logic as the science of reason.

The aforementioned basis of metaphysics and its orientation toward propositional truth is indeed necessary in a certain respect, yet it is *not originary.* It is this lack of originality which has obstructed the proper unfolding of the question of world hitherto. It is this connection between metaphysics and logic that has become self-evident to us which, without our immediately seeing it, has hindered the development of an originary problematic that would open access to the problem of world. Consequently we should not be surprised if certain inappropriate forms of questioning have already crept into our problematic. We should not be surprised if, in this provisional exposition of the problem of the 'as', we already even find ourselves moving within an *inappropriate form of questioning,* one that becomes fateful if it is adhered to *exclusively.*

§70. A fundamental methodological consideration concerning
the understanding of all metaphysical problems and concepts.
Two fundamental forms of misinterpretation.

a) The first misinterpretation: the examination of philosophical
problems as something present at hand in the broad sense. Formal
indication as a fundamental character of philosophical concepts.

We shall go into this issue briefly here, especially since in this connection we encounter a fundamental *methodological* consideration which may act as a pointer for our understanding of all metaphysical problems and concepts. I shall briefly refer to an issue that was first brought to light by Kant in attempting to lay the foundations for metaphysics. Kant for the first time pointed out a certain, and indeed necessary, 'illusion' contained in metaphysical concepts, an illusion that does not condemn these concepts as empty fictions but rather for its part renders a particular problematic quite necessary for metaphysics. He calls this 'dialectical illusion'. It is not the 'designation' which is important here, but the matter itself. By the dialectical illusion of reason Kant understands the peculiar fact that for human thought certain concepts are given that intend what is ultimate and most universal; and that furthermore precisely these ultimate and most decisive of concepts, which guide and in a certain sense ground all concrete thinking, essentially lack the possibility of our demonstrating their legitimacy through any intuition of what it is they properly intend. It is because this possibility of demonstration is lacking that the understanding falls victim to an illusion, for it does not recognize this lack and holds such a demonstration to be quite unnecessary or to be already accomplished in an a priori fashion. Kant broached this problem of dialectical illusion in the second major part of the "Transcendental Doctrine of Elements," i.e., in the Transcendental Dialectic. We shall leave aside the question as to whether this problem of dialectical illusion was developed and grounded in a sufficiently radical manner.

For us there is something else that is essential. For there is *another* illusion which is far more decisive and originary than the dialectical one discovered by Kant, and one which persists in *all* philosophical thinking and exposes it to *misinterpretation*. Philosophizing is something living only where it comes to language and expresses itself, although this does not necessarily imply 'communicating itself to others'. Such coming to language in terms of concepts is not something fatefully unavoidable, but is rather the essence and power of this essential human activity. Yet once philosophizing is expressed, then it is exposed to misinterpretation, and not merely that misinterpretation which lies in the relative ambiguity and unreliability of all terminology; rather it is exposed to that essential *substantive misinterpretation* for which *ordinary understanding* inevitably falls. For ordinary understanding examines everything it finds expressed philosophically *as though it were something present at hand* and, especially since it seems to be essential, takes it from the outset on the same level as the things it pursues everyday. It does not reflect upon the fact and cannot even understand that *what philosophy deals with only discloses itself at all within and from out of a transformation of human Dasein.* Ordinary understanding struggles against this transformation of man demanded by every philosophical step on account of a natural idleness which is grounded in what Kant once called the 'idle flaw' in human nature.[1] Put in terms of our guiding problem, that means: By the term 'world', and here perhaps more strongly than anywhere else, we initially try to seek something that is present at hand in itself and ascertainable, something that we can always appeal to. We must appreciate from the very beginning that this is not how things are, even though we are tempted to make just this mistake. Or to put it in another way: philosophical knowledge of the essence of world is not and never can be an awareness of something present at hand. It is rather a comprehending disclosure of something in a specifically determined and directed questioning, which as a questioning never allows what is questioned to become something present at hand. This specifically determined and directed questioning is itself necessary in order to make world and suchlike thematic in an appropriate manner and to maintain it as such.

If with reference to what was said above we now ask ourselves what we have actually achieved in the *preceding characterization of the structure of the 'as'*, and how we proceeded in that connection, we can express it in the following way: World was indicated by reference to the character of the *manifestness of beings as such as a whole.* The 'as' belongs to manifestness—beings *as* such, as this or that. Closer examination of the 'as' led us to consider the *assertion* and propositional truth. Now how did we elucidate the 'as'? What was the first step we took in order to bring the 'as' closer to us? We said that the 'as' cannot exist on its own account, that it is a relation which moves from one term to the other—something as something. This characterization is formally correct insofar as we can in fact bring the 'as' closer to us in the form of a relation. But we can easily see that with this utterly vacuous determination of the 'as'—an 'as'-relation—we have already relinquished its proper essence. For the 'and' is also a relation between two terms, and furthermore the 'or'—'a and b', 'c or d'. Now one might object that there is no danger in characterizing the 'as' in terms of a 'relation' as long as we remember that the characterization

---

1. Kant, *Die Religion innerhalb der Grenzen der bloßen Vernunft.* Kants Werke. Ed. E. Cassirer. Vol. 6 (Berlin, 1923), p. 178. [Trans. T. Greene and H. Hudson, *Religion Within the Limits of Reason Alone* (New York: Harper & Brothers, 1960), p. 34 (translation modified).]

specific to this relation must be ascertained and taken into account as being distinct from the 'and'-relation, for example. Yet it is precisely here that the fateful character of any formal characterization reveals itself. For it is questionable whether we do thereby grasp the essence of the 'as' at all, even if we attempt to identify its specific character. It is questionable because the whole phenomenon already gets levelled down through the apparently innocuous—because always correct—characterization of the 'as' in terms of a relation. What I mean is this: If for example we designate something as a relation, we thereby suppress the *dimension* within which the relevant relation can be what it is. On account of the suppression of this dimension, the relation in question gets put on the same level as every other relation. We have from the outset taken the relation self-evidently as something which moves between something and something else, as something which is present at hand in the broadest sense. Not only that, but the empty formal idea of relation is simultaneously thought to belong to any equally empty manifold of relational terms whatsoever, terms whose manner of being is taken as quite undifferentiated. Yet following what we have said earlier, that means taken as something *present at hand* in the broadest sense: something as something. And then from that perspective, we certainly found ourselves led to the assertion which expresses this relation as such. The simple form of the assertion, which we are familiar with as the categorical statement, is only the elementary propositional form within the undifferentiated and everyday way we comport ourselves toward and talk about beings (logic, grammar, discourse, and language). Consequently, when we elucidate the 'as' by designating it as 'relation', this implies that we unwittingly take the *dimension* of this relation to be the *realm of the present at hand in general.* Yet from this perspective it is quite hopeless to try to identify the essence of the 'as', unless, that is, we have already glimpsed something of the true essence of the 'as'.

Nevertheless, we can continue to call the 'as' a relation and to talk about the 'as'-relation. Only we must remember that this *formal characterization does not give us the essence.* On the contrary, it merely indicates precisely the decisive *task* of grasping the relation in terms of its proper dimension, instead of levelling down this dimension through such formal characterization. Designating the 'as' in terms of a relation tells us nothing about the 'as' as such, but merely directs us toward our proper and peculiar task. That is why I speak of *formal indication* in connection with such a characterization of the 'as'. The full import of this for the entire conceptuality of philosophy cannot be expounded here.

There is only one thing which should be mentioned now because it is of particular importance for understanding the problem of world—as well as both our other questions. All philosophical concepts are *formally indicative,* and only if they are taken in this way do they provide the genuine possibility of comprehending something. I shall elucidate what I mean by this *fundamental character of philosophical concepts* as distinct from all scientific concepts by means of a particularly incisive example, namely the problem of *death,* and indeed human death. I have developed this problem of death in a quite specific context, which can be disregarded here, in *Being and Time,* §46ff. In a very rough and ready fashion we can say that human Dasein is in one way or another a being toward death. Man always comports himself somehow or other toward death, that is, toward *his* death. This implies that man *can* run ahead toward death as the most extreme possibility of his Dasein, and understand himself from that perspective in the most proper and whole selfhood of his Dasein. To understand Dasein means understanding how to go about being-there, Da-sein; it means being able to be-there. Understanding ourselves from out of this most extreme possibility of Dasein means acting in the sense of being exposed to the most extreme possibility. We described such running ahead in being free for our own death as Dasein's proper and authentic way of being a self, and distinguished the authenticity proper to existence from the inauthenticity of our everyday doings in which we are forgetful of ourselves. Even if we tear this problem out of its original context and simply consider the specific content and manner of its exposition, it should not be too difficult to grasp the decisive point here. And yet, misinterpretation constantly and repeatedly arises with predictable certainty. The reason for this does not lie in any lack of perspicacity on the part of the reader, nor in any lack of readiness to examine what has been presented, nor in this case, as I imagine, in any lack of incisiveness in the interpretation itself. Rather, it lies in the 'natural idleness' of the ordinary understanding in which each of us is caught up and which believes itself to be philosophizing when it reads and writes about, or argues with, philosophical books. With respect to the aforementioned problem, it proceeds in this way: if running ahead toward death constitutes the proper authenticity of human existence, then in order to exist properly man must be constantly thinking about death. And if he attempts to do that, then he will not be able to endure existence at all and the only way for him to achieve this authentic existence would be to commit suicide. But to seek the essence of the man's proper existence in suicide, in the annihilation of existence, is a conclusion that is as insane as it is absurd. Therefore the interpretation which was given above of authentic existence as a running ahead toward death is the purely arbitrary product of an intrinsically impossible conception of life. Where does the misunderstanding lie here? Not in the drawing of a false conclusion, but rather in the fundamental attitude, one which is not explicitly assumed but rather is there in our natural way of getting on with life. As a result we take such claims from the outset as a report about certain properties of man who also happens to crop up alongside the stone, the plant, the animal. A relationship toward death is *present at hand* within man. It is then asserted that this constitutes the proper, authentic existence of man, i.e., the demand is made that this *present at hand* relationship toward death should become a permanent condition in man. But since the human beings who are there cannot endure this and since they are often indeed present at hand in a perfectly contented state, this proves that such a gloomy conception of existence is impossible.

With this fundamental attitude, which unwittingly comes into play from the outset, death, man's relationship toward death, is already taken as something *present at hand.* Since the ordinary understanding considers that which properly is to be that which is always present at hand, it sees the proper authenticity of existence in the permanent presence at hand of this relationship toward death, in this constant thinking about death. In this fundamental attitude, from which none of us may consider ourselves free, what is overlooked from the outset is that the fundamental character of existence, of human existing, lies in *resolute disclosedness* [Entschlossenheit]. Yet this resolute disclosedness is not some present at hand condition that I possess, but on the contrary is something which possesses me. However, this resolute disclosedness is what it is as such only and always as the *moment of vision* [Augenblick], as the moment of vision of genuine action. These moments of resolute disclosedness only come about in time because they are something temporal themselves, and only ever happen within the temporality of Dasein. Ordinary understanding certainly sees the moment within time as well, but it only sees the moment of vision as an ordinary moment, and only sees the ordinary moment in its evanescent character as something which is present at hand only for a short time. It is incapable of seeing the essence of the moment of vision, which rests in its seldomness when seen in relation to the time of any Dasein as a whole. The ordinary understanding is unable to grasp the seldomness of such moments and the ecstatic expanse of this seldomness, because it lacks the power of recollection [*Erinnerung*]. It has a memory only of what was formerly present at hand which has been retained as something now no longer present at hand. What we have called the seldomness of resolute action is a unique feature of the moment of vision, and one precisely by virtue of which the moment possesses a quite specific relation to its temporality. For where the moment of vision is not temporalized, there is not simply nothing present at hand, but rather there is always already the temporality of everydayness. Thus it is not as though man had to steal back once more into the inauthenticity of his actions from out of an unendurable anticipatory running ahead toward death. Rather this return to inauthenticity is an extinguishing of the moment of vision, an extinguishing which does not eventually come about through some external cause or other, but is essentially grounded in the momentary character of the moment of vision. Yet while the everydayness of Dasein—insofar as it maintains itself in inauthenticity—is indeed a sinking back when compared to the moment of vision and its flaring up, it is by no means to be regarded intrinsically as something negative, and certainly never as something simply present at hand, as some persisting state which would be interrupted by the moments of vision proper to authentic action. The whole connection between authentic and inauthentic existence, between the moment of vision and the absence of such a moment, is not something present at hand which transpires within man, but one which belongs to Dasein. We can only understand the *concepts* that open up this connection as long as they are not taken to signify characteristic features or properties of something present at hand, but are taken rather as *indications* that show how our understanding must first twist free from our ordinary conceptions of beings and properly transform itself into the Da-sein in us. The challenge to such a transformation lies within each one of these concepts—death, resolute disclosedness, history, existence—yet not as some additional, so-called ethical application of what is conceptualized, but rather as a prior opening up of the dimension of what is to be comprehended. These concepts are indicative because, insofar as they have been genuinely acquired, they can only ever address the challenge of such a transformation to us, but can never bring about this transformation themselves. They point into Dasein itself. But Da-sein—as I understand it—is always *mine*. These concepts are *formally indicative* because in accordance with the essence of such indication they indeed point into a concretion of the individual Dasein in man in each case, yet never already bring this concretion along with them in their content.

Now it is always possible to take up the content of these concepts without their indicative character. But then the concepts not only fail to provide what they intend but rather—and this is the truly fateful thing—they become a supposedly genuine and rigorously defined starting point for groundless questions. One characteristic example of this is the problem of *human freedom* and the way in which this is investigated in the context of a concept of causality oriented toward the specific manner of being of that which is present at hand. Even where something *other* than natural causality was sought in or as freedom, it was still precisely a *causality* that was sought from the outset; that is, freedom was turned into a problem without following the indications about the character of the existence and Dasein pertaining to the beings we call free. With respect to this problem it could be shown how Kant certainly sees an illusion here, but still falls victim precisely to an original metaphysical illusion himself in this connection. Precisely the fate which befell the problem of freedom within the transcendental dialectic clearly shows that the philosopher is never safely protected from this metaphysical illusion, and that every philosophy must fall victim to such illusion the more it strives to develop its problematic in a radical manner. This concrete example surely reveals the peculiar difficulty facing *us* when we attempt to grasp what we mean by the problem of *world* and by the thesis that man is *world-forming*.

Let us once again summarize the intervening methodological considerations we have been developing. We turned to an apparently purely methodological preparation for approaching the problem of world-formation. But this was not methodological in the sense of being simply a technical matter quite detached from the substantive question, but rather is a method that is intimately bound up with the substantive issue itself. I initially clarified the problem by referring to Kant's achievements in laying the foundations for metaphysics through his demonstration of dialectical illusion. As against this dialectical illusion, which relates to a particular kind of concept—and here to a particular aspect of such concepts, namely the impossibility of demonstrating them by way of intuition—we turned back to a more originary illusion, an illusion that can be grasped in its necessity from out of the essence of man. We cannot go into the grounds of this illusion here. We are merely concerned with the question as to how we might escape, relatively at least, from this illusion with respect to our concrete problem, the question concerning the essence of world. For this we need to reflect upon the thoroughgoing character of philosophical concepts, namely that they are all formally indicative concepts. That they are indicative implies the following: the meaning-content of these concepts does not directly intend or express what they refer to, but only gives an indication, a pointer to the fact that anyone who seeks to understand is called upon by this conceptual context to undertake a transformation of themselves into their Dasein. But as soon as one takes these concepts without reference to their indicative character, like a scientific concept according to the conception of ordinary understanding, then philosophical questioning gets led astray with respect to every single problem. We illustrated this very briefly with our interpretation of the 'as'. We said that it is a relation and thus points back toward the proposition, which is either true or false. We thereby have a connection between the 'as' and the truth of a proposition, and thereby that which we established in the concept of world as the manifestness of beings. With respect to the concrete example of death, we clarified further where the natural error of our ordinary understanding lies: namely in the fact that it takes any philosophical explication it encounters in its own terms, as an assertion about certain characteristic features of beings as present at hand. The inferences which suggest themselves as soon as we attempt to grasp death as a possible characteristic feature of man show that no possible understanding can be expected from this quarter. What I have suggested here with respect to death has just the same consequences with respect to the question concerning the essence of freedom, insofar as this problem in particular was forced in a completely wrong direction in Kant.

Now what we have briefly expounded here concerning formal indication is true in an exemplary sense for the concept of world. What we mean by world is certainly not a being which is intrinsically present at hand, but nor is it some intrinsically present at hand structure of Dasein either. We can never look upon the phenomenon of world directly. It is true that even here we could extract some content from a given interpretation of the phenomenon of world without reference to its indicative character, and set it out in an objective definition which could then be passed on. But this would deprive the interpretation of all its reliable power, since whoever seeks to understand would not then be heeding the directive that lies in every philosophical concept.

b) The second misinterpretation: the false interconnection of philosophical concepts, and their isolation from one another.

On account of this failure, philosophical speculation proceeded to establish— and this is the *second aspect of misinterpretation*—a *false interconnection between philosophical concepts*. We all know that since Kant laid the foundations for metaphysics the tendency toward *system* has made itself felt within Western philosophy to a previously unheard of degree. This is a remarkable phenomenon, the reasons for which have still not been explained. It has to do with the fact that the conceptuality of philosophy, considered in accordance with its inner essence, reveals a tendency to refer one concept to another, and this suggests that we should look for an immanent interconnection between the concepts themselves. But since all formally indicative concepts and contexts of interpretation address whoever is trying to understand with respect to his or her Dasein, a properly *unique* interconnection of these concepts is also given at the same time. This interconnection does not consist in the relations that can be obtained by dialectically playing off such concepts against one another without reference to their indicative character or by thinking up something like a system of Dasein, for example. On the contrary, *the one and only originary interconnection of concepts* is already *established through Dasein itself.* The vitality of this interconnection depends upon the extent to which Dasein in each case comes to itself (and this is not the same as the degree of subjective reflection involved). The interconnection is intrinsically historical and is concealed within the history of Dasein. Consequently there is no system of Dasein for the metaphysical interpretation of Dasein. Rather the intrinsic conceptual interconnection is that of the history of Dasein itself, something which, as history, transforms itself. This is why formally indicative concepts and especially fundamental concepts can in an exemplary sense *never* be taken *in isolation.* The historicity of Dasein refuses, even more than any system does, any isolation or isolated consideration of individual concepts. This temptation also lies within ordinary understanding, where it is coupled in a peculiar fashion with the tendency to take everything encountered as something present at hand. We shall give an example of this as well, though not, let it be understood, in order to illustrate the failure of ordinary understanding, but rather to sharpen our attention to the difficulty and the inner requirements of a correct understanding.

I shall merely propose the example in a rough and ready way here. Amongst other things Dasein means: comporting oneself in being toward beings as such, and indeed doing so in such a way that this comportment also constitutes Dasein's *being* a being [*das Seiend-sein des Daseins*], and such being we designate as *existence*. What Dasein is consists in *how* it is, namely in how it exists. The what-being of Dasein, its essence, lies in its existence (*Being and Time,* p. 42). All human comportment toward beings as such is only intrinsically possible if such comportment is capable of understanding what is *not* as such. What is not and nothingness can only be understood if Dasein in understanding holds itself from the outset and fundamentally toward the *nothing,* is held out into the nothing. The task is to understand the innermost power of the nothing, precisely in order to let beings be as beings, in order to have and to be beings in all their powerfulness as beings. Now if ordinary understanding encounters this clarification of the fundamental relations of Dasein and its existence, and hears talk of the nothing and the fact that Dasein is supposedly held out into this nothing, then it hears only the nothing—which is somehow present at hand—and it also knows Dasein only as something present at hand. Thus it concludes that man is present at hand in the nothing, properly speaking he has nothing and consequently is himself nothing. Any philosophy which asserts such a thing is pure nihilism and the enemy of all culture. And this is all perfectly correct if we understand things the way in which they appear in the newspaper. For here the nothing is *isolated* and Dasein is placed into the nothing as something present at hand, instead of seeing that being held into the nothing is not some present at hand property of Dasein as compared with something else equally present at hand, but is rather a fundamental way in which Da-sein as such brings forth its ability to be. The nothing is not an empty nothingness that allows nothing to be present at hand, but is that power which constantly thrusts us back, which alone thrusts us into being and lets us assume power over our Dasein.

Now if intelligent and even inwardly gifted individuals inevitably fall victim to such an interpretation, utterly reversing its true meaning, this only shows once again that the most sharp-sighted conception, and even the most penetrating presentation of the problem, remains ineffectual until and unless a transformation of Dasein occurs; and this not through the apron strings of instruction, but from out of a free ability to hearken to things. But this is also to say that in this misunderstanding on the part of ordinary understanding we are not remotely concerned with the situation of opponents or reviewers of my work, but rather with a situation that each of us must constantly combat for ourselves—and indeed even more seriously in the case of so-called followers than in that of so-called opponents, which is why the philosopher must treat both as equally important, i.e., as equally unimportant, if he or she understands the task at hand. True understanding never proves its mettle in repeating something after someone, but only in its power to lead understanding into genuine action, into objective achievement, which by no means primarily consists in the production of more philosophical literature. Thus this argument and our reference to the types of ordinary understanding can only help us if we grasp that this ordinary understanding is not peculiar to those who are too stupid or who are not fortunate enough to have heard things more clearly. Rather we all find ourselves afflicted in this way in varying degrees in each case.

If accordingly we now attempt a thematic exposition of the problem of world, we must take care not only to *avoid* understanding *world* as something *present at hand,* but also to *avoid isolating* the phenomenon of world. Consequently we must aim, in accordance with our theme, to let *the intrinsic relationships between world, individuation, and finitude* emerge together. In addition, however, we must not shirk the difficulty of leading ourselves into the problem through a genuine exposition and explication of it. We must renounce the apparently convenient but actually impossible path of providing a direct account of the essence of world, because we can know nothing about world, nor indeed about individuation or finitude, in this direct way.

Let us briefly summarize once again our methodological reflections in retrospect. We undertook a general excursus concerning philosophical concepts themselves, and the way in which they signify meaning: the fact that they do not directly intend what they mean as something present at hand, but that their meaning-function has the character of formal indication. The one who attempts to understand is thereby already challenged to comprehend that which is to be understood in their own Dasein, which does not imply that every philosophical concept is one that can be related to Dasein. We then elucidated the misinterpretations to which philosophical concepts as such are subject, using various examples: the concepts of death, freedom, and the nothing. We came to recognize two fundamental forms of misinterpretation which the conceptions of ordinary understanding tend to adopt, namely [1.] to take what is meant as something present at hand; [2.] to take what is meant as something isolated in each case. Just as death, freedom, and the nothing must be understood in their specifically philosophical sense, so too with the concept of world. And precisely before we begin the exposition of this concept it is particularly important to be clear about such misinterpretation, because this term in particular tends to encourage us to grasp its meaning as something present at hand, to grasp the world as an aggregate.

§71. The task of returning to the originary dimension of the 'as', taking an interpretation of the structure of the propositional statement as our point of departure.

We said that *world* means the *manifestness of beings as such as a whole.* Our explication of the problem began with the 'as'. We found that it is a structural moment of the statement, or more precisely that it expresses something which is always already understood in every propositional statement. But it thereby already becomes questionable whether the 'as' belongs primarily to the statement and its structure or is not rather presupposed by the propositional structure. Consequently it is necessary to ask positively about the *dimension* in which this 'as' originarily moves and within which it arises. But the *return into this origin* must thereby open up for us the whole context within which whatever we mean by the manifestness of beings and the 'as a whole' essentially prevails. Yet in order genuinely to accomplish this return to the origin of the 'as', we must be much more circumspect within the approach we have adopted, i.e., we must ask about the direction in which the propositional structure as such points us back.

There are various possible paths we can take in this interpretation of the propositional statement. Here I shall choose one that will simultaneously lead us toward a phenomenon which, however obscurely, has always already stood at the centre of our questioning: the 'as a whole'. The statement 'a is b' would not be possible with respect to what it means and the way in which it means what it does if it could not emerge from an *underlying experiencing of 'a as b'.* If accordingly the 'as' is not specifically expressed in the linguistic form of the statement, that does not prove that it does not already underlie the accomplishment of understanding the statement. Why must the 'as' underlie the statement and how does it do so? What is a *statement* in general? We talk about sentences and statements in various senses. We are familiar on the one hand with statements of wish, with interrogative statements, with imperative statements, with propositional statements. But we are also familiar with statements of principle, statements of inference, statements of instruction, and auxiliary statements. In both groups the term 'statement' means something different. In the first case we mean particular forms of linguistic expression, which we can also articulate and distinguish through particular signs (the question mark, the exclamation mark, the full stop), but above all through a particular rhythm or tone. In the first group we mean units of linguistic expression, by means of which a particular comportment of human beings is expressed in each case—wishing, questioning, commanding, requesting, discovering, ascertaining. In the second case on the other hand we do not mean the sort of statement which serves to express various kinds of human comportment, but rather statements in which something is established about something (and consequently 'set down'). Statement in this second sense has more to do with statutory expressions of rules and regulations, although a logical statement of principle is naturally different from the statutory rules of a club.

In the first group, in speaking and setting forth questions, commands, and assertions, we have to do with various *ways of proposing something.* In the second group we are only concerned with *what has been proposed,* with the propositional content and its character in the context of the total content that is expounded. If we recall Spinoza's principal work *The Ethics,* for example, then we are confronted by a quite particular concatenation of propositional statements. If we say that we are only concerned with what has been proposed, this does not mean that a certain way of proposing does not also belong to statements of principle, to statements of inference, or to auxiliary statements. For all these statements are, in accordance with their general character, propositional statements, and therefore belong to the first class. On the other hand, the kinds of statements that belong to the first group—as ways in which modes of human comportment toward something proposed is expressed—also possess a content, although the content of statements of wish, imperative statements, and interrogative statements is difficult to grasp in its structure. For what is wished for in a statement of wish is not the content of such a statement. In a statement of wish I do not express myself about what is wished, but express myself rather as one who wishes what is wished. But this moment of expressing oneself on the part of the speaker also lies within every propositional statement, although in the course of everyday discourse, where we attend in advance to whatever is said, we allow this moment to recede completely.

Under the term 'statement' we make a twofold distinction: [1.] the statement as a way of proposing something; [2.] the statement as that which is proposed. However inadequate this distinction is with respect to a thematic examination of the problem of the statement, it will initially suffice as a pointer for our problem. If we now select for examination a particular form of statement, the *simple propositional statement,* we do not do so because this form of statement has played an exemplary role in the philosophical theory of propositions from the beginning. Rather we do so for reasons which precisely led to the fact that it is this form of statement which has decisively determined the doctrine of discourse in general, of the λόγος (logic). What are these reasons? We are already familiar with them. The fundamental trait of everyday Dasein is that undifferentiated comportment toward beings precisely as something present at hand. The corresponding form of discourse in which such comportment at first and for the most part expresses itself—whether in conversation, in narration, in reporting, in proclamation, or in scientific discussion—is this undifferentiated habitual form of assertion: 'a is b'. This λόγος determines the philosophical theory of the λόγος, or logic, because the λόγος first impresses itself upon us in this form, indeed as something that is also present at hand within everyday human discoursing with one another, and furthermore as the kind of discourse which is predominantly and for the most part present at hand. What is more, the logical theory of the λόγος as propositional statement came to acquire the dominant position within the theory of the λόγος in general as discourse and language, i.e., within the field of grammar. The inner construction, the fundamental concepts, and the particular questions of general and specific grammar as the science of languages in the broader sense have stood for centuries and even today still stand under the domination of the logic in question. We are only now slowly beginning to comprehend that as a result of this the whole science of linguistics and thus philology as well rest on shaky foundations. This reveals itself every day in philology with reference to a simple state of affairs. When a poem is made the object of philological interpretation, the resources of grammar find themselves at a loss, and precisely with respect to the greatest creations of language. Such analyses usually terminate in commonplace observations or arbitrarily selected literary phrases. And yet even here these foundations are gradually beginning to shake, even though the new is still hesitant and rather arbitrary. Here too we can see a process of transformation as philology is being transferred onto new foundations. Yet even here we see the remarkable fact that the younger and older generation alike behave as though nothing at all were happening.

When we said that the history of Western logic, and following from that the science of languages in general, is determined by the Greek theory of the λόγος in the sense of the propositional statement, then it must also be mentioned that the same Aristotle who—under essential influences from Plato—first penetrated to an insight into the structure of the statement, also in his *Rhetoric* recognized and undertook the mighty task of submitting the forms and formations of non-thetic discourse to interpretation. It was certainly true for various reasons, however, that the power of logic was too strong to leave open any genuine possibility of developing this attempt.

These indications must suffice to show that the *problem of the statement* represents anything but a specialist question. It entails the task of a fundamental engagement with the logic of antiquity, and one which cannot even be begun without tracing this logic back to ancient metaphysics. From another perspective this task is also that of laying the foundations of philology in the broader sense. And by this we understand neither the unearthing of grammatical rules and sound-shifts, nor gossiping about literature after the manner of the literati, but rather a passion for the λόγος; for it is in the λόγος that man expresses what is most essential to him, so as in this very expression to place himself into the clarity, depth, and need pertaining to the essential possibilities of his action, of his existence. It is only from this perspective that all the apparently technical aspects of philology acquire their inner justification and their genuine, albeit relative necessity.

In the attempt to provide an initial interpretation of the 'as' we have been led to consider the *propositional statement*. We now see that this propositional statement is indeed a necessary form within human discourse and particularly within the discourse of everydayness, of Dasein's everyday comportment to what is present at hand. Yet precisely for that reason it is a form that bears within it all the dangers and temptations with which ordinary understanding besets our philosophizing. But then why should we investigate this form of discourse at all if, as we admit, it is *not an originary one,* not one that immediately displays the problem? Why do we not directly force the problem of the 'as' into its proper dimension? Because the task is to catch sight of *this dimension* as something *entirely other,* and this can only occur if we contrast it with that in which we self-evidently move. But we do not simply wish to set this entirely other, in which the 'as' and the 'as a whole' are grounded, over against the propositional structure, but rather to penetrate to the former *through this structure.* We wish to investigate the propositional statement because this form of statement belongs to the essence of everyday discourse and because we only really comprehend the peculiar and at the same time seductive character of this form of the statement if we are able to penetrate through it to something entirely other from out of which the essence of the statement in this sense can first be comprehended. But this means that the task is to show where the propositional structure itself stands, in accordance with its own inner possibility. The task is to reveal those relations within which the statement as such already moves and rests—relations which the statement as such does not first create, but which it rather requires for its own essence. With such an approach, the statement and the λόγος already enter into an entirely other dimension. The statement is now no longer the central focus of the problematic, but something that dissolves into a much more far-reaching dimension. Of course, this whole consideration of the problem of the statement must restrict itself here to those connections which are best fitted to lead us toward the problem of world.

§72. Outline of the propositional statement (λόγος ἀποφαντικός) in Aristotle.

In order to ensure that our task maintains its intrinsic link with the tradition, as well as to make visible the elementary nature of the problem in all its simplicity, I shall add an outline of the propositional statement as provided by various treatises of Aristotle. First of all, however, we must recall the problem again: world is the manifestness of beings as such as a whole. Here we drew attention to the 'as' and the 'as a whole'. The two are connected to this manifestness. We grasped the 'as' in terms of a 'relation', introduced merely as a *formal indication* of the 'as'. This relation belongs to the structure of the statement. The statement is something that is true or false, i.e., that provides information about something in keeping with whatever the proposition is about, makes it manifest. If we look closely, the entirety of these relations between the 'as'-relation and the propositional structure and propositional truth comes to light in the first decisive interpretation Aristotle provides of the λόγος. This comes to light in such a way, however, that we cannot immediately see or get a grip on the 'as'-phenomenon, nor on the character of the 'as a whole'.

To provide some general orientation as to the way in which I develop the problem of the λόγος as regards metaphysics and its context, I shall point to those places where I have dealt with the logos-problem, and done so in a form that *deviates* from our present approach (in the context of our present problem we shall pursue other directions of questioning): *Being and Time*, §§7B, 33, and 44; *Kant and the Problem of Metaphysics*, §§7, 11, and the entire third part of the book; *On the Essence of Ground*, first section: the problem of the λόγος in Leibniz in the context of the metaphysical question concerning being. These are merely major stages within the history of the problem; they do not provide a complete orientation regarding the development of the problematic itself.

a) The λόγος in its general conception: discourse as meaning (σημαίνειν), giving something to be understood. The occurrence of agreement that holds together (γένεται σύμβολον—κατὰ συνθήκην) as condition of the possibility of discourse.

We shall first consider what Aristotle says in general about the λόγος. λόγος means discourse, everything that is spoken and sayable. The Greeks really have no word corresponding to our word 'language'. λόγος as discourse means what we understand by language, yet it also means more than our vocabulary taken as a whole. It means the fundamental faculty of being able to talk discursively, and accordingly, to speak. The Greeks thus characterize man as ζῷον λόγον ἔχον—that living being that essentially possesses the possibility of discourse. The animal, as the living being that lacks this possibility of discourse, is ζῷον ἄλογον. This definition of man then passed over into the traditional conception of man, in keeping with which (for reasons we shall not pursue now) λόγος was later translated by the Latin *ratio*. It was then said that man is *animal rationale*, a living being with reason. From this definition you can see how the decisive problem in antiquity, where man is defined from the perspective of discourse and language, now becomes lost, and how language is only introduced again as an afterthought, whereby the whole problematic is left without its roots. If in antiquity the λόγος represents that phenomenon with respect to which man is understood in terms of what is proper to him, and if we ourselves are saying that the essence of man is *world-forming,* then this expresses the fact that if the two theses are at all connected, then λόγος, *language, and world* stand in an intrinsic connectedness. We can even go further, and connect this ancient definition with our definition of man. While discussing the second thesis, we heard that the animal is characterized by a being open, namely in its behaviour toward what we call the encircling ring. The animal lacks the ability to apprehend as a being whatever it is open for. However, to the extent that the λόγος is connected with νοῦς and with νοεῖν, with apprehending something, we may say: There belongs to man a being open for . . . *of such a kind* that this being open for . . . has the character of *apprehending something as something.* This kind of relating to beings we call comportment, as distinct from the behaviour of the animal. Thus man is a ζῷον λόγον ἔχον, whereas the animal is ἄλογον. Despite the fact that our interpretation and way of questioning is altogether different from that of antiquity, it is not saying anything substantially new, but—as always and everywhere in philosophy—purely the same.

What, then, is the λόγος, conceived in this general way according to which it means as much as language? Aristotle says: Ἔστι δὲ λόγος ἅπας μὲν σημαντικός:[1] Each discourse, all discursivity, has in itself the possibility of giving something meaningful, something that we understand. In accordance with its essence and its innermost task, all discursivity places us in the dimension of understandability; indeed, discourse and language constitutes precisely this dimension of understandability, of mutual expression, requesting, desiring, asking, telling. Discourse gives something to be understood and demands understanding. By its very essence it is turned toward the free comportment and activity of human beings among one another.

The λόγος gives something to be understood. This essential function of discourse has a character of its own, which Aristotle points to concisely when he says: λόγος ἅπας μὲν σημαντικός, οὐχ ὡς ὄργανον δέ, ἀλλ' ὥσπερ εἴρηται, κατὰ συνθήκην:[2] This giving-to-be-understood of discourse is not a functioning such as we are acquainted with in the case of the organ, a functioning that, set in motion, is necessarily impelled to accomplish something: it is not φύσει. Discoursing is not a series of events, such as digestion or blood circulation—ἀλλὰ κατὰ συνθήκην. At a preceding point in the text, Aristotle provides an explication of this expression which is decisive for an insight into the essence of discourse. The λόγος is κατὰ συνθήκην, ὅτι φύσει τῶν ὀνομάτων οὐδέν ἐστιν, ἀλλ' ὅταν γένηται σύμβολον, ἐπεὶ δηλοῦσί γέ

---

1. *Aristotelis Organon.* Ed. Th. Waitz (Leipzig, 1844). Vol. 1, *Hermeneutica (de interpretatione),* Chap. 4, 17a 1.
2. Ibid.

τι καὶ οἱ ἀγράμματοι ψόφοι, οἷον θηρίων, ὧν οὐδέν ἐστιν ὄνομα:[3] No word of language is what it is on the basis of a purely physical connection, on the basis of a natural event, such as when, in the case of the animal for instance, a cry is triggered off due to some physiological state. Rather the word, indeed every word, is ὅταν γένηται σύμβολον, whenever a *symbol* occurs. The unarticulated sounds that animals produce by themselves indeed indicate something; animals can even reach agreement among themselves, as we are accustomed to saying—though inappropriately. Yet none of these utterances that animals by themselves produce are words: they are merely ψόφοι, noises. They are vocal utterances (φωνή) that lack something, namely *meaning*. The animal does not mean or understand by its call. This has led to people linking what are distinguished as vocal utterances and as the word with meaning attached to it (which is what the expression *meaning* implies), and saying that in addition to vocal utterance, man also has a meaning that is connected to this, and which he understands. We are thereby forced into seeing the problem the wrong way round from the very beginning. The situation is quite the reverse. From the very beginning our essence is such as to understand and form the possibility of understanding. It is because our essence is like this that utterances that we also produce have a meaning. Meaning does not accrue to sounds, but the reverse: the sound is first forged from meanings that are forming and have already formed. The λόγος is indeed φωνή, yet not primarily and then something else besides, but rather the reverse: it is primarily something else and then also . . . φωνή. Primarily what? κατὰ συνθήκην. The fact that there is an essential distinction between the vocal utterance of the animal (φωνή) and human discourse in the broadest sense is indicated by Aristotle when he says that human discourse is κατὰ συνθήκην, which he interprets as ὅταν γένηται σύμβολον. The κατὰ συνθήκην consists in the γένεσις of a σύμβολον.

The question is: What does Aristotle understand by ὅταν γένηται σύμβολον? He does not tell us anything more precise about this. However, we can attain some insight in this context that Aristotle is dealing with if we ask what σύμβολον means. We must beware of translating σύμβολον by symbol and introducing for σύμβολον a concept of symbol that is current today. συμβολή means throwing one thing together with another, holding something together with something else, i.e., keeping them alongside one another, joining them to and with one another. σύμβολον therefore means joint, seam, or hinge, in which one thing is not simply brought together with the other, but the two are held to one another, so that they fit one another. Whatever is held together, fits together so that the two parts prove to belong together, is σύμβολον. In the original concrete sense, for example, the two halves of a ring are σύμβολα

3. Ibid., Chap. 2, 16a 27ff.

which two guest-friends share between them and bequeath to their children, so that if the latter happen to meet later, they can hold together the halves of the ring to see if they fit, and can thereby recognize one another as belonging together, i.e., as befriended via their fathers. We cannot here pursue any further the more extensive history of the meaning of this word. We have here the intrinsic meaning of σύμβολον: being held to one another and simultaneously proving to belong together, or, as we generally say: agreement in being held to-gether, being held-to one another (compared).

Aristotle tells us: Discourse is what it is, i.e., it forms a sphere of *understandability,* whenever there is a γένεσις of a σύμβολον, whenever a *being held together* occurs in which there also lies an *agreement.* Discourse and word are to be found only in the occurrence of the symbol, whenever and to the extent that an agreement and a holding together occur. This occurrence is the condition of the possibility of discourse. Such an occurrence is lacking in the case of the animal, although the animal does produce sounds. These sounds designate something, as we say, they bear witness to something, and yet these utterances are not words, they have no meaning, they cannot give anything as meaningful. Only the genesis of the symbol makes this possible, the entire occurrence in which, from the very beginning, there occurs a holding together: *man's holding himself together with something* in such a way that he can come into agreement with whatever he is holding himself together with, and do so in the manner of referring [*Meinen*]. In accordance with his essence, man holds himself together with something else, insofar as he holds himself in a comportment toward other beings, and on the basis of this comportment toward other beings is able to refer to these other beings as such. Since sounds emerge within such an occurrence, and emerge for this referring, they enter into the service of meanings, which thus befit them, as it were. Only something which is referred to as such in the utterance can be held together, something with which, in uniting it, this holding together agrees. Sounds which emerge out of and for this *fundamental relation of letting something come into agreement and holding it together* are words. Words, discourse, occur in and out of such agreement with whatever can be referred to from the beginning and can be grasped as such, with something that several people can and must simultaneously agree with one another on, as that which is meant to be referred to in discourse. Because the λόγος is grounded in the γένεσις of the σύμβολον, it is κατὰ συνθήκην: by *agreement.*

What Aristotle sees quite obscurely under the title σύμβολον, sees only approximately, and without any explication, in looking at it quite ingeniously, is nothing other than what we today call *transcendence.* There is language [*Es gibt Sprache*] only in the case of a being that by its essence *transcends.* This is the sense of Aristotle's thesis that a λόγος is κατὰ συνθήκην. I have no inclination to recall what people have made of this Aristotelian thesis when interpreting it. Yet it is not by chance, either, that interpretations have gone astray here, because in thoughts on the essence of the λόγος prior to Aristotle there indeed arose two theories or theses that make it look as though Aristotle took one side of this debate. Aristotle states: The λόγος is not φύσει, is not some product of a physical event or process; it is not anything like digestion or the circulation of the blood, but has its γένεσις in something quite different: not φύσει, but κατὰ συνθήκην. Corresponding to this is that part of the earlier theory of the λόγος which says that language is θέσει: Words do not grow, they do not occur and form like organic processes, but are what they are on the basis of reaching an agreement. Since Aristotle also says κατὰ συνθήκην, it looks as though he were of the opinion that language formed in this way, that sounds are produced and humans reach an agreement: we will understand such and such by this. This does happen, but it does not reach the inner essence of the γένεσις of language itself, which Aristotle saw much more profoundly by indeed starting from these theories in a certain way, yet by taking decisive new steps to overcome them. Words emerge from that *essential agreement* of human beings with one another, in accordance with which they *are open in their being with one another for the beings around them,* which they can then individually agree about—and this also means fail to agree about. Only on the grounds of this originary, essential agreement is discourse possible in its essential function: σημαίνειν, giving that which is understandable to be understood.

b) Discourse as exhibiting (λόγος ἀποφαντικός) in its possibility of revealing-concealing (ἀληθεύειν-ψεύδεσθαι).

We have thus achieved some initial understanding of what the inner possibility of the λόγος consists in, taken in this quite broad sense. However, Aristotle says: λόγος ἅπας μὲν σημαντικός, every λόγος indeed gives something to be understood—ἀποφαντικὸς δὲ οὐ πᾶς,[4] but not every discourse is an *exhibiting,* i.e., one which, in the manner in which it gives something to be understood, has the specific tendency merely to exhibit as such whatever it is referring to. By *propositional statement* we mean only the λόγος ἀποφαντικός, discourse that points out. Requesting, εὐχή, for example, is a non-apophantic λόγος. If my discourse is a requesting, then it is not attempting to inform the other person about something in the sense of increasing his or her knowledge. Nor, however, is the request a communicating of the fact that I desire something or am filled with a desire. Nor is this discourse a mere desiring, but rather the concrete act of 'requesting of another'. Aristotle says: οἱ μὲν οὖν ἄλλοι

---

4. Ibid., Chap. 4, 17a 2f.

ἀφείσθωσαν· ῥητορικῆς γὰρ ἢ ποιητικῆς οἰκειοτέρα ἡ σκέψις· ὁ δὲ ἀποφαντικὸς τῆς νῦν θεωρίας:[5] The examination of these kinds of discourse which do not have the character of a pointing out—of ascertaining and letting be seen what and how something is—the examination of these λόγοι belongs to rhetoric and poetics. The propositional λόγος, however, is the object of our current investigation.

Every λόγος is σημαντικός—which is why Aristotle also says that the λόγος is φωνὴ σημαντική, a forming of understandability occurring by way of vocal utterance—but not every λόγος σημαντικός is ἀποφαντικός. The question is: Which λόγος is apophantic, and *how* does it become such? What is the distinguishing feature of propositional discourse compared to all other kinds of discourse? Aristotle says: Only that λόγος is ἀποφαντικός, ἐν ᾧ τὸ ἀληθεύειν ἢ ψεύδεσθαι ὑπάρχει,[6] in which we find truth and falsity. This is the usual translation—the natural one, and if we deviate from this we are accused of arbitrariness. And yet we must deviate from it, because the translation that appears to be literal does not at all render what the Greeks understood by this definition, and only this can lead us to the problem of the λόγος. Aristotle says ἐν ᾧ . . . ὑπάρχει, a discourse is propositional through ἀληθεύειν ἢ ψεύδεσθαι not merely being found in it, but *lying in it as underlying it,* as contributing toward its *ground* and its *essence.* Aristotle employs the medial form ψεύδεσθαι: constituting a deception, being inherently deceptive. That λόγος to whose essence there belongs (among other things) the ability to be deceptive is a pointing out. To deceive means: to pretend something, to present something as something it is not, or to present something that is not such and such as indeed being such and such. This deception, this being deceptive that belongs to the essence of the λόγος—this proffering of something as something it is not—this pretending, with respect to whatever the deception is about, is a *concealing.* That λόγος which has the possibility of being able to conceal is an exhibiting. We have to say: which has the *possibility,* because Aristotle emphasizes: ἀληθεύειν ἢ ψεύδεσθαι, either one or the other, but one of the two, the inherent possibility of one or the other, either concealing—or not concealing, but precisely *taking from concealment,* thus not concealing but *revealing*—ἀ-ληθεύειν.

That λόγος, therefore, to whose essence it pertains either to reveal or to conceal, is a pointing out, i.e., apophantic. This possibility characterizes what is meant by apophantic: pointing out. For the λόγος that *conceals* is *also a pointing out.* If this were not the case, in accordance with its inner essence, then it could never become a λόγος that deceives. For precisely whenever I want to pretend something to someone else, I must first already be in a position

5. Ibid., 17a 5ff.
6. Ibid., 17a 2f.

to want to point something out to him. The other person in general must in advance take my discourse as having this tendency to point out; only in this way can I deceive him about something. This indicates the problem in interpreting the essence of the λόγος. We must ask: *In what is this intrinsic possibility of concealing and revealing grounded?* When we have answered this question, we will be able to answer the question: How does that which we designate the 'as'-structure relate to the inner structure of the λόγος? Is the 'as'-structure merely a property of the λόγος, or ultimately something originary: the condition of the possibility of any λόγος in general being what it is?

Before we pursue these questions, let us summarize once more what has been said concerning the λόγος, and at the same time recall our central problem. In all its behaviourally driven activity, the animal is *taken* by whatever it is relating to in this behaviour. That *to which* it stands in relation is thus never given to it in its what-being as such: it is not given as what it is and how it is, *not as a being.* The animal's behaviour is never an apprehending of something as something. Insofar as we address this possibility of taking *something as something* as characteristic of the phenomenon of world, the 'as'-structure is an essential determination of the structure of world. The *'as'* is thereby given as a *possible approach to the problem of world.* We formally traced the 'as'-structure back to the propositional statement. The propositional statement is a normal form of human discourse, a form which, since the first reflections of the philosophy of antiquity, determined not only the theory of discourse, namely logic, but also the study of grammar. If, therefore, we orient our exposition of the problem of the connection between 'as'-structure and assertion around the λόγος, this is not some arbitrary historical interest, but is intended to lead into the elementary nature of the problem. We are considering the problem of the connection between the 'as' and the λόγος, taking our orientation from what Aristotle says about the λόγος. For ancient reflection reaches its apotheosis in Aristotle. He was the first to establish the correct basis for the problem and interpreted it so extensively that we—if we have the eyes to see—can take from him certain guidelines for our problem. Quite broadly, the λόγος, according to Aristotle, is the possibility of *discourse* and of *speaking* in general. From this perspective, it is quite natural for antiquity to take discourse in the broadest sense as an essential moment of man himself, and thereby to define man as ζῷον λόγον ἔχον, a living being that is open for, and can speak out about, that toward which it is open. This is the general character of their conception of the λόγος. The question now is where we are to see the *pervasive* essence of the λόγος. λόγος σημαντικός is an utterance that inherently gives something meaningful, forms a sphere of understandability. The more far-reaching question is: What does σημαντικός mean? Aristotle says: This event is not a natural occurrence, but something that happens on the basis of an *agreement.* The essence of agreement consists in the fact that the genesis of the symbol occurs, which we interpret as the agreement of man with that toward which he comports himself. On the basis of agreement with beings, man can and must come to utter his understanding, form those alliances of sounds which are the coining of meanings, utterances that we call words and vocabulary. *All* discourse is determined by this γένεσις of the σύμβολον. But *not all* discourse is a λόγος ἀποφαντικός, a *propositional* discourse, one which has the tendency *to point out as such* that which is being spoken about. What is it, then, that determines such a λόγος? The fact that ἀληθεύειν ἢ ψεύδεσθαι occurs in it, *revealing* or *concealing*. The λόγος that points out, therefore, is that λόγος which has the intrinsic possibility of revealing and concealing. We must note, however, that this possibility of revealing and concealing is not a contingent property of the λόγος, but its inner essence. The λόγος that points out must point out even when it conceals. In order to make a false judgement, in order to deceive, I must, insofar as I speak discursively, live in a discursive tendency that is concerned with pointing something out. Even concealing is grounded in a tendency to point out. The other person must have taken my discourse as though it were supposed to communicate something to him. The character of this tendency to point out lies at the basis both of revealing and of concealing.

c) Apprehending something as something in forming a unity (σύνθεσις νοημάτων ὥσπερ ἓν ὄντων), the 'as'-structure, as the essential ground of the possibility of the revealing-concealing pertaining to the λόγος as exhibiting.

If we now wish to pursue this structure of the apophantic λόγος more carefully, we must ask how this *specific* λόγος ἀποφαντικός is connected with the *general* essence of the λόγος, namely σημαίνειν. We have heard that the essence of discourse in general, both non-apophantic and apophantic, lies in σημαντικός, in the γένεσις of the σύμβολον, in the occurrence of this fundamental connection of an agreement that holds together. If a discourse becomes *apophantic,* then this σημαντικός must become transformed in the manner indicated, i.e., what happens is *not simply* an agreement *in general* between the meaning and what is intended, rather the meaning and the meaningful content of the λόγος ἀποφαντικός agrees with what is meant *in such a way* that this λόγος as discourse and in its discursivity seeks *to point out* what is meant itself. Discourse now has the tendency *to let* whatever the discourse is about *be seen*—to let it be seen, and this alone. The 'propositional statement' is a kind of discourse which in itself, in accordance with its discursive intention, is either *revealing* or *concealing*. However elementary this characterization may be, it is nevertheless decisive for understanding the whole problem of the λόγος. It also provides a measure of the history of this problem, of the extent to which that history has distanced itself from its fundamental roots up to the present day. All attempts to reform logic must remain merely arbitrary, unless they arise from an engagement with the core of this problematic. To make just one point: Philosophy today, for various reasons, is impelled toward dialectics, and toward a renewal of the dialectical method in the context of a renewal of Hegelian philosophy. Dialectics moves within a speaking—λόγος—and counter-speaking, thesis and antithesis. The possibility of one speaking, one λόγος, being opposed and counter to another λόγος, the ἀντικεῖσθαι of λόγος and λόγος, can be understood only if we know what the λόγος itself is. Only then can we know what dialectic is, and only then can we know whether dialectic is justified and necessary, or whether it is a stopgap measure, perhaps because it does not comprehend the problem of the λόγος. What is permitted today in philosophy and even in theology with respect to this problem exceeds all imagination.

We shall pursue only *one* thread from the problematic of the λόγος, so as to unfold the problem of the 'as' and the 'as a whole'. We arrived at the result that what is distinctive about the λόγος ἀποφαντικός is its ability to reveal or conceal. This *possibility* of doing one or the other constitutes the positive essence of this λόγος. We shall now ask about the *ground* of this essence. What is it that grounds this possibility of either revealing or concealing? How must the λόγος in itself be, in accordance with its innermost essential structure, if it is to have the possibility of revealing or concealing? Aristotle provides us with some information on this (at a point which is not insignificant with respect to the whole problem) in his treatise Περὶ ψυχῆς Γ6.[7] This deals with the essence of life and the levels of living beings (cf. λόγον ἔχον—ἄλογον above). He does not provide this information within his theory of the λόγος ἀποφαντικός as such, then, although it is also mentioned there (see below). It is odd that there is talk of λόγος precisely in this treatise "On the Essence of Life." Yet it is not so odd as soon as we recall that Aristotle grasps the concept of life in a very broad sense that includes the being of plant, animal, and human. Book Three of this treatise deals precisely with living beings in the sense of man. The distinguishing feature of man is the λόγος. And this is why this treatise deals with the λόγος. At this particular point Aristotle provides us with information about what it is that grounds the possibility for the λόγος to be either true or false. He states: ἐν οἷς δὲ καὶ τὸ ψεῦδος καὶ τὸ ἀληθές, σύνθεσίς τις ἤδη νοημάτων ὥσπερ ἓν ὄντων:[8] In the field of that in relation to which both what conceals and what reveals become possible, something like an assembling (a taking together) of whatever is apprehended has already occurred, and in such a way that whatever is apprehended forms

---

7. *Aristotelis De anima.* Ed. W. Biehl. Second edition, Ed. O. Apelt (Leipzig, 1911).
8. Ibid., Γ6, 430a 27f.

314 Fundamental Concepts of Metaphysics [454–56]

a unity as it were. The *ground of the possibility* of revealing or concealing is this *formation of a unity*. Wherever there is revealing or concealing, we have λόγος ἀποφαντικός; and wherever we have the latter—belonging to its inner-most possibility, lying at the basis of that revealing and concealing—we have "synthesis," assembling, taking together (the positing of a together as such; formation of a unity), ap-prehending [*Ver-nehmen*] of a together, unity—namely of whatever is apprehended. At the basis of the λόγος there lies an *apprehending*, νόησις, νοῦς, an apprehending of something—or rather the λόγος *is*, in accordance with its essence, this apprehending of . . . (cf. σύμβολον above). In accordance with its inner possibility, the λόγος is grounded in νοῦς, *ratio* in Latin, which is why this comes to be equated with λόγος, because the latter is νοῦς. The translation of the definition of man as ζῷον λόγον ἔχον by *animal rationale* also comes from this. In short: An *apprehending that forms a unity* (the apprehending formation of unity) is the essential ground of the possibility of revealing or concealing, not only of one or the other, but of the 'either/or' and the 'both . . . and' of these two possibilities. It is thus the essential ground of each of them as such, such as we find them only *in* this 'either/or' or 'both . . . and'.

The question now is: How does Aristotle ground this thesis, and how does he show that revealing and concealing necessarily demand a σύνθεσις as the condition of their possibility? σύνθεσις, in short, is the condition of the possibility of ψεῦδος. Thus Aristotle can state directly: τὸ γὰρ ψεῦδος ἐν συνθέσει ἀεί:[9] Where there is deception (concealment), there we find such apprehending formation of a unity. This is merely what the thesis says. Aristotle immediately grounds this: καὶ γὰρ ἂν τὸ λευκὸν μὴ λευκόν, τὸ μὴ λευκὸν συνέθηκεν:[10] For if someone says, in such a way that he wants to deceive the other person, that something white is *not white*, he has already brought the 'not white' into a unity with white. This 'together' must in general be formed in advance in order to be able to say by way of deception that something is not this or that. In principle we may say that in order to point out something in general—whether as it is or as it is not—i.e., in order to be able to reveal or conceal by way of pointing out, *whatever* is to be pointed out must already *be apprehended* in advance in the *unity of its determinations,* in terms of which and in which it can be determined explicitly in its character *as such and such.* This is why it is already apprehended in advance as this or that. When Aristotle speaks of σύνθεσις in this context, he means what we call the 'as'-structure. This is what he means, though without explicitly penetrating into the dimension of this problem. The *'as'-structure,* the *prior apprehending of something as something in forming a unity,* is the *condition of the possibility* of *truth* and

9. Ibid., Γ6, 430b 1f.
10. Ibid., Γ6, 430b 2f.

falsity of the λόγος. I must already have had the blackboard in view *as* something *unitary* in order to take apart in a judgement what has been apprehended.

In our first introductory and superficial outline of the 'as' we merely said that it appears wherever the propositional statement appears, which for its part is associated with being true or being false. A connection within the λόγος is now becoming clear, such that the 'as'-structure itself is the condition of the possibility of the λόγος ἀποφαντικός, if the latter is indeed distinguished by ἀληθές and ψεῦδος. The 'as' is not some property of the λόγος, stuck on or grafted onto it, but the reverse: the 'as'-structure for its part is in general the condition of the possibility of this λόγος.

d) The apprehension of something as something in forming a unity in the affirmative and negative assertion as a taking together that takes apart (σύνθεσις—διαίρεσις).

We must see things more clearly if we are to make the most of the interpretation of the λόγος we have given so far, oriented toward our particular problem. In Aristotle the 'as' is to be found under the title of σύνθεσις. Yet is this not the same thing as we have already indicated: namely that a *relation* is thought in the 'as'? We now see, however, that σύνθεσις is not simply a relation in the formal sense in which everything is a relation. The 'as' pertains to a σύνθεσις, to a *relating,* and specifically to a σύνθεσις νοημάτων, to a connecting of representations, to the apprehending formation of a unity or a unity-forming apprehension. If, however, the 'as'-structure belongs to such a synthesis—although how remains obscure initially—then we can glean something more from this. The συν means a together, a unity, and manifestly one that is not a piecing together, but an *originary* unity which, earlier than the parts, is a whole. συν—whole—*as a whole?* The 'as'-structure itself thereby shows an essential connection with the second structure we are asking about here: the 'as a whole'.

We shall let the problem rest. For to begin with, our attempt to ascribe the 'as'-structure to σύνθεσις becomes extremely questionable if we note that Aristotle, immediately after pointing out the connection between ψεῦδος and σύνθεσις, states: ἐνδέχεται δὲ καὶ διαίρεσιν φάναι πάντα·[11] Everything that I have pointed out under the title σύνθεσις, one may also call διαίρεσις, *taking apart,* i.e., one may conceive of it as this. To begin with we shall elucidate this with an example, borrowing from what Aristotle himself cites: Something white is not white. A prior taking together of white and not white underlies this.

---

11. Ibid., Γ6, 430b 3f.

And precisely this taking together is also a taking apart. We can only hold one together with the other if this holding together in itself remains a holding apart. The σύνθεσις νοημάτων is inherently, in itself, also already διαίρεσις. Apprehending is intrinsically *a taking together that takes apart*. As such it is the essential ground of the possibility of revealing or concealing pertaining to the λόγος, i.e., the λόγος ἀποφαντικός.

Aristotle concisely expresses this structural connection right at the beginning of his treatise on the λόγος ἀποφαντικός in the following way: περὶ γὰρ σύνθεσιν καὶ διαίρεσίν ἐστι τὸ ψεῦδός τε καὶ τὸ ἀληθές.[12] The revealing and concealing of discourse as pointing out is to be found only where this apprehending occurs that takes together and takes apart. Furthermore, he states in his *Metaphysics:*[13] Both ἀληθές and ψεῦδος are περὶ σύνθεσιν . . . καὶ διαίρεσιν—stand alongside . . . , are dependent upon . . . , are grounded in taking together and taking apart. For σύνθεσις he also uses the expression συμπλοκή or συνάπτειν. The problem is how it is possible that something, namely human comportment, can in itself simultaneously be a taking together and taking apart, not consecutively, but in accordance with their unitary structure. Unfolding this problem means nothing other than interpreting the essence of the 'as', and thereby an essential component of world in general.

We should take careful note of the fact that every ἀληθεύειν of the λόγος ἀποφαντικός is grounded upon σύνθεσις and διαίρεσις, and likewise every ψεύδεσθαι. This insight is of far-reaching significance not merely for our concrete problem in general, but also for interpreting the whole doctrine of λόγος in Aristotle (cf. *De Interpretatione,* Chapter 5). With respect to its fundamental function, Aristotle also refers to the λόγος ἀποφαντικός as ἀπόφανσις for short—pointing out something in and according to what it is or is not (*De Interpretatione,* Chapter 5, 17a 20). The ἁπλῆ ἀπόφανσις accordingly has two fundamental forms: it is either ἀπόφανσίς τινος κατά τινος or ἀπόφανσίς τινος ἀπό τινος. φάσις, the λόγος, is accordingly κατάφασις or ἀπόφασις (*De Interpretatione,* Chapter 5, 17a 23—Chapter 6,a 26). That which points out is either a pointing out that *points toward* or a pointing out that *points away:* The board is black, the board is not red. The pointing out can be such as to *ascribe* something to whatever the pointing out is concerned with, or such as to *deny* it something in pointing it out, i.e., to point something *away* from it: the board is not red. In each case there occurs a pointing out of the board as such, and this pointing out is in each case a *revealing,* a true pointing out. The board is not black, the board is red: here too we have a 'toward' and 'away', in each case a tendency to point out, in each case *concealing,* false. We can see from this that if every true and every false λόγος can be either κατάφασις or ἀπόφασις, and if every true and every false

---

12. *Aristotelis Organon,* ibid. *Hermeneutica (de interpretatione),* Chap. 1, 16a 12f.
13. *Aristotelis Metaphysica,* ibid., E4, 1027b 19.

λόγος is grounded as such in a σύνθεσις-διαίρεσις-apprehending, then the latter also lies at the basis of every κατάφασις and every ἀπόφασις. Every κατάφασις-assertion is in itself σύνθεσις and διαίρεσις, likewise every ἀπόφασις, and it is not as though κατάφασις is a σύνθεσις, and ἀπόφασις a διαίρεσις. These distinctions lie in quite different dimensions. Furthermore, the distinction between σύνθεσις and διαίρεσις is not of the same order as ἀπόφανσις, but rather a distinction that precisely articulates the originary and unitary essence of a structure or a structured phenomenon. This phenomenon is what we are seeking under the title of the 'as'.

On the basis of the development of the doctrine of λόγος that we have outlined so far, we can define the problem *schematically* in order to gain an overview of the intrinsic context. Aristotle takes his starting point from the λόγος in general. The essence of the λόγος is σημαντικός, meaning. From here he proceeds to a specific λόγος, the λόγος ἀποφαντικός. As we have just heard, every propositional statement is either an ascribing or a denying. If we keep to the example of a true judgement, the blackboard is not red. κατάφασις and ἀπόφασις are the two forms of the λόγος ἀποφαντικός. Both forms have the inherent fundamental tendency to point out. Even in a negative statement I wish to say what the board is or is not. The two fundamental forms have the possibility of being true or being false. Being true or false, and thus the entire structure of the λόγος ἀποφαντικός, is grounded in σύνθεσις, which in itself is simultaneously διαίρεσις. The unity of this structure is the essence of νοῦς. We must keep this contextual order of founding in view in order to understand the next part of our interpretation, in the course of which we shall meet a new element that will enable us to unfurl the 'as'-structure as a whole.

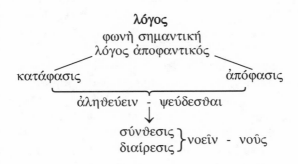

e) The pointing out (ἀπόφανσις) pertaining to assertion as letting beings be seen as what and how they are.

We said by way of introduction that the 'as' is a *relation*. We have now seen, to begin with, that this relating is concerned with a σύνθεσις: it is a relating that *takes together*. Yet not only that. Rather this taking together is *in itself* a *taking apart*. We find not only this dual structure, however, but something else as well: Relating as an action, an activity, an occurrence, is one of νοήματα, a νοεῖν, an *apprehending* (νοῦς), an apprehending taking together and taking apart. This entails that whatever is taken apart is apprehended as such in its togetherness as such. 'a is b'. Let us take another concrete example: This board is badly positioned: the board in its bad position, the board as such and in itself, what it is and how it is. Here we must note that we do not first think of the bad position and then add it to the board, thus subsequently uniting it with the board: the reverse is the case. The board is initially taken in this unity, and on the basis of and with respect to this unity it is then taken apart—yet in such a way that the unity not only remains, but precisely *makes itself known*. σύνθεσις as taking together means: taking with respect to an originary together that already exists and continues to do so (a peculiar kind of unity-forming). Aristotle states:[14] πῶς δὲ τὸ ἅμα ἢ τὸ χωρὶς νοεῖν συμβαίνει, ἄλλος λόγος. λέγω δὲ τὸ ἅμα καὶ τὸ χωρὶς ὥστε μὴ τὸ ἐφεξῆς ἀλλ᾽ ἕν τι γίγνεσθαι: The way in which this νοεῖν occurs, however, which is in an 'at once' and at the same time in a 'separated', i.e., in a taking together and simultaneous taking apart, is the subject of another inquiry; I speak here of an apprehending in an 'at once' and at the same time in a 'separated' in order to show that things do not happen consecutively in this νοεῖν, first the taking together and then the taking apart, but that through this unitary structure a unity emerges. We can therefore say that reason is by its essence unity-forming. Aristotle tells us this in *De Anima*: τὸ δὲ ἕν ποιοῦν, τοῦτο ὁ νοῦς ἕκαστον:[15] The forming of One and of unity in general is in each case the intrinsic task of reason. You can immediately see how far-reaching this whole problem is if I point to the fact that the ἕν is an essential determination of being in general. Where we have the ἕν, there we also find the ὄν. For this reason we already have here a fundamental clue to the question of being.

Yet *what* is it that is apprehended in this apprehending that takes together and takes apart? What is the *fundamental character of whatever is apprehended* and capable of being apprehended as such and in general? We are not to guess the answer to this question, but must catch sight of it from out of the inner structure of the λόγος ἀποφαντικός, namely ἀπόφανσις. The λόγος ἀποφαντικός has two fundamental forms, which Aristotle presents concisely at the beginning of Chapter 6 of *De Interpretatione* in the following way: κατάφασις δέ ἐστιν ἀπόφανσίς τινος κατά τινος. ἀπόφασις δέ ἐστιν ἀπόφανσίς τινος ἀπό τινος. ἐπεὶ δὲ ἔστι καὶ τὸ ὑπάρχον ἀποφαίνεσθαι ὡς μὴ ὑπάρχον καὶ τὸ μὴ ὑπάρχον ὡς ὑπάρχον καὶ τὸ ὑπάρχον ὡς ὑπάρχον

14. Ibid., E4, 1027b 23ff.
15. Aristotelis *De anima*, ibid., Γ6, 430b 5f.

καὶ τὸ μὴ ὑπάρχον ὡς μὴ ὑπάρχον, καὶ περὶ τοὺς ἐκτὸς δὲ τοῦ νῦν χρόνους ὡσαύτως.[16] Pointing out is a pointing toward and pointing away, and there are various possibilities here, which we shall not go into in detail now, but merely treat insofar as we can see a *pervasive fundamental trait* emerge here: Pointing out is pointing out what is at hand as not at hand, what is not at hand as at hand, what is at hand as at hand and what is not at hand as not at hand (formal negative judgement, formal positive as true positive and true negative judgement): what is at hand or not at hand as such or not as such. To put it in a more general way: *Pointing out is letting what is at hand be seen as such.* The being at hand of whatever is at hand, however, as presence, and indeed as constant presence, is what antiquity understood as the being of beings. ἀπόφανσις is *letting beings be seen as beings,* as what and how they are in each case. The assertion, however, is not limited in its pointing out to what is at hand right now. Rather the said possibilities of letting be seen also cover beings outside the time which is now in each case: they do not merely concern τὸ νῦν ὑπάρχειν,[17] but also whatever is past and future.

I shall summarize once more the last steps of the interpretation we have just carried out. I provided a concise illustration of how the pervasive characteristic of the λόγος ἀποφαντικός lies in being true or false, or in the potential for being true or false. We then moved to the question of what grounds the possibility of being true or false. We heard that this possibility is grounded in the fact that the λόγος is in itself a σύνθεσις. We can best elucidate this connection by considering what Aristotle says about the dual structure of the λόγος, namely that every λόγος ἀποφαντικός is either a κατάφασις or ἀπόφασις, i.e., a pointing out that points toward or points away. This has since received the not quite accurate designation of positive or negative judgement. Every pointing toward and pointing away is directed toward its connecting something with something else in advance, so that being true or false is grounded in σύνθεσις. Aristotle says in addition that we can *also* designate σύνθεσις as διαίρεσις. To be able to connect something together, I must simultaneously hold it apart, so that a σύνθεσις and a διαίρεσις lie in every pointing toward. It is not as though the pointing toward, the positive judgement: 'a is b', were merely constituted by a σύνθεσις and the negative judgement: a is not b by a διαίρεσις. The positive judgement is in itself connecting and holding apart, just as the judgement that points away is a holding apart and connecting, so that the inner structure of the λόγος goes back to σύνθεσις and διαίρεσις. We claimed that the latter in turn are linked to what we designated the 'as'-structure. After establishing the schema for the whole construction of the structure of the λόγος, we then proceeded to the question of

16. *Aristotelis Organon,* ibid., *Hermeneutica (de interpretatione),* Chap. 6, 17a 25ff.
17. Ibid., Chap. 3, 16b 9.

what is pointed out in this activity that points out, the question of that *to which* all pointing out relates. Here we saw that all pointing out is either the pointing out of something at hand as at hand, or of something not at hand as something not at hand, or of something not at hand as at hand, or finally of something at hand as not at hand. All these variations relate to what is at hand with respect to how it is at hand or not at hand; they relate to whatever is at hand not only in the way it is at hand precisely now, but also in the way it was or will be at hand. Pointing out is therefore ἀποφαίνεσθαι, bringing something into view, and doing so for our seeing that understands and for our grasping. It is a bringing into view of what is at hand in the way in which it is at hand. The being at hand of whatever is at hand, however, is grasped as the presence of something, and ever since antiquity the presence of something has been regarded as the proper meaning of what we designate as being. ἀπόφανσις, the fundamental accomplishment of the λόγος, is a bringing into view of beings in how and what they are as beings. The assertion is not just limited to whatever is present now, but also relates to what has been and to what will be.

f) Summary of the essential definition of the simple assertion and the determination of its individual components (ὄνομα, ῥῆμα).

Aristotle therefore summarizes the *essential definition of the simple assertion* as follows: ἔστι θὲ ἡ μὲν ἁπλῆ ἀπόφανσις φωνὴ σημαντικὴ περὶ τοῦ ὑπάρχειν τι ἢ μὴ ὑπάρχειν, ὡς οἱ χρόνοι διῄρηνται:[18] The simple assertion is therefore an utterance that means something, and that asserts something while referring, in that it deals with something being at hand or not being at hand, and does so in the manner of holding the *tempora* apart in each case— i.e., grammatically: present, perfect, or future.

From the perspective of this unitary structure of the λόγος ἀποφαντικός we are first able to comprehend what Aristotle asserts concerning the individual *components* of the λόγος. His characterization of these components later passed over into logic and the study of grammar. The components of the assertion are, as we usually say, subject and predicate. Aristotle initally calls them something else: ὄνομα and ῥῆμα. In each case we find time as a criterion for distinguishing the two. To put it more precisely, in the case of one (ῥῆμα) being-in-time belongs to its meaning, indeed essentially so; in the other case (ὄνομα) no such meaning is associated with it. ὄνομα means the word, the name, that which names something. We call it the noun, although this expression can be distorting, since a verb can also assume the function of a noun. What in fact is an ὄνομα, a name, or better a word that merely names some-

---

18. Ibid., Chap. 5, 17a 22ff.

thing? Ὄνομα μὲν οὖν ἐστὶ φωνὴ σημαντικὴ κατὰ συνθήκην ἄνευ χρόνου, ἧς μηδὲν μέρος ἐστὶ σημαντικὸν κεχωρισμένον:[19] Naming, however, is an utterance that is meaningful on the basis of an agreement, without referring to time as such in naming. It is simultaneously a φωνὴ σημαντικὴ, a totality of sounds, of which no individual part taken by itself means anything. Aristotle illustrates this characteristic by referring to the Greek name Kallippos, in German *Schönpferd* [beautiful horse]. The individual syllables and parts of the whole word mean nothing when taken by themselves in this context, because the unitary name in itself also has a unitary meaning: what is referred to is a particular human being with this name, whereas καλὸς ἵππος is a λόγος insofar as the word can be broken down into the statement: The horse is beautiful. Here the individual parts of the λόγος in each case mean something by themselves. Much more essential to this interpretation of naming is that Aristotle says that naming is a meaning without time. How he understands this we can see from the opposing definition of the second component of the λόγος, namely ῥῆμα. Ῥῆμα δέ ἐστι τὸ προσσημαῖνον χρόνον, οὗ μέρος οὐδὲν σημαίνει χωρίς, καὶ ἔστιν ἀεὶ τῶν καθ᾽ ἑτέρου λεγομένων σημεῖον:[20] A saying, a verb, is what refers to time in addition, something to whose essence it belongs to refer to time in addition, namely in addition to what is otherwise referred to in the verb; it is always a meaning which is meaningful in such a way as to be related to whatever is being spoken about. In accordance with its intrinsic meaning, every verb is thus concerned with something that the discourse is about, something underlying as a being, as such and such a being. Thus we can see that the ῥῆμα is distinguished from the ὄνομα by the criterion of time. Although Aristotle did not pursue this any further, there is indeed a quite decisive insight here. The two essential elements characterising the verb are that it also refers to time, and in its meaning is always related to something that the discourse is about, namely to beings. This indicates that all positing of beings is necessarily related to time. In keeping with this, we therefore call the verb a time-word [*Zeitwort*] in German. These are the two structural moments of the λόγος which are important for the problem we are about to meet.

If every assertion is therefore a pointing out of beings according to what and how they *are,* then in such propositional discourse there is somehow always necessarily discourse concerning the *being* of beings—whether of being now, having been, or coming to be. The fact that there is discourse concerning *beings in their being* in the assertion is expressed linguistically by the 'is'. Yet even where the latter is lacking—the board sits badly, the bird flies away—the ῥῆμα (verb) not

---

19. Ibid., Chap. 2, 16a 19f.
20. Ibid., Chap. 3, 16b 6ff.

only has a particular temporal form in each case, but this form also already means a specific *being-in-time* of whatever the discourse is about.

g) Connectedness (σύνθεσις) as the meaning of the 'is' in the assertion.

As a pointing out, the assertion is a pointing toward or pointing away, and so in each case a revealing or concealing. What is revealed or concealed in each case are beings as beings that are or are not such and such. In this discursive form, the discourse is in each case about beings, and yet the discourse is also always of *being*—of the 'is'. The propositional discourse is not, in general, *about* being, yet it is *of being,* of beings as they are, in their being. The Greeks express this incisively in the following way. In the assertion there is discourse concerning the ὄντα ὡς ὄντα, beings as they in each case are as beings, beings with respect to themselves. We say at first, in a consciously ambivalent way: there is discourse of beings as beings. At the same time, however, Aristotle, in a context central to metaphysics, speaks of an investigation aimed at the ὂν ᾗ ὄν, which we again express formally by: Beings as beings. In the first instance I am directed toward beings themselves; I confine myself to their qualities. In the second instance, on the other hand, when I consider beings insofar as they are beings, I am not investigating their properties, but take them insofar as they *are,* with respect to the fact that they are determined by their *being.* I consider them with respect to their being. The assertion refers to beings, and the revealing and concealing is directed toward them. And yet being is concomitantly understood and referred to—not as an aside or afterthought, but precisely in that which is revealing, e.g., "the snow is alternating." The *'is'* here plays a central role. The 'is' thus proves to be an essential structural moment of the assertion, and this is already expressed in the designation given to the 'is' in logic. In linguistic theory the 'is' is the *copula,* the tie or nexus, that which connects subject and predicate. However, that which is linguistic is meaningful in itself. What is referred to in it? Where do we find *what is referred to?*

Let us remember what our interpretation of the λόγος ἀποφαντικός has given us so far: σύνθεσις and διαίρεσις as the condition of the possibility of ἀληθεύειν and ψεύδεσθαι, and this in each case in the form of κατάφασις or ἀπόφασις. All this is grounded in a νοεῖν, a pointing out that apprehends, indeed—as we saw—a pointing out of ὑπάρχον, of beings, and indeed in various tempora. Finally: in all this pointing out and apprehending comportment toward beings in discourse, a guiding understanding of the 'is', of being (not only of beings), manifests itself. *Where does such 'being' belong?* How does it stand within the whole structure of the λόγος? In particular, how does it relate to what we came to know as the fundamental structure—to σύνθεσις and διαίρεσις, to the 'as'? How do things stand concerning the 'is', the copula?

First of all, it is not superfluous to emphasize that—however unlikely the problem of what the 'is' means may appear—we stand at a decisive point, one that is decisive in two senses. [1.] We have already seen in general that the λόγος in the broadest sense, as discourse and language, as the distinction of man, evidently has to do with *world*. This must indeed be so if *world-formation* is likewise distinctive for man, or is such as to harbour within it the possibility of language. Wherever there is world, we find a comportment toward beings as beings. Wherever beings are manifest in such a way, they can be dealt with as something that is, is not, has been, or will be. Something like *being* can be said of beings in a strangely *manifold way*. Precisely this fact that in the λόγος, in language, and thereby within man's formation of world, being can be said, is what the simple assertion expresses in the 'is'. From here we can understand why the assertion—precisely because it carries the 'is' up front—was able to achieve central significance for metaphysics, which asks concerning being. However, for the very reason that the λόγος, distinguished by this 'is', seems to have a central metaphysical significance, the point at which *we* have arrived is decisive in a second sense. [2.] We must ask and clarify whether the assertion should be allowed to play the leading role in the question concerning being, concerning the essence of world and so on, just because being and the 'is' so prominently come to light in it, or whether, *conversely,* it is not a matter of seeing that this prominent form of being, the 'is', indeed rightly and necessarily contains being as manifest, but that this manifestness is *not originary.* In short, metaphysics is decided by our position with respect to the problem of the copula, the manner and way in which we deal with it, and how we fit it into the whole. We know that metaphysics since Aristotle has oriented the problem of being toward the 'is' of the proposition, and that we are faced with the massive task of unhinging this tradition, which simultaneously means: demonstrating its limited legitimacy. You can see from here the far-reaching significance of what is apparently this special problem concerning the dry question of what is meant by the 'is' in the proposition.

Before we systematically develop this problem according to the perspectives that are important for us, we should first examine how far-seeing Aristotle was here, and whether this strange 'is' in the proposition came to his attention here. I shall attempt to provide a brief interpretation of the conception of the 'is' and of being in Aristotle. This should also give you some estimation of how, in these simple interpretations from antiquity, which cannot be related at all to the contemporary literary nonsense in philosophy, the most central problems are seized upon with an assurance and with a power that we ourselves as epigones can never again achieve.

We shall initially let Aristotle himself provide us with an answer to the question of how the 'is' stands within the λόγος and what it properly means. Aristotle formulates this answer in his conclusion to Chapter 3 of the treatise *De Interpretatione:* Αὐτὰ μὲν οὖν καθ᾿ ἑαυτὰ λεγόμενα τὰ ῥήματα ὀνόματά ἐστι καὶ σημαίνει τι (ἵστησι γὰρ ὁ λέγων τὴν διάνοιαν, καὶ ὁ ἀκούσας ἠρέμησεν), ἀλλ᾿ εἰ ἔστιν ἢ μή, οὔπω σημαίνει· οὐδὲ γὰρ τὸ εἶναι ἢ μὴ εἶναι σημεῖόν ἐστι τοῦ πράγματος, οὐδ᾿ ἂν τὸ ὂν εἴπῃς αὐτὸ καθ᾿ ἑαυτὸ ψιλόν. αὐτὸ μὲν γὰρ οὐδέν ἐστι, προσσημαίνει δὲ σύνθεσίν τινα, ἣν ἄνευ τῶν συγκειμένων οὐκ ἔστι νοῆσαι.[21] Translating, and at the same time elucidating, what Aristotle says here is: If we enunciate the time-words in and by themselves, i.e., if instead of "the bird flies" we merely say "flying," then they are nouns which name: 'flying', 'standing', and they mean something. For whoever says or speaks such words in and by themselves—flying—ἵστησι τὴν διάνοιαν, that person brings thought to a standstill, whereas thought is otherwise always a thinking *through,* is always in motion in the form of asserting: this or that is such and such. (This is why propositional and judgemental thinking is also called διανοεῖν by Aristotle: a thinking that passes through, that proceeds from one thing to another). In merely naming, I do not pass from one thing over to another, but rather thinking stops alongside something and remains standing there; it refers to whatever is named itself. Thinking does not run *through.* Correspondingly, whoever hears such words pauses (ἠρέμησεν), he rests by that which is named, he does not proceed to something else in the manner in which 'a is b' proceeds. Taken by themselves, therefore, these ways of naming are indeed not without meaning, and yet they do not yet mean, do not yet refer to the fact that what is named, 'flying', is or is not. The words, employed in these ways of naming, do not say that something flies or is flying. Yet what is it that is missing when the verb is used merely as an infinitive, as a name and noun, as it were: flying like a bird, as distinct from *is* flying? What is referred to by this 'is' that is added on or can be expressed in the form of a verb? Aristotle says negatively, to begin with, that the εἶναι and μὴ εἶναι, this being and not being, do not refer to πρᾶγμα at all, to beings that are such and such, to some matter or thing—not even if you say and name something as being a being [*Seiend-sein*] in itself and purely for itself. For being in itself is nothing (αὐτὸ μὲν γὰρ οὐδέν ἐστι; being and nothing the same). This says that *being is not a being,* not a thing, nor any thingly property, nothing at hand. Yet it does mean something; when I say 'is' and 'is not', I understand something by it after all. Yet what does τὸ εἶναι mean? To begin with, meaning is also-meaning-in-addition, is σύνθεσίν τινα, a *certain synthesis,* connecting, uniting, unity. This unity, i.e., being, however, cannot be apprehended and understood without συγκείμενα, without that which *lies together, lies together before us,* that which I can refer to *as* together.

From this brief yet quite fundamental interpretation of the meaning of being qua 'is' in Aristotle, we shall take three things: [1.] The guiding meaning of the 'is' is *meaning-in-addition.* It is not an independent meaning, such as the naming of something. Rather in its meaningful function as such, the meaning of being and 'is' is already related to something that is. [2.] In that which means-in-addition, the 'is' means *synthesis, connectedness, unity.* [3.] The 'is' does not mean πρᾶγμα, *does not mean some matter* or thing.

Precisely this same interpretation of the 'is' was provided, centuries later, by Kant, perhaps without his knowing this place in Aristotle, yet while being guided by the tradition, which he then managed to grasp more profoundly in this interpretation of the copula. Kant deals with being in general and in particular with the 'is', the copula, in two places: [1.] In his short essay of 1763, his so-called pre-critical period, entitled "The Sole Possible Grounds for Demonstrating the Existence of God." [2.] In the *Critique of Pure Reason* (1781, 1787), namely in the Transcendental Doctrine of Elements, Second Part (The Transcendental Logic), Second Division (The Transcendental Dialectic), Book II (The Dialectical Inferences of Pure Reason), Chapter 3 (The Ideal of Pure Reason), Section 4 (The Impossibility of an Ontological Proof of the Existence of God), A592ff., B 620ff. In the *Critique of Pure Reason,* Kant speaks of the 'is' and being in the same context as in the first essay.

Kant's interpretation is consistent with that of Aristotle with respect to the two main points that he makes in the same way as Aristotle: Being is not the determination of some thing, or, as Kant puts it: Being is not a real predicate. 'Real' here means: not pertaining to a *res,* to a matter or thing. Furthermore, he says: Being, insofar as it is used in the sense of the 'is' in the assertion, is a connecting concept, synthesis, or, as he also puts it, *respectus logicus,* a logical relation, i.e., one belonging to and grounded in the λόγος. The analysis in the first section of the 1763 essay is entitled: 'Of existence in general'.[22] Kant here understands by the term 'existence' [*Dasein*] what we call being at hand, existing, in the sense that existence "is not at all the predicate or determination of any thing."[23] In the second part of the first section Kant says: "The concept of position or positing is completely straightforward and identical to that of being in general."[24] Kant thus says that being means positing, or better: being posited. He continues: "Now, something can be thought as posited merely relatively, or better, we can merely think the relation (*respectus logicus*) of something as a

22. Kant, 'Der einzig mögliche Beweisgrund zur Demonstration des Daseins Gottes'. *Immanuel Kants Werke.* Ed. E. Cassirer. Vol. 2 (Berlin, 1922), pp. 74ff. [Trans. G. Treash, *The One Possible Basis for a Demonstration of the Existence of God* (New York: Abaris Books, 1979), pp. 53ff.]
23. Ibid., p. 76.
24. Ibid., p. 77.

feature of a thing, and being, i.e., the position of this relation, is then nothing other than the connecting concept in a judgement."[25] What Kant is talking about here is the Aristotelian σύνθεσις in the λόγος. "If we consider not merely this relation, but the matter posited in and of itself, then such being means as much as existence."[26] If, therefore, I use the 'is' not in the sense of a copula, but as in the sentence "God is," then it means as much as existence, existing. "This concept is so straightforward that one cannot say anything to unwrap it, other than to take care that it is not confused with the relations that things have to their features. When one perceives that our entire knowledge ultimately ends in concepts that cannot be resolved, then one will also comprehend that there will be a few concepts that are virtually irresolvable, i.e., whose features are scarcely clearer or simpler than the matter itself. This is the case with our explanation of existence. I readily concede that it has only clarified the concept it has tried to explain to a very limited extent. However, the nature of the object in relation to the faculty of our understanding allows no greater degree of clarification."[27] Clarifying the concept and essence of being must be content to ascertain: being = position, or being in the sense of the 'is' = relation.

What particularly concerns us here, however, and must be striking, is that the structural moment of the λόγος, the 'is', the copula, has—according to Aristotle's interpretation—the character of a σύνθεσις. As we heard *earlier,* the potential for being true or false (ἀληθεύειν and ψεύδεσθαι), i.e., the fundamental properties of the assertion, go back to a σύνθεσις. The question arises of whether this σύνθεσις in which the essence of the copula consists is the same σύνθεσις that grounds the λόγος in general in accordance with its inner possibility. If this is the case, then does διαίρεσις also belong to the σύνθεσις of the copula? If 'being' is connectedness, it also means being taken apart. What, then, does being mean in general, such that determinations like connectedness and being taken apart pertain to it? Where do they spring from? The theory of the λόγος thus leads directly into the most central problems of metaphysics. We are not, however, as Kant thinks, faced with ultimate concepts that resist further analysis.

h) What-being, that-being, and being true as possible interpretations of the copula. The undifferentiated manifold of these meanings as the primary essence of the copula.

Despite the fact that precisely the Aristotelian theory of the λόγος ἀποφαντικός became and remained definitive for the ensuing tradition of

25. Ibid.
26. Ibid.
27. Ibid., p. 77f.

logic, subsequent and more recent theories are very diverse precisely with respect to the way in which the *copula,* the 'is', is conceived. Although it would be very instructive, we cannot discuss even the major theories in detail here. However, we shall try to explicate the *possible interpretations of the copula* by way of a concrete example, not in order to prove that philosophers always and everywhere have different opinions, but in order to ask whether this manifold of theories is arbitrary, or whether this manifold springs from the essence of what the theories deal with. Does the 'is' itself give rise to this manifold? Is it inherently equivocal? Is this equivocality necessary, and what is it grounded in? If we pursue these questions in the correct way, we shall return with an improved understanding for the main problem: What is the relation of the 'is' to the overall structure of the λόγος ἀποφαντικός and to what conditions it—to σύνθεσις and διαίρεσις, and to the 'as' (being and 'as')?

Let us first, by way of a simple example, attempt to explicate the *manifold of possible interpretations of the copula,* without going into the individual theories in any great historical detail. We shall choose as an example the statement: "This board is black." How do things stand concerning the 'is'? What does it mean, what does it refer to? What *meaning* does it have? If we ask quite *naively* in the direction of our ordinary understanding, for example, the situation appears to be as follows: We have before us the statement: This board is black. Here we see that the 'is' lies between the subject-term and the predicate-term, and does so in such a way as to connect the one with the other. The 'is' functions as a "connection." This is why it is called the copula. This naming of the 'is' as copula is not a harmless way of naming it, but a particular interpretation of it, oriented toward the way in which the term functions in the structure of the statement. The initial question here does not concern what this 'is' and being mean, but concerns the meaning of the 'is' in the sense of what function the 'is' has, what role it plays in the sentence structure. If one takes the propositional statement in this way, as a given word-structure, then the 'is' indeed appears as a copula. However, when Aristotle and Kant say that the εἶναι and the 'is' are σύνθεσις and a connecting concept, then there is more at stake here than merely characterizing the 'is' with respect to its position as a term in the word-structure of the statement. There is "more" at stake—and yet, when taken as a 'connection', the 'is' is *also* oriented toward the linguistic function of the term. 'Is' and being then mean connectedness, 'is' means: something is connected with, stands in connection with (*respectus logicus*). If we repeat the statement: The board is black, then according to this interpretation we ought to be referring to the fact that the board and black stand in a connectedness. The board's being black means a *connectedness* of black and board.

Is this what we are referring to when we straightforwardly make this statement? Yes and no. Yes, insofar as we are referring to the board's being black. No, insofar as in our everyday saying and understanding the statement we do not specifically think of the connectedness of the two as such. We find the interpretation that the 'is' refers to a connectedness at once too contrived and far-fetched. In part—disregarding the fact that we are factically orienting our interpretation around formal logic in its questionableness—this is linked to the fact that the statement chosen as an example is perhaps altogether too contrived and hackneyed to serve as an example—a statement that we seldom or indeed never tend to make in our immediate factical existence [*Dasein*] here in this room. A better example is the statement: The board is badly positioned. You and I have perhaps already made this statement, if only to ourselves. In so doing—in making the statement spontaneously for ourselves—we are not thinking of any connectedness of the board to its unfavourable position. The board is badly positioned.

In all such interpretations, we are still sticking too closely to the linguistic form of the enunciated statement and failing to pay attention to what we are directly referring to. Only by looking at what is directly understood, therefore, will we manage to grasp the genuine meaning of the 'is'. Initially, we are not contesting the fact that the 'is' indeed ultimately has to do with something like synthesis and connection. If we take up the first example again, 'The board is black', and if, in keeping with this, we try to understand the statement directly, then we are inclined to take the 'is' (being) in a different way. In what sense is being expressed in the 'is'? Evidently, in the sense of *what* the board *is,* its *what-being*. The what-being of something is also designated as its essence. But does the statement 'The board is black' state the essence of the board, i.e., does it state what belongs to a board as such and in general? By no means. The board could be and can be a board, i.e., it could be to hand as something we use and as an item of equipment, even if it were white—we would only need to write on it with black or blue chalk. Being black does not necessarily belong to a thing being able to serve as a board, it does not belong to the possibility of its being a board. The statement in question, then, does not state what-being qua essence, but it does state something that the board is: its *being such and such.* Being such and such is not equivalent to what-being (essence). However, there are statements whose linguistic construction is entirely identical, and which express such a thing: 'The circle is round'. If we note this distinction, and at the same time keep in view both possibilities of saying what-being, grasping them formally as *what-being* in the broad sense (which does not necessarily mean essence), then we can see that the thesis that the 'is' refers to what-being in this broad sense is closer to the primary meaning of the 'is'. This interpretation thus provides a more workable basis for a more extensive interpretation of the copula. Thus the English philosopher Hobbes developed a theory of the copula which is especially significant in the history of logic. He says quite generally: *oratio constans ex duobus nominibus:*[28] The Logos is something that consists of two words. *nomina [copulata] quidem in animo excitant cogitationem unius et ejusdem rei:*[29] The *copulatio*—copula— leads thinking and referring toward one and the same thing. The 'is' does not simply connect words, but concentrates its meaning on one and the same being. The copula is no mere connecting of words, but intervenes in the meaning of the words of an assertion, organizes them around *one* thing, makes them connected in this deeper sense. It thereby accomplishes something specific with respect to the inner construction of the logos. Hobbes says: Copulatio *autem cogitationem inducit causae propter quam ea nomina illi rei imponuntur.*[30] The *copulatio,* in this peculiar concentrating of the meaning of the subject and predicate upon one and the same thing, provides the reason why the sequence of names refer to one and the same thing. Accordingly, the copula is not the sign of a mere connection, but points to that *in which* the connectedness is grounded. In what is it grounded? It is grounded in *what* the thing is, in its *quid* (what), in its *quidditas.* Whatever the attitude we take toward the details of this theory, which presents major difficulties in other respects, the important thing about it is that it indicates how the meaning of the 'is' in respect of its ground points back to those beings as such (the blackboard) which the assertion is about, and that it refers to these beings as the ground of the belonging together of what is connected in the statement. The meaning of the 'is' points back to beings as such in their what, *essence* and *being-such.*

The interpretation just outlined of the 'is' in the sense of what-being points in the direction of a further interpretation of the 'is' which, however one-sided it may be, touches upon something decisive. If we take an assertion in which what-being in the sense of essence is stated, such as the statement "The circle is round," then one can also interpret such a statement as follows: "By circle we understand something round," which is to say: "The word 'circle' means something round." The 'is' does not now tell us what a being whose meaning is referred to in itself is, rather the 'is' means the equivalent of: "The word means"—the circle is: the word 'circle' *means.* The fact that this interpretation is a very narrow one is indicated by the fact that it does not at all fit our example. By 'The board is black' we certainly do not intend to say that the word 'board' means 'being black'. Indeed, the interpretation is not even adequate in the case of the assertion 'The circle is round'. Nonetheless, we may not exclude this interpretation altogether, because there is indeed the possibility of understanding a statement such as "The circle is round" not merely im-

28. Thomas Hobbes, *Elementorum philosophiae sectio prima. De corpore, pars prima, sive Logica. Cap. III, 2. Opera philosophica, quae latine scripsit, omnia.* Ed. G. Molesworth (London, 1839ff.). Vol. 1, p. 27.

29. Ibid., *cap.* III, 3, p. 28.

30. Ibid.

mediately and directly, in the direction of the being referred to in it, but also in relation to the statement itself as a statement, or in the direction of the words used in it. "The circle"—is round: The theme now is not what is referred to in the subject of the assertion, but the subject-term as a word that is meaningful and whose meaning is now provided by the assertion. The circle is round, 'circle' means something round, the word 'circle' means. . . . However contrived we may find this interpretation, it has played a major role in logic under the title *nominalism*. It is primarily oriented toward the linguistic and meaningful character of the statement and not toward that which the statement itself refers to, not toward the relation to beings themselves.

Let us, however, return anew to our example 'The board is black'. The 'is' expresses and refers to the board's being such and such. The board is not any arbitrary board, however, for instance some board that I am imagining right now, but which is not at hand; nor does it refer to a board that was perhaps once at hand somewhere and is now no longer at hand. Rather it is the board *at hand* right here and now that '*is*' black. The 'is' in the statement does not only refer to something's being *constituted* in such and such a way, but also to the board's *being* constituted, its being *at hand* in such and such a way, i.e., it refers also to the fact that the board at hand is at hand as black. In this case, the 'is' also refers to the blackboard's *being at hand,* even though we do not necessarily think specifically of this. One could of course say: This statement is intended to say that the board is black and not red. What is at stake is only the way the board is constituted. However, precisely in any possible dispute over how it is constituted, it becomes clear that in order to decide, we have recourse to this board at hand as such and to what is at hand in it. In other words, in the assertion 'The board is black', we have always already had recourse to the board as this one at hand, and we are referring to *its being* constituted as a board that is *at hand.*

We have now already extracted two *fundamental meanings* of the 'is', if we disregard the first meaning of the 'is' as connection and the meaning of the 'is' as 'it means', which we also mentioned. The two fundamental meanings are, on the one hand, *what-being* in the broader sense of being such and such, and in the narrower sense of essential being, and on the other hand the 'is' in the sense of *being at hand.* We shall see that with these two fundamental meanings of the 'is', which always belong together in some form or other, we have not yet exhausted the ultimate content of the copula—indeed, there is one quite central meaning that we are not yet familiar with. Only when we have elaborated this meaning will we be in a position to understand the enigmatic essence of this unlikely 'is' in its full richness and also in its overall problematic.

To begin with, we shall provide a summary of what has been said so far about the copula. We became acquainted with the structural moment that bears the name copula, and which commonly finds its linguistic expression in the form of the 'is'. We asked what is meant by this 'is' and in general by being as referred to in it. We then summarized the Aristotelian analysis in three points: [1.] The 'is' has a meaning in the specific form of meaning that Aristotle designates as προσσημαίνειν, 'meaning in addition'; what is referred to in the meaning is essentially related to something else which is to be grasped in what is referred to. [2.] The specific content of the 'is', of being, is a σύνθεσις, a certain kind of connectedness, a together. [3.] What is referred to in the 'is' is not some πρᾶγμα, not some thing, not something at hand of which we could say that it is such and such. Following this, we compared the analysis of the copula with the interpretation of the 'is' provided by Kant in the two places mentioned. If we survey in general the entire tradition of logic in the narrower sense, we notice essential distinctions in the way in which the 'is' is conceived, distinctions which point back to an equivocality of the copula, so that the question arises of where this polysemy comes from. Is it merely due to a multiplicity of conceptions, or does this equivocality of the 'is' reside in the 'is' itself as something necessarily demanded by it? In order to shed light on these questions, we attempted to characterize the main meaning of the 'is' by recourse to typical interpretations that have emerged in the course of the history of logic and metaphysics. We took as our basis the trivial example 'The board is black'. From this we saw: [1.] The 'is' is determined as the linguistic coupling of subject-term and predicate-term, a conception which leads to the 'is' receiving the name and designation of copula or connection. [2.] This approach to interpreting the 'is' in terms of its linguistic function of connecting also points toward an interpretation of the 'is' in respect of its specific meaning. Accordingly, Aristotle and Kant say that the 'is' means connectedness, being connected—although what it is that is connected remains unclarified. If we consider more concretely the intention of the statement 'This board is black', however, the 'is' then means being, it means *what* that which is spoken about *is*. [3.] We can therefore say that the 'is' means *what-being,* whereby a distinction emerges between a thing's being constituted in such and such a way and that which belongs to its essence. [4.] We saw the 'is' in the sense of 'it is called', 'it means'. In such assertions or interpretations of the assertion we do not think of the subject as the being itself that is referred to in the subject-term (this board or this thing), rather the subject in this statement is the subject-*term* as such; the word 'board' says and means such and such. [5.] In saying 'This board is black', we are not merely referring to the fact that this board in general is constituted this way as a board, but that this board at hand is at hand as constituted in this particular way, so that the 'is' also means *being at hand.* The 'is' refers to that being as we inquire about it when we ask *whether* something is. To this question of whether it is, we reply *that* it is or *that* it is not, so that we may also designate this meaning of being as *that-being.*

The meanings that lie in this unlikely 'is', and are already referred to in it in an unlikely and self-evident way, are thus accumulating. And yet we have so far overlooked one further and quite central meaning. It comes to light if the statement 'The board is black' is emphasized and spoken accordingly: 'The board *is* black'. We are now referring not only to being such and such, nor only to the being at hand of whatever is such and such. Rather we are also referring to the fact that what I am saying here and expressing in this statement *is true*. The board *is truly* black. The 'is' thus also means the *being true* of whatever is said in the statement. If we leave aside the more extreme and superficial forms of the 'is' and concentrate on those which spring *from its inner content-matter,* we may now say that what is referred to in the 'is' is what-being, whether in the form of being such and such and of essential being, or of that-being and being true.

The last-named meaning of the 'is' also became a point of departure for various theories, particularly prevalent today, concerning the copula, the λόγος, and judgement in general. It has been said that something is affirmed in such statements, the board's being black is affirmed, and so the 'is' properly expresses this affirmation. What is affirmed in this affirming is the fact that whatever is spoken of *is valid,* so that the 'is' also comes to be interpreted as *validity* and *being valid.* The theory of judgement has been developed in this direction by Lotze, and subsequently by Windelband, Rickert, and Lask. Especially in the case of Rickert, this interpretation of the judgement as expressing a validity became an approach for developing a value-philosophy. Rickert said: If a validity is affirmed in the judgement, then this is only possible if validity has a standard; everything valid must be measured by what ought to be. An 'ought' can only be in force and binding as 'ought' if it is grounded upon a value. The orientation toward value-philosophy thus arises in this way.

None of the theories that have arisen concerning the 'is' and being in the proposition are correct, because they are one-sided. Yet why are they one-sided? Because they fail to see and to take account of the multiplicity of meanings pertaining to the 'is'. Will we therefore attain a true theory by assembling all the interpretations that have emerged and by achieving a compromise? Things are not so simple. What is at stake is to see something far more essential. It is not a matter of seeing that all these meanings—what-being, that-being, and being true—are to be found and may be found in the 'is', but rather the fact *that* they all *must* be found in it and *why* they must be found in it, at first and for the most part in an *unarticulated* and undifferentiated way. It is a matter of comprehending this peculiar *undifferentiatedness* and *universality* of the 'is' as the originary and primary essence of the copula or of what is superficially designated the copula. It is by no means the case, therefore, that the 'is' at first merely means *copulatio* (the linking of words) and that the other meanings then accrue to it one after the other, rather the converse is the case:

What is *originary and primary* is, and constantly remains, the *full undifferentiated manifold* out of which, from time to time and in particular cases and discursive tendencies of the assertion, only one meaning or one predominant meaning is referred to. The originary yet unarticulated and unaccentuated multiplicity of what *being* already means in advance in each case becomes a particular meaning via limitation, whereby the whole multiplicity that is already inter alia understood is not eliminated, but precisely also posited. To the extent that a concept of being is achieved, it begins in one or more of these meanings. Limitation is always subsequent to the originary whole. For now, we may only assess the implications of this insight into the multiformity of the essence of the copula in one particular direction—a direction that immediately leads us back into the *guiding* problem that we had *meanwhile suspended.*

§73. Return to the ground of the possibility of the structure of assertion as a whole.

a) Indication of the connection between our inquiring back and the guiding problem of world.

I shall briefly outline once more *the way in which we have thus far unfolded the problem of world. World* is the *manifestness of beings as such as a whole.* We are asking concerning the *'as'* in order to penetrate from there into the phenomenon of world. The 'as' is something distinctive about that which human Dasein is open for, in contrast to the animal's being open for. . . . In the case of the animal, being open for . . . is being taken by . . . in captivation. This 'as' belongs to a *relating.* The kind of relation and its dimension are obscure. However, the 'as' is after all connected to the *assertion.* Accordingly, we attempted to elucidate, by providing an interpretation of such assertion, how the 'as' belongs to the structure of assertion. Our interpretation of the assertion with respect to Aristotle revealed that all essential structures—κατάφασις, ἀπόφασις, ἀληθεύειν, ψεύδεσθαι—are traced back to σύνθεσις and διαίρεσις. This enigmatic collection of mutually exclusive kinds of relating remained obscure and enigmatic for us. Presumably the relation belonging to the 'as' is to be found here. As well as κατάφασις and ἀπόφασις, however, the assertion is equally always an assertion about . . . , λόγος τινός (Plato). What ἀπόφανσις as a form relates to is *beings.* Their *being* appears in a multiplicity of discursive forms in the assertion, as expressed by the *'is'.* According to Aristotle, we likewise find a σύνθεσις here. 'Being' and its multiplicity, as well as the 'as', are accordingly also grounded in this enigmatic σύνθεσις and διαίρεσις. Or, to put it more cautiously, 'being' and the 'as' point to the same origin. In other words, *the elucidation of the essence of the 'as' goes together with the question concerning the essence of the 'is', of being. Both questions serve to unfold the problem of world.* We can already clarify this at this stage from our provisional formal analysis of the concept of world: manifestness of beings as such. This entails manifestness of beings as beings, i.e., with respect to their being. The 'as' and the relation that sustains and forms it makes possible a perspective upon something like being. The question of how things stand regarding being cannot be posed without asking about the essence of the 'as', and vice-versa. We have to ponder which question merits a methodological privilege on the level of factical exposition. The direct question concerning the 'as' and the relation sustaining it always led us straight into obscurity. Only a detour via the λόγος provided an insight into its manifold structures (why this is the case need not occupy us now). It thus seems appropriate to continue along this path, especially since it has led us to the question concerning being in the shape of the copula. It is now a matter of getting a view of the whole of the λόγος-structure and *inquiring back into the ground of its possibility* (σύνθεσις—διαίρεσις), and of doing so via the guiding thread of the 'is' pertaining to the λόγος-structure, the 'is' taken in the multiplicity of its initially undifferentiated meanings.

And yet—can we inquire back behind the assertion? Is it not something ultimate? On the other hand, however, we have heard about components of the λόγος—ὄνομα, ῥῆμα, the so-called parts of speech. The λόγος can thus be resolved into these parts of speech: subject-term, predicate-term, copula. Certainly, yet resolving it in this way precisely destroys the wholeness of the λόγος, so that even the connection becomes free-floating and cannot be what it is, namely binding. That which binds, according to Aristotle too, only has meaning if it can be related to συγκείμενα. After all, we are precisely not asking about individual parts of the λόγος, but about the *ground* of the possibility of λόγος as such taken as a whole, and are doing so via the guiding thread of the 'is' and its place in the λόγος-structure as a whole. Our inquiring back into the ground of the possibility of the λόγος must therefore be something other than resolving and splitting it into its parts. On the contrary, our inquiring back into the ground must attempt *to maintain as a whole* that whose ground and inner possibility we are asking about. This kind of inquiring back, this kind of analytic was first seen by Kant in all its peculiarity, even though he did not ultimately become aware of the extent of his insight in any detail. It is the kind of analytic that neo-Kantianism later called the question of the origin, though while making it shallow in a particular direction. To interrogate the λόγος as to its origin means to point out that from which it springs in each case as a whole, not factically, in its specific accomplishment, but in accordance with the inner possibility of its essence. Analytic and *investigation of the origin* therefore refer to an inquiring back into the ground of the inner possibility, or, as we also say for short, inquiring back into this ground in the sense of *discovering the ground.* Investigating the origin does not mean grounding in the sense of factical proving, but rather an inquiring into the essential origin, letting something spring from the ground of its essence, discovering the ground in the sense of pointing out the ground of the possibility of the structure as a whole. We are inquiring back into the ground of the inner possibility of the λόγος. We are thereby inquiring into the dimension of what makes it intrinsically possible, the dimension of its *essential origin.* We must therefore already be acquainted with this originary dimension in advance. How are we to find it? Evidently we can only do so by catching sight of the whole structure of the λόγος and looking to see what its intrinsic and essential construction itself points to as that which grounds it and embraces it.

Accordingly, we are asking where the λόγος in general stands. We have to say that it is an essential *manner of comportment* belonging to man. We must therefore ask after the *ground of the inner possibility of the* λόγος *in terms of the concealed essence of man.* Yet here too we are not to proceed in such a way as to now acquire a definition of the essence of man from somewhere and apply it; on the contrary, we must proceed from the very structure of the λόγος correctly understood and, by going back to the ground of its possibility that it points toward, first let it be said how things stand concerning the essence of man. All we know is that we must proceed from the unitary structure of the λόγος back into the essence of man. Nothing has been decided concerning this essence. All we have is the thesis: *man is world-forming,* a thesis we appeal to as a statement of essence, of the same character as the thesis that the animal is poor in world. This thesis, however, must not be applied at this stage; rather it is precisely a matter of unfolding it and grounding it as a problem. What we here call *world-formation* is ultimately also the very *ground of the inner possibility of the* λόγος. *Whether* it is this, and above all *what* it is, is something we do not yet know. In the end we shall come to comprehend from the essence of world-formation what Aristotle hits upon as the ground of the possibility of the λόγος ἀποφαντικός, namely apprehending in its peculiar structure of σύνθεσις-διαίρεσις, which we linked to the 'as'-structure. Yet if we recall correctly, it is not only via the thesis 'man is world-forming' that we know something of man, for in the first part of the lecture course we developed a *fundamental attunement* of man within which we were able to attain an essential insight into the *Dasein* of man in general. Now that we are inquiring back into the ground of the inner possibility of assertion, the question is whether we will not ultimately be led back into that dimension which—from a quite different perspective and in a very rich manner—the interpretation of *boredom* as a fundamental attunement of Dasein has already led us to.

b) The point of departure of our inquiry back from the inner construction of the essence of the assertion: the 'either/or' potential of the revealing and concealing that points out and expresses being in the 'both/and' of ascribing and denying.

Our initial concrete task is to start from the λόγος and inquire back into the ground of its possibility. We must do this by taking our point of departure from the *inner essential construction* of the λόγος that has now been illuminated. This is what we constantly have to keep in view above all else, while confining ourselves to the simple λόγος. The formal example of the simple λόγος is: *'a is b'*. However, we must now ask whether we here have the essential construction of the λόγος. What we are advancing here is *one* particular form of the λόγος, namely an example of κατάφασις and—we are assuming—of ἀληθεύειν, that is, the form of the positive and true assertion. Wherever the λόγος, the statement, or the judgement is dealt with in logic, *this* form is always the primary and exemplary one, if not the only one. In addition, however, we have the negative true assertion, as well as the positive false one and the negative false one. Consequently we must also take these into account. And this indeed happens within certain limits in conventional theories of judgement. Precisely here, however, we find the fundamental mistake and the fundamental difficulty of the whole problem. We may neither advance the positive true judgement, nor any other form, as the sole privileged form of the λόγος and then take all the others into account retrospectively (in supplementary fashion). All these procedures still leave us outside the dimension of the real problem. We have not yet attained the correct approach at all. The correct approach is missing in Aristotle too, and consequently throughout the following eras. Nonetheless, Aristotle came closer to the problem. He explicitly emphasizes something that is no longer even noticed in contemporary logic, namely that the λόγος is not true *and* false, but true *or* false: ἀληθεύειν ἢ ψεύδεσθαι. On the other hand, we can understand why the central problematic is not grasped by Aristotle, since his primary and sole intention was the necessity of first making the structures of the λόγος visible in general, in contrast to the provisional and extrinsic theories of his predecessors, including even Plato. If we may speak of "easier" and "more difficult" at all here, then radicalization is always "easier" because it has already been prepared. This is how the problems first come to light.

The form of the assertion taken as positive and true makes an interpretation of the λόγος easier, for reasons we shall not discuss now. This kind of approach in logic which starts with the positive true judgement is justified within certain limits, but for this very reason it gives rise to the fundamental illusion that it is only a matter of simply relating the other possible forms of assertion to this one in a supplementary fashion. I myself—at least in carrying out the interpretation of λόγος—also fell victim to this illusion in *Being and Time* (cf. as exempt from this illusion *Being and Time*, pp. 222 and 285f.[1]). In the interpretation that follows, while it does not really invalidate what I have said before in *Being and Time*, I must deviate essentially and decisively from this.

We are as yet unable to get a central perspective on the inner and essential construction of the λόγος, even if we take full account of the possible forms it can assume: the true positive judgement and the false positive one, the true negative judgement and the false negative one. The essence of the λόγος consists precisely in its containing as such the possibility of '*either* true *or* false', of '*both* positive *and* negative'. It is precisely the *possibility* of all these kinds of transformation—which have merely been outlined in a rough and ready fashion—that comprises the innermost essence of the λόγος. Only when we grasp this will we have the place *from which to leap* back into the *origin*.[2] The λόγος is not some figment at hand that simply appears first in this form, then in that one; rather by its very essence it is this possibility of one or the other. We say that it is an *ability for . . .* [Vermögen zu . . .]. By ability we always understand the possibility [*Möglichkeit*] of a comportment toward, i.e., the possibility of a relation to beings as such. The λόγος is an ability, i.e., it intrinsically entails *having a relating toward beings as such at one's disposal*. In contrast to this, we called *capacity* [Fähigkeit] the possibility of behaving, of being related to something in a captivated and taken manner.

The λόγος ἀποφαντικός is able to allow for an 'either/or' in the revealing and concealing that point out both in the manner of pointing toward and pointing away, that is, in a pointing out in which the 'is' (being) comes to be expressed in some meaning or other. The character of ability having this orientation is the essence of the λόγος ἀποφαντικός; its essential construction is centred in this ability. It is from here that we must pursue the question of whether we can see anything pointing to the *ground* that *makes this essence possible*. What underlies this ability of the λόγος, what *must* underlie it if the λόγος is to be able to prevail in its essence that it proclaims to us, namely *as the possibility of the 'either/or' of that revealing and concealing which points out and which expresses being?* When we have answered these questions we will see how here too, as everywhere in philosophy, this trivial and elementary phenomenon of judgement and of the assertion—a phenomenon that has already been exhaustively pursued in every possible direction—returns us at a stroke to a dimension which is none other than that *expanse* and *uncanniness* to which the interpretation of our *fundamental attunement* was initially to lead us.

1. [Tr: Translation: *Being and Time*, pp. 264 and 330f.]
2. 'Erst wenn wir das fassen, haben wir den Ort des *Absprungs*, von dem aus wir in den *Ursprung* zurückgehen.'

Before we pursue the problem we have indicated, let us recall the context of the problem once again. We concluded our initial interpretation of the copula using the example 'The board is black' by drawing attention to an essential meaning which we characterised and formulated thus: being equals being true. Such being in the sense of being true is inherently referred to in every statement, whether the statement expresses being in the sense of being at hand or of being constituted in such and such a way, or even in the sense of essential constitution. Such being true is bound up with the three previous meanings of being in a strange sense, so that there appears a peculiar unity of these meanings which intrinsically belong together. More precisely, we must ask why there is this polysemy of the copula, and where the ground of its unity is to be found. We recognized this polysemy of the copula quite generally as its positive essence, which is mostly expressed in the strange undifferentiatedness and universality that has given rise to various, inherently one-sided theories. Without seeing its polysemy, Aristotle traced the copula back to a σύνθεσις. The structural moments of the λόγος, which we considered before analysing the λόγος, namely κατάφασις and ἀπόφασις, ἀληθές and ψεῦδος, are likewise traced back to a σύνθεσις or διαίρεσις. We said that this σύνθεσις underlying the λόγος is presumably that relation in which the 'as' and the 'as'-structure we were asking about is grounded. If, however, according to Aristotle, being, the copula—now taken in its polysemy—is also grounded in a σύνθεσις, then we here see the possibility that *the 'as' and being have a common root*. This is already pointed to by the fact that, in our formal indication of the concept of world as the manifestness of beings as such as a whole together with our grasping beings themselves, we use the 'as' and do so in a distinctive sense. Perhaps that very relation in which the 'as' and the 'as'-structure is rooted is the relation that also makes it possible to get a view of something like being, so that the 'as'-structure and being intrinsically hang together in some sense. That this is so, is something we can only see if we also comprehend from our interpretation of the λόγος so far that the λόγος is not independent, but is grounded in something more originary. We shall only find this originary essence of the λόγος if, instead of positing it as constituted in this way or that, we keep the *whole* essential construction of the λόγος in view and inquire back into the dimension of its origin, i.e., into that which makes it possible in accordance with its inner possibility. In considering the origin of the essence of the λόγος, of the assertion, therefore, we are not to take the true positive assertion as the underlying primary example—as commonly occurs—but nor are we to take some other form of assertion as our basis. Rather what is at issue is to see that the deeper essence of the λόγος lies in the fact that it is the intrinsic possibility of this 'either/or' of the potential for being true or false, both in the manner of ascribing and of denying. Only when we orient the question concerning the ground of the possibility of the λόγος in such a way as to ask what makes possible its inner essence, namely its ability to allow the 'either/or' of being true or being false, will we be assured of being able to really *discover the ground* of the λόγος in its essential structure.

c) Being free, pre-logical being open for beings as such and holding oneself toward the binding character of things as the ground of the possibility of assertion.

The λόγος in the form of the λόγος ἀποφαντικός is the ability for a *comportment* that points beings out, whether in the manner of revealing (true) *or* concealing (false). Such ability is possible only as this ability if it is grounded in *being free for beings as such*. It is upon this that *being free in* that pointing out that points toward and away is grounded, and this being free in . . . can then unfold as *being free for* revealing or concealing (truth or falsity). In short, the λόγος ἀποφαντικός as assertion is possible only where there is freedom. Within the particular comportment and ability that can spring from freedom and with which we are now solely concerned, i.e., in the phenomenon of pointing out, something like conforming to . . . and being bound to . . . is possible such that what this binding binds itself to, namely beings, are announced in their binding character. And this is possible only if there is an underlying freedom that is structurally articulated in this way, and for its part itself articulates. Revealing and concealing of λόγος, truth and being false, truth *or* falsity—the *possibility* of both—is to be found only where there is freedom, and only where there is freedom do we find the possibility of something having a binding character. It is precisely possibility and the character of ability pertaining to the λόγος whose *ground* we wish to discover. When we say that this ability to point out is grounded in being free for beings as such, this entails that the λόγος does not first produce a relation toward beings as such, but for its part is *grounded* in such a relation. In each of its forms it always makes use of such a relation in a particular way. How? The λόγος can point out beings as they are, and in such pointing out point *toward* whatever pertains to those beings or direct *away* whatever does not pertain to them, only if it already has the possibility in general of measuring this pointing out and whether it suitably conforms to those beings. However, in order to be able to decide about the conformity or nonconformity of whatever the λόγος says in pointing out, or more precisely, in order to be able to comport himself in general within this 'either/or', man in his propositional discourse must have *leeway* [Spielraum] in advance for the comparative to-and-fro of the 'either/or', of *truth or falsity*. He must have leeway within which those beings that assertion is to be about are themselves manifest. This entails the essential point that not only does the λόγος ἀποφαντικός—as we have shown above—not produce our relation to beings, it does not even produce this manifestness of beings. It always already merely makes use of both *that relation* and *this manifestness* in order to fulfil its potential as a revealing or concealing that points out.

However, in talking about revealing and concealing, are we not saying that the λόγος itself as such makes manifest, is true—indeed, in accordance with general opinion, is it not the proper and sole place of truth? Certainly truth or the possibility of the 'either/or' lies in the λόγος, but this possible being true or revealing that belongs *to it,* the λόγος, is *not an originary* being true, i.e., not that making manifest and revealing through which beings as such lie open for us in general and are unconcealed in themselves. It is not, and indeed never the case that an assertion as such—however true it might be—could ever primarily reveal beings as such. To take an example: in making the true assertion 'The board is black', this being that we call a board does not first become manifest to us in the way that it is through this true statement as such, as though the assertion as such were capable of opening up to us, as it were, this being that was previously closed off. The assertion—although it opens up in *its* own way—*never* brings us *primarily* and *in general* before those beings that are revealed. Rather the converse is the case: the blackboard must already have become manifest to us as such a being in order for us to assert something about it in pointing out. The λόγος ἀποφαντικός merely *takes apart* [legt . . . auseinander], in the assertion, what is already manifest. It does not, however, first form the manifestness of beings in general. There does indeed lie a being true or being false in the assertion—indeed the assertion is even *the* form in which being true and being false are commonly *expressed,* passed on, and *communicated.* Yet this does not at all entail that propositional truth is the fundamental form of truth. Certainly, in order to see this we need to take a deeper look into the essence of truth, something we shall achieve in the course of our investigation. If we recoil from this task and stick from the outset to some dogmatic opinion about what 'true' is supposed to mean, then it can indeed be irrefutably proven—as happens repeatedly today—that the judgement is the bearer of truth. If we say from the outset that what is true is whatever is valid and continue: there is something valid only where there is acknowledgement, and acknowledgement is the expression and fundamental act of affirmation, and affirmation is the fundamental form of judgement, then truth as validity is connected with judgement as affirmation. This simply cannot be refuted. But the question is: Is validity the essence of truth, or is this characterization of truth as validity and validation not the most trivial and superficial interpretation, one that only the sound common sense of routine thought can and must hit upon? We shall later come to see that this is indeed the case.

As assertion, the λόγος ἀποφαντικός certainly has the possibility of being true or being false, but this manner of being true, of becoming manifest, is grounded in a manifestness which, because it lies *prior* to *predication* and the assertion, we designate as *pre-predicative manifestness,* or better, as *pre-logical truth.* 'Logical' is here to be taken in a quite rigorous sense, namely having to do with the λόγος ἀποφαντικός in the form we have interpreted it. With respect to the latter, there is a manifestness that lies *prior* to it, *prior* to it in the distinct sense that this original manifestness grounds the possibility of the λόγος being true and being false, grounds it in preceding it.

We saw, furthermore, that the assertion is expressed—though not always in this linguistic form—in the 'is', being, and that such being at first and for the most part shows an undifferentiatedness and universality of meaning. We can now see that through the assertion, being is not first attributed *to* whatever the assertion is about, and that those beings with which the assertion is concerned do not first receive their ontological character through the 'is', but conversely that the 'is' in all its multiplicity and specific determinacy on each occasion only ever proves to be the *expression* of *what, how,* and *whether* beings *are.* The manifold character of the essence of being can therefore never be read off from the copula and its meanings at all. Instead, it is necessary to return to where every assertion and its copula speaks from, namely *beings themselves as already manifest.* Because the being of the copula—in each of its possible interpretations—is not what is originary, and yet the copula plays an essential role in the expressed statement and the expressed statement is commonly taken as the the place of truth, we are faced with the necessity of a destructuring [*Destruktion*].

The ability we have characterized as the λόγος ἀποφαντικός accordingly points to a manifestness of beings as such which lies *prior* to all assertions. The question arises: Is this pre-logical manifestness of beings as such the originary *ground* of the possibility of that ability, and do we see in this ground that of which Aristotle already had an intimation in speaking of σύνθεσις and διαίρεσις? If this original manifestness of beings is more originary than the λόγος, and the λόγος is a manner of human comportment, where then is this originary manifestness? It is surely not outside man, but must be man himself in a deeper sense, man himself in his essence. We indicated this essence by way of a thesis: man is *world-forming.* Where is this manifestness situated, and what does it consist in?

For the moment, we can already see that if the λόγος ἀποφαντικός leads back to something more originary in respect of its inner possibility, and if whatever is more originary is somehow connected with what we call *world* and *world-formation,* then judgements and statements are not primarily world-forming in themselves, even though they belong to world-formation. The λόγος is an ability, characterized by the 'either/or' of revealing-concealing in pointing out. A being open for those beings themselves which the judgement is in each case concerned with must therefore already be possible in man, as the one who makes assertions, *prior to* the accomplishment and *for* the accomplishment of every assertion. The ability as such must accordingly already be tuned in [*eingespielt*] to the 'either/or' of conforming or not conforming to those beings that the discourse of the λόγος is about. Man's being open for beings themselves, which can become the object and theme of an assertion, is not the being at hand of a gaping emptiness that could be filled, an emptiness that appears in man as distinct from things and their determinacy. Rather this being open *for* beings as they are sustains the λόγος and as such brings with it the possibility of a pointing out that can be bound by beings. Being open for . . . is from the very outset a *free holding oneself toward* whatever beings are given there *in letting oneself be bound*. The possibility, which can become binding, of tuning in to beings, this relating to them in comporting oneself in such and such a way, is characteristic in general of every ability and comportment as distinct from capacity and behaviour. In the latter we never find any letting oneself be bound by something binding, but merely a sphere of instinctual drives becoming disinhibited while remaining captivated.

Not only must a pre-predicative manifestness in general constantly already occur and have occurred, however, if the assertion as pointing out is to be accomplished in whatever way, but this *pre-predicative manifestness* must itself be this *occurrence* in which a particular *letting oneself be bound* occurs. This is the prior relation to that which gives pointing out in assertion its measure: beings as they are. This giving of measure is transferred to beings in advance in accordance with a comportment that lets itself be bound, so that conformity or nonconformity is regulated according to beings. Propositional comportment must intrinsically already be the providing of something that can give a measure for the very making of assertions. This provision of, and subjection to, something binding is in turn only possible where there is *freedom*. Only where there is this possibility of transferring our being bound from one thing to another are we given the leeway to decide concerning the conformity or nonconformity of our comportment toward whatever is binding. If we consider the old, traditional definition of truth from this perspective—the definition *veritas est adaequatio intellectus ad rem,* ὁμοίωσις, conformity, assimilation of thinking to the thing that is thought—then we can see that this old definition of truth is indeed correct in its approach. Yet it is also *merely* one *approach,* and not at all what it is commonly taken to be, namely a determination of the essence, or the result of a determination of the essence of truth. It is merely an approach to the problem of asking what grounds in general the possibility of conforming to something. What must underlie *adaequatio* is the fundamental character of being open. Letting oneself be bound must already bring toward itself in advance, and as something that can be binding, whatever is to provide the measure and be binding in one way or another. This holding oneself toward—toward something binding—which occurs in all propositional comportment and *grounds* it is what we call a *fundamental comportment: being free* in an originary sense.

Whatever is binding, however, announces itself to the pointing out *as a being* that in each case is or is not in such and such a way; one that is or is not in general; one that is of this essence or another. Accordingly, this fundamental comportment having the character of letting oneself be bound in being held toward something must intrinsically occur in such a way that in it beings are manifest as such in advance. This manifestness of beings as such is in turn of such a kind that propositional comportment, because it is an ability, is in each case able to express itself both with respect to being such and such and with respect to that-being, as well as with respect to what-being.

We can see more and more clearly in particular respects the essential contrast between the animal's being open and the *world-openness* of man. Man's being open is a being held toward . . . , whereas the animal's being open is a being taken by . . . and thereby a being absorbed in its encircling ring.

d) Pre-logical being open for beings as completion (as a prior forming of the 'as a whole') and as an unveiling of the being of beings. The tripartite structure of the fundamental occurrence in Dasein as the originary dimension of the assertion.

Yet even with this we have not yet exhausted what necessarily has to occur at all times in this fundamental comportment of our original, pre-predicative being open for beings. We can easily see what is missing if, without any pre-formed theories, we simply inquire once more into the tendency to point out that we find in a simple assertion, and if we remain circumspect about the leeway within which the assertion necessarily moves.

As an example of a simple assertion we shall again take the statement 'The board is black'. It is 'simple' in the sense of the Aristotelian ἁπλῆ ἀπόφανσις because it does not present a complex or artificially constructed sentence-formation. Yet for all its simplicity, indeed perhaps through this very simplicity, this λόγος is in fact not 'simple' in the sense of something spoken staightforwardly and naturally. We can sense straightaway that this statement is, as it were, ready-made for logic and the study of grammar. And here we are trying precisely to free ourselves from the shackles of these disciplines. The other assertion we mentioned, 'The board is badly positioned', is simpler in the sense of something spoken naturally and spontaneously, as it were, if we take it not so much in the form of an enunciation we have made, but rather in the form of something we quietly say and think to ourselves. The question is what we should now do with this example 'The board is badly positioned' with respect to our problem. What is at stake now is no longer the structure of the λόγος itself (for we have established this in various directions), but rather what the λόγος is grounded in, together with its entire structure as an ability: namely in a *pre-logical being open for beings*. We must experience something more about the character of this being open from our interpretation of the statement in question. We must therefore orient our view toward what is being asserted in the assertion: the board that is badly positioned. 'Badly positioned'—what kind of determinacy is that? Is it other than that in the previous example, for instance, namely being black? The position is bad *for those* who are sitting at the other side of the room or bad *for this* teacher, *for the one who* is writing and has to go over to the board each time rather than having it more favourably situated behind him. Accordingly, the bad position is not a determinacy of the board itself, such as its black colour, or its breadth and height, but a determinacy that is merely relative to us who are here in this very situation. This determinate quality of the board—its bad position—is therefore not a so-called objective property, but is relative to the subject.

However, how does this point concerning the determinate quality of the board being relative to the subject serve to *illuminate the pre-logical manifestness of beings?* This manifestness, after all, is supposed to make possible the so-called objective provision of a measure on the part of beings with regard to the λόγος as a pointing out that keeps to this measure. In talking about subject-relatedness, however, we have arrived at the opposite. However, what is at issue is not the subject-relatedness of the property 'badly positioned'. We will perhaps also find such a relatedness in the property 'black' or in the property of colour, only in a quite different respect. What is at issue is neither the relation between the property 'bad position' and the thing, nor the relation between this property and the human being who judges and makes assertions. Rather what is at issue is the question of *what is pre-predicatively manifest in this pre-logical manifestness of the badly positioned board*. It is only because we find the board badly positioned that we can make a corresponding judgement. Yet what do we find here? Its bad position. Certainly, we have already established this and even explained why it is the case. And yet it was precisely the inquisitive cleverness of this kind of explanation that led us astray. We may well think how amazingly philosophical we have been in establishing that the bad position of the board does not pertain to the board itself, but is due merely to its relatedness to those who are reading and writing. And yet even this very explanation is contrived—quite apart from the fact that it leads us altogether off the path of our investigation. The bad position of the board is indeed a property of this board itself—and is far more objective than even its black colour. For the board is not—as this rash interpretation concluded—badly positioned in relation to us who are factically to be found here, rather the board is badly positioned in this room. However, if we think of the room not as tiered, but as a dance hall, then the board would be sitting quite favourably in the corner, out of the way. More precisely, it would not merely be well positioned in that case, but would be completely superfluous. This board in itself is badly positioned in this room, in a lecture theatre belonging to the university. Its unfavourable position is precisely a property of this board itself. It does not pertain to it because a listener sitting on the right at the front has trouble seeing it. For even someone sitting directly in front of it would have to say that the board is badly positioned (in the room), and that it would be better if it were positioned where it usually stands for very good reasons, namely in the middle behind the lectern.

Yet all this has merely served to correct the false, though apparently eminently philosophical explanation of this property of the board. However, we were not meant to get into these discussions at all concerning what kind of property this is. Indeed not—we were to look at what it is about beings that is manifest to us in their pre-predicative manifestness. The concern of our assertion, what we merely explicitly take apart and examine and specifically point to in making our assertion, is the badly-positioned board. It is already manifest. The board alone? No, we are looking at the lectern, at the notebook in front of us, and so on. Many kinds of things—yet all these do not enter the question as far as this assertion and the grounds of its possibility are concerned. What does enter the question, however, is the very thing that is *also already* manifest in the board's bad position correctly considered—the lecture theatre as *a whole*. It is out of the manifestness of the lecture theatre that we experience the bad position of the board in the first place. Precisely this manifestness of the lecture theatre within which the board is badly positioned is what does not explicitly appear at all in the assertion. We do not first attain the manifestness of the lecture theatre via the assertion 'The board is badly positioned', rather this manifestness is the *condition of the possibility* of the board in general being something we can make judgements about. In our making what is apparently an isolated judgement about this particular thing, we therefore already speak out of a manifestness which—we may say provisionally—is not merely lots of things, but something as a whole. This fact that in every individual assertion, no matter how trivial or complicated, we always already speak *out of beings that are manifest as a whole,* and this 'as a whole' itself—the lecture theatre that we already understand as a whole—these are not in turn the result of a pointing out by way of assertion. Rather assertions can only ever be inserted into what is already there and manifest as a whole.

We thus see that the possibility of making an assertion depends not only on the assertion itself assigning the possibility of being binding to whatever it wishes to make a judgement about, and that it depends not only on whatever the judgement is about being conceived and grasped in advance as a being, but that it is equally necessary for *every assertion* to already speak *into a manifestness as a whole* from the outset, and at the same time to speak out of such a manifestness.

We can now see more clearly that the assertion is neither originary nor independent. However, we still want to know precisely what it is that grounds it, what it is that we are calling man's pre-logical being open for beings.

Before inquiring any further into what we have now established as the second moment of the originary dimension of the assertion, let us summarize what we have hitherto seen of this originary dimension. We are interrogating the fundamental structure of the λόγος with respect to its inner possibility, with respect to that which the λόγος as λόγος springs from. This demands that we go back into the dimension of the origin. In doing so, we come across several things which, seen together in their unity, constitute what properly makes the λόγος possible, but also lead us back to what we called the formation of world. The first thing this path led us to see is the following: The λόγος is a λόγος that points out, which is to say: The manner and way in which it makes things manifest is not a primary or originary manifesting, as though a judgement or assertion in itself could ever make accessible that which the assertion is about. Rather all λόγος can only point out, i.e., take apart and examine, whatever *is already pre-logically manifest.* Yet not only this. In order for the λόγος to satisfy this fundamental function of pointing out, it must—in order to be able to point out—have the possibility of conforming to whatever it points out or else going astray in its pointing out. For it also has the possible potential to be false. The λόγος therefore in and for itself requires this leeway of possible conformity or nonconformity. To put it quite generally, it requires in advance something that provides it with the measure for all measurement. There is a comportment that already stretches ahead, in advance of all propositional comportment, in the direction of whatever the assertion is about, a comportment that has the character of holding oneself toward something binding, and it is from here that conformity and nonconformity, the ultimate meaning of *adaequatio,* are possible. The *first* moment that underlies the λόγος is this holding oneself toward something binding. We attempted to approach the *second* moment via the concrete analysis of a particular example: 'This board is badly positioned'. At first, we intentionally attributed importance to making sure of what was being referred to in the said property, and we did so by showing the following: what we here ascribe to the board is not merely a property pertaining to the board relative to us who observe and make judgements about it; rather this property is precisely utterly objective, i.e., a property that pertains to this specific object as such, if only we can see it explicitly in its true objectivity with regard to which we make the assertion in saying 'The board is badly positioned'. Insofar as we spontaneously utter this assertion without any construction or theoretical reflection, but in terms of our everyday being here, we do not have the board alone in view when making this assertion. Rather we have this room here as a lecture theatre in view—although not in the narrower sense of something facing us. In accordance with the actual character it has as such, this lecture theatre demands that the board as a board be put in a quite specific place here in this room. What is decisive in this interpretation of assertion is that we do not make a judgement in relation to an isolated object, but in this judgement we speak out of this whole that we have already experienced and are familiar with, and which we call the lecture theatre.

What further essential character are we to take from the phenomenon indicated regarding this being open? At first one might say that there is no great wisdom in emphasizing that the possibility of the assertion is connected to the lecture theatre being manifest. After all, it is everywhere the case that in making our assertions we can only ever express ourselves concerning *one* object, and accordingly we must always be selective with respect to those remaining. Those remaining indeed belong to the many things that continually press upon us.

This is indeed correct—so correct that for all our alluding to the beings that remain at hand in the room in addition to the board, we overlook what must properly be grasped here. For what is at stake is not the fact that besides and in addition to the board there are other things at hand, and alongside these other things there is the board. As long as we merely approach our investigation in the way that usually happens in logic and epistemology, namely by assuming that we have arbitrary objects that we then judge and investigate as the theme of judgement or supplement with other possible objects, we overlook what we are calling the specific context. As long as we move on this level, it is almost literally true to say that we cannot see the forest for the trees. More precisely, this saying tries to express in a concrete image something that we must grasp in principle. By way of anticipation, we can also express the principle behind this saying as follows: *ordinary understanding cannot see the world for beings,* the world in which it must constantly maintain itself simply to be able to be what it itself is, to be able to pick out this or that being in each case as such in the sense of a possible object of assertion. What we analysed above (cf. pp. 275f.) as characteristic of ordinary understanding was its failure to make any distinctions in encountering all the beings it comes up against. This failure to distinguish in its comportment toward beings—which is itself rooted in something deeper—is part of the reason for this failure to see world.

At the same time, the saying "not seeing the forest for the trees" shows us the major difficulty we are faced with. For—to stay with this image—we not only have to see the forest and see it as such, but also say what it is and how it is. In doing so, we must of course beware of interpreting the world by analogy with the forest. The following decisive point alone is at issue: In relation to the individual trees and the way they are gathered together, the forest is something else and therefore not simply something that we arbitrarily think up in addition to the sum of trees which we believe to be all that is given. The forest is not only quantitatively more than a collection of many trees. Nor, however, is this 'something else' something that is simply at hand besides the many trees. Rather, it is that out of which the many trees belong to a forest. To return to our example: we do not yet understand or grasp at all the pre-logical manifestness of beings if we take it to be the way in which many kinds of beings are simultaneously manifest. Instead, everything depends on already seeing, in the apparently narrow and limited character of the assertion 'The board is badly positioned', how what the assertion is about (namely the badly positioned board) is manifest from *out of a whole*, out of a whole that we do not at all explicitly or specifically grasp as such. Yet precisely this realm within which we always already move is what we initially designate schematically as the 'as a whole'. It is nothing other than what we see to be the pre-logical manifestness of beings in the λόγος. We can now say quite generally: The *pre-logical being open for beings*, out of which every λόγος must speak, has in advance always already *completed* beings in the direction of an *'as a whole'*. By this *completion* we are not to understand the subsequent addition of something hitherto missing, but rather the *prior forming of the 'as a whole' already prevailing.* (Moreover, what is essential in the case of any completion in the sense of craftmanship is not the addition of the missing piece. Rather the central achievement of completion is seeing the whole and forming it in advance, making it into a whole.) All assertion occurs on the basis of such completion, i.e., on the grounds of a prior forming of this 'as a whole'. This 'as a whole' varies in its expanse and transparency and in the richness of its contents, and it changes more or less constantly for us in the everydayness of our Dasein, even though here too we see a peculiar averageness of the 'as a whole' maintain itself. That is a question in its own right. Man's pre-logical being open for beings is accordingly not only a prior holding oneself toward the binding character of things, but together with this it is this *completion* we have just characterized.

This completion that is a holding oneself toward the binding character of things is furthermore—as we can already see—a being open for beings such as to make it possible to express oneself about *beings,* i.e., to speak of *what-being, being such and such, that-being,* and *being true.* Accordingly, the *being* of beings must also already be *unveiled* in a certain way in and through this completion we have characterized.

Our going back into the originary dimension of the λόγος ἀποφαντικός has thus provided *a rich, intrinsically articulated structural context* which evidently characterizes a *fundamental occurrence in the Dasein* of man, one we can record in *three moments:* [1.] holding the binding character of things toward us; [2.] completion; [3.] unveiling the being of beings. These three moments represent a unitary, fundamental occurrence in the Dasein of man, one from which the λόγος first springs and indeed always does so. The question is: How are we to grasp in a *unitary* way this fundamental occurrence in Dasein as represented by the three moments?

Yet does this fundamental occurrence that is supposed to make the λόγος possible have anything at all to do with what Aristotle mentions as the condition of the possibility, and thus as the origin, of the λόγος ἀποφαντικός, i.e., with σύνθεσις-διαίρεσις or with the σύνθεσις expressed in the 'is' of the copula? Is not everything we have come across very much richer and more complicated than what Aristotle indicates in this manner? Certainly, but for us this means only that we must provide an actual interpretation that leads to an understanding of why Aristotle, on his first journey into this originary dimension, had to grasp the fundamental condition in this way. And here we must remark that what Aristotle traces the λόγος back to—σύνθεσις that is also intrinsically διαίρεσις—for all its formality can by no means be taken as something self-evident. If our elucidation of the origin of the entire essential construction of the λόγος is legitimate, then we must also be able to clarify from this how something like σύνθεσις-διαίρεσις is possible, and what we are fundamentally to understand by it.

We said furthermore that what Aristotle posits as the ground of the possibility of the λόγος ἀποφαντικός—namely σύνθεσις-διαίρεσις—is that *relating* and relational comportment in which the *'as'* and the 'as'-structure emerge. If this is so, and if what Aristotle sees only indeterminately and faintly as σύνθεσις-διαίρεσις belongs to the rich and articulated structural context of that fundamental occurrence expressed as holding the binding character of things toward oneself, completion, and the unveiling of the being of beings, then it must be in this context that the 'as'-structure itself emerges. However, to the extent that the 'as' is a structural moment of what we call *world*—world taken as the manifestness of beings as such as a whole—then with this fundamental (tripartite) occurrence we have hit upon that occurrence in which there occurs what we call *world-formation*. This is all the more likely since to the structure of world, according to our formal analysis, there belongs the 'as a whole', which evidently belongs to completion and forms within it.

§74. World-formation as the fundamental occurrence in Dasein. The essence of world as the prevailing of world.

We are thus approaching a direct and immediate interpretation of the phenomenon of world, initially via the guiding thread outlined through our formal analysis: world as manifestness of beings as such as a whole. If we take up this determination of world directly, we find nothing at all said of the assertion or the λόγος. Why then did we investigate these? Was it a detour? In a certain sense, indeed—yet it was one of those detours by which all philosophizing moves around what it is asking about. On the other hand, it was not a detour in the sense of a superfluous journey, if we consider that the philosophical tradition unknowingly treats—under the title of λόγος, of *ratio,* of reason— what we are seeking to unfold as the problem of world. To the present day, the problem has remained unrecognizable for us in its disguises, because these titles and what is dealt with under them have long since been taken as extrinsic questions, and can be freed from their congealment only with difficulty. We will learn from history only if we first awaken it and keep it so. The fact that we are incapable of learning anything from history anymore says only that we ourselves have become ahistorical. No period has known such an influx of tradition, and none has been so poor in genuine tradition. λόγος, *ratio,* reason, spirit—all these titles are disguises for the problem of world.

Through our showing, however, that λόγος, in accordance with its intrinsic possibility, points back to something more originary, we have also made four things clear: [1.] The λόγος is not the radical approach to unfolding the problem of world. [2.] This problem must therefore be set aside, so long as the λόγος in the broad sense (together with its variations) dominates the problematic of metaphysics, so long as metaphysics is "Science of Logic" (Hegel). [3.] If, however, this questioning along the lines of the λόγος was able to assert itself for so long and to lead to major philosophical works, then we cannot dream of eliminating this tradition at one fell swoop. [4.] This can only happen, rather, by our taking upon ourselves the effort to transform man, and thereby traditional metaphysics, into a more originary existence [Dasein], so as to let the ancient fundamental questions spring forth anew from this.

We attempted to undertake what we have identified once more in the fourth point by way of a *dual approach:* initially, without orienting ourselves toward any particular metaphysical question, by *awakening a fundamental attunement of our Dasein,* which is to say, in each case transforming the humanity of us human beings into the Da-sein in ourselves. We then attempted conversely, without constantly or explicitly referring to this fundamental attunement, yet still tacitly recalling it, to unfold a metaphysical question under the title of the *problem of world.* This in turn occurred by way of the wider detour of a comparative examination using the thesis: The animal is poor in world. This thesis apparently brought us merely negative results, until we proceeded to an interpretation of the thesis that man is world-forming. The interpretation as a whole led us back into an originary dimension, into a fundamental occur- rence in which we now claim that *world-formation* occurs. The three things we claimed as fundamental moments of this occurrence, namely holding the bind- ing character of things toward oneself, completion, and the unveiling of the being of beings, are something that, in their specifically rooted unity, we never ever find in any sense in the animal. Yet these things are not simply lacking in the animal, rather the animal does not have such things in and on the basis of a quite specific having, namely its manner of being open in the sense of captivation.

"World" may thus be comprehended in such occurrence. It is now a matter, therefore, of comprehending this *fundamental occurrence in a unitary manner* and, out of this occurrence of world-formation, of simultaneously determining in a direct and positive manner the *essence of world*. This comprehending, however, is not the discussion of something lying before us, nor is it possible as the exhaustive treatment of something we are presented with, something everyone comes across everywhere without any preparation. Nor indeed—which is fundamentally the same thing—is it a matter for some exceptional profundity of intuition. All observation of whatever kind must remain eternally distant from what *world* is, insofar as its essence resides in what we call the *prevailing of world,* a prevailing that is more originary than all those beings that press themselves upon us. The awakening of a fundamental attunement in the first part of the lecture course, and the return we have just undertaken from the λόγος-structure to the fundamental occurrence, both serve one purpose: *to prepare our entering into the occurrence of the prevailing of world.* This philosophizing entry and return of man into the Dasein in him can only ever be prepared, never effected. Awakening is a matter for each individual human being, not a matter of his or her good will or even skilfulness, but of his or her destiny, whatever falls or does not fall to him or her. Everything that contingently falls upon us, however, only falls and falls due to us if we have waited for it and are able to wait. Only whoever honours a mystery gains the strength to wait. Honouring in this metaphysical sense means action that engages in the whole that in each case prevails through us. Only in this way do we enter the possibility that this 'as a whole' and world will explicitly prevail through us, so explicitly that we have the possibility of inquiring about it in a comprehending way.

We have thus already spoken of the prevailing of world and indicated that we have already turned our backs on this prevailing of world if we set about dealing with it as though it were some business affair. Yet we have also indicated that the unfolding of its essence cannot be reduced to some erudite discourse. These false trails will constantly dislodge our entry into the fundamental occurrence of Dasein, and do so all the more stubbornly the less, and the less assuredly, we entrust ourselves to the power of the concept and of comprehension.

We shall recall once more what we have now said in our transition from the assertion to world. Our investigation led us from the λόγος to world, more precisely as a return to the pre-logical manifestness of beings. We are here understanding pre-logical in the quite specific sense of that which makes the λόγος possible as such in accordance with all its dimensions and possibilities.

Pre-logical manifestness is a fundamental occurrence of Dasein. This fundamental occurrence is characterized by three things: bringing the binding character of things toward oneself, completion, and the unveiling of the being of beings. We are claiming that Aristotle, in tracing the λόγος back to σύνθεσις and διαίρεσις, moved in the direction of this intrinsically articulated fundamental occurrence, without having seen this structural context as such. We also recognize this fundamental occurrence in its peculiar relational character, as we shall see, as that in which the 'as' and the 'as'-structure are rooted. We have moved from λόγος to world, world grasped formally as the manifestness of beings as such as a whole, so that the question arises as to why we did not start out directly from this initially formal definition of world and then proceed directly to the interpretation of its structure, instead of choosing a detour via the λόγος. We have seen that λόγος, *ratio,* reason, is what has dominated the entire problematic of metaphysics precisely with respect to the problem of world which failed to come to light. If we wish to free ourselves from this tradition in one respect, then this does not mean somehow pushing it aside and leaving it behind us. Rather all liberation from something is genuine only when it masters and appropriates whatever it is liberating itself from. *Liberation from the tradition is an ever new appropriation of its newly recognized strengths.* For this major step, however, which we are convinced metaphysics must take for the future, some sort of cleverness and acumen, or philosophical discoveries we think we have made, are not sufficient. Rather if we understand anything of this task at all, then it is this: that it is possible only *on the basis of a transformation of Dasein itself.* We have taken *two paths* that serve this transformation and its preparation. In the first part of the lecture course we took the path of awakening a fundamental attunement, while in the second part we took the path of dealing with a concrete problem without relating it to the fundamental attunement. *The two paths now merge,* yet do so in such a way that we are not thereby forcibly bringing about a transformation of our Dasein or effecting it in any sense, but only ever preparing it—which is all that philosophy can do.

§75. The 'as a whole' as the world, and the enigmatic distinction between being and beings.

We shall summarize the state of our interpretation of the phenomenon of world anew and somewhat more concisely. We do so in order to gain a view of the unitary primordial structure of this fundamental occurrence underlying the λόγος. In understanding this originary structure of this fundamental occurrence of Dasein, we shall comprehend what is meant by the thesis that man, in the essence and ground of his Dasein, is world-forming.

On the one side, we have the formal analysis: World is the manifestness of beings as such as a whole. On the other side, our movement back from the λόγος has led us to an occurrence which we characterized in three moments: Holding the binding character of things toward oneself, completion, and unveiling of the being of beings. This fundamental occurrence does not exhaust what we refer to as *world-formation,* but belongs essentially to it. Accordingly, it must be intrinsically related to *world.* Manifestness of beings as such as a whole must occur in it. Can this threefold fundamental occurrence be grasped in its primordial structure, in which these moments belong together as articulated and in the unity of their belonging together make possible what we call manifestness of beings as such as a whole? We can indeed grasp this fundamental occurrence in a unitary primordial structure, so as to comprehend in terms of this structure how the individual moments belong together in it. This is only possible, however, by our taking our interpretation thus far even further, and not simply sticking together so-called results. We are not to construct the primordial structure of this threefold fundamental occurrence of Dasein by having recourse to structures of Dasein; on the contrary: we must comprehend the inner unity of this occurrence and thereby first grant ourselves a look into the fundamental constitution of Dasein.

We can see that the pre-logical manifestness of beings has the character of 'as a whole'. In every assertion, whether we know it or not, and in each case in different and changing ways, we speak out of the whole and into it. Above all, this 'as a whole' does not only concern those beings we have before us in being occupied with them, for instance; rather all those beings that are accessible in each case, ourselves included, are embraced by this whole. We ourselves are comprehensively included in this 'as a whole', not in the sense of some component belonging to it that also happens to be there, but in different ways in each case and in possibilities belonging to the essence of Dasein itself, be it in the form of immersing ourselves in beings, or be it in the form of directly facing them, going along with them, being rebuffed by them, being left empty, being held in limbo, being fulfilled or being sustained by them. These are ways in which this 'as a whole' prevails around and through us, ways that lie before any taking up of positions and before all standpoints, ways that are independent of subjective reflection or psychological experience.

This indicates to begin with that this 'as a whole' is not tailored to any particular area nor even any particular species of beings. Rather this 'as a whole', the world, admits precisely the manifestness of manifold beings in the various contexts of their being—other human beings, animals, plants, material things, artworks, i.e., everything we are capable of identifying as beings. This manifold, however, is poorly comprehended, or is not comprehended at all, if we take it merely as a colourful multiplicity of things at hand. If we only recall the particular domain of the animal realm, we already noticed there a peculiar enmeshing and intertwining of the rings that encircle animals, rings that in turn are incorporated in a peculiar way into the human world. The formally so-called manifold of beings requires quite specific conditions in order to become manifest as such. It does not at all merely require the possibility of being able to distinguish the various specific ways of being, as though these were simply lined up alongside one another in a vacuum. The interweaving of the distinctions themselves, and the way in which this interweaving oppresses and sustains us, is, as this prevailing, the primordial lawfulness out of which we first comprehend the specific constitution of being pertaining to those beings standing before us or even those beings that have been made the object of scientific theory. To give a concrete example: When, in the *Critique of Pure Reason,* Kant inquires about the intrinsic possibility of nature in the sense of those beings that are at hand, this whole way of questioning—radical though it is with respect to what has gone before—has failed to comprehend something essential and central, namely that the material beings talked about here have the character of worldlessness. However negative this determination may be, with respect to the metaphysical determination of the essence of nature it is something positive. The problematic of the Kantian question in the *Critique of Pure Reason* can be placed upon its metaphysical ground only when we comprehend that so-called regions of being are not arrayed alongside one another or above or behind one another, but are what they are only *within and out of a prevailing of world.*

This 'as a whole' that constantly surrounds us, and which has nothing to do with any pantheism, must, however, also be what brings with it that *un-differentiatedness* of the manifestness of beings within which we commonly move. And yet, however undifferentiated the specific manner of being of one particular being may initially be for us with respect to that of another (for example, the manner of being of a human being or of a process), and in particular with respect to any conceptual articulation, our factical comportment toward beings is, after all, correspondingly varied in each case, i.e., different. To the peculiarly undifferentiated character of knowing and understanding there corresponds a quite distinct difference in our comportment toward the relevant beings and in the way we are tuned in to them. Yet this manifold and differentiated comportment toward beings is maintained, after all, on the background of that undifferentiatedness which entails that everything is manifest, in whatever way, i.e., is precisely a *being.* Such is everything that is there and that is in such and such a way. To be a being—every being agrees with every other in this; this is the most undifferentiated, universal, and general thing we can say concerning beings. Here there is no difference anymore. The fact that every being is such and such, the way it is in each case, whether it is or is not, whether it ought to be or not—this is what concerns us, not only regarding those beings that we ourselves are not, but also with respect to the beings that we ourselves are. But the fact that every being is a being is all too empty and unquestionable. Most definitely—such things tell us nothing in our everyday busyness, and above all they cannot represent a serious question for us. What else is there for us to ask about: either beings are in this way or in some other way, either they are not at all or they are. Yet however things stand, in all this we heed the *being* of beings and make constant decisions concerning it. Why? Can we not simply stick to *beings,* to this or that one which concerns us, oppresses us, makes us happy or just happens to cross our path? The *being* of beings is something we can leave to the philosophers for their empty and dubious speculations.

If only we could do that—get by without being! Yet it must be possible. The incontrovertible evidence for this is our own history—up to that moment when we became involved with philosophy and heard something of the being of beings, though merely heard it without comprehending anything. Up to that point we knew and sought after, busied ourselves with and honoured beings, and perhaps suffered from beings, without any need for being. Beings themselves, which is what everything depends on, after all, were indeed immediately accessible to us before, without any tiresome reflection intervening. We can relinquish the being of beings and stick only to beings.

It is incontestable that we can comport ourselves toward beings without ever worrying for a moment about the philosophical question concerning the being of beings. Yet does it follow from this that we have never heard of the being of beings and hear from it only in philosophizing? Or must we not conclude, conversely, that if the philosophical question of the being of beings is possible, indeed perhaps even necessary, then philosophy cannot find what it asks about by *inventing* it. It must somehow *find itself before* it, and indeed find itself before it as something belonging not to the realm of the arbitrary, but to the essential, indeed to the very essentiality of everything essential. If, however, philosophy in all its questioning can only reach its findings and has to find its way with whatever is primarily an essential *find*—a find that man qua man has thus in each case already made without knowing it—is the situation not then that the *being* of beings has *already been found* prior to and apart from all philosophy, althoug it is a find that is so worn and in its primordiality lies so far back in primal time that we pay no heed to it? Do we first hear of the being of beings through philosophy, or have we already found the being of those beings we comport ourselves toward and ourselves belong to? Have we not always already and long since *found our way* with this find, so that we pay no heed to it at all, pay so little heed to it that instead in all our comportment toward beings we fundamentally fail to hear the being of beings—fail to hear it in such a way that we arrive at the opinion, perhaps strange and even impossible, that we could just stick to beings and dispense with being? And yet—the *most profound undifferentiatedness* and indifference of ordinary understanding does not lie in that undifferentiated comportment toward various beings, within which ordinary understanding is able to manage and find its way through. The enormity of that indifference pertaining to ordinary understanding is that such understanding fails to hear the *being* of beings and is able to acquaint itself only with beings. Beings are the beginning and end of its accomplishments. In other words, precisely *that* distinction which ultimately and fundamentally *makes possible all distinguishing and all distinctiveness* remains closed off from ordinary understanding. If the essence of understanding consists precisely in distinguishing (it has been regarded in terms of κρίνειν from time immemorial), then ordinary understanding in all its glory can only be what it is on the grounds of *that* distinction it believes it can do without.

What kind of *distinction* is this: *'being of beings'?* Being and beings. Let us freely concede that it is obscure and cannot straightforwardly be made like that between black and white, house and garden. Why can a straightforward distinction be made in these cases? Because it is a distinction between beings and beings. Such a distinction can be made—in an entirely formal and universal way—both when it is located within one and the same domain and when it obtains between beings belonging to domains that are different in kind, such as, for example, between a motorbike and a triangle, or between God and the number 'five'. Although the distinctions are difficult to determine in detail, the immediate way of approaching every such determination is after all given of its own accord, as it were—namely oriented toward beings, such as those we constantly encounter, even if we do not specifically grasp them or even submit them to a comparative examination in order to make distinctions.

Yet: beings and being. Here the difficulty does not lie in first determining the *kind* of distinction, rather we are already unsure and at a loss to begin with, when we wish merely to attain the field or *dimension* in which to make the distinction. For this dimension is not to be found among beings. Being is not some being among others; rather all the things which we previously distinguished between, together with their relevant realms, now fall on the side of beings. And being? We do not know where to accommodate it. Furthermore, if the two are fundamentally different, then nevertheless they are still *related to one another in this distinction:* the bridge between the two is the 'and'. Thus this distinction as a whole is in its essence a *completely obscure distinction*. Only if we endure this obscurity will we become sensitive to what is problematic, and thereby reach a position from which we can develop the central problem inherent in this distinction and thus comprehend the *problem of world*.

The distinction between being and beings, or the being of beings for short— this is such and such, that is, this is not so, this is. We shall try to set out what is problematic about this distinction in various directions in a series of nine points. We do so in order to gain a foothold in the problem: not so much to solve it, but in order to have an opportunity to continually bring closer to us what is enigmatic about this issue that is the most self-evident of everything self-evident.

[1.] We constantly fail to hear this distinction between being and beings, precisely where we continually make use of it: specifically whenever we say 'is', but before this in all our comportment toward beings (what-being, being such and such, and that-being).

[2.] We *continually make use* of this distinction, without knowing or being able to ascertain that in so doing we are applying any knowledge, rule, proposition or the like.

[3.] The distinction—disregarding its content, namely whatever is distinguished as such in it—is obscure with respect to the very *dimension* in which the distinction is possible. We cannot put being on a level comparable to that of beings. This implies that this distinction is not at all represented or taken note of in the sense of something knowable.

[4.] If, therefore, we do not place this distinction before us in the sense of making an objective distinction, then we are always already moving *within* the *distinction as it occurs.* It is not *we* who make it, rather *it* happens *to us* as the fundamental occurrence of our Dasein.

[5.] The distinction does not happen to us arbitrarily or from time to time, but *fundamentally* and constantly.

[6.] For if this distinction did not occur, then—forgetting the distinction—we could not even stick merely to beings at first and for the most part. For precisely in order to experience *what* and *how* beings in each case *are* in themselves as the beings that they *are,* we must—although not conceptually—already understand something like the what-being and that-being of beings.

[7.] Not only does the distinction occur continually, but this distinction must *already* have occurred if we wish to experience beings in their being such and such. We never ever experience anything about being subsequently or after the event from beings; rather beings—wherever and however we approach them—*already* stand *in the light of being.* In the metaphysical sense, therefore, the distinction stands at the commencement of Dasein itself.

[8.] This distinction between being and beings always already occurs in such a way that "being," although undifferentiated, is indeed understood at all times in an *inexplicit articulation,* at least with respect to *what-being* and *that-being.* Man, therefore, always has the possibility of asking: What is that? and: Is it at all or is it not? Why precisely this doubling of what-being and that-being belongs to the originary essence of being is one of the deepest problems that these terms contain, a problem that indeed has hitherto never yet been a problem at all, but something self-evident. This can be seen, for example, in traditional metaphysics and ontology, where one distinguishes between *essentia* and *existentia,* the what-being and that-being of beings. This distinction is employed as self-evidently as that between night and day.

[9.] From all the eight moments listed above, we may infer the *uniqueness* of this distinction, as well as its *universality*.

We now have to see what essential problems this distinction impels us toward, and—since the unveiling of the being of beings is connected to the fundamental occurrence at issue—how this distinction is an essential moment of world, indeed the central one from which the problem of world in general can be comprehended.

Contrary to our expectations, then, we have already said many pertinent things concerning this distinction, without freeing it from its enigmatic nature. All these things have indeed taken us far beyond the problems of philosophy hitherto, if only by the very fact that we have specifically raised this distinction as such to the status of a problem in general. A broad field of questions is thereby opened up. Our question about the being of beings is not concerned with the specific beings that in each case come to be interrogated with respect to their proper content in the individual sciences. Furthermore, raising this theme exceeds the scope of what is commonly called the doctrine of categories, whether in the traditional sense or in the sense of the systematic study of regions of beings. For the thematic we have touched upon is centred precisely on the so-called universal questions concerning being: what-being, being such and such, that-being, being true. Accordingly, it must seek a *new basis* of possible appraisal (cf. the lecture course "The Basic Problems of Phenomenology," summer semester 1927).[1] And yet we meet with a further obstacle in our exposition of this problem. We are tempted to pronounce ourselves content with the stage of the problem we have now arrived at, i.e., to drag it out into a question that can now be discussed objectively and thereby intrinsically connect it retrospectively with the way the problem has been treated hitherto in the history of metaphysics. All this is expressed in the fact that we give a thematic name to the problem of the distinction between being and beings: we call it the problem of the *ontological difference*. What 'difference' means here is initially clear: precisely this distinction between being and beings. And what does 'ontological' mean? In the first instance, 'logical' names that which belongs to the λόγος, that which concerns it or is determined by it. The 'ontological' concerns the ὄν insofar as it is grasped as seen from the λόγος. The λόγος expresses something concerning beings. Yet not every assertion or opinion is ontological, but only those which express themselves about beings as such, indeed specifically with respect to whatever makes beings beings, the 'is'—and this is precisely what we call the being of beings. The ontological is that which concerns the *being* of beings. The ontological difference is that

---

1. [Tr: M. Heidegger, *Die Grundprobleme der Phänomenologie*. Gesamtausgabe, Vol. 24 (Frankfurt: Klostermann, 1975). Trans. Albert Hofstadter, *The Basic Problems of Phenomenology* (Bloomington: Indiana University Press, 1982).]

distinction that concerns the being of beings, or more precisely the distinction within which everything ontological moves and which it presupposes, as it were, for its own possibility. It is the distinction in which being is distinguished from beings, which it also determines in the way their being is constituted. The ontological difference is the difference sustaining and guiding such a thing as the ontological in general, and not a particular distinction that can or must be made within the ontological.

Even in giving it this name and outlining its features, we are pushing the problem of the distinction between being and beings into the framework of *ontology,* i.e., we are inserting it into a direction of questioning and discussion that has particular intentions and especially limits, both with respect to the extent of its problematic and above all with respect to its originality. Certainly we may say with some legitimacy that ontology first attains a clear problematic with this problem of the ontological difference and its elaboration precisely in the context of the problem of world. On the other hand, however, we must ponder the following: it is nowhere written that there must be such a thing as ontology, nor that the problematic of philosophy is rooted in ontology. If we look closely, we see that already in Aristotle where the distinction irrupts—ὄν ᾗ ὄν—everything is still indeterminate and in flux, still open, so that it is generally questionable (and is certainly becoming more and more questionable for me) whether those coming afterward ever came close to the proper intention of ancient metaphysics at all, and whether the scholastic tradition did not cover over everything, even where we no longer suspect it. Perhaps the problem of the distinction between being and beings is prematurely stifled as a problematic by our entrusting it to ontology and naming it in this way. Conversely, we must ultimately unfold this problem *still more* radically, with the danger of arriving at a position where we *must reject all ontology in its very idea as an inadequate metaphysical problematic.* Yet what are we then to put in place of ontology? Kant's transcendental philosophy, for instance? Here it is only the name and claims that have been changed, while the idea itself has been retained. Transcendental philosophy too must fall. What, then, is to take the place of ontology? This is a premature, and above all superficial question. For in the end, through our unfolding of the problem, we altogether lose the *place* in which we could replace ontology by something else. It is only thus that we shall ultimately come completely into the open, and out of the framework and boundary posts of contrived disciplines. Ontology too and its idea must fall, precisely because the radicalization of this idea was a necessary stage in unfolding the fundamental problematic of metaphysics.

One might object, however, that ontology moves within the realm of the distinction between being and beings with the intent of bringing to light the constitution of being pertaining to beings. Is it not a well-considered task to carry out this undertaking and thereby to take advantage of the horizons that have been increasingly illuminated, instead of rushing into radicalisms? Accordingly, it might be better to take the position of first genuinely carrying out an ontology on whatever basis is possible now; there will be plenty of opportunity to radicalize things afterward.

We speak of the ontological difference as the distinction within which everything ontological moves: being and beings. Regarding this distinction, we can proceed further and distinguish accordingly that questioning which is concerned with beings *in themselves,* just as they are—ὄν ὡς ὄν, and the commensurate manifestness of beings as they in each case are in themselves, the manifestness of the ὄν: *ontic truth.* As opposed to this, we have that questioning which is concerned with beings *as such,* i.e., which inquires solely about what constitutes the *being* of beings, ὄν ἦ ὄν: *ontological truth.* For this questioning makes specific use of the distinction between being and beings, counting not on beings, but on being. And yet—how do things stand with regard to *this distinction itself?* Is it a problem for ontological or for ontic knowledge? Or for neither of these, since each is already grounded upon it? With the intrinsically clear distinguishing of ontic and ontological—ontic truth and ontological truth—we indeed have that which is different in its difference, but not this difference itself. The question concerning this difference becomes all the more urgent when we see that this distinction does not arise subsequently by merely distinguishing two separate things lying before us, but in each case belongs to that fundamental occurrence in which Dasein moves as such.

*§76. Projection as the primordial structure of the tripartite
fundamental occurrence of world-formation. The prevailing
of world as that of the being of beings as a whole in
the projection of world that lets it prevail.*

The distinction between being and beings, which we scrutinized in nine points in all its enigmatic character, is thus only provisionally indicated in general so long as we talk of a 'distinction' and a 'difference'. For these are merely formal titles which, like the term 'relation', fit anything and everything, thus impairing nothing at first, yet providing nothing either. We say deliberately that they impair nothing *at first.* For we know from our previous discussions concerning formal analysis (cf. above regarding the 'as' and 'relation') that the indeterminacy of these terms is taken by our ordinary understanding as referring to a connection that is at hand among things that are at hand. Thus here too: the 'ontological difference' is precisely at hand. Yet this has already proved impossible. We have seen that this distinction is never at hand, but refers to something that *occurs.* At the same time, however, we have seen anew the necessity of transforming our orientation of questioning, which entails our entering into this fundamental occurrence. We approached this fundamental occurrence by returning into the originary dimension of the λόγος. In itself this fundamental occurrence is not primarily or solely related to the λόγος. The λόγος is merely grounded in it in its possibility. Leaving aside the terminological and thematic coining of the distinction, we shall venture the *essential step* of transposing ourselves into the *occurrence of this distinguishing* in which the distinction occurs. To put it another way, we shall inquire concerning the *primordial structure of this fundamental occurrence.* We became familiar with this fundamental occurrence via the three moments of holding oneself toward something binding, completion, and unveiling the being of beings. Yet we are not to take cognizance of these as properties at hand. Rather they are directives for being transposed into Da-sein in an originary and unitary manner.

Let us attempt such transposition, with the intent of discovering the primordial structure of this fundamental occurrence, and of comprehending its originary unity, though not simplicity. The first moment we named addresses us most directly: *Holding oneself toward something binding.* The binding character of things always already prevails throughout our comportment, to the extent that we comport ourselves toward beings and in such comportment also—not subsequently and by the way—conform to beings, without any compulsion, yet nonetheless binding ourselves, but also unbinding ourselves and failing to conform. We orient ourselves toward beings, and yet are never able to say what it is about beings that binds us, or what the possibility of such binding is grounded in on our part. For not all 'standing opposite' necessarily entails binding, and when we speak of something standing 'opposite' as an ob-ject (the subject-object relation, con-sciousness), then the decisive problem has been preempted—as not posed at all—irrespective of the fact that the objectivity of something standing opposite is neither the sole nor the primary form of binding. Yet however things stand in this respect, a binding character prevails throughout all being related to . . . , all comportment toward beings. We cannot explain this binding character in terms of objectivity, but vice-versa.

Likewise in all comportment we become aware of comporting ourselves in each case from out of the 'as a whole', however everyday and restricted this comportment may be. We become aware of both—holding ourselves toward something binding and *completion*—in their unitary prevailing, even, and indeed precisely, wherever there is any conflict about an assertion's corresponding to what it establishes, or about whether a decision is fitting or an action essential. However concerned we are to comport ourselves with respect to various issues and to speak in terms of individual things, we nevertheless already move directly and in advance within a tacit appeal to this 'as a whole'. A binding character and completion prevail throughout all comportment.

Yet how are we to grasp these two—holding oneself toward the binding character of things, and originary completion—in their unity? Most difficult of all, however, is that *unveiledness of the being of beings* which is supposed to belong together with these. Here too, we have the pieces clearly in our grasp, as it were: beings—we constantly comport ourselves toward them; being—we constantly express it. But the being of beings? The unifying connection is missing, or rather the origin of this distinction in which, in accordance with its uniqueness and originary character, the distinguishing is *earlier* than the two terms that are distinguished. That is, we are missing the origin that first lets these two terms spring forth.

We are now asking: What is the *unitary character of the fundamental occurrence* that these *three moments* lead us to? We can comprehend the primordial structure of the fundamental occurrence and its tripartite character as *projection*. We are familiar with what this designates purely from the meaning of the word in our everyday experience of being, as a projecting of measures to be taken and as planning in the sense of the anticipatory regulating of human comportment. With this in view, even my first interpretation of this phenomenon took 'projection' in this broad sense and gave this word, which is familiar in normal linguistic usage, a terminological status. At the same time, however, I was inquiring back into its intrinsic possibility in the constitution of being pertaining to Dasein itself. Thus I also called projection that which made such things possible. Strictly speaking, however, if we are clear about this, it is only the *originary* projection that should in general be named in this philosophical and terminological way—namely that occurrence which fundamentally makes possible all familiar projection in our everyday comportment. For only if we retain this name for what is thus unique can we remain constantly vigilant, as it were, for the uniqueness of the fact that the essence of man, the Dasein in him, is determined by this *projective character. Projection as the primordial structure of this occurrence is the fundamental structure of world-formation.* Accordingly, we can now say not only in a more strictly terminological way, but also with respect to a more lucid and radical problematic, that *projection is world-projection. World prevails in and for a letting-prevail that has the character of projecting.* With respect to our previous terminology, projection is only this originary occurrence, and no longer to be taken as our specifically factical and concrete planning, deliberation, and understanding; for this reason it is also inappropriate to speak of a derivative sense of projection.

We shall now ask more concretely to what extent projection is the primordial structure of that tripartite fundamental occurrence. By 'primordial structure' we understand that which originarily unifies those three moments in an articulated unity. 'Originary' unifying means: intrinsically forming and sustaining this articulated unity. Not only must the three moments of that fundamental occurrence appear simultaneously in projection, but in it they must together belong to their unity. Projection itself must thus show itself in its originary unity.

It may be hard immediately to see through what we mean by projection in the entire unity of its many forms. And yet we can assuredly and clearly experience one thing straightaway: 'Projection' does not refer to some sequence of actions or to some process we might piece together from individual phases, rather what it refers to is the unity of an action, but of an originary and properly unique kind of action. What is *most proper* to such activity and occurrence is what is expressed in the prefix 'pro-' [*Ent-*], namely that in projecting [*Entwerfen*], this occurrence of projection *carries* whoever is projecting *out and away from themselves* in a certain way. It indeed removes them into whatever has been projected, but it does not as it were deposit and abandon them there—on the contrary: in this being removed by the projection, what occurs is precisely a peculiar *turning toward themselves on the part of whoever is projecting.* Yet why is the projection this *turning toward that is a removal?* Why is it not a being lifted away to something in the manner of captivated being taken? Why is it not a turning toward something in the sense of reflecting, either? Because this removal that pertains to projecting has the character of *raising away into the possible,* and indeed—as we must observe— into the possible in its possibly being made possible, namely into something possibly actual. Wherever the projection raises us away to—into the possible that is a making-possible—indeed leaves whoever is projecting no rest. Rather what is projected in the projection *compels* us before what is possibly actual, i.e., the projection *binds* us—not to what is possible, nor to what is actual, but to *making-possible,* i.e., to that which the possibly actual in the projected possibility demands of the possibility for itself in order to actualize itself.

The projection is thus in itself *that* occurrence that lets the *binding character* of things spring forth as such, insofar as such occurrence always presupposes a making-possible. With this free *binding,* in which all that makes possible holds itself before what is possibly actual, there is also always a determinacy proper to that which is possible itself. For whatever is possible does not become more possible through indeterminacy, so that everything possible would, as it were, find room and be accommodated in it. Rather whatever is possible grows in its possibility and in the force that makes it possible through *restriction.* Every possibility brings its intrinsic *restriction* with it. But the restriction of the possible is here that which is in each case precisely actual, that *expansiveness* that can be filled, i.e., that 'as a whole' out of which our comportment comports itself in each case. We must therefore say that this *single* occurrence of projecting in the unity of its essence raises us away in binding us to what is possible, and this simultaneously means: it expands into a whole, holds this before it. The projection is intrinsically *completing* in the sense of a casting ahead that is the *forming* of an 'as a whole' into whose realm there is spread out a quite specific dimension of possible actualization. Every projection raises us away into the possible, and in so doing brings us back into the expanded breadth of whatever has been made possible by it.

The projection and projecting in themselves raise us away to possibilities of binding, and are binding and expansive in the sense of holding a whole before us within which this or that actual thing can actualize itself as what is actual in something possible that has been projected. This expansion that raises us away and binds us—something that occurs simultaneously in the projection— also shows, however, its intrinsic character of *opening*. Yet—as we can now easily perceive—it is not some mere or fixed remaining open for something: neither for what is possible, nor even for what is actual. Projecting is not a gaping at what is possible, and cannot be such, because whatever is possible as such is precisely stifled in its being possible if we merely observe and talk about it. What is possible only essentially prevails in its possibility if we bind ourselves to it in its being made possible. Making-possible, however, as making-possible, always speaks into what is possibly actual—making-possible is a prefiguring of actualizing—and indeed in such a way that in the projection we do not in turn accept and take possession of what is actual as something in the possibility that has been actualized. The object of the projection is neither the possibility nor the actuality—the projection has no object at all, but is an *opening for making-possible*. In making-possible the originary relatedness of the possible and the actual, of possibility and actuality in general and as such, is revealed.

Projecting as this *revealing that pertains to making-possible* is the proper *occurrence of that distinction between being and beings*. The projection is the irruption into this 'between' of the distinction. It first makes possible the terms that are distinguished in their distinguishability. The projection *unveils the being of beings*. For this reason it is, as we may say in borrowing a word from Schelling,[1] the look into the light of a possible making-possible [*Lichtblick ins Mögliche-Ermöglichende*] in general. The look into the light tears darkness as such along with it, gives the possibility of that dawning of the everyday in which at first and for the most part we catch sight of beings, cope with them, suffer from them, and enjoy ourselves with them. The look into the light of the possible makes whatever is projecting open for the dimension of the 'either/or', the 'both/and', the 'in such a way', and the 'otherwise', the 'what', the 'is' and 'is not'. Only insofar as this irruption has occurred do the 'yes' and 'no' and questioning become possible. The projection raises us away into

---

1. Cf. Schelling, *Philosophische Untersuchungen über das Wesen der menschlichen Freiheit und die damit zusammenhängenden Gegenstände* (1809). Sämmtliche Werke. Ed. K. F. A. von Schelling (Stuttgart and Augsburg, 1856ff.). Part I, Vol. 7, p. 361. [Trans. J. Gutmann, *Philosophical Inquiries into the Nature of Human Freedom* (Illinois: Open Court, 1986), p. 36.]

and thus unveils the dimension of the possible in general, and what is possible is in itself already articulated into possibly 'being in such a way or otherwise', into the possibility of 'being or not being'. Why this is the case, however, we cannot discuss here.

What we previously pointed out as individual characteristics have now been unveiled as originarily interwoven into the unity of the primordial structure of projection in a unitary manner. *In projection there occurs the letting-prevail of the being of beings in the whole of their possible binding character in each case. In projection world prevails.*

This primordial structure of world-formation, namely projection, also displays, in its originary unity, that which Aristotle necessarily had recourse to in his question concerning the possibility of λόγος. Aristotle says: The λόγος, in accordance with its possibility, is grounded in the originary unity of σύνθεσις and διαίρεσις. For projection is an occurrence which, as raising us away and casting us ahead, takes apart as it were (διαίρεσις)—in that *apartness of a raising away,* yet as we saw, precisely in such a way that in this process there occurs an intrinsic *turning toward* on the part of whatever has been projected, such that that which has been projected is that which *binds* and *binds together* (σύνθεσις). Projection is that originarily simple occurrence which—in terms of formal logic—intrinsically unites contradictory things: binding together and separating. Yet—as the forming of the distinction between possible and actual in its making-possible, and as irruption into the distinction between being and beings, or more precisely as the irrupting of this 'between'—this projection is also that *relating* in which the 'as' springs forth. For the 'as' expresses the fact that beings in general have become manifest in their being, that that distinction has occurred. The 'as' designates the structural moment of that originarily *irruptive* 'between'. We simply never first have 'something' and then 'something more' and then the possibility of taking something *as* something, but the complete reverse: something first gives itself to us only when we are already moving within projection, within the 'as'.

In the occurrence of projection world is formed, i.e., in projecting something erupts and irrupts toward possibilities, thereby irrupting into what is actual as such, so as to experience itself as having irrupted as an actual being in the midst of what can now be manifest as beings. It is a being of a properly primordial kind, which has irrupted to that way of being which we call *Da-sein,* and to that being which we say *exists,* i.e., ex-sists, is an exiting from itself in the essence of its being, yet without abandoning itself.

Man is that inability to remain and is yet unable to leave his place. In projecting, the Da-sein in him constantly *throws* him into possibilities and thereby keeps him *subjected* to what is actual. Thus thrown in this throw, man is a *transition,* transition as the fundamental essence of occurrence. Man is history, or better, history is man. Man is *enraptured* in this transition and therefore essentially *'absent'.* Absent in a fundamental sense—never simply at hand, but absent in his essence, in his *essentially being away,* removed into *essential having been* and *future*—essentially absencing and never at hand, yet *existent* in his essential absence. *Transposed* into the possible, he must constantly *be mistaken* concerning what is actual. And only because he is thus mistaken and transposed can he become *seized by terror.* And only where there is the perilousness of being seized by terror do we find the bliss of astonishment—being torn away in that wakeful manner that is the breath of all philosophizing, and which the greats among the philosophers called ἐνθουσιασμός—as witnessed by the last of the greats, Friedrich Nietzsche, in that song of Zarathustra's which he called the "intoxicated song" and in which we also experience what the world is:

> O Man! Attend!
> What does deep midnight's voice contend?
> "I slept my sleep,
> "And now awake at dreaming's end:
> "The world is deep,
> "Deeper than day can comprehend.
> "Deep is its woe,
> "Joy—deeper than heart's agony:
> "Woe says: Fade! Go!
> "But all joy wants eternity,
> "Wants deep, profound eternity!"[2]

2. [Tr: Slightly amended version of the translation by R. J. Hollingdale, *Thus Spoke Zarathustra* (London: Penguin, 1988), p. 333.]

Appendix

For Eugen Fink on His Sixtieth Birthday

Dear Eugen Fink,

Two months ago thirty-seven years had passed since you helped me to move my writing desk to the place where it still stands today, in our new house on the Rötebuck.

That is one sign.

The other can be found in my seminar book containing the lists of the participants in each seminar. For the first upper seminar following my return from Marburg on "The ontological principles and the problem of the categories," held in the winter semester of 1928–29, the first entry on the list is the name of our recently deceased and dearly beloved friend, Oskar Becker. At the fourth place on the list there follows the name: Käte Oltmanns, 8th semester—the later Frau Bröcker—and below that at number 14 Eugen Fink, 8th semester.

Both names are underlined in red. This sign means: These students are likely to achieve something.

The third sign I must mention today is the fact that your ancestors on your mother's side come from the same upper-Swabian village as my mother, and that we both had the same teachers in Greek and Latin at the grammar school in Constance.

The first and third signs need no particular discussion in comparison to the second:

The red line under your name.

At that time you were already known as a recognized and privileged student of Husserl's.

You now entered another, and yet the same school of phenomenology.

Of course, we must understand this title correctly. It does not refer to a particular direction of philosophy. It names a possibility that continues to exist today, i.e., making it possible for thinking to attain the "things themselves," or to put it more clearly: to attain the matter of thinking. There would be much to say about this.

Yet for now I am referring to Eugen Fink the "student," and note that from then to the present day he has shown the truth of a well-known saying of Nietzsche's. It runs: "One repays a teacher badly if one always remains merely a student."

Nietzsche's saying only speaks in a negative way. It does not say how one manages not to remain a student any longer. This is something that cannot simply be realized. Showing something to be true has a special sense here.

What characterizes a student, if there is such a thing, is something we can only leave behind us if we succeed in experiencing anew the same matter of thinking, experiencing it as ancient and as sheltering something most ancient within it.

Such an experience continues to be determined by the tradition and by the spirit of the present age.

From this perspective, it seems to me that the worth of your thinking still remains in store for you.

For philosophy today has entered the stage in which it will be most thoroughly tested.

Philosophy is dissipating into independent sciences. They are known as logistics, semantics, psychology, anthropology, sociology, political science, the science of poetics, technology. As well as dissipating into the sciences, philosophy is being superseded by a new kind of unification of all sciences. The overpowering of the sciences by a fundamental trait that prevails in them themselves is happening in the rise of what we see attempting to consolidate itself under the title of cybernetics. This process is promoted and accelerated by the fact that modern science itself accommodates it on account of its own fundamental character.

A year before his collapse (1888), Nietzsche expressed this fundamental trait of modern science in a single sentence. It reads: "It is not the victory of *science* that marks this nineteenth century of ours, but the victory of *method* over science" (*The Will to Power,* No. 466).

Method here is no longer thought as the instrument with the aid of which scientific research works on the objects it has already set out. Method constitutes the very objectivity of the objects, granted that we may still speak of objects here, granted that formulating certain determinations of objectivity in general still has any "ontological valency" here.

Presumably philosophy in the previous style and with its corresponding validity will vanish from the field of view of man in the technical world-civilization.

Yet the end of philosophy is not the end of thinking. The question therefore becomes pressing as to whether thinking can face the test that stands before it, and how it can survive the period of this ordeal.

It is my wish, therefore, dear Eugen Fink, on this the eve of your sixtieth birthday, that it be given to you to make a genuine necessity out of virtue. That is to say: May you, on account of your fittingness for thought, remain in a position—without covering anything over or making overhasty compromises—to endure the test that thought is entering. And more: May you too help to first make visible the need into which thinking is compelled by the unlimited power of science, which in itself is already technical.

The commencement of Western thinking in the Greeks was prepared by poetry.

Perhaps thinking must in future first open the time-play-space for poetising, so that through the poetising word there may again be a wording world.

Prompted by such thoughts, I have selected this small gift for your sixtieth birthday: Paul Valéry, 'The young Parca' (translated by Paul Celan).

Freiburg i. Br., 30 March 1966

Dear Eugen Fink,

Enclosed is the text of my speech for your sixtieth birthday, with our warmest greetings to you for Easter.

Yours, Martin Heidegger.

Editor's Epilogue

The manuscript of the hitherto unpublished lecture course presented here bears the title "The Fundamental Concepts of Metaphysics: World, Finitude, Solitude." Martin Heidegger delivered the lecture course for four hours per week during the winter semester of 1929–30 at the University of Freiburg. Two people who attended the course, Herr Professor Dr. Walter Bröcker (Kiel) and Herr Dr. Heinrich Wiegand Petzet (Freiburg) both report that according to Heidegger's own handwriting announcing the course on the notice board, the subtitle was not "World, Finitude, Solitude," but "World, Finitude, Individuation." This discrepancy also corresponds to the way in which Heidegger formulates the question of solitude at the beginning of the course when providing a general elucidation of the course title (p. 6). However, since he did not delete the word 'solitude' in the subtitle in order to replace it with the word 'individuation'—either in the manuscript or in the first typewritten copy—the subtitle of the manuscript has been retained for this publication.

By contrast to the announcement in the publisher's prospectus, where the course is listed as Volume 30, it now appears as the double issue 29–30. Inquiries made by the administrator of Heidegger's estate, Herr Dr. Hermann Heidegger, have indicated that the lecture course "Introduction to Academic Study," which was announced for summer semester 1929 and envisaged as Volume 29, not only was not held, but was not even worked out in manuscript form.

The manuscript of the course comprises 94 sides in horizontal folio format. As in almost all the manuscripts, the main text is written on the left-hand side of the page. The right-hand side contains the numerous textual insertions, textual improvements, and abbreviated remarks that likewise supplement the main text. These are of varying length and not always fully formulated. Among the pages of the manuscript, which are numbered consecutively, a few additional pages with page references have been inserted, whose text is barely outlined, as well as pieces of notepaper recapitulating the lectures. The editor had at his disposal an initial typewritten copy of this manuscript, prepared for Heidegger by Frau Professor Dr. Ute Guzzoni (Freiburg) at the beginning of the sixties, with the aid of a grant from the Deutsche Forschungsgemeinschaft that Heidegger had applied for, although he did not help to collate the copy. The editor also had available a record of the lecture course in shorthand, made by Heidegger's former student Simon Moser who, after the end of the semester, delivered this to Heidegger in typewritten and bound form. These notes which Heidegger regarded as his personal record were inspected by him, occasionally corrected by hand, and provided with a few marginal comments. He used the last empty page to record a kind of list of some of the basic words and concepts of the course, together with the relevant page references.

The editor's task consisted in attending to the "Directives for preparing a text adequately suited for print," provided by Martin Heidegger. The first task was to decipher the text of the manuscript anew word by word, with the help of the initial copy. Occasional misreadings, which are unavoidable when initially transcribing a text written in German script and in very small and compressed handwriting, were corrected. It was possible to supplement this copy with parts of the text that had yet to be transcribed. These consisted of the additional notes, some textual insertions and marginal remarks, and of the notes made for recapitulation purposes. This supplemented copy was compared sentence by sentence with Heidegger's personal record of the notes. For the purposes of preparing the manuscript for printing, the following additions were adopted from the notes authorized by Heidegger: those thoughts which were extended or further developed in the course of the lecture as compared to the manuscript; all more developed formulations of those parts of the text which are merely sketched or written down in abbreviated form in the manuscript (several sections of the main text, additional material, textual insertions, marginal remarks); a series of recapitulations of the course which were merely formulated orally in the lectures and not only serve as repetitions, but extend the train of thought presented or formulate it in a new way that furthers our understanding. Everything adopted from the notes was included in accordance with the directives provided by Heidegger in this respect.

The editor had the further task of dividing the text of the lecture course into paragraphs, since it was written mainly in continuous form. Because Heidegger for the most part only indicated the syntactic caesurae within sentences by dashes, the preparation of copy for print entailed working out consistent punctuation. Those words which merely serve as fillers and are peculiar to the style of a lecture, but are superfluous and distracting in a printed text (words such as 'but', 'indeed', 'precisely', and 'now'), as well as sentences beginning with 'And' which are not demanded by the train of thought, were deleted by the editor. Where the position of words and in particular the positioning of the verb in the sentence had been chosen so that the listener could understand more easily, it was altered in accordance with the requirements of a printed text. These re-workings of the text of the lecture are similar to those undertaken by Heidegger in those lectures he himself published. The text was prepared in such a way that on the one hand, the demands of a printed text were met, and on the other hand the overall style of a lecture was nevertheless retained.

The overall structuring of the text into a Preliminary Appraisal, Part One, and Part Two has been provided for by Heidegger to the extent that in the course he speaks both of a preliminary appraisal and a first and a second part. In the manuscript he gives Part One the title "Awakening a Fundamental Attunement in Our Philosophizing," while Part Two bears the abbreviated, albeit central title "What Is World?" Apart from these two titles, the manuscript contains only the title for a section clearly separated off from the preceding and subsequent text of the lecture: "Summary and renewed introduction following the vacation" (the reference is to the Christmas holidays). In the table of contents this section with the title provided by Heidegger is to be found as Section 44. The remaining structuring of the overall text of the lecture into chapters, paragraphs, and subsections of paragraphs, as well as the formulation of all titles except the three mentioned, was undertaken by the editor. As the reader can see, the titles were selected solely by using phrases formed by Heidegger in each of the relevant sections. The detailed table of contents reflecting the actual construction and thought-sequence of this comprehensive lecture course is in place of a subject index, which was firmly rejected by Heidegger.

Despite intensive and wide-ranging inquiries, it has proved impossible to locate in Leibniz' works the sentence ascribed to him on page 24 of the German text.

The occasional page references to *Sein und Zeit* relate to the separate edition (15th edition, Max Niemeyer, Tübingen, 1979); they can, however, also be consulted in Volume 2 of the *Gesamtausgabe* via the page references to the separate edition provided in the margins.

* * *

At the time of preparation of his *Gesamtausgabe,* Heidegger gave the editor the present lecture course in person for editing. When the editor came on working visits, Heidegger repeatedly directed the conversation toward this lecture course, and emphasized the detailed analysis of boredom, in addition to the significance of the course for the concept of world.

Shortly before beginning his preparation and elaboration of this lecture course, on 24 July 1929, Heidegger had given his inaugural Freiburg lecture, "What Is Metaphysics?," in which he dealt with the attunement of boredom for the first time. The comprehensive analysis of boredom and its three forms, which constitutes the first part of the present lecture course, must be read in the context of this inaugural lecture. In his equally wide-ranging attempt to determine the essence of life in the second part, aimed at attaining the concept of world, Heidegger undertakes a task which he merely mentions in *Sein und Zeit* (Section 12, p. 58 of the Niemeyer edition; p. 78 in Vol. 2 of the *Gesamtausgabe*), but does not undertake. There he formulates the task as an a priori delimitation of the "constitution of being pertaining to 'life'."

* * *

When Martin Heidegger heard the news of the death of Eugen Fink, who passed away on 25 June 1975 in Freiburg, he decided to dedicate this volume of the lecture course to the deceased. He sent the text of the handwritten *dedication* to the widow, Frau Susanne Fink. The text of the dedication speaks for itself and tells the reader something about the motivation for this posthumous homage.

The text reproduced in the Appendix also gives us an insight into Heidegger's friendship with Fink, which extended over decades. This is the birthday speech which Heidegger gave on the eve of Fink's sixtieth birthday, on 10 December 1965, during a celebration in the Viktoria Hotel in Freiburg.

Because the speech was to be reproduced in the form in which Heidegger had originally composed it for Eugen Fink, discrepancies in the two quotations from Nietzsche (which were presumably quoted from memory) were not corrected for consistency with Nietzsche's text. The first quotation comes from the section "Of the Bestowing Virtue" from *Thus Spoke Zarathustra*.

* * *

I am indebted to Herr Dr. Hermann Heidegger for continual consultation during the editing work, and the valuable help he has contributed toward the preparation of this volume. For his helpful support in editing I must especially thank Herr Dr. Hartmut Tietjen. My warmest thanks go to Frau Dr. Luise Michaelsen and Herr cand. phil. Hans-Helmuth Gander for the correction work which they undertook with great care and circumspection. In addition, I must thank Herr Gander for his generous help in preparing the various stages of the edition. I thank Herr Dr. Georg Wöhrle (Freiburg), to whom I am greatly indebted for correcting final layout and checking through the entire volume.

My cordial thanks go to Herr Professor Dr. Bernhard Casper (Freiburg) and Herr Professor Dr. Wolfgang Wieland (Freiburg) for their valuable assistance.

F.-W. v. Herrmann.
Freiburg i. Br., December 1982.

Postscript to the Second Edition

Some minor typographical errors in the first edition have been corrected in the second.

Regarding the lecture course announced for the summer semester of 1929, "Introduction to Academic Study" (originally intended as Volume 29 of the *Gesamtausgabe*), it was stated in the Epilogue to the first edition that inquiries had shown that this course "not only was not held, but was not even worked out in manuscript form" by Heidegger. Just after publication of the volume, however, two written transcripts came to light, one by Herbert Marcuse, the other by Alois Siggemann. The conclusion arrived at by the editor following diligent inquiries thus proved to be incorrect.

This conclusion on the editor's part was not arrived at hastily, but as a result of inquiries made in three directions. A search of Heidegger's entire archive for the manuscript of the course was undertaken, but proved negative. Inquiries were also made of two people who attended Heidegger's lectures and were also present in Freiburg in the summer semester of 1929. They were able to remember the other academic activities taking place that semester, but had no recollection of this particular lecture course.

The most reliable source, however, was taken to be a list drawn up by Heidegger himself entitled "Lectures and Seminars since the Publication of *Sein und Zeit* (all those fully worked out)." This list mentions only the lecture course "German Idealism" for summer semester 1929, while no reference is made to the course "Introduction to Academic Study."

The two transcripts, each comprising only nine and seventeen typed pages, suggest that in that course Heidegger was concerned with grasping the genuine essence of science and philosophy, while keeping their unity in view. In interpreting the proper essence of theoretical comportment, Heidegger referred to Plato's allegory of the cave from Book VII of the *Republic*. The interpretation of this constituted the major part of the course.

The fact that Heidegger did not mention this lecture course in his otherwise complete overview of the courses he held between 1927 and 1944–45 leads one to suspect that, unlike the other courses listed, this course was not fully worked out.

It is impossible to reconstruct and to edit the text of this lecture course on the basis of these two very short typescripts.

F.-W. v. Herrmann.
Freiburg i. Br., March 1992.

Glossary

ability: *Können, Vermögen*
absorbed: *eingenommen*
absorption in . . . : *Eingenommenheit in . . .*
to agree: *übereinkommen*
ambiguity: *Zweideutigkeit*
ambivalence: *Doppeldeutigkeit*
to announce: *ansagen*
(telling) announcement: *Ansagen*
apprehending: *Vernehmen*
assertion: *Aussage*
attack: *Angriff*
to attend to . . . : *sich einlassen auf . . .*
to attune: *stimmen*
(fundamental) attunement: *(Grund)stimmung*
behaviour: *Benehmen*
being: *Sein*
being taken: *Hingenommenheit*
beings: *Seiendes*
beings as a whole: *das Seiende im Ganzen*
beings as such: *das Seiende als solches*
being true: *Wahr-sein*
benumbed: *benommen*
benumbment: *Benommenheit*
binding: *verbindlich*
binding character: *Verbindlichkeit*
(profound) boredom: *(tiefe) Langeweile*
to be bored with . . . : *sich langweilen mit/bei . . .*
to become bored by . . . : *gelangweiltwerden von . . .*
boring: *langweilig*
capability: *Fähigsein*
capable: *fähig*
(rendered) capable: *befähigt*
capacity: *Fähigkeit*
captivated: *benommen*
captivation: *Benommenheit*
casualness: *Lässigkeit*
changeover: *Umschlag*
closed off: *verschlossen*
to compel: *zwingen*
compulsion, compelling force: *Zwang*
completion: *Ergänzung*
to comport oneself: *sich verhalten*
comportment: *Verhaltung*

to comprehend: *begreifen*
comprehensive concept: *Inbegriff*
(fundamental) concept: *(Grund)begriff*
concealed: *verborgen*
to conform: *sich anmessen*
conformity: *Angemessenheit*
connectedness, connection: *Zusammenhang*
(mood of) courage: *Mut*
deprivation: *Entbehrung*
(the ontological) difference: *(die ontologische) Differenz*
disclosedness: *Erschlossenheit*
discourse: *Rede*
to disinhibit: *enthemmen*
disinhibition: *Enthemmung*
distinction: *Unterschied*
distinguished: *unterschieden*
to drag: *zögern*
time as it drags: *der zögernde Zeitverlauf*
to drive away: *wegtreiben*
to drive (time) on: *(die Zeit) antreiben*
(instinctual) drive: *Trieb*
driven activity: *Treiben, Umtrieb*
drivenness: *Getriebenheit*
during: *während*
to eliminate: *beseitigen*
to encircle: *umringen*
encircling ring: *Umring*
to endure: *währen*
to entrance: *bannen*
entrancement: *Bann*
equipment: *Zeug*
essence: *Wesen*
everyday: *alltäglich*
everydayness: *Alltäglichkeit*
expanse: *Weite*
to express: *ausdrücken, aussprechen*
finitude: *Endlichkeit*
to form: *sich bilden*
(world-)formation: *(Welt-)bildung*
fulfilled: *erfüllt*
future: *Zukunft*
to grasp: *fassen, begreifen*
to grip: *ergreifen*
gripped: *ergriffen*
ground: *Grund*
to ground: *begründen*

to discover the ground: *ergründen*
to be (present) at hand: *vorhanden sein*
to be (ready) to hand: *zuhanden sein*
having-been: *Gewesenheit*
(being) held in limbo: *Hingehaltenheit*
horizon: *Horizont*
immersion: *Aufgehen*
to impel: *hinzwingen*
indifference: *Gleichgültigkeit*
individuation: *Vereinzelung*
(working) instrument: *Werkzeug*
(being) left empty: *Leergelassenheit*
to let be: *seinlassen*
(structural) link: *Fuge*
linkage: *Gefüge*
linking: *Fügung*
long: *lang*
manifold: *Mannigfaltigkeit*
manifestness: *Offenbarkeit*
(specific) manner of being: *Seinsart*
meaning: *Bedeutung, Sinn*
(mood of) melancholy: *Schwermut*
moment of vision: *Augenblick*
necessity: *Notwendigkeit*
need: *Not*
the 'now': *das Jetzt*
occurrence: *das Geschehen*
openness: *Offenheit*
to oppress: *bedrängen*
oppressiveness: *Bedrängnis*
origin: *Ursprung*
original, originary: *ursprünglich*
to pass the time: *die Zeit vertreiben*
poor in world: *weltarm*
possible: *möglich*
to make possible: *ermöglichen*
potentiality: *Können*
poverty: *Armut*
poverty in world: *Weltarmut*
the present: *die Gegenwart, die An-
    wesenheit*
to be present: *gegenwärtig sein*
to prevail: *walten*
to prevail essentially: *wesen*
to produce: *erzeugen*
product: *Erzeugnis*
to project: *entwerfen*
projection: *Entwurf*
proper: *eigen*
proper authenticity: *Eigentlichkeit*
properly: *eigentlich*
proper being: *Eigentum*
properly peculiar: *eigentümlich*

proper peculiarity: *Eigentümlichkeit*
(being) proper to oneself: *Sich-zu-
    eigen(-sein)*
propositional statement: *Aussagesatz*
readiness: *Fertigkeit*
ready: *fertig*
ready-made: *verfertigt*
to refer: *meinen*
to refuse: *versagen*
(telling) refusal: *Versagen*
relation: *Beziehung, Bezug*
relatedness: *Bezogenheit*
relationship: *Verhältnis*
to release: *entlassen*
releasement: *Gelassenheit*
not being released: *Nichtentlassensein*
resolute disclosedness: *Entschlossenheit*
to retain: *behalten*
intrinsic self-retention: *Sich-einbehalten*
ring: *Ring*
satisfied: *ausgefüllt*
self-proposing: *Sichvorlegen*
self-pro-posing: *Sich-vor-legen*
serviceable: *dienlich*
serviceability: *Dienlichkeit*
solitude: *Einsamkeit*
the standing 'now': *das stehende Jetzt*
standing time: *die stehende Zeit*
statement: *Satz*
to stretch: *sich dehnen*
subservience: *Diensthaftigkeit*
subservient: *diensthaftig*
temporal: *zeitlich*
temporality: *Zeitlichkeit*
to temporalize: *sich zeitigen*
time: *die Zeit*
the course of time: *der Zeitverlauf*
that-being: *Daß-sein*
to transpose: *sich versetzen*
transposability: *Versetzbarkeit*
unconcealment: *Unverborgenheit*
undifferentiated: *indifferent*
undifferentiatedness: *Indifferenz*
to vacillate: *zaudern*
way of being: *Seinsweise*
what-being: *Was-sein*
the while: *die Weile*
to withdraw: *sich entziehen*
withdrawal: *Entzug*
withholding: *Genommenheit*
world: *Welt*
world-forming: *weltbildend*
worldless: *weltlos*